THE CONFRONTATION

THE CONFRONTATION
WINNING THE WAR AGAINST FUTURE JIHAD

WALID PHARES

palgrave
macmillan

First published in hardcover in 2008 by PALGRAVE MACMILLAN® in the
US–a division of St. Martin's Press LLC, 175 Fifth Avenue, New York, NY
10010.

Where this book is distributed in the UK, Europe and the rest of the world, this
is by Palgrave Macmillan, a division of Macmillan Publishers Limited, registered
in England, company number 785998, of Houndmills, Basingstoke, Hampshire
RG21 6XS.

Palgrave Macmillan is the global academic imprint of the above companies and
has companies and representatives throughout the world.

Palgrave® and Macmillan® are registered trademarks in the United States, the
United Kingdom, Europe and other countries.

ISBN-13: 978-0-230-61130-6
ISBN-10: 0-230-61130-3

Library of Congress Cataloging-in-Publication Data is available from the Library
of Congress.

A catalogue record of the book is available from the British Library.

Design by Letra Libre

First PALGRAVE MACMILLAN paperback edition: April 2009
10 9 8 7 6 5 4 3 2 1
Printed in the United States of America.

CONTENTS

To my mother, Hind, who left this world on December 17, 2007, seventeen years after we were separated by the frontier between freedom and oppression. She was the spiritual force that propelled my learning and teaching. Her sacrifices have allowed me to work for a better future for all parents and children. This book is dedicated to her memory.

ACKNOWLEDGMENTS

I WOULD LIKE TO THANK AGAIN THOSE PERSONS IN MY LIFE WHO deserve my full attention but have given me the time I owe them to write these pages. In particular I thank the "scholar" and the "commander" for their support. I thank them above all for understanding the important reasons behind this work, and for sacrificing our time together to all those who would eventually read this book.

I wish to acknowledge my literary agent, Lynne Rabinoff, for her faithful dedication to my work and her presence at all stages of the making of this book. Also I thank my publisher, Airíe Stuart at Palgrave Macmillan, who encouraged me to write this book and patiently oversaw the complex process of its production. Her patience, advice, and suggestions have impacted its final shape. I also thank the entire team at Palgrave Macmillan with whom I worked diligently for many months to ensure the book's quality. In particular, Alan Bradshaw's input was essential.

I am grateful for the work of my host institution, the Foundation for the Defense of Democracies in Washington, which is now influencing many minds and hearts both in America and on other continents. I'd like to thank FDD's President Cliff May for making my fellowship possible, as well as Mark Dubowitz, my colleagues, and the staff for their support. In addition, I thank the European Foundation for Democracy and its President Roberta Bonazzi for assisting me in my research in Europe. A particular recognition goes to Adela Zacharides, the tireless manager of our Future Terrorism Project.

Acknowledgment is due also to the legislators and current and former officials in the United States, Europe, and worldwide who have understood the importance of my previous books *Future Jihad* and *The War of Ideas*, and have acted upon the recommendations in their own fields. Also, I thank the various foundations, NGOs, government entities, and military and defense institutions who have interacted favorably with my work and who have expressed their anticipation for this book, *The Confrontation*.

My gratitude goes also to my colleagues in the media, past and present, who have been my route companions in discussing and sharing these ideas and writings with the public. Particularly I thank the leadership and producers at Fox News who entrusted me to become their expert beginning in 2007. I also thank my friends and colleagues at other national and international networks, on radio shows and Web sites, and in printed media worldwide with whom I have and I am still working to broaden the debate and better inform and educate the public.

I wish to acknowledge and thank my readers, those faithful ones who have followed my work for years and those new readers who are now turning this page. The measure of success of this book may be measured in the number of its readers, but more important are their satisfaction and their actions after finishing the book. Messages I have received from readers of my previous publications have impacted *The Confrontation.*

My last acknowledgment goes to my family. To my brother, Sami, whose early ideas impacted me; to my loving sister, Liliane; and to my father, Halim, who taught me justice, and mother, Hind, who taught me faith, now united in the other world. Thank you for what I became and for what I gave and will give to others.

Walid Phares
Washington D.C., January 12, 2008

PROLOGUE

WHY THIS BOOK?

IN NOVEMBER 2005 I PUBLISHED MY FIRST POST-9/11 BOOK, *FUTURE JIHAD: Terrorist Strategies against America.*[1] Its purpose was to present an explanation of the War on Terror that differed from what had been offered after September 11, 2001, when the American and international publics sought answers to the "they" in the primitive but much publicized question of the moment: "Why do they hate us?"

I felt I had to write about "them"—the Jihadists—because of the failure of those participating in the public debate to identify and call them what they call themselves. Scholars, experts, and politicians were wandering around in various directions, talking about who the West and the Free World were facing in the new age of terror. Apologists for the attackers advanced the shady argument that the attackers are people frustrated with Western policies; Western responses were weak and incoherent. It was said that the new war was a War on Terror, meaning a war against a *form* of violence and not a war against an *enemy* that was using violence. In fact, this enemy has an agenda that it pursues with the many weapons at its disposal, terrorism being only one of them. Now, seven years after 9/11 and three years after the Iraq campaign began, the American-led coalition has dispatched troops from China's borders to the Persian Gulf and spent billions of dollars on a conflict with a problematic name and few effective arguments in favor of it.[2]

Worse, those democracies not engaged broke the international solidarity against terror, claiming that the war in Iraq had no legitimacy and the War on Terror, aside from "retaliation for 9/11," had no basis. But the failure in understanding wasn't only about the identity of the terrorists; it was also about hate. Too quickly, the Western debate over the perpetrators of terror—in New York, Washington, Madrid, London, and beyond—shifted from the haters themselves to the so-called root causes of this hatred. The Jihadi propaganda machine, from al Jazeera to websites and critics within the West, claimed that the roots of rage were legitimate and bound up with the unresolved Arab-Israeli conflict, neocolonial policies, and the rest of a familiar litany. Years after the first conflict of the twenty-first century, liberal democracies did not yet even agree on the existence of a Jihadi ideology, nor on the strategies and long-term goals of the Salafists and Khumeinists, two currents that constitute the bulk of worldwide Jihadi forces.[3] In 2005, from an intellectual standpoint, it looked bad for the West and for the embattled civil societies in the Greater Middle East. This major party to the conflict—the West—lacked a clear vision and had nothing resembling an operative and effective assessment of the confrontation.

AN OBSERVER

Having been among those observers who had seen the ideological threat developing for decades, and having been able to analyze it early on and publish as much as circumstances allowed in a high-risk location (my native Beirut in the 1980s), I had immigrated to America in 1990 with a major project on my mind: an academic contribution to Western democracy that would help the Free World see the mounting menace and act against it before it was too late. The first need I saw was to defend my soon-to-be adopted country, and, after that, to salvage the societies that had already lost freedom because of Jihadism.

My scholarly and journalistic work had begun with my very first book in Arabic, *Pluralism*.[4] In it I dedicated a whole section to the "relationship between civilizations" and the "historical development of Jihad" in the Middle East and beyond. I published this book while I was still a law student. In the 1980s, I published (also in Arabic) a number of monographs and books dealing with the ideological clash between regional ideologies, including Pan-Arabism, Islamism, Marxism, liberalism, and extreme nationalism. In 1987 I put out *Background of the Islamic Revolution of Iran*, analyzing its future strategies.[5] And during that last decade of the Cold War, I published article after article (mostly in Arabic, a few in French) about what I was projecting as the next global menace to democracy and pluralism.

But six books and hundreds of articles were like a drop of rain in an oceanic tempest, because in the 1980s Europe and North America were—for good reason—still thinking in terms of containing the USSR, and, later, of how to deal with its fall. There was no need to worry about some marginal Jihadism coming from the Middle East. In addition, Western centers of learning were already influenced by oil lobbyists, who had convinced them (sometimes with contributed funds) that Wahabism, Salafism, and even Baathism were legitimate expressions of a people marching toward liberation and modernity! So books and articles by this Beirut-based author in the 1980s that argued otherwise didn't stand a chance of attracting academic interest.

The dominant paradigm in Western geopolitics at the time had two pillars: The Soviets had to be contained at any price, whatever the effect on any other crises, including human rights; and it had to be done in collaboration with the oil-producing regimes, both fundamentalist and nationalist. My work to expose the oppression of minorities, women, students, and nationalities and the suppression of pluralism was not picked up by key opinion makers in the West. In short, Middle Eastern dissidents had no place yet in the Western debate. A Jesuit intellectual who wrote the preface to one of my booklets likened my work to that of Soviet dissident Andrei Amalrik, who in the 1970s was predicting the fall of the Soviet Empire and wasn't listened to at the time.[6]

Language, and not just location and subject, was also a barrier. Having published mostly in Arabic decades before the development of the Internet and globalization, there remained little trace of my early analysis, other than perhaps unread copies in the Library of Congress and the Bibliothèque Nationale. Realizing my isolation from the international debate of ideas in the mid-1980s, I managed to launch a weekly magazine (quickly converted to a monthly) in English and French, with a handful of subscribers overseas.[7] As world events unfolded rapidly in those years, from glasnost to the rise of Iranian and Wahabi "Jihadisms," I saw that in the following decade—the 1990s—the threat would spread, take root in the Arab Muslim world, penetrate the West, and wreak havoc there as it did in the Middle East. As a lawyer, publisher, and lecturer, and as a policy activist, I had many opportunities to meet local and regional politicians as well as diplomats, journalists, and intellectuals; in the decade before I immigrated to the United States, I interacted with thinkers from almost all the ethnicities and religions of the region: Arabs, Kurds, Jews, ethnic Aramaens, Africans, Chaldo-Assyrians, Berbers, Iranians, and others. I also had the fascinating opportunity to be part of an exchange of arguments and articles (in Arabic) with intellectuals representing Jihadi and Baathist thinking.[8] The picture that emerged was clear. While the West was still concerned about the ailing Soviet Union, the forces of Jihadism and their counterparts in the authoritarian regimes of the region were bracing for a new Dark Ages and an attack on the Free World.

MOVING ON

In 1990, when Soviet-built Syrian tanks rolled into Lebanon and the forces of the American-led coalition were preparing to roll northward into Kuwait and southern Iraq, I was in Florida, working on a doctorate in international relations and strategic studies, having made a decision to educate the West. The global Jihadi and Middle Eastern authoritarian threat was rising. Furthermore, it was expanding too fast for the development of any classical containment strategy by the United Nations or its Western membership. I was among those few writers (mostly in the region and some in the West) who understood that the decline of the Soviet menace would be accompanied by the rise of the Jihadi menace. And while Soviet studies had flourished in America, and the East-West conflict was a mainstream field of research in the West, Jihadism studies were practically nonexistent.

It was a sudden and massive loss of freedom around me that prompted me to make the leap and officially emigrate. By October 13, 1990, as the world was watching the unfolding of Saddam's occupation of Kuwait, thirty thousand Syrian troops backed by Sukhoi bombers crushed the last enclave of freedom in Lebanon. The Syrian Baathists and their pro-Iranian Khumeinists thus added a once-democratic country—my mother country—to their roster of subject regimes. This move changed the geopolitics of the region for years to come and convinced me that liberty would be scarce there for a while. Developing research and publishing articles about the threat of Jihadism and radicalism was impossible in Lebanon; I had to pack and leave for freer lands.

THINKING FREELY UNDER FREEDOM

As I was working hard on my Ph.D. courses in Florida, I thought that the United States and the West, freed from Cold War obligations and having sent a strong message to the region, would eventually realize the mounting menace of fundamentalism and come to understand the immense abuse taking place in the Greater Middle East. I assumed that the policy planners in Washington—as well as those in London, Paris, and perhaps even Moscow—would gradually begin to set in motion a confrontation with Jihadism and totalitarianism in order to open spaces for freedom in the Arab and Muslim worlds, and in former Soviet areas, in the western hemisphere and beyond. In early writings and lectures, I warned of a spreading war of terror from the East. I collected these pieces in a monograph titled *Radical Islam and the Middle East.*[9] In it I discussed the Jihadi intention to strike inside America, and I saw the future of an international Jihad unbound. The 1992–1993 meetings of the Pan Islamist Conference in Khartoum, attended by dozens of Jihadi cadres, including those who would form the core of al Qaeda, were a watershed.[10] Reading the minutes of the Pan-Islamist conference was enlightening: The Internationalist Jihadists wanted to attack the West, while others wanted to widen operations in the Arab and Muslim worlds. Wahabi powers wanted to continue to penetrate the Free World, and Iran's Khumeinist leadership planned on building strategic power. That was my reading then; the rest is history.

THE WEST MISSING THE PICTURE

Months and years passed. I realized by 1993—not without frustration—that Washington and the West as a whole were missing the picture. It was clear by mid-decade that a War of Ideas waged by the Jihadi powers during the Cold War had already been won; the proof was that Western understanding of the nature of the Salafist and Khumeinist ideologies and agendas was almost nonexistent. Even worse, the Jihadists were also winning a second War of Ideas. By then, as a professor of comparative politics and Middle East studies at a state university in Florida, I attended the annual meetings of the Middle East Studies Association of North America (MESA), the American Political Science Association (APSA), and other bodies, and read thoroughly the literature dispensed to millions of young people in classrooms across the nation. I realized that the battle for the minds of the public was taking place on campuses, in classrooms and libraries. The defeat of the Free World was happening at the hands of its own elites while the public was looking forward hopefully to peace and global prosperity after the end of the Cold War. As I argued in *The War of Ideas: Jihadism against Democracy*,[11] the Jihadists and their allies used the 1990s to complete their domination of public debate on the Middle East and all things related to it.

Observing classrooms and media reporting about world events, it became very clear to me that the citizens of most liberal democracies were being conditioned not to absorb the reality of the mounting threat. Civil societies in the Greater Middle East were being intimidated and sometimes terrorized into submission. As I analyzed the mechanisms by which U.S. and Western academic programs were funded, I observed how the elite was painting geopolitical realities and ideological evolution in a way that served the interests and goals of the funding regimes, all of them authoritarian. Americans (and many Western democracies) were headed for an immense shock: Instead of being gradually educated about the rise of Jihadism and its different forms, such as Salafism, Wahabism, and Khumeinism, instead of being informed about the goals of al Qaeda, the Taliban, Hezbollah, and the Iranian, Sudanese, Syrian, and Iraqi regimes, audiences were being served up a totally different analysis. Ninety percent of the discussion of the region was about the Arab-Israeli conflict, and that was narrowed to the Palestinian-Israeli question. Every other drama, from Sudan to Iraq and from Lebanon to Iran, was marginalized, shrunk, and eventually wrongly explained. The shattering conclusion to this second War of Ideas came on September 11, 2001. Then a misinformed public could only wonder, "Why do they hate us?"

While I was trying to warn the West, a few of my colleagues in America and in Europe were making similar attempts. I was often called a voice in the wilderness, heard by the audiences but not listened to by decision makers. In eight years (between 1993 and 2001), I delivered more than four hundred public lectures and made several media appearances to analyze the trends that would lead to the twenty-first century's first global war. But as I wasn't appearing on C-SPAN and National Public Radio in America or on CNN and BBC worldwide, the message didn't travel very far in the pre-9/11 world. The wall was too high, too thick. Too much money and too much power were at stake. But Osama bin Laden's deadly strikes into the heart of the West changed everything. As the planes were destroying the Twin Towers, damaging the Pentagon, and bringing death to thousands, a window opened and light at last shone on the universal and most imminent threats to international relations.

JIHAD ISN'T YOGA

An enlightened public's first conclusion on the morning of September 12 should have been that Jihad isn't yoga. Instead, the mainstream media came up with "Why do they hate us?"—revealing just how dramatic the West's shortcomings were in perceiving the attackers and their motives. Academics widened the gap by throwing out dozens of decoy arguments: The attack is about U.S. foreign policy; it is because of social injustice and economic disenfranchisement; it is the result of the West's colonial past—an endless series of smoke screens were released by a gigantic spin machine. The average citizen in the Free World wanted more answers, and clearer ones. Bin Laden, Ayman Zawahiri, Abu Masa'b al Zarqawi of al Qaeda, and, later on, Mahmoud Ahmedinijad of Iran and Hassan Nasrallah of Hezbollah, would raise even larger questions, as would the photos of corpses in Madrid, London, Casablanca, and other cities, along with the images of beheadings and massacres across the Greater Middle East. The citizens of the West and elsewhere could no longer be fooled into believing that Jihad was yogalike or rooted in frustration at Western policies. The bearded men who commanded the violence (appearing on al Jazeera since the fall of 2001) speak of Jihad as war, not as a spiritual experience. They have introduced troubling terms such as *kafir* (meaning infidels), identifying them as an enemy[12]; they speak of apostates, the enemies of Allah, Crusaders, and so on. They invoke the return of the Islamic caliphate, the resumption of *fatah* (conquest), and the forcing of the *hijaab* and chador on women. In the post-9/11 era, ordinary people in the West are troubled by the contradiction between the terrorists, who openly call for Jihadi blitzkriegs, and their apologists, who continue to assert that the Jihadist campaign results from ordinary people's support for their elected governments and, more particularly, their foreign policies.

In the years since 9/11, two streams of opinion have developed. In the West, most citizens feel the danger but do not understand it (and their elites aren't helping them much). In the East, most men and women feel the oppression, but do not understand why many in the West are reluctant to help them. Between these publics lie a myriad of institutions, organizations, and interests. Most regimes in the Greater Middle East are authoritarian; many are oil producers; some are Arab nationalist, while others are Islamist. All countries in the West are democracies,

but not all governments targeted by the Jihadists are liberal. Meanwhile, most political elites with influence over the destiny of the region are influenced by
petrodollars. The products of these contradictions have been the crises and conflicts that we've been witnessing since the war began—or, more precisely, since the
Free World began responding to the Jihadi threat.

With 9/11, a third War of Ideas began. Academics, journalists, writers, and
analysts are all producing arguments and pushing agendas. Their intent is to sway
nations, powers, and the public into entering, continuing, or exiting the war with
Jihadism. The confrontation rages across continents in a global conflict over the
future of humanity. Will the peoples of the world live under the diktat of the
Salafists and Khumeinists and the regimes they aim at establishing, or will they
not? That is the bottom line.

In 1979 I wrote a three-volume study of Lebanon's ethnic conflict, the history of
the region, and a third issue relevant to my future scholarship: the clash of civilizations. My analysis of *civilizational* world politics attracted some criticism by local
reviewers. My thesis was dismissed on the ground that civilizations do not exist in
the realm of world politics. Fourteen years later, however, I read—with great ex-
citement—the first article by Professor Samuel Huntington on the subject, in *Foreign Affairs*.[13] The clash of civilizations is now of course a hotly debated issue.

In the early 1980s, from the so-called cultural capital of the Arab world, I ex-
changed views with intellectuals of Arab nationalist, Marxist, and Islamist backgrounds, including not only scholars but even muftis and clerics. The debate
centered on the identity of the Greater Middle East: Was it Arab, Islamic, Middle
Eastern, or all of the above? During that same period, I lived through and observed the conflict in Lebanon, the Arab-Israeli conflict, and the Cypriot partition
and visited divided capitals in lands in crisis. Interacting with erudite intellectuals
in the region, as well as with visiting Western scholars, I refined my ability to compare cultures and claims and to see similarities and differences. I had the chance to
meet with diplomats, journalists, academics, politicians, and activists from many
countries.[14] This fabulous interaction with a world of minds, research, and agendas, as well as with multiple ideologies, formed the groundwork for my immense
interest in comparative studies.

In the 1990s I further interacted with the academic and intellectual community of my adopted land on topics ranging from the Middle East, terrorism, and
slavery to ethnoreligious studies. I was able to interact with senators and representatives, and I testified before congressional committees and advised on legislation,
including an act on international religious freedom in 1998. I worked on regional

issues, such as the genocide in Sudan, the persecution of minorities in the Middle East, the Syrian occupation of Lebanon, and the Arab-Israeli conflict.[15] Toward the end of the decade, I had my first contacts with missions at the United Nations.

Above all, I enjoyed a career of full-time teaching at Florida Atlantic University, where I witnessed a much-needed transformation among students, who went from a poor understanding of world politics to a mature absorption of the international crisis.

THE CONFRONTATION

After the attacks of September 11, 2001, the confrontation became inescapable and at last visible to many more people. The scope of this battle is enormous, taking in four continents (Asia, Africa, Europe, and North America). The countries involved with the Jihadi networks are numerous. Salafist organizations exist in dozens of countries, including some in Latin America and Oceania. The Khumeinist regime has alliances across the Middle East, and its surrogates are found everywhere around the globe. The Jihadists are causing mass violence everywhere from Sudan to Iraq; their cells are wreaking havoc in the West and in Russia and India. Their ideologues are attempting to capture the minds of millions in the Muslim world, and their apologists are feverishly trying to blur the vision of the public in the Free World. America's forces and its allies are in Afghanistan and Iraq and may be forced to intervene in other places, while the Jihadists are moving from one area to another, from one tactic to another. The United Nations is shaken by realities it has been slow to confront, including conflicts in Darfur, Lebanon, and Iran. European governments are split over U.S. initiatives in Iraq and hesitant to engage terror cells on their own soil; the Arab world is deeply divided over politics, but maintains a consensus on obstructing democratization.

From day one, after Washington declared a war on terror and bin Laden reaffirmed his Jihad against the *kuffar* and the apostates, I had no hesitation about reaching out through national and international TV, radio, publications, and websites to stimulate a deeper, wider, and clearer exchange about the first great war of the twenty-first century, which, if not ended quickly, might well become the longest war of modern times.

GETTING THE INFORMATION THROUGH

Over the past seven years I have appeared on all the major networks and cable channels in the United States, Canada, and Great Britain, as well as outlets in France, Russia, Portugal, Spain, Belgium, and other countries.[16] Between 2003 and 2007, I was an MSNBC terrorism analyst before I moved to Fox News. I have spent many hours a week on radio programs. I have written scholarly articles and published them in newspapers and major websites, including my own.[17]

On media around the world, I have used my multicultural identity to delve into the real debate taking place at the core of the cultures involved in these issues. My Francophone identity allowed me to interact with French, Walloon, Canadian, and African media as well as with European, North African, and West African intellectuals. And, of course, the Arab education I had received, with its inherent Islamic sociology, allowed me to absorb—though a non-Muslim born and raised in an East Mediterranean civilization—the very core of the Islamic vision. To my advantage, Beirut was indeed the cultural capital of a vast Arab and Muslim world, a Mediterranean learning center with historical ties to Europe and the West. Along with opportunity came family history: My great-uncles, father, older brother, and other relatives were part of a Levantine educational circle that, trained by Jesuits over the generations, thought, wrote, spoke, and even produced poetry in both Arabic and French. They sat at the center of a vast cultural chessboard. I took this farther by delving into the history of the Arab Muslim civilization and tracing the roots of its philosophy and politics. This educational process allowed me to see what most non-Muslims cannot, and helped me understand how ethnic minorities in the Greater Middle East and Western nations are perceived.

As a result, I have been able to travel throughout the Arab Islamic cultural sphere and grasp the goals of ideological movements aiming at global domination. More, after 2001 I frequently appeared on al Jazeera, on its toughest crossfire shows, interacting directly with representatives of aggressive ideologies, shrewd scholars, and Jihadist propagandists. My participation in the Arab media's forums was and remains the high point in my engagement in the raging War of Ideas. From the young liberal media of Iraq and Lebanon to perceived centrist TV channels such as al Arabiya, al Hurra, and others, all the way to the Jihadi ones such as the Qatari-funded al Jazeera and the Iranian state-run al Aalam, one can see a spectrum of views in the Arab and Muslim worlds. But the most dramatic discoveries I have made in the Arabic sphere of my research are undoubtedly the famous Jihadi chat rooms in the underworld of cyberspace. Having been a frequent visitor to and sometimes a debater in these online discussions since the late 1990s, I am no stranger in this world. My research interest isn't limited only to the growing Jihadi communities, but extends also to the civil society blooming in the region despite state oppression and Islamist dominance, to students, liberals, democracy advocates, and women activists.

SHARING THE KNOWLEDGE

With such a body of discoveries, research, and experience behind me, I attempted to share my scholarship with decision makers who might alter the course of the conflict, impact events, and educate the public. Since 2001, my contribution to public policy bodies in the United States and overseas has multiplied several times over. I offered frequent lectures and analyses to many sectors of the U.S. government: the departments of Justice, Homeland Security, Defense, and State, as well as national security institutions. In addition to the U.S. Congress, I consulted with the European Parliament and Commission, as well as with French, British, Spanish, Belgian, and Dutch officials in those and other countries. I have frequently met and discussed issues with politicians and government officials from Iraq, Lebanon, Algeria, Morocco, and other parts of the region. For several years I was privileged to be part of discussions with all the ambassadors leading the permanent UN missions holding veto powers and other members of the Security Council.

Last but not least, I interacted with military leaders, commanders, and experts around the world, retired and on duty; I had the chance to sit down with men and women from all branches of the U.S. armed forces, as well as their counterparts in NATO and other countries in Europe, the Arab world, the Greater Middle East, South Asia, Latin America, and Africa.

This sudden increase in my research and outreach compelled me to move to Washington, D.C., so as to interact more closely with this world and offer better perspectives on matters of interest to the media, decision makers, and the public. The relocation was made possible by the Foundation for the Defense of Democracies (FDD), which I joined in 2001. As a senior fellow at FDD and as a director of its Future Terrorism Project, I continue to observe the developing global conflict with Jihadism and to analyze the evolving War of Ideas. I am also often a visiting fellow at the European Foundation for Democracy. Though I left my tenured position at the Department of Political Science at Florida Atlantic University, I continue to offer specialized courses on terrorism and global conflicts there and at the National Defense University and other colleges when I can.

This personal prologue was motivated by requests from many of my readers who have wanted me to go beyond the intellectual analysis and place my writings in a historical context, including in relation to my own experience. I hope that it can shed further light on the analysis I advance here and treated in my previous two books. Readers, listeners, and viewers who have contacted me over the years wanted to see the road I have taken to my ideas and conclusions. I still feel that each one of us—whether writer, essayist, scholar, media person, analyst, or even policymaker, at whatever level—is at work discovering clues to the solution of the giant puzzle that envelops us. It just happens that some among us have been given the opportunity to learn in a wider range of circumstances. Ultimately it is up to the readers, of this and future generations, to judge the fruits of our efforts.

Walid Phares

INTRODUCTION

WORLD HISTORY CONSTANTLY EVOLVES BUT THE PREDICTIONS AND assessments of its evolution aren't constant or always successful. With the rise of technology at the end of the nineteenth century many expected the twentieth to be the century of the grand peace. World War I shattered those prophecies. Then observers called the 1914–1919 conflict the "war to end all wars" and looked at the Versailles Treaty and the establishment of the League of Nations as the beginning of a bright new era of hope. President Woodrow Wilson's famous Fourteen Points and the reorganization of the world community promised the advent of an ideal international order, but just less than two decades later the most horrific of all wars led to the massacre of tens of millions of people across several continents: Nazi Germany, Fascist Italy, and militaristic Japan—all modern and industrialized countries—perpetrated genocide, a Holocaust, and global devastation. This disaster showed how unready the international community was for the League of Nations, which failed to prevent the surge of fascism and World War II. The level of education wasn't enough to contain the barbarism produced by such ideological regimes; actually, education multiplied barbarism's effects through the technological advancement of weaponry.

With the end of World War II, the founding of the United Nations in 1945, and the issuing of the Universal Declaration of Human Rights in 1948, again the world thought (for just a few months) that the Allies had produced a much better world for the next generation and that human freedom had been elevated to a higher level of protection. But again the predictions were proven wrong. The emerging Cold War turned bloody in many regions and ravaged the second half of the supposedly peaceful century. Human rights suffered within the Soviet bloc, China, and parts of the southern hemisphere. Idealist observers didn't immediately take account of the continuous suppressive behavior of post–World War II Stalinism or Maoism, even after the fall of their totalitarian predecessors in Europe: Nazism and fascism. During this period millions around the world were persecuted, killed, tortured, and jailed. Military regimes on more than one continent responded to the Communist threat with their own authoritarian wrath; the spiral of violence continued until the rise of reformers in the Soviet Union and the collapse of the Red Empire.

After the fall of the USSR, hopes for a better world again blossomed among the thinkers of international relations. It is the end of history as we know it, claimed many writers.[1] With the fall of the Berlin Wall, the non-Soviet intervention in the Kuwait war, and the Soviet collapse, a "new world order" appeared to have solidly emerged. The elites of the sole remaining superpower felt their country had actually defeated all sources of evil on the planet; throughout the 1990s it engaged in futurist missions of globalization and international policing of what it perceived as lower forms of conflict in Bosnia, Haiti, and Kosovo, while claiming human rights victories against South Africa's apartheid regime and Latin America's last military juntas. There were even celebrations of what was thought to be a breakthrough in the Arab-Israeli conflict, the so-called Peace Process of 1993. American and Western commentators looked at the last decade of the twentieth century as the final passage into the promised land of world peace.[2]

When the world mutated from its multipolar form (at the time of World War I) to a bipolar system in 1945, international relations experts believed that a balance of power between two superpowers would freeze world politics—no victor and no vanquished. This was the projection of the realists: Washington and Moscow would be the antipodes of a world stability based on fear. The development of the concept of mutually assured destruction (MAD) added credibility to the views of these realists: With each side having thousands of nuclear warheads aimed at the other, an end-of-days nuclear war wouldn't happen, as everyone knew it would consume all parties, and the world, forever. But the peoples of the Eastern bloc rejected the idea of becoming the human price for this international stability. Central and Eastern Europeans, as well as the peoples of the Soviet Union itself, produced a long, gradual, tectonic opposition to the expectations of the ruling Communist elites, and abstained from delivering the "glorious days" of the victorious proletariat. In other words, the masses inside the Soviet bloc didn't fight to the death against the capitalist enemy, neither in the factories nor on the battlefield of Afghanistan. This passive attitude of the populations brought down Soviet Communism. By 1991, hopes renewed around the Free World that totalitarianism would not prevail ideologically, and thus would not win the final stage of any confrontation with the West. China and the few remaining Communist regimes were left for what was believed to be a long, agonizing decline of a failing ideology until its inevitable collapse.

Thus, in September 1991, the world was set for a rebirth from out of the rubble of universal threats. Local and regional conflicts could be isolated, addressed one after the other, and ultimately solved, either by long negotiations or through massive military action sanctioned by the United Nations. Western analysts, particularly Americans, ruled out future world wars. But once again history was playing a trick on the self-styled great strategic thinkers of the world. Emerging from the dust of past centuries, an ideological movement claiming religious legitimacy reignited violence across the oceans, from the vast Arab Muslim world to the urban centers of the West: Jihadism. Once again hopes for an international society organized around a lasting peace were shattered, from Mogadishu to Manhattan, as early as 1993. In the center of the new storm were two violent strains of Jihadism, both embracing violence and seeking world domination: the Salafists (encompassing Wahabis, Takfiris, Deobandis, and others), on the one hand, and the Khumeinists, on the other. The Jihadi powers, both regimes and organizations, were fueled by radical religious establishments and backed by endless oil revenues.

In my book *Future Jihad: Terrorist Strategies against the West,* I analyzed the rise of these ideologies and movements since the 1920s, and then again in the 1970s, and described their global strategies against their enemies, the so-called *kuffar* (infidels).[3] I described the trends they followed and the debates they engaged in before unleashing their worldwide offensives in the 1990s in what became the road to 9/11. My essential point in *Future Jihad* was that the West failed to realize a war was being waged against it by an ideological movement manifested in different forms of power: regimes, circles within governments, indoctrination institutions, and other organizations. The Jihadists and other radicals were able to rise in the Greater Middle East region, target the West, and strike deep—culturally, politically, financially, and finally with terror—before the international community, the West, or the United States realized they were in a war. The book asked readers a major question: How come leaders, decision and opinion makers, weren't able to see the growing threat as it infiltrated and targeted the Free World, eventually attacking democracies directly? And how come the Jihadists—believers in fascism and terrorism—were able to spread through the Arab and Muslim world, both during and after the Cold War, while democracy and dissident movements were persecuted by the regimes in the region, some of which actually supported the West? The book explained clearly how the Salafists and Khumeinists took all the time they needed, moved stealthily, and maneuvered with success during the Cold War and throughout the 1990s, and then launched their final leap into open, world confrontation. As for why the West and other democracies failed to detect the menace, the answer was clear: They were defeated intellectually in a War of Ideas.

The War of Ideas: Jihadism against Democracy was published in March 2007.[4] In it I wrote about two main subjects: one was the irreconcilable contradiction between the ideology of Jihadism and the political culture of democracy, including all aspects affecting public life, such as pluralism, international law, human rights, women's rights, minorities' rights, religious freedom, and other basic values. All of these are rejected by the Jihadists. From a theoretical perspective, liberal democratic countries should have been the first to understand the depth of the ideological conflict with the rising fundamentalist movement. Instead, Western elites avoided questioning the fascistic nature of Salafism and Khumeinism and, worse, denied their own public the knowledge it needed to understand the nature of Jihadism. The second subject I covered was the three "wars of ideas" waged by the various Jihadi movements to defeat their opponents—first inside the Arab and Muslim world, and then within the West and across other regions of the world.

The essence of the problem today lies in the obstruction by the "teachers" (read: the mainstream educational and cultural elite) of the transfer of critical knowledge to their "classroom" (read: the people) about the War on Terror. In previous works I have explained why the academic establishment and its derivatives in the private and public spheres have denied their audiences the brutal truth about the growing power of Jihadists and their real agenda. Among many other factors contributing to this power was money: With significant Wahabi (and eventually Khumeinist) funding of Middle East and Islamic studies, international relations, sociology, and other related departments, our schools and colleges (including the Ivy League universities) produced two to three generations of experts, diplomats, analysts, strategists, lawyers, judges, political scientists, and cultural cadres who were either blind to Jihad or Jihadophiles themselves. But since the terrorist attacks beginning in 2001, the public, from Los Angeles to Vladivostok, has wanted answers about the perpetrators and their motives. It became extremely difficult, if not impossible, for the apologist elite to remain silent about the threat.

Though cornered by the mounting and unexplained violence committed by the Jihadi terrorists and pressed by the "consumers" of education for answers, the Western elite (or at least its overwhelming majority) continued its obfuscation. Not only had it hidden the reality of Islamism as a geopolitical and ideological force before 9/11, it now began resisting any attempts by a minority of intellectuals, a majority of professional experts, and national and international leaders to inform the public about the gravity of the threat. Incredibly, six years after the triggering of the so-called War on Terror, the bulk of the cultural establishment, a majority of artistic talents and celebrities, and a segment of the political elite are blocking the full mobilization of liberal democracies in what may be a fight for their existence.

The picture in the first decade of the twenty-first century seems bleak when colored by the dismal hopes of winning the War on Terror in this generation. For if the Jihadists are really expanding within the Arab Muslim societies, reaching out to younger generations, penetrating Western and other democracies, and growing both classical and unconventional resources, it does not take a great deal of reflection to see that the Free World should be acting faster, coordinating better, reaching out across the continents, and striking strategically at the foundation of the threat. However, a half decade of observation of the Western debate, an analysis of the various national policies, and the biased expertise provided to governments, which favor disengagement from the War on Terror, tells us that a systemic problem is hampering strategic victory at this stage. In short, I would argue that the path taken by the main forces of democracy till now leads to a longer, more uncertain, and bloodier fate for the international community and world peace.

This conclusion springs from a very simple equation: If the Free World is not confronting the expanding terrorist threat, or is not doing so in the right ways, the threat will grow stronger and more enduring in the near, medium, and long term. This was the case before World Wars I and II and during the Cold War. The systemic error is about to be repeated, but on a larger scale and with the threat commanding more destructive and powerful technologies.

At the dawn of the new millennium, the key factor in the War on Terror is the awareness of democratic societies. If they don't believe that they are in the middle of a global confrontation with their nemesis, they will fail to resist, and so they will lose the will to survive. The long and violent history of the human race has shown that a failure to address a challenge in one generation will automatically transfer it to future ones. In crude terms, if international society today doesn't confront terrorism, and more specifically the threat of contemporary Jihadism, with every means available to it, its principles will be delegitimized, its communities bled, and its freedoms shrunk, until a more clairvoyant generation undertakes a laborious resistance and somehow manages to salvage or restore its foundation.

The first principle, if civilized societies are to survive and thrive, building higher levels of freedoms and individual rights, is to recognize a threat to these values when it arises and to identify the source. Principle number two is to possess the will to resist the threat, and maintain that resistance until the threat is defeated. Principle number three is to be conscious of the confrontation, and to plan how to win it in the least costly manner, in the shortest time, and, most conclusively, with the greatest possible victory. These principles haven't just been discovered; they have shaped the strategies and policies of states, nations, and communities for centuries. All that is needed is to apply them to the present conflict.

How would they apply to today's tragic situation? Following these principles, one has to realize that the forces of terror have a vision of the world, life, society, and the future of humanity that differs radically from that of the Free World. If that primary reality isn't clear in the minds of policy makers, strategic planners, and educators, the other principles will be nullified. But if the ideological divide is crystal clear, then the commitment by democracies and their civil societies to struggle against terror and its fascist components is legitimated and receives the full backing of the public. If the Free World identifies the threat as existential (as it did with Nazism, fascism, and Bolshevism), the corresponding policies will have to be undertaken and whatever hardships arise will have to be endured. If the Free World should waiver, fall into doubt, or retreat, the forces of terror will press on and defeat democracies around the world. The international community must be conscious of the fact that it is confronting an anti–human rights hydra backed by endless waves of foot soldiers and vast financial resources. In short: there must be a realization that the battle is on and there aren't any other options.

After five years of battling around the world, from Kabul to Beirut, from Bali to New York City, the forces of Jihadism and their allies have shown unequivocally that they are primarily driven by sheer ideology and a determination to crush their opponents absolutely. With modern roots going back to the 1920s and the 1970s, the terror networks have at their disposal oil power, financial empires, regular armies, militias, underground connections, radical clerics, influential media, madrassas, regimes, circles within governments, biochemical arms, a totalitarian ideology, wide webs of collaborators and sympathizers within the Free World, and, potentially, nuclear weapons. That is one camp. On the other side, democracies are divided on the inside as to the principles of the War on Terror; are divided among each other as to the policies to adopt toward the terrorist threat, particularly the Jihadist one; and are tackling the crisis in a confused way. While the authoritarians and the Jihadists are moving forward, converging on their enemy and penetrating its defenses, the other side (which it wants to destroy or take over) has many fragments, and each one of them has its own little wars on terror. Arab and Muslim moderate governments fight for their internal security but not for the world's; Russia fights on its soil only; India fights over Kashmir, Israel over the West Bank, France in its suburbs. Spain's politics paralyses its efforts; China feels remote from the War on Terror; Latin America can't unite against it; and Africa's sub-Saharan countries are too weak to face it. The big picture is troubling: The confrontation is on, but the determination to win the War on Terror is proportional to the awareness of the players, the interests involved in prosecuting it, and a public understanding of it. In other words, the Jihadi terror forces—regimes and organizations—have been surging ahead while democracies of all sorts are uncertain about the confrontation.

In this book, I will ask the hard questions historians should ask and try to provide the harder answers the public wishes to obtain. The final judgment will be made by you, the readers.

Do we have to redefine the War on Terror? Should we move backward and give the pre-9/11 world another chance, or should we move forward and give space to alternative thinking? While it is true that we may have two directions to consider in the phase ahead, do we really have a choice if we wish to achieve a democratic stability?

Within the United States, but also in any liberal democracy challenged in the confrontation, the highest priority is the survival of the homeland, of its lifestyle and identity, its national security, and the rights of its citizens. Such things are what is at risk in the United States, Europe, Russia, India, Africa, Australia, and some parts of Latin America. Civil societies in the greater Middle East also face the threat of fascism and genocide. The question of survival is global, but each nation has to address its own homeland security. Is the very existence of societies, either physical or cultural, at risk when confronted with Jihadism?

To answer these pressing questions a Western rethinking of the War on Terror is needed. New alliances must be reached, accompanied by a series of revolutions in world economics and international diplomacy, reform of the United Nations, and, above all, a cultural revolution in the Arab and Muslim world. The War of Ideas will have to intensify; the isolation of terror ideologies would change the landscape of conflicts taking place everywhere at the instigation of Jihadism and its allies. Such a revolution in politics, ideology, academia, and media would not only bring cohesiveness to the international campaign against terror but also provide long-term answers to the crises in Iraq, Lebanon, Sudan, and Iran, as well as to menaces rising in the Greater Middle East and adjacent areas.

The confrontation is happening now and will grow wider, but the appropriate response to it must come in stages. Many are still confused about what our objectives ought to be. How should efforts be organized to roll back the Jihadi powers and undercut the Jihad looming on the horizon?

CHAPTER 1

REDEFINING THE WAR

HALF A DECADE AFTER 9/11, EIGHTEEN YEARS AFTER THE END OF THE Cold War, and fifty-two years after the founding of the United Nations, the question arises again: How can the Free World survive and how can it win in a confrontation with an authoritarian, hegemonic enemy?

For the last seven years, some democracies have begun responding to the ideological attack they have been under—even as their soldiers fight on the battlefields, their civilians are killed by terror attacks, and the political debate wears on the nerves of citizens and taxpayers in the West. The dominant establishment seems to disagree on why the war started, on the steps leaders have taken or not taken, and on how to end the conflict. Peoples throughout history have consented to extreme sacrifices and deprivations in the hope of ultimately winning the wars imposed on them. But in the War on Terror the public seems lost in such questions as, Could we have avoided the war? and, since 2001, Have we made the right decisions?

But the mother of all questions remains unaddressed: How can we still win this global war and defeat the forces of Jihadism? This is the center of today's debate. One camp says we have to fight the war but isn't telling us how to win it, while another says we were wrong to engage the enemy—we have made the enemy stronger and are losing the conflict. The latter camp, however, isn't telling us how we should have engaged the Jihadists differently or how we should do so in the future. Within the West, unfortunately, narrow political interests prevent the development of strategic policies. The focus is more on who sits in the White House, 10 Downing Street, or the Élysée Palace than on global, relentless, and long-lasting steps to end Jihadi terrorism and its derivatives.

THE FREE WORLD CAN STILL WIN

In this book I argue that modern and free societies can win the War on Terror, including the conflict with Jihadism. I will try to demonstrate that the public has not been served well by the intelligentsia, who miseducated and misinformed them and who are mired in one sterile debate after another. But since the start of the great counteroffensive in 2001 by the United States, the coalition of the willing, and the new dissidents in the Middle East, breaches have been opened in the defenses of global Jihadism. Now we can see the real state of affairs inside their realm. And with a better understanding of their ideology, we have begun to understand their strategies within the West. We are now at a critical stage. The conflict can evolve in either of two directions: the Jihadists break down the democracies, or the forces of freedom defeat Jihadism. From the confrontation with Salafi and Wahabi powers and organizations in Iraq, the Arab peninsula, Sudan, elsewhere in Africa, and south Asia to the clash with the Khumeinist axis of control in Iran, Syria, and Lebanon, the frontiers of terror are endless. From London to Mumbai and from New York to Madrid, the cells of the urban Jihad are growing, menacing security and stability.

I argue that if the engaged democracies can "see" the global map of Jihadism, they can defeat it. However, this ultimate victory in the War on Terror will require a clear vision, determination, coordination, and perseverance by leaders and the public. But the gigantic task, which will consume efforts and talents and require greater sophistication and education, rests on a simple equation: If we want to win the War on Terror, we have to defeat the phenomenon of Jihadism. It will require a reconstruction of strategies, a new discourse with citizens, and a revolution in thinking. Can we in the Free World gain this victory? Yes, if we adopt a new direction.

DEFINING IS HALF OF WINNING

Defining the threat is already halfway to victory. Since 9/11, there has been a war over the definition of war among the various parties to the conflict. The stakes are high. The faster a party can frame the conflict, the quicker that party can isolate its enemy by dominating the debate. In modern times, and with high technology, winning the framing can bring victory on the ground. The radical forces, particularly the Jihadi networks, have learned quickly from past Communist propaganda and the first post-Soviet decade that with speed and overwhelming media they can shift the center of debate, enabling them to project themselves as the legitimate defenders of their societies and their foes as the aggressors. The tactics of Salafists and Khumeinists reflect a principle of psychological war known in the Arab world as *Darabani wa baka, sabaqani wa ishtaka:* "They hit me and cried, beat me to court, and sued me." The propaganda of the Jihadists, whether through regime-backed media or dispersed groups, operates on two main principles: Be first to frame the conflict, and demonize the other side as the attackers. That's how al Qaeda, their allies, Wahabis within regimes, Muslim Brotherhood operatives, Tehran's intelligence network, Syria's Mukhabarat, Hezbollah, and their allies have operated on satellite TV and online, in forums around the world—and how they won the 1990s War of Ideas and are winning it still.[1]

In each conflict, the Jihadist attempts to isolate one major target. The different groups of Jihadists, despite their inner crises, tensions, and subconflicts, focus one set of arguments against one particular target, be it Israel, France, Southern Sudan, or Kurdistan. In each conflict the Jihadists, through multiple groups extending around the world, close in on the target. The target is demonized, isolated, and marked for punishment by "all." The Free World watches these witch hunts passively. While the global Jihadi propaganda machine launches its political offensives, encircling and weakening the morale of its adversary, the democratic camp divides over "the issue," if it is even aware of the threat, and ends up losing more ground. The Jihadi camp has a better knowledge of the weakness of democracies than the latter has of Jihadists, which brings us to another advantage the terror groups have over the Free World.

Under authoritarian and totalitarian regimes, public opinion, coalitions, free media, polls, debates, and other features of liberal democracies are irrelevant: Either they do not exist, as under the Taliban and in Saudi Arabia, Iran, Syria, Libya, and Cuba, or they are manipulated by antidemocracy forces, as in Egypt, Pakistan, and Indonesia. In full-fledged democracies, the process of setting a national agenda is complex and difficult and dependent on whoever manages to persuade the public of its views. And this is precisely where the Jihadists have been winning for years: using the mechanisms of democracy and basic freedoms in liberal societies to win the battle of framing the conflict. With huge funds at their disposal, the enemies of pluralism use media, intelligentsia, and academia to spread propaganda that labels Western governments as the bad guys in international relations. Once so branded, all efforts by the Free World are doomed to fail. Once a government, or even a country, is successfully labeled by its foes, it loses international support, the opportunity to rally allies, and most important, the confidence of the public. Hence, the first battle is over the image of the foe. When fighting India in an effort to erect an emirate in Kashmir, the world Jihadi machine accuses New Delhi of human rights abuses, war crimes, and aggressiveness. The world watches. When the Jihadi engage Russia with the aim of establishing a Wahabi principality in Chechnya, the same techniques are applied. And the world watches. Then comes France's turn (over the *hijaab* and the rioting in the suburbs): France is demonized, and the world blasts French political culture. Likewise Great Britain, in its battles against the terrorists after 2005: It is British political culture and government that are made responsible for the violence. In other, similar reversals of blame, it was the rebels in Sudan, not the Islamist regime, who were made responsible for the genocide; the government in Lebanon, not Fatah al Islam and Syria, who was blamed for the violence there.

And, of course, this is how America found itself blamed on the morning of 9/11—portrayed as the aggressor rather than the victim. In the very first hours after the strikes, a formidable conglomeration of media, Internet, and propaganda operatives, from the heart of the Middle East to the American Middle West, explained the roots of the attacks and attempted to deflect the U.S. response, and perhaps even with time reset the national and international agendas. From bin Laden's (and later Ahmadinejad's) speeches, to Sheikh Yusuf al Qaradawi's "sermons" on al Jazeera, to the "academic analysis" by Ivy League professors, the sentence was rendered swiftly: It was America's fault—Western plundering and meddling in Islamic lands prompted the attacks, and of course, at the center was the Israeli-Palestinian problem.[2] America was blamed for the Arab-Israeli conflict, for Iraq's situation since 1991, for having forces in Saudi Arabia, and even for European colonialism and the Crusades. An old Middle Eastern proverb aptly describes this distorted portrayal: *Aanze walaw taret*, meaning, "It is a goat, even if it flies!"

"THERE IS NO THREAT"

The first line of attack by the Jihadist propaganda was to deny the threat altogether and thereby convince the democracies (their decision makers and the public) that there is no global threat menacing the West and the Free World. In order to achieve this goal the propaganda machine moved quickly on two tracks: One was to accuse the West, or at least the corporate powers on the one hand and Christian-Zionist lobbies on the other, of concocting the idea of a threat, so that business or political interests appeared to be the cause of the war. This is a sort of preemptive strike to cut off the international campaign at the start. The advocates of such arguments are found among the Trotskyites, the extreme left-wing and some self-declared progressive forces within the West, and, strangely enough, also the racist-motivated extreme right wing.[3]

This assertion that a threat is nonexistent is developed directly by the apologists for Jihadism. They are found mostly in academic circles, and their argument is that Jihad is essentially spiritual; thus the Jihadists are a force for spiritual change. This argument was dominant in the mainstream thinking in the West until 9/11. With the ensuing exultant videos of celebrating Arab crowds, violent attacks in European cities, and the wars in Afghanistan and Iraq, the first wave of Jihad apology receded as the Salafi ideologues and cadre, including al Qaeda, demonstrated to the world that a Jihadi ideology existed, and it was manifestly violent.

At this point, a second wave of arguments claimed that if indeed there is violence it is caused by U.S. policy, past colonialism, and other Western sins. We'll explore some of the latter in this chapter. A third wave of arguments—which I call the save-Jihad doctrine—was produced by Wahabi and Muslim Brotherhood clerics and conveyed via lobbyists in the United States and the West. It basically said that the real Jihadists aren't the problem, only those who conduct nonsanctioned terror activities.[4] Again, one after another, these attempts to deflect Western anger came up against the hard reality of the statements and the actions of the Jihadists themselves. The apologists used all their resources to convince the world that Jihad is not a war enterprise and that Jihadism is not a threat, but the Jihadists proved all these apologetics wrong. And yet the clash of arguments is still going on both in the West and throughout the Arab and Muslim worlds. The efforts and resources of the apologist scholars and the Jihadi tacticians are gigantic. If successful, their efforts would make the War on Terror seem like a quixotic campaign against an imaginary enemy, and would lead the West to let its guard down for another decade, if not more; such a defeat in the War of Ideas would cause the conflict to last another generation, for it is clear that Jihadists will continue to use terror as a tactic.

"THERE IS NO WAR!"

A more daring attempt to defeat the identification of the problem was a campaign to deny that the War on Terror or the campaigns by the Jihadists are in fact a war. Even after 9/11 in the United States, 3/11 in Madrid, 7/7 in London, as well two major campaigns in Iraq and Afghanistan, and all the car bombs, massacres, and blowing up of mosques and churches by Jihadists (not to mention the Islamic courts coup in Somalia, the terrorist assassinations and explosions in Lebanon, the bloody assault on the Beslan school in Russia, the discovery of terror cells in Canada, Australia, and Germany, and the bombings in Morocco, Algeria, Tunisia, Saudi Arabia, Yemen, Turkey, and Israel), critics incredibly persist in saying the war is a mirage. Such an attitude has no parallel in history. No ostrich politics has dug so deep to oppose one specific conflict.

Peace movements, including the most left-leaning (worldwide) and the most extreme conservative isolationist (in America), have traditionally opposed war, but never maintained that it didn't exist. Recent fierce opposition to the so-called War on Terror seems to have reached intellectual hysteria; the opponents claim that the confrontation is nothing but a conspiracy to secure oil, scare politics, or the work of some sort of cabal. The "there-is-no-war" party in fact demonstrates the determination by the Jihadophile camp to block the awareness of the American people and other Westerners, and the rest of the Free World.

Such blindness gives the opponents of the West the opportunity for initiatives and surprises and, ultimately, the power to dictate the course of the conflict. The

European theater in the Jihadi campaign illustrates this dimension clearly. Until 2007, most European governments, following the advice of the intelligentsia and of Islamist lobbies, dropped the term "War on Terror," not to replace it with a more efficient description, but to pull back linguistically, culturally, and ideologically. As a result of this tactical intellectual defeat, the terrorist groups were emboldened, the militant networks grew less fearful of authorities, and mobilization for urban intifadas in Europe proceeded. The Europeans opened the floodgates to further legitimization without—as they had been led to believe would happen—containing radicalization.[5]

A WRONG FOREIGN POLICY

As all arguments refuting the reality of a clear danger and a real war collapsed, the apologist camp retreated to another line of defense. The critics advanced the idea that terrorists are attacking the West because of a negative, faulty, and irresponsible U.S. and Western foreign policy. They charged Washington with plunder, unilateralism, and unfairness in its attitudes and long-term strategies. The first charge was about the biased U.S. backing of Israel. They portrayed the United States as ideologically committed to the Jewish state and under the domination of the Jewish lobby. Washington, they said, rejected the Palestinians and all other Arabs, or at least treated them less fairly than its ally Israel. Another charge was America's constant support for Arab regimes portrayed by the Jihadists and other radicals as "authoritarian" and opposed to democracy. An additional charge was that the United States maintained troops and bases in the region. Jihadists and Jihadophiles in the West claimed that al Qaeda's and others' radical strikes against the United States were directly linked to this matter, though their only evidence was bin Laden's statement to that effect. Last was the argument over sanctions against Saddam's regime. For years, and increasingly after 9/11, critics said that U.S. and British policies of economic sanctions and no-fly zones in Iraq actually caused terrorist attacks.

A thorough comparative analysis of these accusations reveals the pro-Jihadi lobby's hidden strategic agenda: distracting attention from the Jihadi projects in the region. A simple deconstruction of the volley of arguments shows the real equation behind the charges. The Americans' constant support of Israel, although an undeniable fact over the past decades, isn't eternal, isn't unconditional, and doesn't exclude support for other countries and other players in the region. Between 1947 and 1966, U.S. policies weren't fully supportive of Israel's actions. In 1956, during the Suez crisis, President Dwight D. Eisenhower forced Israel, France, and Great Britain to pull out of the Sinai immediately. Until 1966, it was France that provided Israel's best weapons, not America. By the end of the 1980s and the early 1990s, Washington was providing very advanced military systems to moderate Arab governments, sometimes in opposition to Israeli concerns. In reality, if the United States maintained a strong support for the state of Israel it was because of the nature of the Israeli political identity: a Jewish pluralist democracy.

One can add two more reasons, both rational: In the Cold War, Israel was counted in the Western bloc, and Israel supporters in America pressed the right buttons in their advocacy of the Mediterranean nation. Most other ethnic pressure groups, including Arabs, Muslims, and Palestinians, tried to emulate it. Ironically, the charge that the United States supports only Israel conflicts with the second charge, that Washington supports Arab authoritarian regimes. When examined closely, the Jihadi argumentation becomes clear. What they are saying is that the United States should support the Arabs over Israel in general but not their authoritarian regimes. And since all Arab governments are portrayed as repressive by the Jihadists, therefore (in Salafi and Khumeinist fantasies) Washington's best policy should be to fully support the Jihadists!

The argument about the presence of U.S. troops in the region (before 2003) also doesn't stand up well, since the forces were requested by Arab Muslim governments before and after the Saddam invasion of Kuwait. Saudi Arabia, the most closed of Sunni Islamic regimes, opened its bases, ports, and airports to the infidels, as did other Gulf states, to defend the peninsula against the Baathist "apostate" invasion. The proponents of this view fail to note that British bases and a European military presence preceded the United States' full offensive of 1991, which was basically undertaken to liberate one Arab Muslim country from another.[6] As to the self-declared "pure" bin Laden group that invented this argument, they had no objections to getting training, logistics, and weapons from the same *kuffar* during the 1980s in Afghanistan. As I argued in *Future Jihad*, the Salafi ideologues are very pragmatic: America is good when it provides them with weapons and when they can raise funds within its borders, but it is bad when it obstructs their regional agenda.

But to be fair, U.S. foreign policy was indeed very problematic during the Cold War and the 1990s when it came to the Greater Middle East. For while it clearly stood by Israel, it abandoned all other bastions of resistance against authoritarianism and terrorism. Lebanon was abandoned to Syria, the Kurds to Saddam, Southern Sudan to Turabi's regime, Iran's opposition to Mohammed Khatemi's so-called reformism, Syria's dissidents to Assad, and in general terms there was a systematic failure to support human rights and democracy movements under friendly and adversarial regimes alike. Even further, American policy at times opened its arms to Jihadists under the auspices of what it conceived of as a "dialogue with the forces of change." In hindsight researchers can see that U.S. and Western diplomats were enticed to engage the Islamists rather than engaging and supporting the democrats in the region. Hence, failure to back up real partners strengthened the radicals. By the time the latter began launching their attacks against the West, the liberals were too weak to make a difference in the battle, and they still are.

Ironically, if American foreign policy is to blame for the rise of terrorism, it is because it didn't prevent it, because it gave the radical movements credibility, and because it abandoned the only real alternative to them: the liberals in the region. The apologists for Jihadism and critics of U.S. policy are really bold when they blame Washington for not supporting them enough—as if American policy hadn't actually opened the doors for them to rise in the region, crush the democrats, and finally strike America and other democracies. In short, American foreign policy is to blame, but not for the reasons advanced by the Jihadis and Jihadophiles; rather, it simply allowed the threat to grow to almost irreversible levels.

TOWARD A NEW DEFINITION

It is a fact that a world movement that adopted a Jihadist agenda, based on multiple Jihadi ideologies and doctrines, has declared war, has waged it, and is pursuing the goal of world domination. The global Jihadi forces combine regimes, institutions, segments within regimes, economic interests and powers, organizations, sub-groups, and individual terrorists. Western democracies, other democracies, developing countries, and even the remaining Communist countries, in addition to Arab and Muslim moderate governments, are all targeted by the global Jihadi forces.

The Jihadi camp, although composed of two main trees (Salafi and Khumein-ist) and multilayered, is actually at war, an all-out conflict aiming at the downfall of twenty-one Arab states and more than fifty Muslim governments, hoping to re-place them with a caliphate (or an imamate, in the case of Iran) that would reject international law and its institutions, including the United Nations, and revive what they believe would be a renewed *fatah* (conquest of the lands outside the caliphate, that is, the rest of the world).

The Jihadi camp would establish oppressive regimes with anti–human rights and counterdemocracy programs. A dark foreshadowing of the future was the Tal-iban regime in Afghanistan. There are currently full or partial models in Iran and Sudan. Governments that have been applying various segments of this ideology are Saudi Arabia and Libya. Regimes that are supporting Jihadi terror without neces-sarily applying their doctrines include Syria's.

The Jihadi forces are hurtling forward in the Greater Middle East, backed by a gigantic propaganda and indoctrination machine with media icons such as al Jazeera and al Manar, and a widening web presence. These forces, connected or not, have extended their influence and recruitment process within the West, both culturally and with militants. The geopolitical map of the global Jihadi deployment has to be clearly understood if the Free World is to be able to define it. Thus a re-definition of the War on Terror is vital for the West, the rest of the Free World, and the international community. Hence, the responses by civil societies within the Arab and Muslim world are legitimate; the defensive moves by the Free World are warranted; and an international condemnation of Jihadi terror is a precondition for ultimate future success in defending peace.

The key terms in defining the war are that it is:

1. waged by the global Jihadists;
2. targeted at civil societies and human rights around the world;
3. aimed at world domination; and
4. threatening international security and peace.

Thus, only repeated failures in the War of Ideas have been able to obscure the stark facts supporting a defense against Jihadi terror.

CHAPTER 2

WESTERN RETHINKING

THOUGH MANY SOCIETIES AND REGIONS ARE TARGETED BY INTERnational terrorism, the West is undoubtedly at the center of the attack. But ironic as it may be, the leader of the international resistance is among the weakest in perception. Liberal democracies in general, and those of Western Europe, the Americas, and the United States in particular, seem to have lost sight of the big picture by retreating in the War of Ideas. By not winning the battle of identification (as I argued in chapter 1), Americans and other Westerners spend tremendous resources without focusing on the global target. For example, U.S. and coalition spending in Iraq and Afghanistan since 2001 and European trans-Mediterranean aid policies over the decade could have already reversed the course of the conflict with Jihadism. Not only hasn't this happened, but the foes of the West have gained time, penetrated deeper into the Arab and Muslim world, and prevented democratic movements within the Middle East from scoring decisive victories. Worse, Jihadi penetration of Western democracies since the 1980s and the continuous mollification of the Western response have succeeded in stretching the bounds of the conflict and weakened the resistance on other continents. For if Americans, Canadians, Australians, and Western Europeans are slow to resist and incapable of identifying the global threat, how can Russians, Indians, Africans, Asians, and Arab Muslim moderates do better? The West will have to rethink its past intellectual approaches to the conflict and apply this new thinking in the confrontation. Such a revolution seems to be the only path to a reinvigoration of the Western response, which in turn would help set the stage for a true cross-*civilizational* and transnational campaign to deal with the widening confrontation. Following are the main ideas to consider in rethinking the principles of the revolution.

SOCIOECONOMIC ROOTS

Relentlessly since the first War of Ideas (1945–1990), actively throughout the second (1990–2001), and continuously ever since, the Jihadis and their apologist followers have been pounding the West with a socioeconomic explanation of terrorism; in particular, Salafi-Khumeinist radicalism has advanced this idea. This thesis, with deep roots in the democracies, has been one of the most successful platforms preventing the identification of Jihadism as an ideology per se and blocking mass mobilization against it. It was concocted on European and North American campuses by a number of liberals and Marxists favorable to the Islamist offensive against the West. It is founded in a massive literature on both sides of the Atlantic, and it argues that terrorism in general and Jihad-inspired groups in particular are an emanation of economic disparities, social injustices, and sheer poverty. To consolidate the concept, the intellectual elite provide many examples of underdevelopment in the Third World and postulate that al Qaeda, other Salafi groups, Hezbollah, and the regimes backing them are representatives of the disenfranchised in the Greater Middle East and beyond. The socioeconomic argument goes so far as to claim that even well-off individuals would commit terrorist acts in the name of the dispossessed. This paradigm has dominated most research in academia, influenced media and politicians, and in many instances swayed defense strategists. To Marxists (and Neo-Marxists as of 1990) the basic idea is that militant action is the direct result of social inequalities and is a proletarian manifestation. To liberals (those who sympathize with the Jihadists and other radicals) terrorism is the product of the weak and disenfranchised. Both Marxists and liberals (with many exceptions) conclude that terrorism is about the West's failure to do enough to ameliorate economic disparities. But over the years the inquiry into the roots of terrorism, and specifically Jihadism, has demonstrated otherwise—dramatically.

In Europe, Jihadi militants, it seems, come mostly from the middle class. The bombers in Madrid and London, the assassins in Amsterdam, and the Jihadists who attacked the United States from Europe hail from educated backgrounds. Examples abound: Mohammad Atta and Ziad Jarrah, the 9/11 ringleaders, and many of their colleagues had a good life, though ideology corrupted it. France's urban intifada in the fall of 2005 was given as an example of disenfranchised Arab Muslim émigrés taking to the street. But investigations showed the prime influence on this movement was radical clerics. Across Europe, as research has shown, Salafi ideology is ravaging the minds of youth, using indoctrinating educational systems, and under pressure, the governments have abandoned educational control to the clerics. The circle is closed: Gulf regimes fund the radical clerics and spread radical ideologies among émigré communities; the indoctrination process creates Jihadists; the latter are recruited by organizations that adopt terror as a strategy.[1] In 2007 British authorities uncovered and disrupted terror plots in London, Glasgow, and elsewhere: Among the alleged perpetrators were forty-five physicians who were planning violence. These upper-class Jihadists weren't motivated by social injustice. They spoke of the will of Allah, *kuffar*, the caliphate, and all things related to Islamist ideology. Ayman Zawahiri was a physician in Egypt, not a Gdansk factory worker. Osama bin Laden, the Iranian ayatollahs, and the Wahabi emirs who fund the terror groups are rich, very rich.[2]

A review of the three main financial centers that support Jihadism—Salafism, Wahabism, and Khumeinism—shows a picture that undermines the disenfranchisement thesis. Flowing out of rich Saudi Arabia like the oil of its deserts are billions of petrodollars, and they have been used over the decades to spread Wahabism around the world. High-living emirs have showered money on artistic, financial, educational, and other undertakings in the region and overseas as a means to indoctrinate young minds. These millions could have been spent in emancipating poor and uneducated Arabs, Muslims, and even the citizens of Saudi Arabia itself. Instead, much of the oil revenue was devoted to waging an ideological war. Following in the footsteps of the Saudis, the Qatari regime has become a promoter of the Muslim Brotherhood agenda—from funding al Jazeera and providing immunity to its radical incitements to leading diplomatic activities against the spread of pluralist democracy in the region (e.g., countering the Cedars Revolution in Lebanon, blocking the protection of Darfur's population, and shielding oppressive regimes, as in Syria and Sudan). Across the Persian Gulf, the Iranian regime has been using oil revenues to fund Hezbollah in Lebanon, Hamas in Gaza, and other Jihadi organizations everywhere. These hardly sound like campaigns for lifting up the proletariat.

In fact, almost 90 percent of the funding of Jihadi networks comes from oil-rich regimes, whose elites enjoy a lifestyle superior to any authoritarian, fascist, or totalitarian establishment in the modern age. The root cause of Jihadism is basically manufactured, drawing on a capital investment in the hundreds of millions of dollars to the vast networks of Salafi and Khumeini operatives—who in turn recruit, indoctrinate, and train thousands of Jihadis. Had the patrons of Jihadism really cared about lower-class frustration and poverty in their region, they would have invested the gargantuan oil royalties in developing the Hijaz and Ihsaa provinces in Saudi Arabia,[3] helping Gaza's economy stand up, supporting Egypt's fellaheen, aiding the disenfranchised sectors of the Iranian population, and spreading scientific and social knowledge among their youth. Instead, they have spent their millions on reasserting doctrines of war, exclusion, and inequality that date to the Middle Ages. Ironically, the deepest, broadest socioeconomic root of Jihadism in the Middle East is the rich regimes' practice of depriving their masses of the benefits of the region's enormous wealth; instead of guiding the region toward modernity, they have deliberately pushed it backward. It is not the wealthy West that keeps the Middle East poor, it is the rich segment of the Middle East itself that does so. Instead of offering youngsters education, they have provided indoctrination, raising a generation not of doctors and lawyers but of Jihadists and suicide bombers.[4]

To be sure, socioeconomic frustrations exist, independent of ideology and culture. This is always true. But in the region, the link between these injustices and inequities and the solutions that can bridge the gaps is poisoned by ideology and political indoctrination. If the poor are indoctrinated by Marxists, they will become Communists, and may end up as activists in political parties or labor unions. The same is true for other forms of indoctrination as well. One can become socialist, corporatist, fascist, liberal, feminist, environmentalist, conservative, religionist, or nationalist, depending on who provides the enlightenment or indoctrination. It is a question of the medium, of the way the teaching and education come. Muslims become Islamists not because of socioeconomic conditions, but because their teachers are Jihadists. That is the conclusion not only of scientific observation and logic, but also of Muslim liberals and progressives. For the difference between those in the Arab and Muslim world who end up in the fundamentalist camp and those who end up in the liberal camp is found not in their socioeconomic backgrounds but in their educational experience.[5]

The most important argument debunking the apologist thesis is certainly the Jihadi agenda itself. Stunningly, while social scientists and lobbyists in the West still insist that disenfranchisement and social disparities are the direct roots of suicide bombings and terrorism, the Salafist and Khumeinist agendas reject that claim altogether. From bin Laden and Zawahiri to imams Khumeini and Khameini, and all other leaders in the two trees of Jihadism, the message can't be clearer in this regard: Their motivation is not to establish social and economic justice. They seek a *divine* satisfaction (*rida ilahi*) that their project is moving forward. Jihadism needs the poor and the rich, the disenfranchised and the socially integrated, in its march toward the caliphate or the imamate. "It is not for material gain that our sons wage Jihad," the mullahs keep repeating online and in the media: "It is about fulfilling our neglected duty and satisfying the Creator (*al Khaliq*)." The long agendas advanced by the Salafists and the Khumeinists do not call for jobs, the redistribution of land, progressive taxation, the reorganization of the means of production, commercial laws, universal health care, social security, or women's equality. Their claims are doctrinal, and have to do with destroying the *kuffar* (infidels), the apostates, and the polytheists; their strategic aims are to defeat twenty-one Arab governments and dozens of Muslim states in order to replace them with a worldwide caliphate, in which a caliph and his administration regulate the society and economy through divinely inspired wisdom. Technically, the caliphate could be as socioeconomically unjust as many other governments and regimes are today. There is no guarantee that the poor will be transformed under a caliphate into a middle class.

The West's vision of the Jihadists has been blurred by oil-funded lobbyists who depict Jihadists as Robin Hoods, or at least (even if violent) as a legitimate resistance against socioeconomic oppression. Ultimately, the West has failed to see the Jihadist agenda for what it really is: another neofascist program that wants to install a totalitarian regime, to expand across the globe and install its own social structure complete with elites, the rich, the middle classes, and the disenfranchised, oppressed, and marginalized. Thus the West and the Free World in general must rethink their understanding of the Jihadi conflict with democracy: This is not the struggle of the poor against the rich, but a war by a form of totalitarianism against all free people, a war to empower an ideological elite who would rule all strata of society according to a so-called divine model defined by them.

PAST COLONIAL ROOTS

Beyond the myth of socioeconomic causation comes the historical claim that terrorism is rooted in past colonialism. Jihadi scholars and commentators, as well as apologists and Jihadophiles in the West, often blame today's violence on what they say is a "reaction to colonialism, imperialism, and Western plunder of the Middle East and North Africa." They try to establish a direct link between al Qaeda's attacks on North America and Europe and the European occupation of vast areas of the Arab and Muslim world in the past. Western apologists emphasize the resulting economic devastation and call for modern reparations, while Islamist ideologues stress the historical injustices and call for systemic punishment, that is, the reestablishment of the caliphate and the dismantling of the modern international system. Both approaches are selective in their historical analysis and obscure.[6]

To begin with, the West has extensively apologized for its own colonial wars, but the Jihadi (and authoritarian) elites have never addressed the colonial wars waged by caliphates and sultanates, entangled with and sometimes the cause for European enterprises.[7] Here are a few examples:

1. The Crusades: Often cited by Western apologists as the source of Arab Islamic anger at the Christian West and considered by the Jihadists as a current casus belli, these European incursions into the eastern Mediterranean (eleventh through thirteenth centuries) are perceived as ongoing wars against Muslim and Arab lands.[8] Bin Laden's speeches and the entire rhetoric of his followers centers on the *Salibyeen* (Crusaders) from the Middle Ages up till this very moment. But the Jihadist conveniently neglects some of the main historical reasons behind the Crusades: the preceding Arab Islamic conquests launched from the seventh century A.D./C.E. onward, out of Arabia into the upper Middle East, including Palestine, Syria, Mesopotamia, Egypt, and North Africa, and into Sicily, Italy, Spain, and France. Western apologists are silent about the four centuries of *jihad* and *fatah* that preceded the Crusades and actually invited the latter into the

eastern Mediterranean. A truncated study of world history places the Crusades as the first move by European Christians against the Islamic empire, but it fails to explain that, centuries earlier, the armies of the Rashidun, Umayyads, and Abbasids invaded, occupied, and dominated lands dozens of times larger than what the Crusades, all together, conquered in the Levant. From a twenty-first-century perspective, of course, all religious wars of conquest are illegitimate. Neither crusades nor *jihad* and *fatah* are permissible today under international law. But Western apologists and Jihadists find it acceptable to legitimize today's Jihadic attacks as a response to medieval crusades. This *diachronic* fallacy cannot stand up to legal and historical scrutiny. Either one would have to link all contemporary actions to all historical events, or the opposite. Bin Laden cannot strike New York while claiming revenge for Richard the Lion-Hearted's crushing of the Abuyyid army in the twelfth century without then allowing the French to strike at Damascus for invading its lands under the Umayyads. This *Stargate* logic would totally dismantle international law.[9] It goes without saying that all military campaigns of the past were brutal, mostly unnecessary, and surely deserving of condemnation by modern standards—including the Crusades. But the Jihadophiles slice these two centuries of European warfare in the eastern Mediterranean from a thousand years of Arab Islamic conquest and occupation to shape a case for modern terrorism, justified as retaliation. In modern terms both invasions would be illegal; hence the West shouldn't fall for the charge that it is "crusading" and that the Jihadists therefore have a legitimate claim to revenge. Historically, the wars of religion across the Mediterranean had a beginning (the Arab Islamic conquest) and an end (with the Ottoman decline). These wars deserve an equal and balanced review, so that the present may profit from their lessons and not be hostage to them in the future.

2. The Spanish Reconquista: As with the Crusades, Jihadi and apologist literature keeps blaming the West, and particularly the Spaniards, for what has been called the Reconquista of the Iberian Peninsula. Intellectuals in the West and ideologues in the Arab world decry the brutality of the Spanish and Portuguese forces' southern advance, pushing back the various dynasties ruling Arab Muslim Andalusia. The critics have gone as far as to link modern Jihadi terrorism to what they perceived as the "bloody" takeover of al-Andalus (the name of Spain under the Islamic empires) by "Europeans." Iberian Christian forces did indeed take Andalusian fortresses one after the other and move their inhabitants south, and these medieval battles and postcombat actions were—like all military encounters of the age—violent and ruthless. But the critics, making a chronological leap similar to

that over the Crusades, mislead their readers. First of all, the Spanish and Portuguese moving south were returning to lands taken by *fatah* and *jihad*. The chronology is as follows: In 715 A.D./C.E., Tariq bin Ziad, leading an expeditionary army sent by the Umayyad caliph, invaded Spain in stages and ruled over its native population. The occupation of the peninsula lasted roughly seven centuries before Spain and Portugal were liberated by their own people. Cruelty was practiced on both sides, but the initial invasion was staged by those whom the Jihadists today claim as their ancestors, and the subsequent liberation was at the hands of those whom the modern Jihadists accuse of being in the wrong. Clearly, a historical gap has been created by apologists so that the Iberian Reconquista is made responsible for injustices committed now, despite the fact that it was a response to an Arab Islamic "Conquista."[10] The apologists blame the defenders for defending themselves and endorse terrorist retaliation today based on legitimate liberations that occurred centuries ago. The West has to reject the argument of "just retaliation because of the Iberian Reconquista." The unfair and harsh treatment of Jews and Muslims at the hands of the Catholic monarchy and the mistreatment of Christians as *dhimmis* (non-Muslim populations living under the Islamic state) at the hands of the Islamic caliphate are both to be deplored.[11] But that is entirely different from supporting the Jihadists' legitimization of terror in the twenty-first century based on what Iberians did in liberating their country in the fifteenth century, which cannot be acceptable.

In the final analysis one has to factor in the emotions involved in all wars, historical and current, and analyze the political sociologies of nations, ethnicities, and larger cultural blocs involved in past events. History has a clear impact on the collective psychologies of groups and will continue to do so. But these radical ideological groups excise a moment in history, even a very long one, and shape it to accommodate current political agendas. Nations have occupied nations and powers have bled and exploited other societies throughout history. Contemporary Jihadists have been trying to hold liberal democracies psychologically and morally responsible for a particular colonialism. But the democracies, and the West in general, must reject the Jihadi ideological warfare for three reasons: first, because the West has already rejected colonial practices and withdrawn from these regions; second, because the Jihadists and the apologists have been selective in their condemnation of colonialism by not criticizing other, similar enterprises such as Arab colonialism and Islamic imperialism; and third, because the Jihadist agenda aims at erecting a new imperialist institution, a twenty-first-century caliphate.

A WAR ON ISLAM

The most serious charge leveled against the West (and other democracies, such as India and Russia) is that it is waging a so-called War against Islam. *Al harb al Islam* has been an almost daily slogan on al Jazeera since 2001 and on all Salafi and Khumeinist websites. In an amazing strategic response to the Western-initiated campaign against terrorism, the forces of Jihadism have turned the concept upside down; they accuse their foes of actually waging an offensive against Islam and against Muslims, not against specific terror groups or regimes. The design of the War on Islam is clever, as it shields the radicals beneath the mantle of a worldwide religion. Hence, instead of allowing an international coalition to encircle al Qaeda and its kind, the Salafists transformed the debate—mainly in the Muslim world but also in the West—into a discussion of the *kuffar* War on Islam, engulfing whoever is involved in the War on Terror. The Iranian network (along with Hezbollah) also propagates this view of Islam under attack. Such a war of words allows the Jihadi powers to remain on the attack.[12]

The strategy has been very successful in at least two respects. The Western elite has been induced to accept this formulation and to initiate campaigns to disengage from this alleged war on Islam. The accusation alone has pushed Western governments, nongovernmental organizations, and institutions to blame their own societies for being the perceived aggressors against a whole civilization. Implicitly, if the West is the attacker, then the Jihadis are the defenders. Merely by accepting the hypothesis of the *harb al Islam*, the Free World, with its various cultures and regions, including non-Jihadist Muslims, has been morally defeated in the confrontation with the forces of terror.

The second aspect is correlative: The strategy isolates the moderate segments of the Muslim world. By cornering the non-Jihadi elements as "unfit to defend Islam," the radicals devastate democrats and liberals in the Greater Middle East. How can progressives defend themselves when fundamentalists charge them with treason against their civilization? And to make it even more difficult, Western acceptance of the idea that the Islamists represent the true feelings of the majority puts Muslim moderates in an indefensible position, converting them, the actual numerical majority, into a conceptualized political minority. The Wahabi-Khumeinist strategy is remarkable in that it has used Western acquiescence to further weaken the West's best allies in the region. And here again, the Free World must come to realize that this slogan of a War against Islam was devised to divide the planet into two parts: a Muslim zone represented by the radicals, who pretend that there is a global conspiracy against their religion and civilization, and the rest of the world, including Muslim moderates. The War on Islam is used as a pretext to prevent moderates from giving aid to the attackers (that is, the West). The West and the international community must dispel this notion, reach out to the moderate majority within the Muslim world, and isolate the Jihadists.

AN ISLAMIC WAR

In reaction to the flurry of literature spread by the Jihadist movements over the past two decades, an oppositional literature has flourished in many parts of the West and the rest of the world. It affirms that an Islamic war is under way against the Free World. Just as the Jihadists have succeeded in portraying their foes as waging a War on Islam so that they can seize control of the Muslim world, growing sectors in the regions targeted by the Jihadists (India, Russia, Africa, and the West) have been claiming that not just the Jihadists, or the Islamist movement at large, but the entire Muslim world is at war with the world's non-Muslims. This extreme reaction has its roots in the radical attitudes of the Salafists and Khumeinists. Declarations and statements made by bin Laden and his supporters and by Iran's Khamenei and his followers have caused a ripple effect on the other side. And with the absence of serious, universal, and (Muslim) state-generated condemnations of the ideology behind the radical statements, radicalism produces alarmism. For when al Qaeda and its emirs threatened to massacre millions of citizens in the West, there was no unconditional and systematic condemnation by the official voices of the Muslim world—or that is what many in the West have come to believe.[13]

In fact, the Organization of the Islamic Conference Muslim States, the Arab League, and many governments condemned the 9/11 attacks, branded al Qaeda a terrorist organization, and instructed their security forces to arrest its members. Most mainstream governments of the Muslim world joined with the international community in stigmatizing the attacks as an act of terror. But many in the West still saw 9/11 as the result of global Islamic hostility. The reasons? First, most official and ideological spokespersons in the Arab Muslim world linked the attacks to the so-called root causes—such as Palestine, colonialism, disenfranchisement, and so on. Second, the appropriate religious authorities didn't respond theologically to bin Laden's citing of sacred texts. In short, many in North America, Europe, India, and Africa awaited a series of strong state rejections of the Jihadists' claims and a clear-cut theological rebuttal of the Salafi religious justifications, but when this did not occur, arguments emerged that a global Islamic attitude had developed to back the agenda of al Qaeda even though Islamic leaders distanced themselves from the terrorist acts. With al Jazeera and other Jihadi media pushing the confrontation to the extreme, radical voices from the Greater Middle East were amplified and triggered irredentist exultation across the continents. "It is Islam as a whole, not just the fundamentalists," many intellectuals affirmed, "which is moving against the

West." The Jihadists were successfully transforming the perception of the confrontation into a clash of civilizations.

But political reality is otherwise: The Jihadists have made progress within many Muslim countries, but they remain—according to most polls—a political minority. Even when they take the control of a regime, as with the Taliban in Afghanistan or the mullahs in Iran, the Islamists have a hard time transforming the majority of the population into convinced radicals. It is true that their constituency grows when they are in power, but as soon as they are removed from government, as was the case with the Taliban in 2001, subsequent elections, polling, and other manifestations demonstrate their unpopularity. More than one election in Afghanistan in the past half decade has failed to bring back the Taliban democratically. The political victories of the Muslim Brotherhood in Egypt and of Hamas in Palestine were said to show that civil societies are choosing Islamists when given the opportunity. The myth was quickly dispelled, however: In Egypt, the Muslim Brotherhood is seizing seats because the other side—pro-regime parties—is tainted with corruption. Over the decades, the liberals have been crushed by both the authoritarian government and the radical Gamaat Islamiya (an offshoot of the Muslim Brotherhood), and thus made irrelevant to the political process.[14] Hence the Brotherhood moves forward to occupy the void. In the Palestinian territories, Hamas gained a majority of parliamentary seats in the last elections (before the 2007 coup against the Palestinian president)—but it was funded as a terrorist organization by circles in the Saudi regime, and then by the Iranian regime. Besides, it is an armed militia omnipresent in a significant Palestinian territory. This combination of overwhelming foreign funding and security control produces domination of the political process ideologically, financially, and psychologically. It took less than a year for Hamas to show its nondemocratic face as it massacred the partisans of Fatah, its competitor in Gaza, and established a Taliban-like regime. In Lebanon, Hezbollah put on a similar show in the Shiite areas when it collected a number of seats during legislative elections: Hundreds of millions of dollars and heavy security in these zones produced a regime-like control of the representative power in the parliament.

The conclusion to be drawn is that Islamist forces in the Muslim world are strong, can seize power, and will muster support when they use this power. They can project the region as a whole as supportive of their goals. And with a global regime-supported media, such as the Qatar-funded al Jazeera or the Iranian-funded al Manar and al Aalam, the masses find themselves sandwiched between the power of the radicals to act and the power of the media to proclaim. The result is to raise a perception in the West that the antiliberal attitude and pro-Jihadi positions are global, endemic to the Muslim world, and supported by a unanimous public: hence the slogan, War by Islam.

But this slogan doesn't match geopolitical and sociological realities. As in Germany and Italy during World War II and in the Soviet Union during the Cold War, the numerical majority of the people are not fully integrated into the agenda of the dominant regime. At times, because of the regime's control of the masses or cultural pressures by the militants, the public seems to be acting against itself, against its own freedoms, or for radical ideologies. But as soon as such a regime falls or the radical networks recede, civil society's normal distribution of political choices and opinions reemerges. That is not to say that the public in the Muslim world will shift to pro-American and pro-Western stances; but when given the opportunity, the masses rapidly reveal a trend toward peaceful management of their own lives. Jihadism—like any other radical ideology—corrupts what is naturally a public space for debate. So the Muslim world, once Jihadism is no longer a dominant factor, will produce the political and cultural phenomena that permit coexistence with other nations and societies under international law.

LIBERATION OF THE EAST

The West's most important rethinking of the so-called War on Terror is to reexamine the strategic goals of this confrontation. Surely the immediate reaction to aggression is to resist it, contain it, and roll it back. This defense would comprise shielding homelands, coordinating international response, dismantling terror networks, and destroying their capacity to wage war. One might add to this the component of justice, depending on the legal systems in place in various liberal democracies. But the real challenge is to decide whether the West and the Free World should stop short of tackling the root causes of the terror wars or cross that line.

The choices are few: Either established and developing democracies selfishly defend only themselves, which is dangerous in the long run, or they leap forward to meet great challenges now and bring long-lasting freedom and liberty to the other side. Historian Bernard Lewis put it in dramatic terms: "Bring them freedom or they will destroy you."[15] In fact, despite the way some may misunderstand the sentence, the "them" here means the oppressed peoples of the Greater Middle East, victims of Jihadism and totalitarianism. The "they" are the Salafists, Khumeinists, and the like, who are using their control of the region to stage offensives against the Free World. Simpler slogans were President George W. Bush's "Spreading Democracy," and "Forward Freedom." The American approach to the War on Terror between 2001 and 2008 was not only to respond to 9/11 and the subsequent acts of terror but go beyond that specific response—and here lies the root of the biggest debate ever since. The United States' and its allies' efforts in Afghanistan and Iraq, as well as some other initiatives in the War of Ideas promoted by the Bush administration, aimed (not always successfully) at containing the terrorist forces on the one hand and somehow bringing democratic changes to the Greater Middle East on the other. Against this push for democracy a large convergence of interests formed a series of overlapping alliances. The Jihadists—both Salafists and Khumeinists—formed the antidemocratization frontline. Behind them stood formidable propaganda and financial machinery: the Qatari al Jazeera in the center surrounded by myriad journalists, media, PR groups, and oil and gas multinational corporations—all of them starting from the East and thrusting Westward. In the West, the massive Wahabi interest groups intertwined with the Western interests in the Arab Muslim world to form a powerful resistance to Washington's pro-democracy campaign. Across the oceans the coalitions opposing democratization now stretched from regimes in the Middle East to European governments, including many radical segments of the political spectrum (both extreme left and extreme right) and their various emanations, such as the antiwar and isolationist movements.

Until 2008, this political confrontation led to a failure in the grand design of liberation conceived in the White House and in the offices of the U.S. Congress before 2006. The idea of spreading democracy as a way to defeat terrorism had been advanced years before by many NGOs, human rights groups, and dissidents from the Arab and Muslim world. Immediately after 9/11, think tanks in the United States and some government advisers picked it up as a working concept to strengthen the moral basis of the War on Terror. Washington rushed out with the new discovery, displaying it in speeches, filling the debate with its shining arguments for liberty and human rights, and challenging political opponents with its undeniable appeal. And as U.S.-led forces were bringing down the Taliban, releasing women into freedom in Afghanistan, downing Saddam Hussein, and freeing millions in Iraq, the military action by the coalition of the willing seemed to match the Forward Freedom strategy.

The campaign to liberate the East sounded legitimate by Western standards and vital by Middle Eastern needs. It had precedents in the sacrifices of the Allies in the war to free Europe from Fascism and Nazism and in Western assistance to Soviet dissidents during the Cold War. The battlefields seemed comparable: Millions of Afghans and Iraqis were enjoying freedom after the Taliban dissolved and the Baath were marginalized. In Lebanon, the Cedars Revolution marched alone, having no financial assistance or foreign boots on the ground to help end the Syrian occupation. Hopes for a new era have grown high: Blacks in Darfur and Southern Sudan, women and students in Iran, reformers in Syria, ethnic minorities across the region, and independent thinkers throughout the Greater Middle East began counting the days, months, and years until their lives would improve. In its rhetoric and in some of its ground actions, the coalition of the willing was moving in the right direction: securing more freedom for more people in more lands. But the advance began to falter, hesitate, become confused, and, in many areas, even regress.

The campaign in Iraq stalled, and the bulk of the United States' energy went into managing the conflict, not winning it. On Iraq's eastern and western borders, Iran and Syria counterattacked by opening their borders to Jihadists who launch suicide bombings, and by equipping and training insurgents. Across the southern border, the Wahabi regime struck at its antigovernment cells but not at the ideology of the Salafi forces feeding the war in Iraq and elsewhere. The growth of democracy in Afghanistan was contained by Neo-Taliban action on the ground, backed by Waziristan-based al Qaeda networks in Pakistan. General Pervaiz Musharraf's government is at war with al Qaeda but spent years before engaging the Jihadi movements. In Lebanon, the Cedars Revolution, although successful at first, has been under attack since its rise in 2005, its leaders the target of assassins, the organization subject to terror attacks and an urban coup d'état. In Darfur, despite international pressures, the Janjaweed are still uncontained.[16] And in many countries south and east of the Mediterranean, oppression of peoples and suppression of freedoms is still the norm. The reality has not yet matched the leadership's 2001 vision of liberation. Why?

In fact, the issue is not about net results in terms of the immediate physical liberation of peoples and rapid democratization. The process of liberation is a gigantic task that cannot be accomplished during one American administration or one session of the UN Security Council or under a single secretary-general; liberation will take decades. The process of democratization is even longer, full of traps, setbacks, and countereffects; it will take generations. The issue is not time, but direction and policies. Was the campaign to spread democracy based on a real doctrine, on comprehensive strategies, on a clear vision of processes? Was the Forward Freedom strategy designed to move by trial and error and to stop at the first sign of the foe's counterpressure? Was the War of Ideas, as declared by top U.S. leaders and a few Western politicians, grounded in analysis and entered into after consultation with its main beneficiaries? Were the right alliances in the War on Terror built on the basis of democratization or on pragmatic considerations? Were other forces involved in the counter-Jihadi conflict, but who present on the battlefields in the Middle East, approached and engaged? A hundred questions remain to be answered.

In this third War of Ideas, which began in 2001 and is still raging in 2008, the adversary's propaganda machine seems to have won simply by denying the coalition of democracies full achievement of its aims. The Jihadists and their allies worldwide were able to block the path of liberation in the Middle East by obstructing Western efforts. The U.S. government spoke of spreading democracy but wasn't able to pinpoint the ideology and the global movements that are threatening it.

When one looks closely at the Western campaign to free peoples in the Greater Middle East, one sees that it was mostly, if not solely, led by Americans. With the exception of a few moves by the British government under Tony Blair and the election of Nicolas Sarkozy in France, or during an uprising, or when rampant abuse was too obvious, as in Darfur or in Lebanon, European governments failed to pursue a systematic policy of promotion of liberation and containment of Jihadism. The War of Ideas in Western Europe has almost been won by the terror ideologies and by their apologist allies. Inside the United States, the opposition to the doctrine of Middle East liberation has been very efficient. While the Bush administration has put some effort and lots of money behind its plans, critics in the media and academia assail and ridicule them. Congress initially backed the principle and granted financial support, but since early 2007 it has limited its support to "aiding opposition movements," and the new Democratic majority (or at least its leadership) has sought to deal directly with the Iranian and Syrian regimes and engage the Muslim Brotherhood over the future of the region. But most troubling of all has been the reluctance of many sectors of the U.S. State Department to further the stated objectives of the top executive leader and of the recommendations of the 9/11 Commission. The teams in charge of waging the War of Ideas, principally against the radical ideologies, stunningly followed the advice of experts covering up for these same ideologies and for the regimes fueling them.[17] In short, the initiative to bring liberation to the East was not even followed thoroughly in the West, within the United States, or inside its government. Hence, with tremendous political and economic powers fighting against the democratization efforts led by the United States, with domestic obstruction, and with limited strategic vision, the campaign to bring more liberties to the Greater Middle East has produced much smaller results than many anticipated.

In rethinking the confrontation, the Free World and liberal democracies must place the principle of liberation of the world's oppressed civil societies at the top of their agenda. They should pursue a conscious philosophy and policy of liberty, independent of 9/11 and the War on Terror. For the peoples of the Arab and Muslim world, the nations of the Greater Middle East, and their counterparts in Central and Eastern Europe and Africa have a right to be liberated, a right inscribed in international principles, at least since Woodrow Wilson enunciated them in 1917. Ideally, the West should have moved in a unified way some while ago and with all its resources to break the grip of neofascism and totalitarianism that rules over a fifth of humanity. It took the bloodshed of 2001 and after to trigger an American initiative of this kind. It also took a linkage between Western security and Eastern freedom for U.S.-led efforts to open spaces of liberty in Afghanistan and Iraq and begin better policies in Lebanon and Sudan. Unfortunately, these miraculous efforts and important sacrifices have been opposed by many other political forces within the West—those in cahoots with the dominant establishment in the Greater Middle East. This ironclad axis of obstruction is cemented by the power of oil and Jihadism from the East and of intellectual decline in the West. Nevertheless, as the West searches for its soul and tries to rethink its survival, it can and must move forward in liberating the East.

CHAPTER 3

CULTURAL REVOLUTION IN THE WEST

TO WIN THE CONFRONTATION WITH JIHADI TOTALITARIAN FORCES, THE center of the Free World, that is, the West, must undergo a change, a massive change. The major missing component in the Western War on Terror is undoubtedly: public action and knowledge. The man or woman on the street is strangely absent from the raging debates on the conflict, whether in New York, Paris, or London. In World Wars I and II, or during national resistance struggles against aggressors and occupiers, the masses of the democracies mobilized, but in the present crisis they have not organized against the forces of terror. On the afternoon of September 11, 2001, one might have expected to see millions in the streets demonstrating against al Qaeda and its ideology, and in some cases burning its flags. A president later spoke at ground zero and then to a joint session of Congress, but the people of America didn't show a visceral anger. Lighting candles, holding ceremonies, and displaying the flag showed that they were touched, hurt, and concerned. But the question most often asked was "Why?" This innocence showed how shielded the American public was from what had happened. The dominant elites had performed a lethal brainwashing.

Three years later, the 9/11 Commission was still asking why: "How come a war was declared against the United States (in 1998) and we haven't been informed?"[1] The answer is clear: The public was denied the truth, and actively miseducated.

This was the case not only in the United States, but also in the United Kingdom, Spain, France, and other European countries. True, to express their opposition to terror, Spanish citizens demonstrated after the Madrid attacks on March 11, 2004; but the apologist propaganda machinery dragged them to vote against their Iraq-involved government because the citizens were made to believe that al Qaeda struck their country only because of the Spanish presence among the Coalition forces. In short, the public was defeated by its own establishment, itself guided by international oil-controlled interests. In Great Britain, too, citizens expressed their anger and fear after the Jihadi attacks of July 7, 2005. They acted as their counterparts did across the Atlantic. But again the public was misled by its own expert elites; this time, the claim was that the root causes of the attacks were to be found in socioeconomic disenfranchisement. Two years later, as the Jihadi plot by forty-five medical doctors was unveiled, the citizens of the United Kingdom were shocked again by the scholarly misrepresentation of who the Jihadists were. In France, elite universities and media asserted that there was a unique social root of the fall 2005 youth uprising. But French citizens were not informed about the Jihadi organization behind the intifada of the *banlieues* (suburbs). In almost every European country where manifestations of political Jihadism occurred, the same patterns played out: a wondering public, and elites diverting the analysis. Intriguingly, the Jihadis also targeted Middle East dissidents, anti-Jihadi Muslims, and liberal Arabs, who were suppressed by apologist and Jihadophile pressure groups— obviously a necessary suppression, in order to prevent the public from being informed by live witnesses and dissident intellectuals. In short, the Jihadist political powers used all available methods to isolate the Western public and put it to sleep.

The marginalization of the masses in the West denies them their basic right to resist the Jihadi onslaught. It denies the public the right to obtain information and to act. Ordinary men and women in societies under attack knew with their basic instincts that their culture and their very existence were being assaulted. But they were deprived of the knowledge needed to transform their feelings, their frustration, and their real aspirations into action—and by their own establishment, which pursues the continued enjoyment of its social privileges and economic status. The elite—or a large part of it—has acted in conjunction with the terror campaign, in fact betraying the confidence of its constituency. Thus, it is time for the masses to revolt politically.

In a besieged political culture, where the command-and-control systems are solidly in the hands of the oil-backed (and mostly Jihadi) cartels, the only choice when survival is at issue is for the public to rise. With revolutionary and democratic traditions going back to the American and French revolutions and reform movements that brought enlightenment to both Old and New Worlds, Westerners have a foundation upon which to build an uprising against the petrodollar powers backing the Jihadi wars. This is the sine qua non of a new cultural revolution. Readers, viewers, listeners, and audiences must rise and pressure the press and audiovisual media to end the dominance of the apologists and open the media to a plurality of views on the terror wars. The public also has to look beyond the traditional media to new media now available to civil society: bloggers, direct news from the field, YouTube, chat rooms, free media—at least until the traditional media, and particularly public outlets, readjust to the reality of the Jihadi menace.

Citizens will have to educate themselves on the most dangerous development of the twenty-first century and begin electing officials on the basis of their understanding of the threat and their will to combat it. We must have among our legislators a majority who have at least a minimal understanding of what Jihadism is and how liberal democracies should use resources in a confrontation that may last decades defending the West, on the one hand, and liberating the East on the other. Without legislators profoundly conscious of the challenge they face, it will be hard to establish a Western global plan for conducting and winning the War on Terror. With legislative chambers changing composition every few years, a Western strategy to defend the Free World and sustain a War of Ideas is impossible unless a new political culture is developed: a culture where the public insists on the spread of freedom to other nations as a fundamental value of liberal democracy, not as a political convenience. Unless the public educates itself on the issue and changes the political landscape, the Western response will be diffused, divided, and chaotic. It is perhaps surprising, but oddly fitting, that the last line of defense in the West is the people, the makers of politicians and the constitutional owners of the government. In the past the masses were led toward revolutionary change by an intelligentsia, but in this global confrontation the masses will have to free themselves from their own intelligentsia (at least the dominant elites) and save their own societies. Certainly, many intellectuals and artists are responding to the challenge. The link between the masses and these dissidents will create the conditions for a new cultural revolution. When the audiences of these alternative intellectuals begin to act politically, the revolution will have begun and with it the global resistance to Jihadism.

New leaders are needed not only in Congress and Parliament but locally, statewide, and nationwide, on school boards and in public libraries, cultural councils, teachers associations, and academic institutions. A better-educated public would also form new and efficient social entities, NGOs, and pressure groups to ensure that the nation is better informed about terror strategies and tactics. Urban Jihadism will have to be countered by an enlightened public in the same way that Neo-Nazism, racism, extremism, violent Trotskyism, and other plagues have been isolated in liberal democracies: with the help of the people, acting culturally, educationally, and legally.

NEW LAWS

The first task of these newly enlightened assemblies would be to produce laws to counter Jihadi terrorism. Legislation against terror ideologies is crucial to mobilize societies against the threat. The Salafi, Takfiri, Khumeinist, Wahabi militant doctrines, which establish discriminatory categories and legitimize violence against people in those categories, must be the object of legal sanction. To begin with, it is unthinkable that in the midst of Western secular democracies, organized movements could spread ideologies that clearly call for urban apartheid within the national communities and advise acting physically to implement them. Jihadi ideologies promote the agenda of separating Muslims from non-Muslims— even within democracies—and of establishing separate spaces in which the Jihadi version of the Sharia would be the exclusive system of laws. That alone contradicts the basic pillars of secular societies. For while it is legitimate for ethnoreligious groups to demand autonomy if a historical ground is established in a specific country, breaking down the rule of law in *national* societies on the grounds of *ethnic* discrimination between groups is antidemocratic. In addition, the Jihadists claim legitimate violence (from low intensity to a much higher level, depending on their readiness and physical capacity to wage it) to establish this apartheid system within the West. Claiming false persecution, the Jihadists use violence to force democracies to relinquish their sovereignty over enclaves, which in turn would become the springboard for additional advances.[2]

But let us be clear that in pluralist democracies there is no ban on ideas. Individuals can develop any ideas they wish, including the worst, the most violent, and the most contradictory to freedom and democracy. Persons who wish to believe in any political future, including the reconstitution of a caliphate at the expense of democracy and national sovereignty, can freely do so. Individuals can express their enmity toward any group (within the bounds of hate-crime laws in some places) under a democratic system. But militants who have sworn allegiance and are acting on behalf of antidemocratic ideologies with the objective of terrorizing society and annihilating its democratic essence should be opposed by these societies via legal means. Hence, as for Nazism, Neofascism, racism, violent anarchism, and subversive Trotskyism, Jihadism (as a militant and radical ideology and movement) has to be addressed by liberal democracies' legislative and judicial branches.[3]

The first step in banning Jihadism as a movement is to make a clear distinction between religion and ideology. Regrettably, West European and North American commentators, legislators, and scholars have for many years confused faith and political doctrine. Jihad, as a religious phenomenon, as the sixth unofficial pillar of the Islamic religion, will remain as part of the theological, sociological, and possibly political debate. As long as it remains in the domain of historical and social studies, it will be discussed like any other doctrine. But once the concept is dragged by political activists and violent militants into the political-ideological sphere, it should be examined in terms of what is permissible and acceptable under current international law. Religious wars are not legitimate, nor are terror movements. Hence, Jihadism as an ideology and an actual movement (not a concept or religious idea), would be subject to legal action and possibly be banned.[4] Anti-Jihadism laws are the first necessary Western—and ultimately international, including Arab Muslim—response to present-day terror.

REFORMING EDUCATION

As the 9/11 Commission found in 2004, there was something odd about this particular conflict: The public seemed to have been purposely misinformed, hence misled. The 9/11 Commission postulated a "lack of imagination" on behalf of Americans.

Reforming education is another fundamental measure in a new intellectual revolution. It will not be easy to reverse decades of cultural invasion by the Jihadi economic and political powers. Billions of petrodollars have been pumped into Western economies to secure political influence, with hundred of millions lavished on campuses and other educational institutions to ensure academic backing.[5] In the three decades after 1973, most teaching and research programs dealing with Middle East studies in the West, particularly in the United States and the United Kingdom, fell under Wahabi dominance. And what is said in the classroom ends up in the newsrooms, art industry, movie theaters, libraries, courtrooms, and, eventually, the war rooms. American and Western analysis of terrorism and its root causes was already derailed years before 9/11 and the Jihadi assault.[6]

This may well be the most difficult task of the intellectual revolution that is needed to salvage the liberal West: How can a change be implemented if the intellectuals are the ones obstructing the reform? Who can investigate the teaching programs if the professors are sitting on Wahabi grants? Who can write the articles and books demanding such a reform when the ranks of the review boards are solid with apologists? At first sight, reforming Middle Eastern studies and the wider scholarly curricula in the West, corrupted by funds and influence from overseas, seems to be impossible. But at a second glance, there could be a way: Students and younger faculty can rise. This wouldn't be the first time a change came from within the campuses; in fact, it is the norm. Argument for argument, research for research, younger minds can push for the needed reform. It may require many more Western students to learn Arabic, Farsi, Pashto, and other languages in order to gain access to primary materials and avoid established apologist interpretations. NGOs would be needed to help young researchers accomplish this task. Junior faculty, despite academic and administrative pressures, should lead the reforms and open the space for debate. Governments and societies must challenge the old teaching materials, investigate grants from Wahabi and Khumeinist regimes, and expose the habitual failures to provide balanced instruction. It would certainly be more difficult to produce an academic reform in the

West than to spread democracy in the East. For it is stunning to realize in the final analysis that the defeat of the Free World might occur at the lecterns of professors, not in the battlefields of the Middle East.

EDUCATING PUBLIC MEDIA

After reforming education, the battle for a more balanced media is the next most needed step. It will entail a confrontation with titanic financial empires, with oil influence running deep. The crisis is not necessarily about freedom as a principle—although many on both the conservative and progressive sides would argue otherwise. Indeed, since the end of the Cold War a heated debate has raged: Who controls the mass media? The far left has argued for ages that the multinational corporations (MNCs)—charged with all sorts of conspiracies—are blocking the liberation of the masses in the West. And the conservative segment has argued instead that those who control the media are the left-wing liberal elites. The clash over media control has been about social, economic, financial, and cultural values. Each side has a view, and the views are irreconcilable. But that is part of the everlasting post–World War II world.

However, in the post-9/11 War on Terror, the battle of ideas is at the center of the conflict. In the West, public opinion can make or break strategies and cause victories or defeats on battlefields. The crises in Vietnam, Algeria, Lebanon, Somalia, and many others show clearly that a shift in the public mood within the West can be decisive for the direction of events on the ground. Since 2001, the propaganda wars have left indelible marks on the confrontations in Afghanistan, Iraq, Lebanon, Somalia, Darfur, Pakistan, and also inside the West. Volumes could be written on the warfare in the media when it comes to the conflict between democracies and terror forces.[7] Since 1991, at least, the Jihadi propaganda machine has scored some of its greatest victories in public opinion.

The question is, Why? How is it that nondemocratic forces, such as Salafists and Khumeinists, have been able to dominate the arguments in the mainstream press and keep almost all liberal democracies (such as the United States, the United Kingdom, France, Israel, India) and democratic movements (such as the Cedars Revolution, Arab and Muslim reformers, Southern Sudanese, etc.) on the defensive? Why can radicals exert better control of the agenda of prime-time debates in the Western media and dominate the interpretation of the campaign against terror (for example, in Iraq or Lebanon)? Furthermore, how have they become such masters in the use of media and free speech, which are anathema to them and universally banned in Wahabist and Khumeinist regimes? The answer seems to be simple: It derives from the fact that whoever controls the academic realm controls the message in the mainstream.

Ironically, both left-wing and conservative arguments hold when it comes to the War of Ideas. For it is true that multinational interests, heavily influenced by Middle Eastern oil-producing powers, have a large degree of influence in Western media circles. Saudi, Qatari, and, indirectly, Iranian interests can reach decision-making processes in editorial rooms, via corporate control. This long arm stretches into American and European journalism spheres thanks also to the collaboration with Western petroleum and related interests; oil dominates the MNCs and MNCs have a significant effect on media. But it is also true, on the other hand, that the self-described liberal media elite exercises influence on the editorial line. This elite comes from the Western classroom already under the influence of the oil powers and the Wahabi message. They then arrive at the news desk, where they find themselves both predisposed to and at the mercy of Wahabi financial influence. Hence the circle is complete. No wonder that CNN, BBC, CBS, NBC, CBC, and PBS and their counterparts in Europe and other democracies have adopted a similar attitude toward the War on Terror, regardless of their left-right tilt. The Jihadi global power has managed to frame issues and direct debate in ways to delay, if not block, the advance of democracy. This is why elections in Afghanistan and Iraq, popular demonstrations in Lebanon, genocide in Sudan, and the strife of dissidents in the region have been framed as "America-related phenomena" instead of as democracy rising, while the terrorist attacks across the Arab Muslim world have been portrayed as "genuine" anti-Western expressions, instead of as Jihadi-manufactured activism. In short, the marriage of convenience between the vast influence of oil and the Jihadi agenda to obstruct liberal change has kept most mainstream Western media in the trenches with the reactionaries against the progressives, at a time when media newsrooms often describe themselves as the front line of liberalism. The result is confusion, and encirclement by the Jihadists.

So how can the West reestablish a balanced media and boot out the Wahabi and Khumeinist influence? First and foremost, new alliances have to form between the "consumers" of the informational industry and an alternative media free from oil influence. Such a convergence has already begun. With the rise of Jihadism and its network of apologists, and the open collaboration the latter found in mainstream media, an "alternative medium" started in the cyber underground. As the icons of the Western media swallowed (and regurgitated) the Jihadi arguments of the "disenfranchised" and the "weapon of the weak" and the rest of the litany, more citizens, older and younger, dived into the newly discovered Web space. By early 2001, a "cyber resistance" to Jihadism had propagated. Immediately after the 9/11 attacks the "alternative" media—in America first—began to converge: the popular rebel Fox News, the prestigious *Wall Street Journal*, a constellation of radio talk shows, and a world of bloggers and websites. The free anti-Jihadi media would soon impact other mainstream media to cater to an increasingly dissatisfied public, almost in revolt. CNN would develop a show to expose "Islamist radical-ism."[8] Other mainstream media would also allot some airtime to tackle terrorism, such as MSNBC and the Discovery Channel. But still, in 2008, the global balance is in favor of the old paradigm. Across the Atlantic, Western Europe's media re-main largely pre-9/11 in outlook. More than 90 percent of the mainstream press still plays the tunes of the second War of Ideas, attempting to find roots other than Jihadism to explain post-9/11 terrorism. But even there, anti-Jihadism in the small media is exploding, often also in the cultural space. The cultural section of the Danish *Jyllands-Posten* triggered an earthquake among Islamist movements after it published cartoons of the Prophet Mohammed that Muslims considered offensive. Despite its large material and financial superiority over the "minority media," the mainstream information industry is faced with a challenge: The longer the third War of Ideas drags on, the more likely the rebel media will steal the thunder of popular communication. The rise of the public toward awareness is causing a shift in media preferences. It may well take years before a full shift takes place. But if the collective consciousness of a nation is not satisfied with the analysis the established media is providing during an ongoing and dramatic con-frontation, it will—as will all manifestations of life—seek its own means of sur-vival, in this case cultural survival.

The web of mainstream media affected by Middle Eastern oil power is simply gigantic and difficult to reeducate or counterbalance. The global Wahabi and Khumeinist influence in the Western media is based on a vast pool of oil invest-ments. A thorough reading of the work of news agencies around the world can de-tect the aspirations and projections of the Wahabi or Iranian international policies. At times, one can compare the clashing stories between the two influences. Re-porting out of Iraq, Lebanon, Gaza, and Sudan is particularly indicative of the sto-ries' backgrounds and political languages. But the influence over news agencies is exponentially amplified as customers in editorial offices around the globe repeat the stories. Trickling all the way down to small-town newspapers or publications on remote islands, the party line promotes a culture of severe criticism of any Western support for liberation forces in the Greater Middle East and a culture of sympathy for Jihadi activities. But the democratic public can reach a very powerful web of information by bypassing the already contaminated private sector: the pub-licly funded media.

Statewide and local broadcast outlets are funded by taxpayers. These can be the first outlets to be reclaimed by citizens. They could become the most powerful means to leading and widening the intellectual revolution in the United States, and then, through similar instruments, the West. What schools and private media are denying to the public, a rebalanced public media would offer. Citizens concerned about their national security and their right to learn the truth about the global Jihadi war on their societies can and should demand from their elected officials an open space for vital information. The reshaping of public media to serve citizens would be a major victory. The public can reestablish balanced, free, and unimpeded access to debate. This would also put pressure on private media to adjust, and an awakened audience would oblige the media tycoons to open up their own space to pluralism for fear of losing their dearest commodity: viewers and listeners.

Indeed, the intellectual revolution in the West can only begin if the public is educated about world realities. Once that happens, however, citizens will reclaim what is theirs—the public media. And as the media begin serving the interest of their owners—the people—it will affect wider circles of opinion-making: academia, private media, and entertainment. From that point on, liberal democracies will begin thinking about the fundamental principles of their national security in terms of a global, decades-long assault by an antidemocratic, antisecular, and state-financed Jihad that has already won two wars of ideas and successfully lodged itself within Western elites and ethnic communities, from which it has already launched successful and bloody attacks. Such sobering analysis will instigate consideration of the appropriate judicial processes, homeland security measures, and military strategies needed to face the rapidly growing challenges of Jihadism within the nation and around the world.[9]

CHAPTER 4

ECONOMIC REVOLUTION

OFTEN PEOPLE IN LIBERAL DEMOCRACIES ARE TOLD THAT CONFRONTING terrorists (ideologies, regimes, and organizations) will bring about all sorts of problems, including "complications in international relations," "frustration with foreign policy," or "negative economic consequences." The 1990s saw many high-profile cases in which Western democracies considered an initiative to rescue an endangered population or counter a terror power, but political lobbies opposed such action on the grounds of economic harm. The following are a few examples.

Throughout the decade prior to 9/11 a genocide was taking place in Sudan. More than a million black people had already been killed, ethnically cleansed, or enslaved by the Islamist regime in Khartoum. Foreign services on both sides of the Atlantic were frequently approached by human rights groups asking for humanitarian intervention. But executive branches were also put under pressure by the Sudan regime and the oil industry associated with it not to go to the rescue of the African tribes in the south. North America and Europe would suffer the economic consequences of an action against Khartoum, the lobbyists and government analysts affirmed. Western financial interests (in reality, multinational corporations and their affiliates) would risk losses. Meanwhile, hundreds of thousands of Southern Sudanese continued to be killed, maimed, kidnapped, or forced to flee their villages. Western companies trading with the Sudanese regime became indirect lobbies for the Jihadi establishment in Khartoum, forcing Washington, London, Paris, and other capitals to abandon the underdogs of East Africa to their bullies.

In October 1990, Syrian forces invaded Lebanon's last free enclaves, crushing its government and exiling, jailing, and torturing thousands of citizens during the following years. Syria has no significant amounts of oil—but it seized control of Beirut's powerful banking and financial nerve center. Lebanon's business, catering to Arab oil regimes, passed under President Bashar al Assad's domination. Damascus provided "protection" against co-profit to the Arab capital hurdling to Syrian-controlled Beirut. In more sinister words, the Assad regime offered protection for the business elites in return for a share of the profit, which explained partially how a socialist system in Syria, absent of oil revenues, could continue to survive and its elites to thrive. And, parallel to the Gulf states and Saudi meddling in Baathist-dominated Lebanon, another oil power, Iran, also moved in to have its share. While Wahabi money flooded downtown Beirut, hundreds of millions of Khumeinist petrodollars poured into the small country to feed Hezbollah. Lebanon came under a financial and oil consortium, and its population was forced to submit to Syrian and Hezbollah domination. Europe and the United States in particular were kept from acting by the power of economic intimidation. Despite calls by Lebanese exiles to intervene and free Lebanon's civil society from Syrian occupation, the West placated Syria and the Arab League and allowed the former democracy to remain in bondage.

When Saddam Hussein invaded Kuwait, the multinational corporations (MNCs) entered the fray. Iraq's oil lobby attempted to reason with Saddam and bring him to an accommodation and diplomatic solution. Kuwait and Saudi Arabia meanwhile urged the United States and Europe to send the troops at once. The balance of power between oil companies and their respective dominance in the international market decided the outcome before the battle even began. The United States, the United Kingdom, France, and many other nations, in addition to the nations of the peninsula, threw their forces against the Iraqi forces occupying Kuwait. Iran's regime—read: Iranian Oil—didn't oppose Iraq's defeat after years of bloody war with it in the 1980s. In a few weeks, the Iraqi forces were smashed in Kuwait, and Coalition forces were chasing the Republican Guard inside Iraq. President George H. W. Bush called on the Iraqi people to rise against Saddam, which they did—at least in the north and south. But while U.S. and Coalition tanks were rolling north in the desert, inside Iraq's borders, diplomatic whispers advised Washington and its allies not to push for regime change in Baghdad, even though Saddam had breached many international law redlines. Ironically, those who had called on Uncle Sam to defeat Hussein in Kuwait were the very ones who asked him not to remove the Iraqi dictator from power. If an Arab dictator should fall at the hands of liberal democracies, it seemed, it would mean that a democracy might be installed in its place; other authoritarian regimes in the region would not see this as in their interest. Saddam's invasion of Kuwait should be stopped, but a regime change in Iraq should also be stopped; so went the logic. The oil MNCs agreed to have the Iraqi regime expelled from its southern neighbor, another producer of oil, but not to be toppled from its own pedestal, because it suited the world oil interests to have Saddam's dictatorship continue. He had to be put in his place but left *in* place, so to speak. Thus the petrol-equation governing the geopolitics of the post-Soviet Middle East led to the continuation of the dictator for another thirteen years and to the massacres he subsequently perpetrated against Shia and Kurds. The West's bondage to the oil powers was as responsible for this tragedy as it was for the previous ones.

Then, in 1996, the Taliban came to power in Afghanistan, eliminated all political pluralism, destroyed religious liberties and brutally suppressed women. In addition, they gave sanctuary to al Qaeda, the top terror group worldwide. On much less weighty grounds, the military regime of Gen. Raoul Cédras in Haiti had been pressured to step aside one year before, yet the Taliban remained entrenched in Kabul till 2001. Why? Here again, the financial dependency on oil played a role in the uneven application of policy. The United States and the European nations treated societies struggling against Jihadi fascism differently from societies struggling toward democracy in other parts of the world. The oppression of women, minorities, and religions in Afghanistan under the Taliban triggered some limited protests from human rights groups, but provoked no action by the United Nations. The Organization of the Islamic Conference deeply influenced by a number of Middle East regimes that belonged to the Organization of Petroleum Exporting Countries (OPEC), gave protection to the Taliban. It cautioned Western governments to weigh carefully the possibility that intervention would produce another oil crisis of the 1973 type—they should think carefully before acting to free the Muslim women in Afghanistan

The same argument was also made about persecuted religious and ethnic minorities. Intervening on behalf of the Copts of Egypt; the Kurds and the Assyro-Chaldeans of Iraq, Syria, and Iran; the Berbers of Algeria; the southern Sudanese and even the Black Muslims in Darfur was a no-go, because of the petroleum cartels connected to the great powers, whose economies ran on cheap energy. The misery of oppressed nationalities in the Greater Middle East was rooted in oil-producing regimes' veto power in the West and at the United Nations. Ironically, the Jihadist and apologist propaganda machine argued that the West was so avid for Arab Muslim oil that it provided continuous support to the authoritarian regimes in the region.[1] They were making the case for the Europeans and the Americans to drop their backing of Saudi Arabia, the Gulf monarchies, Algeria, and others, but they weren't calling for the liberation of minorities. Instead, Islamists wanted to use the argument that the West should not support authoritarian governments precisely in order to remove moderate governments and make way for future radical ones. The Neo-Wahabis and Khumeinists were no more interested in freeing the Berbers, Kurds, and Copts than were the likes of Saddam; in fact, their own long-dreamt-of caliphate, if achieved, would suppress the minorities even more.

What was more compelling was the fact that in the Greater Middle East basic resources are located in areas where minorities are suppressed. Iraqi oil is found in the Kurdish north and Shia south; mineral resources and oil are found in Southern Sudan and Darfur; oil and gas fields are located in the Berber area of Algeria; Iranian oil is mostly located in the Arab areas of Khusistan (Or Ahwaz). All these ethnic groups have and continue to pay the price of Western oil dependency and suffer from the regimes' unwillingness to allow them international rescue.

Oil politics have also hamstrung the peace process for years. Since its beginning, the Arab-Israeli conflict has had several opportunities for the sides to reach a solution. The UN partition plan had proposed the creation of two entities in the British mandate over Palestine: one for the Jews (Israel) and another one for the Arabs (Palestine). I needn't review the long-held positions of both sides on the issues of security and land and the labyrinth of ethnic conflicts. Suffice it to say that, at one point in the Cold War, the Arab allies of the United States could have persuaded the Palestinians to accept a two-state solution, but they refrained from doing so; they used their control over oil to prolong the conflict instead of shortening it. After the Soviet collapse in 1991, the Madrid peace talks and the breakthrough of 1993, oil regimes again had multiple opportunities to put all their weight behind the process—but they didn't. Instead, Iran extended its full support to Hamas in order to sink the peace process, and the Saudis and other petroregimes allowed support to flow to the Jihadists so that they could conduct their suicide operations, thereby shattering the peace arrangements. In ethnic territorial conflicts, where the core of the problem is entrenched in historical claims, emotions, and local politics, external factors can sabotage the resolution of a crisis. The West, particularly the United States, leaned hard on Israel to induce it to accept a two-state solution from the early 1990s, but it wasn't able to pressure the Palestinian side to meet the process halfway. The rejection of a negotiated two-state solution was principally the work of Jihadist forces, who until recently were shielded by the economically decisive influence of Peninsula monarchies. Once again, Western reliance on economic interests in the region stalled the resolution of a conflict often considered to be one of the psychological feeders of terrorism.[2]

It is on the terrorist front that the oil influence has produced the most lethal disasters. It has been clear for the last two decades that American and Western policies intended to counter Jihadi terror have been weakened under pressure from the oil regimes and interests. Not that all petroleum companies and every single member of OPEC were following the same obstructionist policies; but it is a fact that Arab members, including Saudi Arabia, Qatar, Sudan, Libya, and somewhat the United Arab Emirates, Algeria, and others (and mainly the Iranian oil-backed regime) have opposed the concept of a War on Terror and deflected efforts to engage the Jihadists as a global threat. One must note, however, that some enlightened individuals and leaders in these governments have attempted to help the world community tackle the ideological roots of Takfirism and combat Salafism, but have failed to generalize the struggle as a means to strike at the root doctrines of Jihadism. Hence the global trend among oil-producing regimes in the Greater

Middle East, with few exceptions, has been to pressure Western democracies not to engage Jihadism through ideological confrontation, mass awareness, and, ultimately, regime change when horrors are discovered. The negative influence of regional oil producers on the worldwide resistance to terror is stronger than it has ever been before. By taking hostage Western economies and the perceived well-being of North American and Western European societies, the petro-establishment of the region (and their financial partners in the Free World) have actually aided the forces of terror and allowed them to gain time, power, and position. Had such an analysis been available during the hearings of the 9/11 Commission in the summer of 2004, there would have been a clear answer to the question, "How come a terror war was launched against us, and we didn't know it?"[3] The answer would have been: "Because our oil industry partners in the Middle East didn't want us to know it; because our responses to it would have curtailed their extreme power and profits and endangered our partnerships with these same oil regimes."

Another good question the 9/11 Commission could have asked was how this obstruction was allowed to materialize in the first place. In 1993, after the first attack on the Twin Towers, the Clinton administration was advised by the experts not to "go ideological" (meaning strategic) in its response, but to confine itself to trying the terrorists as criminals. The community of Middle East scholars and experts, inside the foreign policy establishment and within the private sector, and especially in academia, made a case against a War on Terror in 1993.[4] One of the most compelling arguments was that it would harm U.S. financial interests abroad. As has been shown, the foundation for this argument was a fear of repercussions in the Arab Muslim world, to which was added a fear of a reduction in arms purchases by Arab states. But as is now proven, the bulk of Middle Eastern studies in America were (and still are) funded by Wahabi states and oil producers; the petro-powers of the region were thus able on the one hand to influence the advice given to Western governments and on the other to threaten financial sanctions if the Free World confronted the terrorist ideology.[5]

Three years after the first attack on the World Trade Center, the Taliban came to power in Afghanistan through a coup d'état. In a few months, they established an antidemocratic regime there and began fostering terror groups. The "advice" of the Arab peninsula's oil cartels was, predictably, that the Taliban should be recognized as a government having international standing. In 1998, a Taliban-backed organization, al Qaeda, launched two terror attacks in East Africa against U.S. embassies. Washington responded with missile attacks on a factory in Sudan and al Qaeda targets in Afghanistan. But when the Clinton administration considered taking action against the Taliban regime, a "whisper" came from the oil powers: Such an attack would jeopardize U.S. interests in the region. This scenario was repeated after the attack on the USS *Cole* in 1999: There must be no retaliatory measures against the Jihadist movement as a whole or the ideology of Jihadism, or else the flow of oil to the United States and the West will be affected.[6]

But the most critical influence of the oil powers in the fight against terrorism came on the domestic front—and it is going on still. Throughout the 1990s, the petroleum-producing regimes gave massive support to Jihadi pressure groups in the Free World. These donors targeted religious, cultural, social, and other related centers and funded the spread of radical ideologies. A constellation of Islamist groups, funded either directly or indirectly by the oil regimes, created a pool of in-doctrinated Salafists (or, in the case of Iranian funding, Khumeinists). The end product was a generation of cadres who would further penetrate the system, and from whom organizations could recruit terrorists.

So where is the link between domestic terror, Jihadi homegrown networks, and the oil powers? The answer is complex but not impossible to describe. The initial funding to spread the ideology (whether Salafism, Khumeinism, or Tak-firism) comes from petrodollars. In the second stage, pools of indoctrinated Jihadi cadres insert themselves in the system and influence it, while actual Jihadi terror-ists strike violently at the democracies. Stunningly, the petrodollars continue to support two levels of activity, for as the militants undermine the Western response to Jihadism, they receive additional support. And when the Jihadi terrorists act, petrodollars fund their legal defense.

These branches of Jihadism inside the West and the oil money that backs them are visible in a number of cases on both sides of the Atlantic. When you re-search the educational programs of madrassas in the West that spread radicalism, you find that their funds come from the oil-producing countries. When you inves-tigate the terror cases, you see propaganda campaigns aimed at undermining the court proceedings that are being funded by the same sources.

But the most powerful tool used to affect United States and European policies on national security and terrorism is the threat of an economic catastrophe if red lines are crossed. Indeed, sporadically before 9/11 and intensely since, the political machinery of Jihadism and its apologist allies have been keeping the lid on a Western assault on the terrorists by using the economic threat. In the United States, the pro-Wahabi lob-bies frequently warn the government not to put pressure on Jihadist circles for fear of the economic consequences. If Washington cracks down on the Jihadists, so the argu-ment goes, or engages in a War of Ideas against these ideologies, or even promotes democracy in the region, the Arab states will organize another oil boycott, sell their petroleum to China, buy their weapons from Russia, and change their dollars into euros. Thus, the more actively America defends its homeland security, the more it loses economically. So says the academic and lobbying establishment.

Such a threat is not taken lightly in capitalist nations; a threat alone can pro-duce a shift in national security policies. It can bring Europe to its knees. And in almost every case where Western authorities have dismantled a terrorist cell, arrested a Jihadi, or indicted Islamists, the Wahabi lobbies and allies have moved forward to minimize the negative impact on the Jihadi ideology. When the cases are very clearly framed by the terms of indictments and evidence (principally if the case is about al Qaeda or if the terrorists have admitted their responsibility), the lobbies hurry to separate the doctrine from the terror and the actual terrorists.[7] And when the cases have been about incitement to violence but not necessarily about a violent act that has already occurred, the pressure groups insist that this is a Western government conspiracy to alienate Muslims, Arabs, or Middle Easterners. Similarly, when Salafists or Khumeinist sympathizers take action to force Western societies to accept their ideological demands, as when they attempt to erect nondemocratic, Islamist enclaves within Western democracies, in contradiction of the principle of separation of church and state, the defenders of secular democracy and religious freedom are depicted as tyrannizing Muslims and discriminating against them. In almost all these cases, the lobbies invoke the specter of negative reactions in the Arab and Muslim worlds that could be triggered by Western, democratic opposition and warn of dire financial and economic consequences. At the center of the threat is, naturally, the ability of oil-producing regimes in the Greater Middle East to affect Western economies, and thus their social stability. The petroleum menace supports the entire Jihadi pressure within the West and throughout the industrialized world. This global subjection of the Free World to the will of oil regimes is at the heart of the confrontation with terrorism. In short, oil power, in many complex ways, protects Jihadism and even promotes it worldwide. Logically, we should ask how this came about, why it wasn't contained, and what the Free World should do about it.

PETRO-JIHADISM

The use of oil as a weapon by the Jihadi forces began before the Cold War ended and was openly identified as such. The historical roots of Petro-Jihadism are discernable in post-1945 statements made by Baathist and other Arab nationalist propagandists and politicians. As the countries of the region were emancipating themselves from the colonial powers and gaining independence, their intellectuals insisted on regaining control as well over oil and other natural resources. From Algeria to Iraq, ranging over Libya, Sudan, Iran, Kuwait, the Gulf monarchies, and, of course, Saudi Arabia, the "luckiest" states (among other less lucky Middle Eastern countries) quickly gained control of the oil fields and developed a lucrative trade with the outside world via multinational corporations on whom they had to rely for technology, management, and distribution. Midway into the Cold War, all oil-producing countries in the region possessed and enjoyed these resources. In addition, they had developed a partnership with mostly Western—but also East-ern—financial powers, based on gigantic transactions and contracts.[8] But these miraculous resources weren't transformed into economic wonders for the civil so-cieties ruled by the oil regimes (at least until very recently, and then only in some countries in the Gulf). Instead, the ruling petro-elites, across the ideological spec-trum, consolidated their power with the revenues. From the socialist states of Iraq and Libya to the fundamentalist regimes of Saudi Arabia and post-shah Iran, the dominant parties, dictators, clerics, and monarchs tightened control over the rev-enues and used them to shore up their authoritarian policies and to crush dissent.

The first political function of oil economies in nondemocratic countries is to keep the regimes running at the expense of democratic change and social mobility. The seemingly limitless supply of oil money has helped dictators like Saddam and Qadhafi crush all opposition, marginalize minorities, and stunt the evolution to-ward a liberal state. Oil royalties permitted the Wahabis to freeze the kingdom under Salafism and allowed this ideology to spread around the world; it also al-lowed the mullahs in Tehran to massacre their opposition, fund Hezbollah, and bankroll the race to develop Iran's own nuclear weapons. Ideologues from all back-grounds have praised oil as a weapon for decades. Pan-Arabist and Islamist intel-lectuals often called for the use of *silah al naft* (the oil weapon) against the "enemies of the *umma*," that is, the Islamic "nation." High-profile doctrinaires such as Jihadi ideologue Sayyid Qutb, Imam Ruhallah Khumeini, Baathist activist Salah Bitar, and countless other intellectuals and clerics urged governments to use these natu-ral resources to further strategic objectives. The use of natural advantages in inter-national bargaining is accepted in world affairs—as long as they aren't used to affect security or to destroy world order. But the ideologues of the authoritarian club of the Middle East particularly envisaged oil as a weapon, not to improve con-ditions within their societies, but to achieve ideological projects at a planetary level. The redlines between economic independence and economic imperialism were crossed by the Jihadists and their fellow travelers.

Even non-oil-producing regimes such as Nasser's Egypt and Assad's Syria stood by the doctrine, as they enjoyed influence among Arabs arising from their military power and radical policies. Although it was not a state actor, during the Cold War the Palestine Liberation Organization called for the weapon to be used in the conflict with Israel. At the helm of the Arab-Israeli conflict, numerous voices, mostly from the pro-Soviets among the Arab nationalists, urged use of the "oil weapon." Syria, Egypt (until 1977), the PLO (including its Marxists), southern Yemen, and others constantly urged the oil-producing states to purchase weapons from Moscow—as Iraq, Libya, and Algeria did—and to distance themselves from the United States and Western financial interests. But the highest pressure was ap-plied to the conservative camp in the Arab world, to Saudi Arabia, Kuwait, Qatar,

Bahrain, and the UAE, to get them to adopt the same attitude. The pressure cul-
minated in 1973 after the so-called Yom Kippur War between the alliance of Egypt
and Syria against Israel. Launching a military offensive in the Sinai and on the
Golan Heights, Anwar Sadat and Hafez Assad shocked Israel in the first days of the
offensive. But soon after, aided by an American materiel air lift, the Israeli forces
pushed back the Arab armies and thrust into their lands. A few days afterward, as
this crisis was escalating, with the two superpowers threatening to intervene, a
cease-fire agreement was signed under UN supervision. The failure of the Arab offensive and America's unquestioning support of the Jewish state triggered ideological reactions throughout the region. Arab nationalists, and with them the Islamic
fundamentalists, decided at last to use the *silah al naft*. Seizing the initiative within
OPEC, an alliance of oil producers in the Arab world, including both socialist
regimes and monarchies, organized a cataclysmic boycott of Western petroleum
markets. The oil shock was felt across the Free World, especially in Western Europe and the United States. Europeans increasingly rode bikes for their daily
transportation needs and, in America, long lines of disgruntled drivers formed at
gas stations. For the first time in postwar history, the oil producers had acted
strategically to strike at what they perceived as "illegitimate and unfair" support of
Israel by the West.[9]

But in another way, it was a reassertion of power by the oil-funded elites in
the region against the Western elites. In Marxian terminology, it was an Arab
Muslim bourgeoisie creating a new balance of power with the Western bourgeoisie. Realists would have described the 1973 crisis as a readjustment of the
balance after years of colonialism. Riyadh and Baghdad, as well as Cairo and
Damascus, wanted to tell Washington, London, and Paris that east of the
Mediterranean there was another great power in world affairs, even though it
did not have a seat on the UN Security Council. By first lowering and then
stopping the flow of oil to these industrial democracies, the Arab oil producers
sent a shiver that reverberated deep inside the West. To Arab nationalists, it was
a resurgence of Pan-Arabism. But to the authoritarian regimes, the 1973 boycott sent another lethal message across the oceans: Do not dare try to intervene
in our domestic affairs. Since then, a complex relationship has developed between the elites of Western liberal democracies and the ruling classes of the oil-
producing lands; in effect, an unspoken pact was created. The oil powers would
continue to fill the pipelines, ensuring the comfortable lifestyle of the West; and
in return the latter would treat these regimes as global partners in world affairs,
protecting them from their external foes—while also insulating them from ex-
posure to criticism. The authoritarian powers of the region won the Mother of
All Deals: a boundless influence inside the most powerful sphere of technology,
military strength, and international diplomacy, as well as political cover for their

authoritarian, antidemocratic, and anti–human rights regimes. Since then, the dictators and strong men of the Greater Middle East have survived unchecked.

But the regimes' success in using *silah al naft* also emboldened the Islamists, who for a long time had been calling for economic warfare against the infidels. Salafists, Wahabis, Takfiris (and, after 1979, Khumeinists) saw in oil a divine instrument for the reconstitution of a world Islamic power. "It is a weapon from Allah," the Islamist ideologues constantly repeated.[10] Thus, the use of the vast natural resources of the region in a global confrontation with the infidels became a fundamental element in Jihadist strategy. But it should be remembered that the Islamists, the regimes, and movements envisaged the oil weapon as a means to achieve long-term strategic goals, not just to respond to the Arab-Israeli conflict. Oil money could purchase the best Western weapons, buy influence inside Western democracies, shield the region's authoritarian regimes from international sanctions for their human rights abuses, and protect the growth of Jihadism worldwide. Oil, in the eyes of the Islamists, became the ultimate source of power for use in Jihad.[11] In other words, petro-Jihadism was born.

ECONOMIC IMPERIALISM

Petro-Jihadism as a weapon of the rich authoritarian regimes has led to the emergence of an economic imperialism, by which the ruling elites of oil-producing countries, while unable or unwilling to help their own societies advance economically, have instead invested in political influence inside Western economies that are increasingly dependent on the oil industry. The equation is complex but lethal. By aggregating their power over oil exports and relying on their Western partners (the MNCs and other entities), petro-regimes have obtained significant influence over markets, mostly in the West.[12] Market control of oil prices, partnership with powerful multinational companies, purchases of military equipment, Western participation in Middle East development, investment in the educational systems of the West, and financial backing of pressure groups, lobbies, and militant entities in the Free World—all these have combined to produce a new world power, the Economic Jihadi Imperialism (EJI).

The chain of relationships and connections that led to the rise of EJI took about three decades to raise a competitive world power, one not bound by a single nation-state as are the other great powers, such as the permanent members of the Security Council or the industrialized G8. EJI begins with a very ideological hard core and ends with far-reaching tentacles deep inside the enemy's zones. Everything in between functions through sheer financial and economic power and relationships. Indeed, the center of that new economic imperialism is populated with radical theological ideologues. In the region, the main hubs are located within the

Wahabi power circles of Saudi Arabia, the Muslim Brotherhood in Qatar and other oil-producing regimes, and Iran's mullah establishment. This troika of Jihadi hard cores has alliances and influences across the region and in other regimes that are also producers of energy: Sudan, Libya, Indonesia, Malaysia, Algeria, UAE, and so on. Through that wider circle, the core impacts nonproducers and poorer countries alike, affecting the policies of their governments (for example Egypt, Syria, Pakistan, Bangladesh, Somalia, and Mauritania). Hence, while the core group designs and develops the mode of attack and means of Western penetration, governments on the periphery follow suit, with varying degrees of engagement. This chain of economic power has in fact seized diplomatic control of both the Arab League and the Organization of Islamic Conference. So, while many problems plague the membership of these two large organizations, and many participants are foes, the ideological pro-Jihadi centers have been able to manipulate these institutions as a tool in their confrontation with the rest of the world.

To take some examples: from Iran, Saudi Arabia, and Qatar, and also Libya (before 2004) and Iraq (before 2003), a long arm was reaching inside the decision centers of liberal democracies, as well as affecting countries such as Russia, India, China, and Brazil. The EJI naturally had a leading impact on OPEC as well, because most influential members were from the Middle East, and most of the latter were ruled by sympathizers to one or another form of Jihadism. In turn OPEC plays a tremendously important role in the industrialized democracies, such as the European Union, Japan, the Asian free economies, and the Latin American transitional economies, as well as in the United States, Canada, Australia, and New Zealand.

The imperial oil power has exercised its influence as a bloc—in world markets and at the United Nations—but also via individual regimes having their own special relationships with countries in the West. Obviously, the Wahabi monarchy of Saudi Arabia comes at the top of the list as one of the most influential oil producers. From inside the kingdom, radical clerics and emirs (though not all of the rulers and bureaucrats in the Middle East are devout Wahabis) can affect capitals, local governments, and small schools in any country in the West via this oil-related influence. The 1973 syndrome is still omnipresent in the psyche of politicians, economists, academics, and even defense analysts. One button pushed in Riyadh and the flow of oil can be slowed and eventually cut off. The question is, Who can press that button?

The Saudi state apparatus knows all too well that such a game, though successful on one occasion during the Cold War, may not be as successful in the twenty-first century. But the syndrome in the West remains, regardless of the changes in world affairs. Radicals may have it in their power to activate this weapon. Salafists in Saudi Arabia, the Muslim Brotherhood's influence in Qatar and other principalities, Islamists in Sudan, mullahs in Iran, and their potential allies in southern Iraq (if things go badly there)—all might use oil to gain a choke hold over the world's free societies. Libya has shifted to a neutral position since 2004,[13] but until it reforms and democratizes, it could revert under Muammar Qadhafi or even his son, Sayf al-Islam. The Islamists in Algeria are also a potential element of menace against their country's secular establishment. Thus it is not only individual regimes that could affect the oil trade and use it for global confrontation, but also forces within these countries. In the final analysis, one can see clearly that the West and other regions, including the Arab Muslim world itself, have been compelled to adopt various policies in accordance with EJI strategies, goals, and actions.

EJI'S IMPACT IN THE EAST

Oil imperialism's first targets were found in the East or the South: the poorer, weaker, and most disenfranchised populations of the Third World. The oil regimes' policies for influencing the West (as I have argued above) aimed principally at deflecting Western intervention while the regimes oppressed minorities, majorities, and marginalized communities in their own midst. Following are some striking examples.

In Saudi Arabia, the Shia minority, women, and political dissidents are denied basic human rights; the country has no secular constitution; and political parties are illegal. But the country's oil influence has kept any outside power from coming to the aid of the disaffected and disenfranchised. The Wahabi elite have enough economic clout to shield their form of apartheid, unlike the white elite of South Africa. In Iran, the "mullocracy" can oppress Kurds, Arabs, women, students, and other elements of the society at will, so long as Iranian oil is pumped and sold to the world. The same rule applies relatively in Sudan and Libya, and it used to apply in Iraq before its liberation by U.S. forces. But the producers' abuse of human rights within their national boundaries wasn't the only impact on the Greater Middle East; they also endorsed their brothers' similar work on other oppressed peoples. Lebanon was invaded gradually by Syrian forces beginning in 1976, finally falling into their hands in 1990. That clear breach of international law was only possible because of the support that the Syrian regime got from the oil family, particularly at different times from Saudi Arabia, the Arab League, and Iran. These countries were instrumental in blocking international intervention on behalf of a free Lebanon.

A simple statistic graphically displays how oil is related to oppression: In many cases, the oppressors use the revenues from resources found on the lands of minorities to fund their oppression—90 percent of Saudi oil fields are located in the

90-percent Shia-inhabited al Ihsaa provinces, and yet the Shia are marginalized there. Iran's most important oil fields are located in the Arab minority province of Khusistan, where the population has been persecuted by the Khumeinist mullahs. Saddam's oil fields were located mostly in the Shia areas in the south and Kurdish areas in the north, two ethnic minorities he brutally oppressed. In Sudan, the most precious minerals are found in the southern provinces and in Darfur, areas that the Islamist regime has been repressing for decades. Even in Algeria, the Berber community claims that the government has asserted direct control over natural resources owned historically by the native ethnicity. Ironically, most of the petroleum royalties used against minorities come from their own property, which have been looted by the oppressive regimes.

In addition to domestic oppression facilitated by oil imperialism, petro-Jihadism has fueled terrorism across the region. The Arab League's wealthiest regimes have been funding the most radical organizations, including Palestine's Hamas and Chad's Islamists (aided by Saudi sources according to Ndjamena), Hezbollah and Islamic Jihad (backed by Iran), and the Janjaweed (supported by the Sudanese regime). Pressures by the West have chipped away only at the edges of this massive oppression, because of counterpressures applied by these regimes and their MNC partners within the West. But beyond direct support to terror groups (on the grounds of ethnic or religious brotherhood), the single most devastating role oil imperialism has ever had in the region was to provide a constant lifeline for the growth of Jihadism in all its forms. From the mid-1970s until today, billions of petrodollars have been spent on the spread of Wahabism, Takfirism, and Khumeinism, and on radical Pan-Arabism, in the Greater Middle East and beyond. Saudi Arabia spent the largest share of these sums on madrassas, religious and social centers, universities, media, and other institutions from Indonesia to Palestine, producing hundreds of thousands of Wahabi adepts. Beyond the region, oil royalties financed hundreds of institutions and mosques in Europe and North America, with a particular focus on disseminating Salafism. Iranian petrodollars went to their Jihadi affiliates in the Middle East, Lebanon, the Palestinian territories, and the West. Sudan's regime funded propaganda in Europe with natural-resource revenues to cover up for the genocide in the south and in Darfur.[14] Libya and Iraq's dictatorships used oil revenues to feed media networks and to defend militants accused of abuses of human rights. In a nutshell, economic Jihad imperialism blighted the Greater Middle East's chances to evolve toward pluralism, democracy, and social justice. Oil brought tremendous potential to a region in great need of development; instead, the income generated by this natural resource has been greatly responsible for the miseries of most of its people. And beyond the frontiers of the region, petro-imperialism produced another drama: It obstructed the West's ability to come to the rescue of the East.

WESTERN ECONOMY TAKEN HOSTAGE

After 1973 Western economies and governments were slowly taken hostage by the economics of oil. By the end of the 1970s, and increasingly through the 1990s, the oil-producing regimes—building on the psychological effects of the oil shock—used their partner entities to penetrate Western Europe and North America with a new agenda. The Western multinational oil corporations such as Aramco, Total, Esso (now Exxon), Mobil, and scores of trade, construction, and import-export companies invested heavily in promoting their Middle Eastern partners within the West. And here lies the salient point of the oil regimes' offensive inside the Free World: Incapable of acting directly themselves, the regimes tasked their partners and mediators with obtaining influence for them within the territories of their customers, who happened to be the most powerful nations of modern times. The multinationals established a vast web of advisers and experts, including former diplomats, scholars, journalists, and politicians, who worked to consolidate the region's relationships with the United States and the West, portraying the region as essential to the world economy. By doing so, the oil powers were able through their army of advocates and lobbyists in Western capitals to steer international decision making at the United Nations, NAFTA, the European Union, NATO, the World Bank, UNESCO, and other agencies. The web created by the corporate associates of the oil regimes was by far more powerful than any other on the planet because it represented the interests of the main producers of energy, perhaps the crucial element in the well-being of all Western economies and thus of the well-being of its socioeconomic and political establishment. The bridge between the petro-powers in the region and large sectors of Western economies was built by the middlemen—for example, the Western MNCs and many other entities having a financial interest in it, which were actually living off that flow of oil wealth. With this equation, Arab Muslim elites partnering with Western interests have succeeded in shielding themselves and their power moves from international scrutiny (and from resistance or interference). Future historians will find that oil imperialism was jointly created by the main power elites of the region's regimes and their counterparts in the industrialized world. The eastern end of this linkage was protecting its own power, while secretly preparing for a future campaign against the infidels; the Western end was content with preserving its own comfort, after years of world war and Cold War. Western economies made all the concessions demanded by the oil producers, including turning a blind eye to human rights abuses and oppression in the Greater Middle East, and in return gained stability in the international economy.

During the Cold War, Western bourgeoisies, mostly concerned with the Soviet (and Communist) threat, ignored the enterprises undertaken by ideological petro-regimes. By the time the Soviet Union finally collapsed, the liberal and capitalist elites of the West were already too penetrated by the Jihadists and their apologists to notice their dependence on oil powers. Volumes could be written on the ways in which oil money and influence penetrated the various layers of culture, politics, diplomacy, media, and social strata in the West. The end of the Cold War could have provided an opportunity for reforms and change in the Greater Middle East. As I have argued before, the deepest penetration of the West took place through education, and from there the influence spread in all directions and across all layers of public life.[15] Tens of millions of petrodollars were spent on U.S. and Western campuses to impact the teaching of and research about the Arab and Muslim world. The grants, donations, gifts, and financial favors aimed at Middle East studies, Islamic studies, international relations, history, and related fields were intended to produce generations of graduates whose perceptions of the region and its crises, ideologies, and political cultures would suit the dominant establishments of the region. And the campaign succeeded. Hence, for decades, the basis of Western understanding of the Greater Middle East has been corrupted by petrodollars, and the poison has spread to other layers of public perception, such as newsrooms, courtrooms, art rooms (including theater, Hollywood, etc.) and war rooms, and eventually to legislatures and business suites. Decision makers in the democracies were caught in a pincer movement: On the one hand, the persuasiveness of the intellectual products of oil-funded education, and on the other hand the looming menace of another oil shock like that of 1973.

The consequences of this penetration of the system brought real, significant, and dramatic policy decisions, from the Cold War to 9/11 and after. Some examples of Western behavior tainted by petro-Jihadism have already been given, such as the abandonment of Southern Sudan's people (1983–2008) and, later, the loss of Darfur's population to the regime's genocidal behavior; the failure to confront Syria's occupation of Lebanon and its vast human rights abuses (1976–2005); and the disregard for the plight of the Berbers in Algeria (1980s–2008). The democracies also ignored the massacre of the Shiites in Iraq (1992–2003), disregarded the persecution of the Copts in Egypt (1980s–2008), dismissed the Salafist onslaught on civil society in Algeria (1992–2008), and turned a deaf ear to East Timor's struggle for liberation (1975–1999). Above all, the Western intelligentsia and political establishment collaborated in portraying the Jihadist movements as revivalist and reformist.

The dependency of the West on oil resources created a strange trilateral equation, extending influence even farther. Many Third World countries rely on multinational corporations for vital services and technology. Many of these MNCs are involved with oil production, trade, and financial transactions. Hence oil producers promoting ideological agendas have been able to score more influence in the Third World thanks to the associations these petro-regimes have with international companies. Sub-Saharan Africa, Latin America, and Asia have all felt the political heft of the oil bloc. This weight has been disproportionate to the small size of the oil producers' national economies; for example, Spain's gross domestic product alone was greater than the combined GDP of the Arab countries, but the oil regimes had even more foreign policy influence in Europe than in Washington, and they were more assertive in Brussels than in the United States.

With so much power at the service of the Oil Jihadi Empire, it was almost impossible to resist the Wahabi and to some extent the Khumeinist agenda for the fate of the region's peoples. With perhaps two exceptions, Israel and Turkey, the region's nation-states were at the mercy of the empire, albeit in a disorganized fashion. This power to make and shape Western decisions about the Middle East crisis extended to the United Nations. For decades, observers have been stunned by the ineffectual reactions of the United Nations to genocides, famines, natural disasters, and injustices across the Third World, including those in Biafra, Sudan, Lebanon, East Timor, Kurdistan, and more. It is only via the deconstruction of the oil power's Jihadist network that the behavior of the UN's General Assembly (and till very recently the Security Council) could be understood. The core Jihadi circles inside the main oil-producing regimes in the region control the international policies of these governments. The latter control OPEC, which, in turn, with the regimes, sets the agendas of the MNCs. All these parties together have the Third World countries under their economic wings (or thumb, perhaps). Since the 1970s no opposition has been able to counter the oil powers—with two exceptions.

One exception occurs when two oil powers in the Middle East clash with each other. The industrialized world then rushes in to contain the conflict and bring it back in balance. Take, for example, the Iran-Iraq War. It ended with no one victor and no one vanquished, as both Saddam's army and Khumeini's Revolutionary Guards were eventually brought back within their national boundaries after seven years of bloody fighting. Examine also the Iraq-Kuwait War: Although it was obvious that Saddam was the invader, the oil equation demanded a return to the status quo ante. Iraq's regime was put in check by Washington and London, but, again, no regime change was permitted under the oil umbrella, even if the offending regime was responsible for breaches of international law, massacres, and even genocide (e.g., Sudan). Iran's regime has committed massive abuses of human rights and openly supports terror; yet it is under a UN check, not for these reasons but for another: the development of nuclear weapons. Syria's regime brutalized Lebanon for decades; it was only after Damascus backed the Jihadists in Iraq and assassinated former prime minister Rafik Hariri that UN action began. The list is long but the pattern is clear: With Western economies under threat by the oil empire, international proactive policies toward the region come under the supervision of the region's regimes. A popular theory among some elite critics of the U.S. intervention in Iraq argues that the war was all about direct seizure of oil. In fact, the era of intervening lawlessly and seizing natural resources in other countries—as was the case in the nineteenth century—is over. First, international law forbids it, but more important is the fact that the economy of oil is open. Saddam's and any other regime were selling petroleum at will. The real oil dimension nowadays is that as a result of American and Western companies' deals with oil producing regimes, U.S. policy has been affected and human rights have been abandoned.

Even after 9/11, oil imperialism continues to affect U.S. plans and decisions. Despite the fact that America has declared the War on Terror, removed the Taliban and Saddam, and established a Department of Homeland Security, the power of Jihadi oil is still omnipresent within the most powerful democracy on earth. The jury is still out on the U.S. conflict with Jihadism because the forces that represent the financial interests of the oil empire are still opposing this war, attempting to deflect it and to discredit its leaders and thinkers, and preparing for a dimming of the national consciousness that was briefly raised after 2001. The influence of oil power took Spain out of the equation in 2004. Al Qaeda attacked the trains in Madrid, and the Jihadi apologist network in the media did the rest—eroding the national will that had sustained the efforts against terror in Iraq. In Amsterdam, a lone Jihadi assassinated a leading anti-Jihadist artist, but the sum of Dutch interests in the oil market stopped the Netherlands from engaging the forces of Jihad on a national scale. In the United Kingdom, al Qaeda repeatedly brought horrors to London and other cities, but the immense influence of Gulf oil prevents Great Britain from mobilizing against the terrorists' ideology. The same problems apply in Canada, Australia, Germany, Italy, France, Argentina, and Denmark. The economic price that has to be paid for a global engagement of the ideologies of terror seems to be too high for the establishment. India and Russia, despite the terror attacks on their soil, are still constrained by economic considerations, mostly linked to oil or to markets linked to petro-regimes. In 1975 the leading financial center of the Arab world fell to the racket as well: Either that small country would accept the diktat of the Arab League (at the time) or it would be left to the forces of radicalism without any Western help. Indeed, Lebanon was delivered to chaos and destruction. Israel, however, has managed to survive despite the conflict with many Arab states. The oil powers couldn't break the Jewish state militarily (due to strategic U.S. support), but thanks to their royalties they were able to keep peace away, thereby maintaining the region in a state of war and conflict and so also denying the Palestinians a home.

THE REVOLUTION

The international community is faced with big dilemmas. As long as the oil-producing regimes are involved in promoting and financing a radical ideological agenda, world peace and security are at great risk. And as long as the democracies, most industrial powers, and the leading members of the UN Security Council are hostages of the petrodollars empire, the peoples in the Greater Middle East will continue to be oppressed and the terror forces will grow. In view of these geopolitical realities and the ongoing War on Terror and War of Ideas, it becomes imperative that the Free World engage in a liberation movement to free their national economies from entanglement with the oil powers. Such a radical change in political economy obviously cannot take place separately from the cultural revolution suggested in the previous chapter. Actually, a revolution in the politics of international economics can only be an extension of a massive change in the political strategies of the West and the rest of the Free World. And as cultural and intellectual reforms will be fought fiercely by the ideological and political forces of Jihadism and their apologists and allies, a serious repositioning of Western and international economics to free democracies from the hegemony of the Oil Jihadi Empire will be obstructed and resisted by the entire spectrum of interests involved. In other words, an economic disengagement by the West will cause much higher resistance among oil producers and their networks than they showed in opposition to the regime changes in Afghanistan and Iraq. An economic revolt against Middle Eastern oil power would be sure to eliminate the hegemony of the Jihad oil power, even more than military action. For a Western economic revolution against oil imperialism would certainly—over time—erode the political order that has been established in the Greater Middle East by the combined efforts of authoritarianism and Jihadism.[16]

So, if the intellectual, mental, cultural, ideological, and political conditions for an uprising against the plague of petrodollars are mustered, how would an economic revolution be possible?

1. *An economic revolution: Control oil influence*

   The very first move to be considered should be the removal of oil-generated influence from political debates. One must think in terms of what the empire has already achieved in its penetration of the West and other blocs (Russia, India, Latin America). Reversing that infiltration is the goal. Legislation must make public the donations coming from oil-producing regimes to colleges, schools, and universities and filter them to allow for transparency.[17] Donations by oil regimes and their associates to public libraries, public media, and government agencies dealing with education, defense, and national security should be controlled. Special legislations dealing with donations by oil-based MNCs (or any business associated with oil regimes) or financing of public debates must be created. The involvement of MNCs in promoting their clients' ideologies within the educational system, pressuring national authorities to provide endorsement to anti-democratic regimes, and lobbying against human rights should come with penalties.

2. *Diversify imports*

One logical step that can be taken to liberate Western economies from the cartels established by Wahabis and Khumeinists in the world markets is of course to diversify suppliers and in that way defuse the *silah al naft*. It is essential that customers break the hold that the main producers have over them. Naturally, the step toward liberation has to be organized according to its economic and financial feasibility, as determined by experts. However, new national and international guidelines must be created in favor of creating new economic relationships. At first, diversification must take place within the region. More oil should be purchased from countries not engaged in ideological propaganda and warfare. There should be fewer imports from, and also less trade, technological assistance, and engagement with, regimes that use natural resources to penetrate liberal democracies, develop dangerous weapons, or violate human rights. New policies should be adopted toward OPEC that would depoliticize the organization and disable the regimes' capacities to seize control of the agency in order to achieve ideological goals. Moves to import more oil from Russia, Canada, Nigeria, and other countries and to tap other regions for oil and energy will contribute to gradually diminishing reliance on the hard-core petro-Jihadists from the Middle East.

3. *Create a mega reserve*

Western powers and liberal democracies should create a petroleum mega reserve under Western—but also international—supervision so that a future oil shock, masterminded by Jihadists and other radicals (including new rogue regimes such as Hugo Chavez's), wouldn't affect the world economy and take it hostage again. America on its own, but also along with Western democracies and other countries, should create these reserves to protect against what could become a massive Oil Jihad against the West, which is likely to occur when the latter begins to free itself from economic dependence on the hard-core petro-Jihadists. This possibility should be prepared for, even if dramatic developments in the region may push civil societies to provoke and achieve a democratic change.

4. *Arrange international cooperation*

In the framework of reassessing the world political economy in light of the War on Terror and the prospect of future Jihadist campaigns, it is imperative that Americans and Europeans engage in negotiations with Russia, China, and India, as well as other industrial powers such as Japan and Brazil, to contain the oil imperialism now centered in the Middle East.

Based on the reality that the ideological Jihadi hard core in the region is projecting a worldwide dominance, following an ideology that aims to create a caliphate that is completely at odds with the principles of sovereignty and self-determination, the leading democratic powers should come together to contain the threat economically by denying the Jihadists and the radicals effective control over oil markets. All the above economies are strategic targets in the eyes of the hard core—and the United States, Europe, India, and Russia are already battlefields. Asian and Latin American economies are next on the Salafists' and Khumeinists' list. Hence the international economic community has an interest in containing, blocking, and then reversing Jihadi oil imperialism as a first stage in freeing the Greater Middle East from war economies and unleashing the real economic and financial talents of the region in the direction of progress, freedom, and prosperity.

5. *Empower minority groups*
   Another important dimension of the economic revolution is support for minorities in the Greater Middle East who wish to assert and reclaim the rights to their natural resources. Ethnic and other minorities in Iran, Saudi Arabia, Iraq, Sudan, Algeria, and Indonesia must receive their royalties from oil profits. This recommendation is aimed at empowering minority groups financially and economically so that they can develop their own regions, alleviate socioeconomic disparities, and participate in the diversification of oil trade worldwide.

6. *Distribute royalties (or dividends) fairly*
   Mirroring the international policies on liberation of women and minorities, righting injustices, addressing human rights, and promoting self-determination, a parallel track must be followed to create a fair distribution of oil revenues within the oil-producing countries, especially for those living under authoritarian rule. A new approach by the international community, particularly by democracies, should be adopted towards petro-regimes. These enormous resources bring gigantic revenues and should address the needs of the local populations instead of being spent overseas in ideological warfare and in support of terror. Producers in the Gulf states, Iran, and North Africa, as well as those in other countries having the same status, must prioritize spending for the weaker segments of their societies: to eradicate poverty and illiteracy; to provide healthcare, jobs, eldercare, and cultural events; to advance technology and care for the environment; and to effect rapid deradicalization. The tens of millions of Arabs, Iranians, and other nationalities living under the Jihadi oil regimes should benefit from the huge wealth now garnered by emirs,

mullahs, and dictators. They are entitled to participate in a more peaceful and prosperous twenty-first century.

7. *Reconsider foreign investments*

   The Jihadi and authoritarian oil-producing regimes should be asked to divert their investments in ideological or political warfare to reasonable and humanitarian assistance in their region. Billions in petrodollars spent by Saudi Arabia, Qatar, Iran, Libya, Sudan, and other governments on radicalization politics should be redirected to help societies in Egypt, Palestine, Morocco, Tunisia, Lebanon, Syria, Jordan, Bangladesh, and Afghanistan, too. The oil producers' foreign aid to the region's needy peoples should gradually replace Western aid, which must be redirected to sub-Saharan Africa and other parts of the developing world. The Oil Empire must begin to help the weak and disenfranchised from within so that its emigrating youth can be transformed from seekers of jobs overseas into happy, fulfilled workers in their own societies.

8. *Develop other energy sources*

   All seven of the above recommendations would help free international society from the onslaught of oil imperialism and Jihadist economic dominance. They would also help the peoples of the region reclaim their rights and gain access to their own resources and the benefits derived there from. In addition, they would also consolidate peace and security. But at the end of the day, and beyond these hard strategic decisions, the one most important shift—although far from attainment just now—would be the development of an alternative source of energy. The oil Jihad will only really recede when an alternative to a petroleum economy is found. Evidently, it will take years, if not decades, to convert the oil-based industries to other forms of energy. It would take worldwide scientific and economic revolutions going beyond world politics to achieve that goal. Perhaps one or two generations will pass before such a transformation can occur. But keeping the pressure in that direction will further hopes among the public, thrill the victims of terrorism, excite environmentalists, and enable humanity to envision a safer, better future than the miseries caused by the *silah al naft*.

However it proceeds, this economic revolution, so essential in the confrontation with terror, will need all the skills of a diplomatic revolution—a new art of truth telling, uncovering of propaganda, and the creation of appropriate alliances—to roll back the ever-present menace.[18]

CHAPTER 5

DIPLOMATIC REVOLUTION

IN THE NEW ERA THAT FOLLOWED THE ATTACKS ON THE UNITED STATES, Spain, and Britain, and included the wars in Afghanistan, Iraq, and Lebanon, and the terror and violence at the heart of matters, a major question arose in the capitals of the world: Why have Western and international policies failed to contain terrorism and the Jihadi movement? Other questions followed logically: Why weren't the policies of all nations threatened by Jihadi terror geared toward one purpose, that is, the defeat of the menace? Even worse, why were the foreign policies of all these governments colliding with each other? Why did each country—especially those targeted by either the Salafists or the Khumeinists and their allies—have its own policies on containment, and why did some governments actually grant recognition to a terror group even though it was at war with another democracy?

Ironies and contradictions abound. While Europe perceived Hezbollah, Hamas, and other similar groups as political movements, the United States saw them as terrorists. America supported the Wahabis during the Cold War and its foreign policy establishment ignored the teachings of Jihadism until 9/11. Russia supported the Syrian and Iranian regimes during the War on Terror, while Jihadists committed atrocities in Moscow and Beslan. The web of interactions since the end of the Cold War and after September 11, 2001, will no doubt intrigue chroniclers in the future. If one surmises that Western priorities before 1990 were to shield their countries from a Soviet first strike and penetration and win the Cold War, then understandably the conflict with any other force, including Jihadists and extremist authoritarians, was secondary. Yet with the collapse of Moscow's Communist leadership, the West should logically have turned to the problem of Jihadi terrorism. Instead, the diplomacies of the Free World went off in different—and often contradictory—directions. One Western democracy would block the efforts of another on the basis of economic or political competition, with the encouragement of authoritarian regimes in the Greater Middle East. The United States,

Western Europe, Russia, the Asian powers, and countries in Africa and Latin America have struggled to keep markets open to their economic interests, while the forces of terror penetrated their decision-making systems and profited tremendously from what they learned. The confusion in dealing with the worldwide Jihadi threat was obviously fed by the Oil Jihadi Empire, which wanted to divide the international community, disorient its major powers, and so rise higher in a divided world order. These crises in international politics had a natural impact on law and diplomacy, especially at the United Nations. More than ever, the leading international organization became the silent bystander at ongoing genocides and human dramas provoked by the Jihadi powers, and at times its bureaucracies ignored the spread of dangerous ideologies.

It is now time to untangle this diplomatic snarl to determine the changes—and they are large—that will be needed to address the challenges as the conflict widens and persists.

WESTERN POLICIES TOWARD JIHADI TERRORISM

Not only have the policies followed by liberal democracies in the West over the last three decades failed to confront the threat; in many instances they helped, advertently or inadvertently, radical ideologies and movements to rise and to spread. Western policies toward Jihadism, both Salafi and Khumeinist, are to blame for the disasters that occurred—at least since the early 1990s—all over the world. But that blame, contrary to the Islamist and Neo-Marxist criticism, is due not to the West's intervention in Arab and Middle Eastern affairs, but rather the democracies' abandonment of the region to bullies and terror groups.

The debate about Western (and particularly American) foreign policies toward the Middle East and the Arab and Muslim world, and the ideologies of radicalism in those areas, follows from the questions originally posed in the War on Terror: What were these policies? Were they actually the root causes of the emerging violence? The Islamists, Baathists, and Marxists claim that colonialism and imperialism, as embodied by the United States and Western Europe, are the reason violent movements arose in the Third World. But the Jihadi networks use their criticism of Western policies to further their own agendas in the Third World. By weakening the international community's stance on human rights and self-determination for countries living under authoritarian regimes, the radicals shield their area of operations from outside intervention. Although pitted against each other in a deadly struggle over control in the Arab Muslim world, the various streams of radical movements and ideologies display a common front against liberal democracies. As I argued in *Future Jihad* and in *War of Ideas*, the long-term strategy of the Jihadists is to seize political and economic control of the Greater Middle East,

Africa, and south Asia, as a first step to declaring a new caliphate. And from there, according to the grand designs of the Muslim Brotherhood, the Wahabis, and other Islamists, they plan to launch a campaign for world domination. Hence blaming the West for the sufferings of the Middle Eastern peoples is a winning strategy concocted by a transnational Fascist-Jihadist axis.[1]

Ironically, Western policies were in many ways responsible for the perpetuation of the oppression of these nations—but by way of omission and abandonment rather than by suppression (at least in the postcolonial era). The authoritarian and Jihadi elites seized power in the Greater Middle East and established their own culture of oppression as the colonial powers withdrew. From Iran to Sudan and from Libya to Afghanistan, the shadow of absolutism descended on the region's masses after World War II. As the French, British, Italians, Portuguese, and Spanish repatriated their forces from North Africa and Asia and shrank their direct domination, absolute monarchies, Arab socialists, Wahabis, Baathists, dictators, sectarian oligarchies, and Communists competed mercilessly for control of dozens of countries. Liberal and democratic elites were rapidly weakened, marginalized, suppressed, and ultimately eliminated, as we will note in the next chapter. The region's peoples were ruled by one or the other of these oppressive systems and ideologies, but always they were denied freedom of choice. And in this environment of mass violence and oppression, more radical movements with terrorist agendas surged forward, organizing within the rubble of fallen authoritarian regimes, as in Iran, or inside the madrassas funded by existing powers, as in the case of the Taliban. And as radicalism was reaching its apex in the Greater Middle East, what did the policies of the West achieve? What were the diplomatic strategies and political choices of the United States and Western Europe regarding Jihadi extremism and terrorism?

United States foreign policy plays a central role in world politics in general and in the struggle against terrorism in particular. Hence the various attitudes of Washington toward Jihadism throughout the second half of the twentieth century and during the current War on Terror are at the core of Western and international policies, and thus bear enormous responsibility in this regard. The sheer resources and moral power of America during and after the Cold War could have played a tremendous role in containing the growth of Jihadi terror. The first question is: Did the United States rise to this task? The second question: If not, why not?

After 1946, the United States found itself in a strategic confrontation with the Soviet Union. After the warning sent by "Mr. X" in 1947[2] to the United States, all energies and resources were directed to containing the Soviet threat. The Cold War, and its multiple bloody subconflicts around the world, including those in Korea, Vietnam, Africa, Latin America, and Asia, was naturally preeminent in the war rooms of NATO and many Western capitals. Even ethnic and nationalistic conflicts such as the Arab-Israeli and India-Pakistan wars and internal disputes in Sudan, Nigeria, Cyprus, and beyond were perceived by Washington and Moscow as East-West generated. In short, because the main threat to America's security was coming from the USSR, it concentrated all its energies and attention on the Soviets and their proxies. But it also recruited allies against the Soviets from camps that would ultimately become future enemies: the Jihadists.

The main strategic error during the Cold War was a poor analysis of Jihadism as a real and long-term enemy. The American-Islamist "components" against the Soviets and Communism had two legs: one was the importance of Middle East oil to the American economy, and the other was the convergence of the interests of capitalism and Islamic fundamentalism in opposition to Marxism-Leninism. This alliance against the Soviets afforded the Wahabis and other oil powers a greater influence within the West in general and the United States in particular. During the Cold War, the general perception in America was that the enemy (Islamists) of our enemy (the Communists) was logically our ally. Hence most Soviet studies and international relations centers, in addition to the multinational corporations, promoted Saudi Arabia, its Jihadists, and even at some point the Muslim Brotherhood as objective allies against the Soviet threat. Such a global policy had strategic consequences. For when Islamism (and inherently Jihadism) was projected as an ally, a whole package of interests developed from the original perception. Cultural leaders in the arts, academics, and other kinds of intellectuals painted the Islamists as allies, and in this way shielded them from public scrutiny. The public perception of Jihadists as anticommunists discounted the fact that the Jihadists were calling at the same time for the downfall of the United States and the erection of a caliphate. Hence wrongly defining the Islamists as natural allies in the resistance to the Soviets shaped a cultural and ideological trap, when, in fact, ties with the real allies of the United States should have been forged, with, for example, moderates in the Middle East. But the Jihadi lobbies transformed the convergence of interests into a strategic choice by the United States, even though American leadership had little education and information about the deeper agenda of the Islamists. From 1947 to 1973, U.S. perception of the Middle East was strictly based on anticommunism. Egypt, Syria, Iraq, and southern Yemen were Soviet clients and therefore foes of the West. Saudi Arabia, the Gulf monarchies, Jordan, Morocco, Lebanon, and Iran sided with the West.

The United States perceived Israel as a Western cultural ally, even though Israel was at war with other U.S. allies in the Arab world. This exception, similar to the Turkish-Greek situation, was an awkward situation, but acceptable nevertheless.[3] The Jewish state had cultural foundations in sympathy with the West (Jewish identity and the democratic system), and in addition it fought efficiently against powerful Soviet allies in the region and defeated them (Egypt, Syria, the PLO, and others). Hence U.S. policy was supportive of Israel on the grounds of cultural and ideological commonalities as well as the anti-Soviet alliance.

With Arab anticommunist regimes, the United States also had two grounds for alliance: oil and anti-Marxism. But following the Yom Kippur War in October 1973 and the subsequent petro-crisis, the United States took the ties to the oil producers much more seriously. Although Washington didn't lessen (much) its commitment to Israel's security, it became more conciliatory to petro-regimes, with a corresponding increase in their influence. The links built rapidly: Washington needed the oil regimes, and the latter responded with an ideology that opposed Communism. Washington locked in the new allies in its struggle against the USSR, but in 1973, the Oil Empire retaliated against U.S. support of Israel; the Wahabi-Jihadi powers put Washington on notice that, without them, the West would suffer economically. Hence the latter was forced to partner strategically with the petroleum-Islamist bloc. In short, the oil Jihadists posed a dilemma for the United States and its allies: without oil, you will crumble; with the oil powers you will survive and ultimately win the Cold War. U.S. foreign policy absorbed the lesson, and after that, on all issues related to the geopolitics of the Arab Muslim world, Washington would defer to its Arab Islamist allies. Thus, one of the major effects of the oil crisis of the mid 1970s was to "subcontract" U.S. policies in the region—with the exception of Israel—to the Jihadi Oil Empire, which included a slew of local regimes, intellectuals, MNCs, and academics, all intertwined with diplomatic circles, incumbents, and former rulers within America's foreign policy establishment.[4] The interplay between the oil powers, U.S. Middle East policy elites, and American academic experts in fact constituted a takeover of Washington's major policy bodies by an establishment subordinate to the Wahabis, the authoritarian regimes, and other Islamist forces. The political influence of oil was managed by the so-called Arabists in the U.S. government, particularly in the State Department. By the late 1970s Washington's ability to pursue a policy of democratization and human rights and its capacity to identify the Jihadi threat were effectively undone by the oil party.

This explains how U.S. foreign policy was practically stifled till 9/11. For almost three decades American diplomacy was—willingly or not—swinging between ignoring Jihadism and legitimizing it. It was no wonder the rest of the world wasn't mobilizing against Jihadi terror when the greatest power on earth was flirting with religious fundamentalism in order to use it as a tool for the containment of the Soviet Union. However, in 1979, an anti-American (yet also anti-Soviet) type of Jihadism emerged from the Khumeinist revolution in Iran. The taking of the U.S. embassy in Tehran and holding of American hostages, along with Iranian-funded Hezbollah's subsequent relentless terror attacks on American personnel in Lebanon, opened a new front in the midst of the Cold War. The outburst of Islamist violence against America in the 1980s provided an opening for a counterstrategy and a strong diplomatic response by Washington. Instead, the policy architects refused to globalize the containment of Iranian-inspired Jihadism and narrowed the conflict to a purely U.S.-Iranian crisis. American diplomacy missed the boat again by failing to confront rising Islamic fundamentalism. Realists would rationalize this attitude as a necessity of the Cold War: one enemy at a time. But seasoned observers of U.S. diplomacy argued that the oil lobbies, and behind them the gigantic Organization of the Islamic Conference, hamstrung U.S. containment of Tehran's regime early on. Confronted by Hezbollah terror on the one hand and the ongoing Soviet menace on the other, Washington preferred to concentrate on Moscow while conceding influence in Lebanon to the Iranian regime of Ayatollah Khumeini. Thus America's response to the ayatollahs in the 1980s was limited to backing Saddam for seven years in his bleeding of the Iranian regime. Whatever the logic, the United States was clearly backpedaling from Jihadism—until it was hit on its own soil in 2001.

U.S. allies fell into this trap as well. Generally, the United Kingdom adopted the U.S. attitude toward the Salafi Wahabis of the Arab peninsula and to some extent also to the Muslim Brotherhood. Historically, though, British Arabists, that is, sympathizers of the Pan-Arabist ideologies, were notorious for backing Arab regimes. In fact, they had preceded their American counterparts in cozying up to the region's authoritarian elites. With the exception of the moderate Hashemites of Jordan, London's foreign policy elite stood by most strongmen of the Greater Middle East and rationalized its attitude toward Islamism. Incredibly, the British established excellent relations with the oil regimes while simultaneously opening their metropolitan centers to Islamist dissidents from the 1970s on. Canada, Australia, and New Zealand remained distant from the Jihadists, but didn't initiate their own campaign against terror ideologies, particularly when the big brothers in Washington and London were in business with the Wahabis and unwilling to take on the Khumeinists ideologically. Canada's establishment, slowly attracted to the riches of the Greater Middle East, particularly in Sudan and the Levant, also effected a rapprochement with the two Islamist branches, the Saudis and the Iranians, until the War on Terror of this century began to shift Canadian policies to tougher stances.

In Europe, France, too, backed away from its traditional strong cultural support for liberty and self-determination in order to follow narrow economic interests with oil-producing regimes (and sell weapons to the region). French policy toward the Greater Middle East was hampered during the transition between colonial rule and the Cold War. Immediately after World War II, France began pulling out of its colonies; still, it engaged in two colonial wars, in Indochina and Algeria. The economic bleeding caused by the two conflicts and the political cost internationally (as well as the political defeat of Paris and London's campaign in the Suez by the United States), transformed French policies for the rest of the century. But it was with the advent of the Fifth Republic and the presidency of Gen. Charles de Gaulle that Paris adopted what it called *la politique Arabe de la France* (France's Arab policy). To confront the influence of the Anglo-Saxons on the one hand (mainly the United States) and to refurbish France's image in the (mostly oil-exporting) Arab world, French governments adopted the position of the Arab League in general and the petro-regimes in particular in their foreign policies. As early as 1966, this Gaullist policy distanced France from Israel, to the advantage of the Arabs in general and Saudi Arabia and Iraq in particular. In the 1970s, French attitudes toward Lebanon shifted from a traditional alliance and protection to mediation between Lebanon and the PLO and Syria. In the 1980s, French support for the most Francophone of all Middle Eastern countries dropped to a minimum, and in 1989 France's aircraft carrier the *Clemenceau* stood watch as the Syrians bombed the last free enclave in Lebanon before Assad ordered the invasion in 1990.

Gaullists and socialists had different agendas on many fronts, but on the general policy toward the Greater Middle East, they made the same concessions to the regimes at the expense of the underdogs and minorities. France stood with Saddam as his regime was butchering the Kurds; in the 1990s, French intelligence provided helpful information to the Sudanese regime on the Southern Sudanese resistance. And with billions in contracts with Gulf regimes, French foreign policy remained as silent as its American and British counterparts toward the rise of Salafi Jihadism. By the end of the decade, not only was Paris entangled with the gigantic oil interests in the region, but it had also opened the doors of its country (as did many other countries in Europe and the West) to radical Islamists seeking refuge there (or more likely, bases on French soil from which to operate). The French attitude toward Hezbollah, particularly under President Jacques Chirac, reached extreme limits, as the latter participated in conferences alongside Hassan Nasrallah, the secretary general of the Iranian-backed group, which (among many other terror attacks in the 1980s) was behind the massacre of the French Peacemakers in Beirut in 1983. Of all European countries, and despite the continuous action of the gendarmerie against the "radical cells" in metropolitan France, French governments made the most significant concessions to Wahabism, Salafism, and Khumeinism for more than three decades. It was only in 2004 that France made a turnabout—for reasons still shrouded in mystery—against Syrian and Iranian influence in Lebanon by co-introducing, along with Washington, a UN Security Council resolution (later coded 1559) asking the Syrian dictator to pull his troops out of Lebanon. Subsequently, President Chirac—despite his disagreement with the United States on Iraq—sided with President George W. Bush in ordering Assad out of Lebanon, most likely because of the assassination of former Prime Minister Rafik Hariri in February 2005. Hariri was a close friend and partner of Chirac. In the fall of 2005, then interior minister Nicolas Sarkozy (elected president in the spring of 2007) broke the silence on the urban threat posed by the Jihadists, but did not name them directly. A French political condemnation of "Jihadi" terrorism still failed to materialize.[5]

The other Western European governments have vacillated between the United States and French attitudes in their foreign policies during and after the Cold War. They, too, had to address the Soviet threat first and so didn't contain the Jihadi menace strategically—even after the collapse of the Red Empire. Generally, European members of NATO during the Cold War mostly followed the trend of the Western alliance, giving priority to the Soviet threat and seeking good relations with the oil regimes. This attitude opened the door for Wahabi influence to creep into the continent, just as it did in the United States. The following are some examples.

Spain's policy toward the region emulated France for decades, until Prime Minister José María Aznar sided with the United States in the campaign to remove Saddam in 2003. But his mostly left wing opposition and Wahabi apologists used a attack by al Qaeda in March 2004 to restore the status quo, which is to say, is a relative disengagement.[6]

In Italy, the Berlusconi government, initially engaged in the Iraq campaign of 2003, was brought down by a left-wing coalition. The move was hailed by the Wahabis and the Khumeinists. Both Italy and Spain, countries having extensive Mediterranean coasts, have alternated between strong stances against terrorism and dialogue with the Islamists. Both withdrew from the Coalition of the Willing in Iraq but offered forces for the United Nations Interim Force in Lebanon (UNIFIL).[7]

In the Benelux countries, the domestic penetration by Jihadophilia, fomented through financial interests, academia, and pressure by the oil-producing regimes, left a deep impact on foreign policies. Their economies were severely affected by OPEC's 1973 boycott, and they submitted to the redlines imposed by the Oil Empire. Even though Holland maintained its support for liberalism as a universal ideal, Benelux in general backed away from confrontation with Jihadism as an ideology. In the post-9/11 era in these three countries, intense Jihadi activities increased, culminating with the assassination of filmmaker Theo Van Gogh in Amsterdam in 2005 after he made a film perceived as critical of Islam. Belgian foreign policy in particular followed a conciliatory line; Brussels' policies were hampered by the weight of large contracts with the region's regimes.

The same factors more or less dominated the foreign policies of Germany, Denmark, and the Scandinavian countries. During the Cold War, Bonn's priorities were the containment of East Germany and the Warsaw Pact. After German reunification in 1990, Berlin's diplomacy lined up with the European Union regarding the Middle East, with a major interest in oil, arms, and other types of contracts with Iran and the Arab world, particularly Saudi Arabia, Libya, Iraq, and Syria. Denmark and Sweden followed a parallel model in their foreign policies. But while Copenhagen maintained a minimal balance between the needs of national security versus binding relations with oil producers, Stockholm covered up for many Islamist movements, including Hezbollah in the 1990s. Norway, benefiting from its self-sufficiency in oil, was more immune to the political pressure of the Jihadi Oil Empire; nevertheless, in its foreign policy it wasn't able to distance itself from the global Western mollification of Islamism-Jihadism. In general, Western Europe succumbed to the influence of political Islamism as a result of petrodollars and Jihadi militant activism.[8]

Using the influence of oil-producing regimes on the one hand and the penetration of Salafists and Khumeinists within the Muslim immigrant communities in Europe on the other, global Jihadism was able to hamstring European political responses. Thus, when al Qaeda and other Jihadists attacked Madrid and London and committed violence in the Netherlands, France, and elsewhere in Europe, the continent's elites had a hard time accepting the fact that the terrorists were emboldened by the spread of their doctrines and the weakness of European foreign policies toward them.

THE FORMER COMMUNIST EUROPE

When the Iron Curtain vanished from central Europe, the continent's policies toward world conflicts, including international terrorism, divided sharply. When Western Europe had banded together under NATO to confront the Soviet threat, Central and Eastern Europe were obliged through the Warsaw Pact to defend Soviet interests and their Communist allies around the world. The countries in the Soviet sphere strictly followed the Kremlin's policies toward the West, including those relating to terrorism. Their intelligence and security agencies opened their doors to a multitude of radical organizations, mostly Marxist, but also ultranationalist, including Pan-Arabists such as the Palestinian Popular Liberation Front (FPLP) and the Palestinian Democratic Popular Liberation Front (FDPLP), Lebanese radicals, Black September, the Red Army Faction, Baader-Meinhof (a German Communist terror group), and the Red Brigades. Eastern Europe thus became a hub for training and assisting socialist and Communist forces recruiting from the Arab and Muslim world. In a way, that part of Europe was aiding the rise of a Marxist Jihadism—a phenomenon that would reemerge later in Latin America under Venezuela's populist leader, Hugo Chavez. But after the Soviet Union collapsed, the Central and East European nations freed themselves from Communist foreign policies and joined NATO and in some cases the European Union.

The Central and East European governments also broke sharply with the Communist terrorism of the past, and didn't fall abruptly into Jihadist apologetics. Perhaps this was because the decades under totalitarianism kept the former European members of the Warsaw Pact distant from and suspicious of the other totalitarian ideologies, such as Salafism and Khumeinism. This attitude—luckily for the Central Europeans, so far—blocked the rapid penetration of these countries by the Wahabi and Iranian influences. Hence the Jihadist lobbies and by extension their terror networks from Prague to Warsaw are still limited, though growing nevertheless. It is evident that, with time, the Islamists will spill over into that part of Europe via various windows: Western Europe, petroleum lobbies, and alliances with trans-European mafias coming from the Balkans and Russia. Meanwhile, the Polish, Czech, Slovak, Romanian, Bulgarian, Hungarian, Slovene, and Baltic states have military personnel deployed alongside U.S., British, and other allies in the battlefields of Afghanistan and Iraq. Ironically, diplomats and politicians from Estonia, Latvia, Poland, and Romania are more vocal against ideological terrorism than Western European bureaucrats in Brussels and Strasbourg.[9]

In the Balkans, particularly in the former Yugoslavia, state policies still reflect regional and local ethnoreligious conflicts. The dismemberment of the former Communist federation led to two wars and Western military interventions in the 1990s, in Bosnia and Kosovo. In the midst of the fray, the Jihadists, political lobbies, and terror networks enhanced their positions and took advantage of the West-East tensions in the area. In the early 1990s, Slovenia and Croatia broke away from Yugoslavia. While the most northern republic swiftly moved to independence, the Serbian minority in Croatia rebelled against Zagreb's secession and declared their own. An ethnic war involving Serbian-controlled Yugoslavia ensued. Simultaneously, the Muslim-controlled Republic of Bosnia also rebelled against the federal government in Belgrade. Automatically, the Serbian and Croatian communities of Bosnia seceded from Bosnia. Serbia got involved and a multiethnic and bloody war spread across the area. The Dayton Accords acknowledged Bosnia's independence (as well as that of Croatia) but kept all ethnic minorities within the breakaway republics. Croatia maintained the Serbian province under its control, and Bosnia maintained both Croatian and Serb provinces under its control. Meanwhile, the Jihadist networks moved to establish Wahabi bases in Bosnia, despite the secular image of the government. And out of these launch pads, Jihadist cells began operating throughout Europe and North America.[10]

The second Balkan conflict, in Kosovo, was triggered by an ethnic Albanian insurgency against Serbian authorities in 1999. Bloodshed and ethnic cleansing compelled the West (the United States first and Europeans later) to intervene. However, unlike the outcome in Bosnia, where Serbian and Croatian provinces were kept under the central rule of the Muslim-dominated government, the Western foreign policies endorsed the right of the mostly Muslim province to separate from the Serbian Orthodox country. This display of Euro-American diplomacy was perceived by Serbs as siding with Bosnian Muslim claims for separatism from Yugoslavia, and against Serbian Christian claims for separation from Bosnia. In this ethnically heated environment the great powers divided along the lines of their allies on the ground. Throughout the 1990s, with the oil lobbies very influential, the United States and Western Europe sided strongly with the Muslims and the Croats against the Serbs. The Wahabi international circles hoped to create the conditions for the emergence of at least two Muslim states in Europe: Bosnia and Kosovo. Hence they threw their financial and political weight behind Washington and Brussels in pressuring the Serbs to relinquish the Serbian province to Muslim Bosnia and the Albanian-majority province to an independent Muslim Kosovo Republic. Countering the Western pro-Muslim move, post-Soviet Russia used its veto power at the United Nations to support Belgrade in the rejection of Kosovo's separation. Entering the fray, al Qaeda and other Salafi Jihadists declared it their aim to build a base in Kosovo to spread their power in the area. The three-way struggle between Serbs (supported by the Russians), the Muslim Albanians supported by Western foreign policy, and the emerging Jihadists will eventually boil down to two levels of conflict: The Salafists (or Neo-Wahabis of al Qaeda) will attempt to seize control of the province as it heads toward separation, and thus will find themselves facing off with the Serbs. This in turn could lead to an awkward choice for the West at some time in the future: side with the Wahabi-Salafi power rising in Kosovo, or with the traditional foe, the Russian-backed Serbs?[11]

In the current War on Terror with al Qaeda, Western choices in the Balkans seem to be very difficult. These challenges will soon encompass Western attitudes toward Eastern bloc policies regarding Jihadism.

THE EASTERN BLOC POLICIES

By Eastern bloc policies I mean the policies of the former Soviet bloc toward the Jihadist and authoritarian regimes and organizations in the Greater Middle East from 1945 till the present. Even though the USSR is no more, Russia has played and continues to play a central role in designing these policies and directing strategic agendas. However, the benchmarks in these relationships with the region are and have been different from Western interests and activities. Russia removed itself from European politics abruptly in 1917 by becoming the leading Bolshevik regime and turned against the rest of the world as it sought to establish a global Soviet dominance. And like the Wahabis, the Soviet Communists spent the first two decades of their regime consolidating their own state and deepening their ideological hold on their own population. But after 1945 Moscow's Communists moved to assert control within Eastern and Central Europe as a whole, and furthermore tried to penetrate countries around the world. The Salafists followed a parallel path by spreading Jihadism within the confines of the Arab and Muslim world. But almost all the camps (pro-Soviet, U.S.-allied, and Islamist), with few exceptions, developed a common front against Israel and jointly repressed minorities and any democratic opposition. The USSR supported authoritarian regimes, both nationalist and socialist, in opposition to the liberal sectors and minorities in the region.

However, as the Soviets and Salafi Islamists spread, they faced each other and clashed in many spots. In 1979, the Khumeinist Islamists joined the confrontation with the USSR and the Communists, from their own trenches in Iran and Lebanon and less directly in Iraq. This confrontation between Jihadists and Soviet Communists raged throughout the globe, and it gave some credibility to the Islamists in the capitalist West before and even after the end of the Cold War. Russians and their Warsaw Pact allies faced off with the Muslim Brotherhood via Soviet allies in the region, such as Assad's Syria, Abdel Nasser's Egypt, Saddam's Iraq, and Nimeiri's Sudan. But it was the direct military confrontation in the mountainous Central Asian country of Afghanistan in the 1980s that fatally weakened the Soviet position in the Arab Muslim world. By 1990, when the Soviet Union collapsed, the Wahabis had already infiltrated many countries in Central Asia and the Caucasus, and were making progress in the Balkans, which had also been freed from Communism.

After the collapse many former satellites of the USSR drifted away from old Cold War policies and stances. As noted, most Central and Eastern European countries joined or are integrating with the European Union. And reemerging democracies such as Poland, Hungary, the Czech Republic, Slovakia, the Baltic states, Bulgaria, Hungary, and Romania are developing diplomatic positions of their own, moving away from Communism and yet not embracing the Wahabi oil influence. However, most of the former Soviet republics in Central Asia returned to their Muslim heritage, with a few keeping Communist elites in power. Kazakhstan, Turkmenistan, Tajikistan, and Kyrgyzstan survived the end of the Cold War by moving to transitional governments, still influenced by former secular socialists but attempting to modernize their old tribal structures. These Central Asian elites are confronted actively by two streams of Jihadism: The Wahabi networks, which have already formed guerrilla groups within some of these republics, and the Iranian influence from the southwest. Russia maintains its friendship with the local authorities and the U.S. has attempted to attract some into a partnership. Again, a three-way dance is taking place between the Russians, the Americans, and the Jihadists. China's influence in that area will depend on how Beijing deals with its own Islamists in Sing Kiang. The future struggle will be determined by who gains power among the Muslim populations of the region.[12]

In the post-9/11 era, Russian foreign policy zigzagged between previous Soviet inclinations and post-Communist transformations. During the 1990s, Moscow abandoned its open policy of backing rogue states. The Russian Federation kept its ties with Libya, Iraq, Syria, and Sudan, but without giving them carte blanche as in the old days. Moscow, like any other world power, considers these resource-rich countries as assets in the struggle to find export markets. On the other hand, the Wahabi-led intifada in Chechnya, in the heart of the country, put the governments of Boris Yeltsin and Vladimir Putin on a collision course with Jihadist forces. Russian intelligence fought the terror networks not only in the Caucasus but also in the Arab world.[13] With the Beslan school massacre on September 1, 2004, the Russian conflict with Jihadi Wahabism and their allies became as intense as the U.S. war on al Qaeda. But Russian foreign policy, unlike its Western counterparts, didn't take the fight overseas, as the West did in Afghanistan and Iraq. While Moscow's resources in Asia could have put pressure on the Islamist forces, its policy was to limit its operations to counterterrorism inside the country and not engage in a world war against the international networks of Jihadism. There are many rationales for this conservative position, including the fear of enflaming other areas inside Russia (e.g., in Dagestan and other provinces close to Central Asia, where Muslim communities are large and the Wahabis are on the rise). But another reason for Russian isolation from the West in its confrontation with the Jihadists is its resentment of the United States and NATO, which are moving eastward, increasing their influence in Ukraine, Russia's southern neighbor. In addition, there is Russian frustration because of the Euro-Western attitude toward the Serbs and in defense of Wahabism in the Balkans.

Hence Russian discourse on the War on Terror has been ambiguous. On the one hand, President Putin has accused the Islamists of perpetrating hateful terror attacks on the Russian people "in order to launch the Caliphate."[14] On the other, Moscow's government has stood against the United States in Iraq and continued to sell weapons to Iran and Syria, even though the latter never stopped backing Hamas, Islamic Jihad, and other Jihadists in Gaza and Lebanon. Russia's foreign policy, like that of many Western states, still struggles with contradictions when it comes to the Jihadi wars. The Kremlin knows all too well the threats coming from the Salafi web, but then stands firm in support of other Jihadi regimes and organizations. The strategic planners in Russia should know better: The Syrian-Iranian axis fuels not only Hezbollah's terror networks but also Sunni Islamists, many of whom have ties to the Chechen Wahabis. This will come back to haunt the Russians' national security. Similarly, protecting Iran's nuclear weapons program could dramatically endanger Russian populations long before it harms Europeans or Americans. A shift in alliances between the mullahs and regional Jihadi groups would put those nukes in the hands of radicals in Chechnya and even in Russia's cities.[15] Also, arming Syria could end up backfiring by strengthening Islamist factions manipulated by Damascus. Arab Islamic politics are constantly shifting and at the mercy of the most radical forces until a real democratic revolution takes place inside the region.

ARAB ISLAMIC POLICIES

The Arab Muslim world underwent cataclysmic changes in the last century, some of which will be explored in the next chapter. The politics of the twenty-one Arab and about fifty Muslim countries are of course extremely relevant to the confrontation with Jihadism. Did Arab policies and the diplomatic initiatives of Muslim states contribute to the rise of Jihadism? Were any regimes directly responsible for the development of terror ideologies and movements? Are there Arab and Muslim governments actively involved in countering, containing, or even reversing the tide? These are dramatically important issues to consider if there is to be a massive and concerted change in world diplomacy to defeat terror.

To summarize: certainly, there were and are regimes directly responsible for the spread of radical ideologies, and at the same time there are initiatives by a number of governments or NGOs aimed at opposing the spread of Jihadi terror. In this regard, Arab and Muslim foreign policies are as complex as Western policies. A main benchmark in Muslim policies regarding the Islamist agenda was the collapse of the Ottoman Empire in the mid-1920s: when the sultanate was abolished by Turkish secular nationalists the caliphate evaporated, and with it the supreme spiritual and political authority in the Muslim Sunni world. This transfiguration of Islamic politics opened the way for two competing trends. A multitude of Muslim states embraced the modern world and its legal foundations (international law); simultaneously, a constellation of movements and regimes began striving to bring back the caliphate (Sunni Salafists) or to invent an imamate (Shia Khumeinists). The Saudi Wahabi Kingdom was the oldest independent country of the Arab and Muslim world, along with its secular competitor, the republic of Turkey. The Arabian absolute monarchy promoted full Salafism, while Kemalist Turkey followed an aggressive separation of state and religion. Between these two extreme models emerged a host of governments, regimes, and states espousing an amalgam of ideologies, systems, and political cultures.

The most important characteristic of Arab and Muslim state policies, with very few exceptions, was that almost all ruling elites refrained from condemning Jihad as a tool of statecraft, and most governmental establishments ignored the rise of Jihadism as an ideology. This reality was the black hole that absorbed immense resources that Arab and Muslim diplomacies instead could have used to eliminate the most dangerous phenomenon of post-Ottoman history: radical ideological subversion of international relations and political economy. Jihadism was spared effective opposition for almost a century, until 9/11 and the subsequent Jihadi wars. While Saudi, Taliban, Sudanese, Libyan, Iranian, Qatari, Pakistani, Malaysian, and other governments promoted the politics of Jihadism, each for its own geopolitical reasons, other regimes such as those of Syria, Iraq (under Saddam), Egypt (under Nasser), the PLO (under Arafat), Algeria (under the National Liberation Front, FLN), and Somalia (when under radicals) allowed various forms of Jihadism to take root and spread. Countries such as Jordan, Morocco, Bangladesh, Senegal, Lebanon, the UAE, Kuwait, Turkey (before the Party of Justice and Development, AKP) and central Asian secular governments tried often to contain the ideological challenge and the terror threat. But at the core of the Arab League and the Organization of Muslim States, the oil-producing regimes wielded more power than the states on the periphery; hence, despite resistance by some countries against radicalism, the ideological elite at the center of the most powerful and wealthiest regimes imposed the party line on the combined diplomacies of the rest of the bloc. In the final analysis, the key players in world politics either adopted Jihadism or ignored it. Both attitudes led to the rise of fundamentalism. Combined with the overarching political culture of antipluralism, this agenda led to the obstruction of democracy, human rights, and social progress and the creation of an atmosphere that was a lethal incubator of crisis and conflict.

UNITED NATIONS

For much of the time that ideological and political Jihadism was wreaking havoc on the agreed-upon norms and systems of world politics, the United Nations sat at the summit of international relations, a supranational organization that was supposed to embody the consensus reached by nation-states on peace, security, and prosperity. Regrettably, the organization founded in 1945 to defend the security of international society failed in its original mission (not to mention the specific task of confronting the roots of genocide and collective threats). Objectively, the United Nations has achieved much, through the efforts of patient administrative servants and staff and diplomats from member states. Its successes—notably in economics, social affairs, jurisprudence, and even some political initiatives—have to be recognized; yet it has been incapable of combating wars and—most relevant to our analysis—terrorism. And because of lesser international stability, its struggles for human rights and literacy, and against famine, illnesses, and drought, have been affected. Its political failures may be understandable, given that the main powers involved in the East-West confrontation before 1990 were the five permanent members of the Security Council, the very body that presides over the questions of war and peace. No office at the organization could have ordered the

United States, NATO, the USSR, the Warsaw Pact countries, and China to stop bickering when they were aiming nuclear missiles at each other. That was impossible. It took the players in that conflict to stop their own arms race as Soviet power waned toward the century's end. But even beyond the big challenge of the Cold War face-off, the United Nations was incapacitated from within when it came to dealing with the second most important threat: the Jihadi terror movement.

Slowly during the Cold War, and rapidly from the late 1980s, the core forces of oil Jihadism pressured their allies in the Arab League and the Organization of Islamic Conference (OIC), as well as their client states in the Non-Aligned Movement, to form a voting bloc in the General Assembly to obstruct the actions of the Western or industrialized bloc. (They also gained some influence on the Security Council.) The strategic aims of the Jihad bloc were to set the agenda according to their interests. The latter revolved around blocking democratization within the authoritarian states of the Third World and maintaining the Jihadi agenda as legitimate. During the Cold War, the "third bloc" played off both the East and the West and positioned itself as an alternative to the two superpowers. For example, it voted against the United States on the Arab-Israeli conflict and against the Soviet Union on Afghanistan; against France and Great Britain on the Suez campaign, and with France when it opposed the United States. The examples are numerous and deserve a study of their own, but the cases reveal a strategy embodying the subtle rise of the Jihadi agenda. The bloc backed Nigeria against Biafra in the 1960s, Sudan against the southern rebellion in the 1970s, Syria against occupied Lebanon till the 1980s, Indonesia against East Timor until a policy reversal in the 1990s, and the Arab League against Israel until the Peace Process. However, just as important were the trends developed by the bloc in defense of Jihadism. While the international community (both for itself and through the United Nations) condemned Nazism, Fascism, and apartheid, and praised the wave of liberation from Soviet rule in the 1990s, there were no similar condemnations of Jihadism and its terror derivatives as an intolerant ideology. Such actions would have addressed the threat at its roots. But the voting power and the influence of the Wahabis, Khumeinists, and Baathists prevented the idea from even being considered, not only in the General Assembly but also in the Security Council—even though the towers of the World Trade Center that al Qaeda destroyed in 2001 were less than five miles away.

The battle at the United Nations obviously is waged not only *about* ideas, but also *through* them. It is evident that the Jihadi oil regimes and the other authoritarian powers of the Greater Middle East won't release their diplomats for a dialogue that might lead the international community to gear up for a struggle against terror ideologies, an event that would soon lead to questioning the sources of these doctrines and their funding, and ultimately to an investigation into the human rights conditions in that region of the world. The United Nations, as a political culture, has dared to criticize democracies when they committed errors but blasted wrongdoers only if they weren't on the magic list of oil-producing regimes (if they weren't caught red-handed). South Africa's Apartheid regime was sanctioned, the Milošević government punished, Haiti's military removed, and Kuwait freed from Saddam, but Sudan's regime was not touched, the Taliban oppression went unchecked, Syria's occupation of Lebanon went unquestioned, and, awkwardly, Saddam's oppression of the Kurds was not put on the agenda until 9/11. Some would argue, though, that the same treatment happened with regard to the Soviet Union's oppression of its peoples and China's mistreatment of Tibet. True, the weight of Moscow and Peking has blocked the discussion of internal matters in their empires. But that is precisely the point: There is another totalitarian empire that has used the organization, though not necessarily through a Security Council veto, to protect its militant agenda. More troubling is the influence the Oil Empire had (and continues to have) within the institution. Following the launching of the War on Terror, the secretary-general, Dr. Kofi Annan, made the incredible statement that the United Nations "stands neutral between terrorism and those fighting it."[16] With the bureaucracy of the United Nations insensitive to the menace of terrorism as a world plague and its post–Cold War policies still unmoved by the genocides perpetrated by the Jihadi-inspired regimes and organizations, without doubt, a major change in the confrontation with terror cannot be successful short of a radical reform, itself caused by a diplomatic revolution worldwide.

THE BASIS OF THE DIPLOMATIC REVOLUTION

U.S. DIPLOMATIC OVERHAUL

If the United States is the greatest democratic power at the beginning of the twenty-first century, its responsibilities include the duty of being true to its political essence, which is freedom and democracy. In other words, if America wishes to intervene at the international stage, it shouldn't contradict its own beliefs, which are the moral and historical values of its citizens. But should America get involved in world politics in the way it has been involved since the collapse of the Soviet Union and, more importantly, after 2001?

The answer in liberal democracies is found at the polls. It is there that citizens decide. From American modern history one can conclude that the people of the United States have often authorized the government to come to the rescue of oppressed nations, as in World Wars I and II and in the Korean and Vietnam wars, as well as interventions to restore democratically elected governments. The interventions per se were always debated and discussed under the principle of helping other peoples defend themselves or free their lands, a principle that has been accepted by a national consensus in America. Apart from an activist political minority—across party lines—which believes in complete isolationism (and has arguments for it), a majority of Americans still believes that the resources of their nation can and sometimes should be used to serve the cause of justice outside its borders. This attitude may well be the result of sociological factors peculiar to the nation: the ideals of the founding fathers, which have passed into the political culture; the memory of the injustices and horrors many immigrants lived through in their motherlands; the fact that America (at least since British colonial rule) hasn't experienced military occupation. Nevertheless, the question about justification for foreign intervention does surface. Why should citizens agree to spend dollars on foreign nations instead of their own? Why should American families suffer the loss of loved ones on some distant overseas battlefield? Hence it will take definitive efforts by the leadership of America in powerful causes to convince its public to engage in an overseas campaign.

As the War on Terror stretches closer to a decade, the psychosociological reading by the masses (with the help of new schools of analysis unavailable before) perceives the conflict as being about survival, a far graver matter than "security." So the crux of the debate in this new conflict isn't about its essence (despite the claims of ideological opposition), but about the rationale of engagement. The American public is developing its ability to understand the danger; hence the heart of the battle of the Jihadi propaganda machine is to deny Americans a complete understanding of the real ideology behind the war, and to substitute misinformation about Jihadists' intentions and aspirations. Hence, to proceed with the massive changes in foreign policy that are needed, the American public must be fully educated about the issues. Otherwise, as was the case with the war in Iraq and other salient crises in the war with the Jihadists, enemy propaganda can create devastation and undermine public support for U.S. policies (assuming the latter were aimed in the right direction). The intellectual revolution discussed earlier is a prerequisite for an overhaul of U.S. foreign policy; there must be a relentless education of the public about the essence of the conflict, the nature of the Jihadist agenda, and the deep desires of the peoples of the Greater Middle East. Only then can reform in diplomacy take place.

To overhaul American strategic policies for the long conflict ahead, the following steps are necessary:

1. Create a new generation of U.S. Foreign Service personnel with a profound knowledge of the political culture of the Arab and Muslim world,

the ethnic, religious, and human rights crisis within the Greater Middle East, and the ideologies and strategies of Jihadism. This must begin with a reform of the qualifications for diplomats, analysts, and bureaucrats at the various departments and agencies dealing with international politics and conflicts. In short, the teaching programs preparing students for foreign service have to be reformed, for no diplomatic revolution can be possible with the same body of academic teaching that led to the disaster.

2. Initiate a debate in the U.S. Congress to set the guidelines for a new foreign policy based on supporting human rights, self-determination, pluralism, and democratization on the one hand and a confrontation with the regimes, movements, and ideologies that promote threats to international law, security, peace, and liberty on the other. Specific legislation should identify Jihadism, as promoted by the terrorists, as an illegal and criminal ideology comparable to Nazism, Fascism, and racism, and enable U.S. foreign policy to set strategies to combat the spread of its derivatives and branches.

3. Make appropriate choices to support democratic movements, assist dissidents, and combat Jihadi (and other) terrorism, and make the necessary efforts to build coalitions and reach out to civil societies under international law to enable them to fight their own struggle for freedom. Hence the American interventions in Afghanistan and Iraq, and the initiatives in Lebanon, Somalia, Sudan, and beyond, should be carried out under the principle of assisting peoples in distress while confronting terrorism.

This new approach should be the platform upon which U.S. diplomacy builds the necessary alliances around the world.

U.S.-EUROPEAN ALLIANCE

The next step in the diplomatic revolution is to base U.S.-European relations in the War on Terror on a strategic alliance. While there are many European policies, each one impacted by the Oil Empire, there is only one official U.S. policy (also influenced by petrodollars). But if Washington follows a new revolutionary doctrine on human rights and democratization (a comprehensive, bipartisan, and strategic one), it can negotiate with each European government to find a common thread of purpose against Jihadi terrorism then move to negotiate with the European bloc as a whole to develop a comprehensive program. A new energy for American reform in foreign affairs would also energize many in Europe who see eye to eye on these issues. A better informed and focused United States can establish better alliances with western, southern, central, and eastern Europe against Jihadi terrorism, despite the political influence the Wahabi, Salafists, and Khumeinists have achieved already on the continent. American diplomats, legislators, and NGOs should work with their counterparts in individual countries as well as at the European level to achieve basic understanding and strategic coordination. Among the many areas of common interest are domestic threats from cells and radicalization, as well as efforts to engage and support Arab and Muslim NGOs at home and overseas, educate the public, and so on. A priority should be the consolidation of the Anglo-American alliance that goes beyond a reliance on the personalities of the leaders. The Jihadi political and ideological penetration is parallel in both countries, and coordinated awareness campaigns should be mounted. The very core of the resistance to the world Jihadi threat begins in the strategic bridge between Washington and London. This was demonstrated clearly in the twentieth century and again during the post-9/11 conflict. The enemy knows this equation very well, as its strategy of driving wedges between the two democracies shows.

The second special relationship to repair and rebuild is the U.S.-French alliance. Both the Americans and the British can and should partner with the French to combat the common mortal enemy infiltrating their societies: Salafi Jihadists. Despite a disagreement on Iraq, mostly provoked by the oil regimes, Washington and Paris were able to move together on liberating Lebanon from the Syrian occupation. The two democracies should build on the new areas of understanding and widen it to encompass strategies on Syria, Iran, Sudan, and North Africa. The United States should recognize French leadership where its experience is salient, as in the Levant, the Maghreb, and sub-Saharan Africa, and thus France's foreign policy will become an equal partner with U.S. and U.K. policies in the War on Terror.

Once this triple counterterrorism alliance is firmed up (with their respective veto powers joined on the Security Council), the three countries should establish a solid dialogue with the governments and civil societies of Spain and Italy to address the need for common Mediterranean strategies against terrorism. The moral weight of the three powers can influence their European partners in an alliance based on new principles of counterterrorism (within national frontiers) and meet the various challenges in a unified front. Each European country is at a point where it fears counterstrikes by the Jihadists if they resist them: The Netherlands, Denmark, and Germany are examples. But with a genuine bridge rebuilt between the three powers, most liberal democracies in Europe would join the diplomatic revolution, finding strength in solidarity as they face the taboos imposed by the Jihadi propaganda machine. Belgium, Scandinavia, and other European democracies realize the depth of the urban Jihad menace. They cannot but unite their efforts with a revolutionary policy across the West. No single European country would engage alone, but all of them would join a collective effort of liberation from the Jihadi lobbies.

Central and Eastern Europe would be even faster to join efforts to identify and marginalize the terror ideologies and then eradicate the terror. As mentioned above, these countries have less of a stake than the wealthier democracies to their West in placating the oil lobby; besides, they have more recent and more profound experiences with totalitarianism. Once a U.S.-European joint strategy is devised, the integration of most European countries will be faster than expected. Their publics also have been learning swiftly from the statements and misdeeds of the Jihadists.

THE WESTERN ALLIANCE

The European-American recalibration and reorganization of a new, informed, and intelligent confrontation with the terrorist forces and movements will quickly rally the other countries of the West. Canada, Australia, and New Zealand would join, as their peoples are culturally in harmony with the European-American core. Not one single player in the West should be left out of the new diplomatic revolution. Even the most critical among them, such as Greece and Cyprus, should be sought out. For example, Athens has turned a cold shoulder to most international efforts against Jihadism, claiming these initiatives are strictly American. But in a new mass effort against terrorism, the Greeks and the Cypriots should be consulted. The new Western campaign must take into consideration all its partners' security perceptions as it moves forward to isolate the terrorists. The overwhelming power of a united front can offer incentives to Western countries attracted by the oil powers in the region to make their choices more rational. This principle of the widest Western alliance must also include the Balkans—all the former members of the Yugoslav Federation, particularly the parties to ethnic conflicts such as Serbia, Croatia, and Bosnia. These three countries must be enlisted in efforts against Wahabism and Khumeinism in their own area. Defense and security organizations such as NATO, ANZUS, and the European Security Organization would become the vanguard of the struggle against terror. A gathering of Western and global democratic powers would create the most formidable alliance in history; it would be able to respond to the most lethal of all menaces to international society today. The regrouping and coordination of all these foreign policies would even have a powerful effect at the United Nations and among non-Western parties as well.

AMERICAN-RUSSIAN JOINT FRONT

Western and international efforts in counterterrorism cannot be fully effective without a crucial readjustment of the strategic relations between the United States and the Russian Federation. In fact, a direct alliance between the two powers is a shortcut to globally deterring the Jihadists. The latest developments in Russian-American relations, in light of the War in Iraq, the general conflict with terrorism, and the crisis over missile deployment in Europe are setbacks for international efforts in this direction, however. After decades of Cold War, Western and Russian policies should have evolved faster toward cooperation against Jihadi terrorism. There are objective reasons for that rapprochement. The Salafi Jihadists, who fought the Russians in Afghanistan in the 1980s, were also involved in the Wahabi struggle in Chechnya in the 1990s, and are planning an all-out war against the Russian hinterland. The internationalist Jihadists led initially by Abu Abdul Rahman al Hattab in the Caucasus are still waging a relentless war to seize control of Chechnya, create an emirate, then spill over into Dagestan and other Muslim provinces within the Federation. Al Qaeda and the Salafist movements have Russia at the top of their enemies list.

The Jihadist strategic project in Russia at this stage isn't meant only to strike at national security for political dividends; it is about dismembering the country and establishing pieces of the caliphate on its soil. On that ground alone, an American-Russian common interest should materialize in a tight alliance against a common enemy. Memory of the genocidal targeting of civilians on 9/11 and the school in Beslan should be at the core of the U.S.-Russian strategic response to the Jihadists. Any U.S. administration's or Russian presidency's first move should be to sign a mutual defense and security treaty to strike back against Jihadism wherever it appears and deny access to weapons of mass destruction to any form of Jihadi regime and movement. It is urgent that a direct link between the two centers be established, but, unfortunately, the deterioration of diplomatic relations in the years following the onset of the Iraq War has been a disservice to both superpowers. This is tragic, because by joining forces, the United States and Russia could win half of the War on Terror alone. The powers have enough military, strategic, logistical, diplomatic, and human resources to conduct that confrontation as a duo, breaking down the layers of penetration by the oil powers in the region and sharply turning the international agenda in an antiterror direction. A Washington-Moscow alliance would rapidly attract the other players on the world stage to join in, from Western countries to Arab and Muslim governments to Third World groups—even China would see an interest in cooperation with a worldwide campaign to eradicate terrorism. Summer joint maneuvers of Russian, Chinese, and Central Asian forces against a virtual terrorist enemy already have taken place, in 2007. Add NATO, and the balance of power would shift dramatically against the Jihadi forces.

The obstacles to cooperation involve geopolitics, diplomacy, and economics. Among the issues at stake: the Russian selling of weapons to Iran, Syria, and Sudan, a matter of concern in the War on Terror; the U.S. support for anti-

Russian movements in Ukraine; the deployment of antiballistic missiles (ABMs) in Europe, aimed at potential Iranian and possibly Syrian intercontinental weapons; the U.S. and European support for the separation of Kosovo from Serbia. These and other tensions require mediation and resolution. Despite these challenging problems, a Russian-American entente on the greater threat could minimize most of these crises and reduce them gradually. The two powers could be led to pursue complementary strategic tracks, and even eventually to sign a treaty. The ABM networks can be transformed into an international response to the Jihadi strategic threat with Russian participation, which would eliminate the Russian export of weapons to a number of regimes. A regional focus on the Wahabi and al Qaeda threat in the Balkans should minimize the acuity of Kosovo's crisis; and so on.

INTERNATIONAL ALLIANCE AGAINST JIHADISM

The above steps would turn the international community from witnesses and viewers into active participants. For example, a major player in the resistance to Jihadi terror is India, which has been targeted by and is battling the same type of radical organizations fighting Russia, America, and Europe. India and Pakistan are confronting the same kind of ideologies and movements, yet they have no common front against this one enemy. Because of the proximity of the terrorists to the nuclear weapons of both countries, Islamabad and New Delhi should both be integrated in an international alliance led by the West and Russia. The world campaign must go beyond traditional bilateral security arrangements, drawing in Black African countries challenged by Jihadi penetration and Wahabi and Khumeinist financing. Ethiopia, Eritrea, and Somalia should be helped to build a regional front against al Qaeda and the Mahakam Islamiya. Chad, Kenya, and the Central African Republic must be considered as frontline countries against Sudan's radicals. Oil-producing Nigeria is a potential target for Salafi recruitment, and South Africa also should be incorporated in the world effort against terror.

In Asia, the alliance has to accommodate countries with various engagements against terror movements: Indonesia, Malaysia, and Bangladesh would follow one model of counterterrorism, while Thailand, the Philippines, and Singapore would develop another model. China naturally has a tremendous role to play. Aside from the debates about Taiwan, Tibet, and the shipping of Chinese weapons to rogue regimes in the Greater Middle East, Peking realizes that it is on a collision course with al Qaeda and the Salafists and Wahabis, particularly over the Uygur province of the Xinjiang region (the westernmost region of China). The Jihadists claim this mineral-rich region has a Muslim majority and therefore must separate and establish an emirate. As in similar domino setups, a breakaway province under a Wahabi program could drag China into a ferocious fight with terror. As with Russia and

India, the potential conflict with the Jihadists concerns the integrity of the country, more than its policies; such an overarching threat to national unity establishes a common ground for an international campaign to contain it.

Last but not least, Jihadi activities in Latin America, particularly in Brazil, Argentina, Paraguay (the tri-border area), as well as in the Caribbean, must be contended with. The latest transformation of Venezuelan politics by populist leader Hugo Chavez, whose regime is cozying up to the Iranian regime, Hezbollah, and al Qaeda's sympathizers, is an area of common concern that should bring about a Latin American consultation on the spread of Middle East-originated terrorism across the continent.

Finally, this projected diplomatic revolution would have a direct effect on the behavior of the United Nations. For when the permanent members of the Security Council, on the one hand, and a majority of the members of the General Assembly, on the other, produce a consensus on containing Jihadi terrorism and assisting its victims everywhere, the confrontation will become a downhill battle. And when the United Nations as an organization is enabled to identify the threat, is supported financially to perform its peace and educational missions, and is politically allowed to legislate against the ideologies of mass death, a new era will have begun on earth.

CHAPTER 6

REVOLUTION IN THE ARAB MUSLIM WORLD

SINCE THE BEGINNING OF THE FIRST WAR OF THE TWENTY-FIRST century, questions have arisen about the root causes of terrorism. The initial questioning came as part of a War of Ideas waged by the Jihadis and their apologists that sought to hold the liberal West responsible for the violence because of its foreign policy. Naturally, this position reflects the interests of the region's oil-producing regimes, and is intended to deflect attention from brewing social unrest in the region and turn attention back on Western democracies. This stratagem was successful for a while with the mainstream media, and it continues to prevail in the academic world of Western Europe and North America. However, the campaign to embarrass the West began to fail as criticism from within the Greater Middle East turned against the very regimes and movements leading the Jihadi propaganda efforts. Dissidents, opposition movements, and advocates for democracy burst from under the oppression of governments and militant Islamists and accused the latter of massive abuses of human rights and sometimes genocide. A three-way struggle has developed between authoritarian and Jihadist forces (though they were at each other's throats), who blame the West, dissidents who accuse the region's fascists, and liberal democracies, who are divided on how to respond to the challenges. With the collapse of the Soviet Union and the Warsaw Pact, the acceleration of democratization in Latin America, the decolonization of Africa, and the modernization of China, the main area of contention in terms of dictatorship, fundamentalism, and oppression is now the Greater Middle East. And as the Jihadi terror forces strike both inside and outside the region, the future of this part of the world will determine peace or conflict in the ongoing confrontation with terrorism.

MIDDLE EARTH

The region's challenges make it into a "Middle Earth." From Western Sahara to Jammu and Kashmir, various ethnic and ideological forces are vying for political and economic dominance, military powers are growing, and international coalitions are involved in containment and peace missions. Whoever seizes power in the oil-producing countries will be able to control world markets and use them in the conflict. Whoever can establish Jihadi emirates will be able to supply cells operating inside the West. Whoever can challenge the oppressive regimes and provoke reforms will hold the keys to peace and progress, not only in the region but internationally. So what is this Middle Earth?

First we should take a look at the geopolitical map. Morocco, Jordan, Kuwait, the United Arab Emirates, and Oman are constitutional monarchies, which in the big picture want peace and are moving—very slowly—toward liberalization. Tunisia, Algeria, Egypt, Yemen, and Mauritania are republics transitioning from authoritarianism to pluralism, albeit at a very low speed. Syria and Libya have Arab ultranationalist socialist regimes controlled by dictators. Saudi Arabia and Iran are Islamist theocracies. The first, Wahabi, is an absolute monarchy, and the second, a so-called Khumeinist republic, is totalitarian. Sudan is an Islamist republic, and Somalia has a transitional government vying for power against a Jihadi regime on the run. In Afghanistan, the democratically elected government has a mix of conservative Islamic parties and secular elements, but is still struggling against the Taliban, who briefly erected the most extreme Islamist state in modern times. Iraq, freed from the Baath, has a pluralist constitution but is riven by opposing forces: pro-Iranian Shia elements, Sunni conservatives, autonomous Kurds, and a panoply of Salafists, Khumeinists, and progressives. Qatar is a constitutional monarchy supporting Islamism and hosting al Jazeera. Lebanon, which has had a democratic (but sectarian) past, is a battlefield between Hezbollah and the Cedars Revolution. Pakistan, although not in the Middle East, is nevertheless a major player in Middle Earth. It is a nuclear power and, under an elected presidency influenced by the military, hosts the largest contingent of Jihadists in the world. The Cypriot Greeks and Turks have partitioned their island but not reached an agreement. Israel and the Palestinians haven't resolved their ethno-territorial conflict, despite the signing of a peace process agreement fifteen years ago; Palestinians and Israelis still trade fire. The Palestinians themselves are divided between those who want peace with Israel (in principle) but want more land, and those who do not want any form of peace with Israel (the Palestine Authority) and want all of the land (Hamas), which of course implies the destruction of Israel and the creation of an Islamic state in the land.

Throughout Middle Earth minorities are not faring well. Only recently the Kurds developed autonomy (in Iraq) on just 20 percent of what they believe is their national homeland in the region, since pieces of it reside in four different countries. The other three governments (Turkey, Iran, and Syria) oppose Kurdish local self-determination. Everywhere across the region ancient minorities are suppressed, regardless of the form of government they live under: Assyrians and Chaldeans in Iraq, Berbers in Algeria, Copts in Egypt, and Black Africans in Sudan. But even ethnicities that constitute majorities in one place are suppressed elsewhere when they find themselves to be numerical minorities, as is the situation of the Arabs in Iran, the Turks in Iraq, and Shia in Afghanistan (under the Taliban). Equally persecuted are women, who were without rights under the Taliban, enjoy few rights in Saudi Arabia, Iran, and Sudan, and generally suffer discrimination in most countries of the region. Political parties, disallowed under the Taliban, are still not legal in Saudi Arabia; one party is legal in Libya, one is dominant in Syria, one is always in power in Egypt, and many are armed in Lebanon. There have been more political prisoners, prisoners of conscience, tortured people, and disappeared in the Arab world than there are people in the entire population of Gaza. Yesterday's students endorsed the coming of the mullahs in Iran, and today's students are calling for their departure. In short, the status of human rights in the Greater Middle East, with very few exceptions, is the worst on the planet.

In addition, Middle Earth is plagued with extreme, radical, and violent ideologies. Ancient and medieval ideas have caused endless bloodshed on all continents. Even in the twentieth century, and despite modernity and the rule of law in Europe, Nazism resulted in genocide, Fascism in crimes, and Bolshevism in purges, gulags, and oppression. The Middle East in the past century has had its own oppressions, crimes, and genocides perpetrated by totalitarian ideologies such as Baathism, Salafism, Wahabism, Khumeinism, and ultranationalism and sectarianism. But unlike the rest of the world, Middle Earth continues to live under these murderous doctrines, the infamous *"Thaqafut al Maout"* (Culture of Death). These ideologies, married to power and money, have been devastating to the peoples of the region and to the outside world.[1]

From this overview of the state of affairs of twenty-four countries between the Atlantic Ocean and the China Sea, one can conclude that life is far from easy (and usually far from free) for the millions of people there. War and terror have ravaged most if not all of these countries, where basic freedoms are still an unattainable dream. Why is Middle Earth so miserable still, even after the end of colonialism and the Cold War? Why is it that Eastern Europe, Latin America, and large parts of Asia are moving from authoritarianism to sunny democratization, while the Greater Middle East still stagnates in a twilight of misery and oppression? Why was the democratic revolution possible elsewhere and not here?

THE MISSED PASSAGE

Each part of the world has taken a different path from the Dark Ages to modernity, with reversals of fortune at times. The Greater Middle East, known previously as the Levant and the Near East, is no exception. In antiquity, the area from Numidia (North Africa) to Persia was constantly invaded and reinvaded. Empires sliced up the deserts and steppes for centuries; Assyrians, Persians, Hittites, Carthaginians, Egyptians, and Hebrews clashed. Old colonialisms preceded the European imperialist enterprises by centuries: Persians, Greeks, Romans, Byzantines, Arabs, Crusaders, Mongols, Mameluks, and Ottomans dominated the land, each in turn, rising and falling, for more than twenty-three centuries, with thirteen hundred years under various Islamic caliphates.

By the beginning of World War I, all of North Africa had come under French, Spanish, Italian, and British domination. Persia was on its own as a Shia monarchy. The rest of the Arab world was part of the Ottoman sultanate. The central deserts of Arabia were controlled by the Wahabi tribes, mostly the Saudis. The Ottoman collapse at the end of World War I led to the abolition of the last caliphate by a Turkish nationalist and a secular revolution in the early 1920s. Two unlikely phenomena followed: the League of Nations awarded France and Britain mandates over most of the Levant, and there was a rapid rise of radical ideologies in the region. The European nations ruled Iraq, Syria, Palestine, Egypt, and the Maghreb until the end of World War II, after which London and Paris began to withdraw from the colonies and protectorates. It is important to keep in mind that the period between the crumbling of the Ottomans and the Franco-British pullout determined the ideological, political, and military trends until 9/11. And here is where an opportunity was lost. In historical terms, the passage from empire to modern nation-states and from religious statesmanship to secular statehood was missed, or at least affected by ultranationalism and fundamentalism and by the emergence of a new imperialism made possible by the oil power. Instead of undergoing a natural transformation from post-Ottoman society and postmandate laws into transitional democracies, as happened in Latin America and many Asian societies (and even in Eastern Europe), the region was seized by frenetic ideological trends and their offshoots: chauvinistic ultranationalisms such as Pan-Arabism, various Salafist doctrines (including Takfirism), and imperialist Khumeinism. The radical and totalitarian ideologies that spread after the Ottoman collapse and as countries were achieving independence, reinforced by Communist activism, turned the Middle East into an ocean of seething hatreds, irredentism, and extremism. Instead of addressing the systemic crisis of modernity and the basic needs of their populations, the ideological elites rushed to destroy the liberal elements of the region and erected regimes that waged wars, inculcated new generations with doctrines that led to endless conflicts, and dodged the pressing need for educational and economic reform, progress, and peace.

Arab nationalists, known as *al Qawmeyeen al Arab*, postulated that no issue was more important than the unification of all Arab lands in one *umma*. This slogan was meant to eliminate any opposition to their project of an Islamic *Reich* extending beyond mere national boundaries. The mythical and chauvinistic struggle for *Uruba*[2] deprived all other social, economic, and political claims not only of legitimacy, but even of the right to be heard. If "Arabness" wasn't achieved—according to the Baathists, the followers of Abdel Nasser, and other Pan-Arabists—no other progress could be achieved. Which in practice meant that, like National Socialism, the ultranationalists of the Arab world linked all politics to the achievement of the final goal of obliterating all other venues of social development. This is why, unlike liberal patriotism in the West and Latin America, which persisted as a third option to authoritarian nationalism or Communist totalitarian internationalism, Arab liberalism was smashed by Arab ultranationalism. Immediately after the decolonization of North Africa and during the first decades of the Cold War, Arab ultranationalist regimes suppressed, marginalized, jailed, tortured, and eliminated the bulk of their liberal elites under the slogan of "unification." Liberalism—one component of a successful transition to democracy—was crushed by the Pan-Arabists, Nasserites, Muammar Qadhafi, and other dictators.[3]

The second component of transition from the long Ottoman Sultanate and the brief European mandates was secular reform. Having lived under a religious legal system for centuries, as had the Christians in medieval Europe, the societies of the Middle East had to be introduced to cultural and political pluralism so that they could move toward modernity. The Ottoman state, although a caliphate in essence, had instituted some constitutional and legal reforms starting in the nineteenth century. Though these limited but still needed changes were resisted by the Wahabi camp in Arabia and the Salafi circles across the empire, when the sultanate collapsed after World War I, the way was open to a massive reform. That was an existential moment, a historic moment, when the peoples of the region had an opportunity to begin to catch up with the rest of international society. But unluckily, totalitarian ideologies and movements arose to obstruct the way forward. A stunning convergence of interests among the Arab ultranationalists, the Islamic fundamentalists, and the authoritarian regimes cut short the crucial social reforms so essential to modernization and democratization. The Pan-Arabists' sin was to marginalize all issues of social justice beyond the narrow and almost racist drive toward *Uruba*. Often the Qawmeyeen Arabs crushed democracy as they asserted their nationalist doctrines. In fact, they delegitimized social causes, and by doing so allowed authoritarian regimes and dictatorships to eliminate liberal elites as traitors to the ultimate and only cause, that is, the *Uruba*. The nationalists destroyed the basis of liberalism, and then the regimes destroyed the liberals. This provided an unparalleled opportunity for the Islamists to fill the void left by the ideas (and people) that had been erased. With no competing public causes beyond their goal of reconstituting the Islamic state, and no significant surviving movements to oppose them, the Islamists occupied the cultural public space. Hence the Jihadist movements were able to continue their uphill struggle against ultranationalists and regimes as well. The most formidable weapon of the Islamic fundamentalists was the absence of reform. Many governments opposed them and suppressed them, but no one in the Muslim world could stop their ideology from thrusting into the political culture of the region, which was already antiliberal and authoritarian. The philosophical groundwork—unity instead of plurality, authority instead of democracy—had already been laid for them. And since there was no caliph to represent the official state position on Islamic issues, and since the secularists and modernists had been crushed by the Arab nationalists, the path of ascent was open to the Salafists, Wahabis, Muslim Brotherhood, and Khumeinists. It took them a long time to rise, but one major consequence of their efforts in the region was the failure to transform civil society—to make the passage from the old order to modernity and democracy. The new (and pre-9/11) order of the region was based on two basic pillars: ultranationalism (mainly Arabist) and Islamic fundamentalism. So long as one or both of these held power, all sorts of regimes and elites could claim legitimacy, at the expense of pluralism, human rights, and freedom. From the 1920s till 2001, the region was frozen ideologically and rendered miserable politically.

THE ARAB ISLAMIC ORDER

What regional system replaced the Ottoman Empire and the European presence in the Greater Middle East? And how successful was the integration of these nation-states within the international community, and particularly into the set of international laws covering the basic rights of communities and individuals? The debates and discussions of these two matters are too voluminous to compass in a paragraph. But a general survey of the region's geopolitics, the contemporary political system of the Greater Middle East, and its responses to the principles agreed upon by international society can be summarized as follows.

After the Ottoman collapse its territories fell under Anglo-French control, with the exception of Saudi Arabia, Turkey, and Iran. Inside the Arabian kingdom, the al Saud absolute monarchy developed Wahabism as a state ideology and later expanded it through the region. Turkey's Kemalist doctrine repositioned the new Turkish republic outside the realm of Islamic statehood and instituted a very secular system of government. Iran was ruled by Shia dynasties, politically allied with the West but under the scrutiny of its suspicious clergy. All the remaining lands, mostly created from former Ottoman provinces, were managed, under League of Nations mandates, by the French (Syria, Lebanon) or the British (Palestine, Jordan, Iraq). North Africa remained under British (Egypt), Italian (Libya), and French (Tunisia, Algeria, and Morocco) rule. The Europeans attempted to impart their constitutional, social, and economic models until the end of World War II. While Turkey, and to some extent Iran, began experiencing the transition to secularism and modernity—with varying degrees of success and failure—the bulk of the Arab world fell to the mounting influence of the radicals, both Arab nationalists and Islamists. The radical Arabists participated in the national struggle of many Arab countries against foreign rule, only to end up establishing authoritarian regimes themselves. Examples include Nasser in Egypt, the National Liberation Front in Algeria, Bourguiba in Tunisia, the Baath in Syria (first Nureddine Attasi, Syrian president 1966–1970, followed by Assad) and in Iraq (al Bakr, then Saddam), Nimeiri in Sudan, and Qadhafi in Libya. Israel was essentially a Western democracy and Lebanon a multiethnic democracy (till 1975), but there were no real liberal democracies in Arab lands after World War II. There were moderate monarchies moving slowly toward constitutionalism and pluralism (Jordan, Morocco, Kuwait, and the Gulf principalities), and then there were the rest, entangled in authoritarianism to one degree or another.

On top of the failure to transition to democracy, most of the region's countries slowly sank under totalitarianism. Till the mid-fifties, minimal liberal and reformist currents survived from Cairo to Damascus, from Khartoum to Baghdad. Urban middle-class intellectuals still wanted to emulate the international model that combined a market economy with social justice, while adding a Middle Eastern and Arab dimension; such a mixture was the form assumed by Asian and Latin American democracies. But the passage to liberalism, either conservative or progressive, was hampered in the Middle East by a lethal convergence of Islamist regimes and organizations allied to the Arab nationalist elites. With very few exceptions—such as Beirut's open cultural space, which flowered from 1943 till 1975—the debate in the Arab world was captured by the radical establishment. Even in countries where business with the West was flourishing, as in the Gulf, the rhetoric of Arabism and Islamism crushed the themes of pluralism and self-criticism. In addition to the oil-supported ideologies of Baathism and Arabism (Iraq and Libya), the petrodollars backing Wahabism (Saudi Arabia), Salafism (Qatar), and Khumeinism (Iran) set the limits to intellectual engagement. Totalitarian and authoritarian regimes and elites shut all doors to internationalization, human rights, and democratization; they had the upper hand in funding and control of the two major organizations representing the Arab and Muslim countries: the Arab League (twenty-one members) and the Organization of Islamic States (about fifty-two members).

Oddly, in contrast to other supranational organizations (the United Nations, European Union, etc.) that were supposed to help civil societies, nongovernmental organizations, and individuals voice their protests and demand solutions to the injustices of nation-states, the two Arab Islamic international organizations cater

more to the ideologies and interests of its member regimes than to minority struggles and the demands of the disenfranchised in the region. The Arab League's officials stand firmly behind the authoritarian regimes, while hundreds of thousands of
political prisoners die in Arab jails, from Iraq to Libya. Instead of intervening on
behalf of oppressed Muslims, the Organization of the Islamic Conference stood by
both Iraq (against Shiites and Kurds) and Sudan (against black Muslims in Darfur).
In the Greater Middle East, from ideologies to radical movements, from regimes
to regional organizations, the power structures unite to maintain an Arab Islamic
order that keeps the majority of Arabs and Muslims suppressed and non-Arab and
Muslim minorities oppressed.[4]

THE OPPRESSED MAJORITY

Not so different from pre-Enlightenment Europe and colonial Latin America, and
relatively similar to Communist Europe, the Greater Middle East, particularly its
Arab countries, witnessed a generalized oppression of its own peoples for long peri-
ods of time. Despite the assertiveness of the liberal West on the grounds of human
rights and the globalization of justice (through such agencies as the International
Court of Justice, Interpol, and the UN Commission on Human Rights), Middle
Earth clung strongly to oppressive systems. This one region continued to escape
the norms of even minimal democracy and freedom. Although human rights are
considered universal and not relative, in this region—which has different traditions,
forms of government, and socioeconomic contexts—ideologues, particularly from
the Islamist background, and their supporters in the West have been arguing for
many years that what is a right to one is not so to another, at least in the Arab Muslim world. In reality, this cultural-relativist argument is a tool used to justify repression and preserve the existing situation. The issue of women in the Arab and
Muslim world has been presented often by the Jihadists and their apologists overseas as a matter of relativism: Arab and Muslim women, the Salafists and Khumeinists boast, have the *umma* as their priority, not a feminist agenda as in the West. In
reality, thorough analysis reveals the Jihadis' gender discrimination in these assertions, for the liberation of women in the Arab and Muslim world would crumble the
fundamentalist or authoritarian power from the Mediterranean to Central Asia. In
different shapes and forms, the rulers of the region (with the exception of those in
the democracies in Turkey, Lebanon, and Israel) keep the natural gender majority
that exists in all nation-states in a condition of inferiority. Obviously, the oppression
of women is not uniform, but it reaches a nadir in many Muslim countries. Jordan,
Kuwait, Morocco, and Algeria, for example, have made significant progress in advancing the rights of women. But ideological forces within civil society—mostly the
Salafists—are obstructing the pace of change. Arab socialist regimes, as in Iraq

(under Saddam), Egypt (under Nasser), Syria, Libya, and southern Yemen (before unification) have elevated women to quasi equality in the factories and in some social settings but have left them at the mercy of the Islamic fundamentalists at home and in matters of personal status, particularly in terms of equality before the law. In these nationalist countries the status of women swings between a general political suppression, under which they suffer along with their male companions, and social suppression, based solely on gender, which arises from societies' ideological sectors when an authoritarian regime weakens. In Egypt, the opening of the government toward the West alleviated the women's oppression suffered under a national security apparatus but opened the door to the Muslim Brotherhood and the Gamaat's Islamiya persecution of secular women. As national socialist regimes tilt toward the West on economic grounds, ironically, pressures are applied on Arab and Muslim women to wear the *hijaab* and show a militant identity. The dramatic choice becomes: either political fascism and oppression for all people, but with allowances for women to work, or market economy for all, with fundamentalist oppression of women in the religious and social spheres. In addition to Egypt, the hard choice between social or religious status has been present in Algeria, Iraq (after liberation), Syria, and Libya, and for Shia women in Hezbollah-controlled Lebanon. In the Gulf, Qatar claims that it is making steps forward but its Jihadi TV, al Jazeera, promotes the *hijaab* for Muslim women worldwide. In the UAE, Bahrain, and Oman, the status of women depends on the wealth and luxurious lifestyle of its financial elites. While all of these areas are experiencing a skyrocketing increase in the number of foreign women visitors, as tourists and as workers, the number of *muhajjabaat* (covered women) is also increasing almost proportionally. These data and other evidence show that the imposition of so-called religious garb on women, intended supposedly for their spiritual uplift, is in reality nothing of the sort. Such measures are legislated by fundamentalist and radical clerics to advance an ideological system of governance linked to their grand design of reestablishing the caliphate. But this troubling status for females in many so-called moderate countries remains still less dramatic than the notorious gender apartheid of regimes in the region, for example, among the Taliban and in Saudi Arabia, Iran, and Sudan. Under the draconian rule of the Taliban in Afghanistan, women were removed from the public space and kept in a social "concentration camp." The experience was so lethal psychologically that seven years after the regime succumbed, many women there still fear the Taliban's oppression and wear the blue burka of apartheid. In Saudi Arabia, women can't drive, walk alone, or work alongside men. In Iran, women may be seen in public offices but are under the tyranny of their husbands and fathers at home. In Sudan, all of the above restrictions apply, but to an even worse degree for black women. Not only do they live under the Jihadi apartheid, but many have been reduced to slavery. In fact, approximately 55 percent of the region's population (again, with exceptions) is oppressed: Women are the majority in most of these countries and in most they suffer varying degrees of disenfranchisement.[5]

But the oppressed majority includes not only women; it encompasses also men who happen to be in disagreement with those in power. According to international human rights groups and UN and NGO reports, political dissenters are widely (and often horribly) oppressed, tortured, and persecuted. In fact, there are no countries in the region (with the exception of Turkey and Israel) where physical harm isn't part of the regime's treatment of political opponents. And even Turkey and Israel are condemned by their critics for harsh treatment of prisoners accused of taking part in violent insurrections. The Greater Middle East typically deals with political opposition harshly—legally, physically, and politically. Some regimes and militant ideological groups have resorted to genocide. Saddam massacred not only Shiites and Kurds, but also his opponents inside the Baath Party. Hafez Assad sent his tanks to roll over the Sunnis in Hama. Iran's Khumeinist regime executed liberals, Communists, and rival Islamic party members by the thousands. The Taliban killed their opponents (and even past comrades in the mujahideen) wholesale. Sudan's regime committed crimes against humanity in the south and in Darfur. Syrian-controlled Lebanon tortured its opposition and transferred detainees to Damascus, in a manner reminiscent of Vichy France's collaboration with Nazi Germany. Libya's security services were notorious in the disappearance of its citizens and of Arab visitors. The list is endless. Putting aside the ruling elites (who comprise about 4 percent of the region's entire population) and their entourages, the overwhelming majority of even the largest nationalities, Arabs and Persians, are oppressed.

Adding to the complexity is that the dominant political culture in authoritarian regimes is merciless even toward its own founders. Fascist elites suppress one another as they seize power. For example, the Arab nationalists who supported Nasser oppressed the Muslim Brotherhood in Egypt; the Wahabis suppressed the Arab nationalists in Saudi Arabia; in southern Yemen, the Marxists crushed the Islamists; Saddam persecuted the Baathist left wing; and Assad sent his tanks to crush the Muslim Brotherhood (but later armed the Islamists in Lebanon). Ayatollah Khumeini's followers marched against the shah along with the Communists, only to massacre them after the fall of the monarch. Not only do the oppressors maintain themselves in power with violence against the people, but even against each other in their race toward totalitarian supremacy.[6]

THE SAGA OF NATIONAL MINORITIES

The Greater Middle East has not had a good record on the treatment of national, religious, and ethnic minorities throughout history and particularly in the post–World War I era. Along with Nazism in the West and Stalinism in the East, ultra-Arabism and Jihadism have been responsible for widespread persecution and genocide. But while Nazism and Soviet Communism have disappeared, Jihadi oppression of minorities is still alive. The brutal regimes and elites continue to ignore the plight of oppressed groups and to deny genocides already perpetrated. Some of these minorities are victims of geography and historical bad luck; their ethnic identity is the same as the majority in another country, but they are a minority in their own. Foremost among the Muslim minorities (and better known to the public in the West) are the Kurds, the Berbers, and the Africans of Darfur. The Kurds, a non-Arab people whose language belongs to the Iranian group, have suffered from persecution under the Baath of Iraq and Syria, especially since the departure of British and French forces in the late 1940s. Under Saddam, they were subjected to cultural ethnocide inasmuch as they were brutally crushed by the state military machine. In 1987, in the ultimate modern tragedy, Saddam used chemical weapons and gas against them during the bombings of Halabja in northern Iraq. Kurds are also claiming rights in Iran and Turkey.

The Berbers, the pre-Arab native peoples of North Africa, were particularly marginalized in Algeria after the withdrawal of the French in the early 1960s. Denied cultural autonomy, they rose against oppression multiple times only to be suppressed by the Arab nationalist regime in Algiers. In the 1990s, Berbers were particularly targeted by the Salafists, who accused them of secularism and liberalism, and assassinated intellectuals, pop singers, and journalists from the Kabyles.[7]

Ironically, the ethnic Arabs in Iran—a majority in the Khusistan province—have been suppressed by the Persian-dominated regime in Tehran. In this case, the Islamists accentuated the oppression. Indeed, since the Khumeinist revolution in 1979, Khusistani Arabs have been under increasing pressure by the Iranian regime. Other minorities in Iran (Kurds, Baluchis and Azeris) are also marginalized.

The most striking recent abuse has been taking place in Darfur at the hands of the Islamist regime of Khartoum. The Arab Jihadist power of the north has launched a terrorist militia, the Janjaweed ("mounted Jinn"), to devastate and ethnically cleanse western Sudan of the black tribes living there. Only since 2004 has the international community began to characterize the massacres as genocide. The people of Darfur are Muslim, but they are Black Africans. The regime in Khartoum is Muslim, too, but it is dominated by Arab Islamists. In Sudan, one can see extremism in the guise of racism merging with radicalism in ideology—another marriage of Arab ultranationalism and Islamic fundamentalism. The result, as in the previous examples, is an extreme, inhuman treatment of a minority.

However, the treatment of non-Muslim minorities in the region by Arabists and Jihadists has reached much higher levels than the oppression of Muslims both in the past and in modern times. Lacking the protection of "co-religionism,"

Christians, Jews, Zoroastrians, Mandeans, Hindus, and followers of local African religions have been subjected to different levels of statutory discrimination (mainly under regimes interpreting Sharia laws narrowly) and to physical, political, and cultural oppression. The status of non-Muslims under Islamic rule has been debated for decades, particularly to assess it in light of the principles of international law, the charter of the United Nations, the Universal Declaration of Human Rights, and other regulations voted since 1945. Islamist and radical regimes in the Greater Middle East, as well as their apologists in the West, have attempted to convince the international community that, in theory, Sharia doesn't discriminate against Jews and Christians. Furthermore, the advocates of the Islamization of laws assert that, throughout history, non-Muslims have lived peacefully and happily under the Islamic legal system. The debates continue to rage, but two facts show that discrimination exists.

The first has to do with the texts of Sharia: the Koran, hadith, and jurisprudence. Discriminatory status for Christians and Jews under the Islamic state were known as the "*dhimmi* conditions," and they did indeed exist.[8] Beyond the historiography and exegetical reinterpretations of the political debating between apologists and critics, it is still a fact that the *dhimmi* status hasn't been condemned, reformed, or replaced by mainstream international organizations, such as the Organization of the Islamic Conference (OIC, representing all Muslim states in the world), let alone by religious authorities, such as al Azhar University and religious research center in Egypt, considered the central theological authority in Sunni Islam. Till that happens, legal discrimination will continue to exist. Second, beyond historical analysis, is what is happening right now, namely the real oppression of non-Muslim minorities (and all other minorities as well), including the invocation of the *dhimmi* status and the Jihadists' use of the concept of "infidels" (*kuffar*) in their justification of violence and massacres. Seven years after 9/11 and the declarations by Osama bin Laden against the "infidels" worldwide, the Copts of Egypt are accusing the Jihadists of kidnappings, church burnings, and assassinations. The Assyro-Chaldeans in Iraq—notwithstanding the presence of U.S. and Coalition forces—are subjected to the same type of persecution.[9] In Lebanon, despite the end of a fifteen-year war (1975–1990) during which more than 100,000 Christians perished in massacres and shellings, Jihadist violence against Christian villages, politicians, and activists is still going on, even after the withdrawal of Syrian troops in 2005. Christians, Jews, Bahais, and other minorities are harassed and targeted in Iran, Algeria, Pakistan, and Syria. Again, the greatest number of Christian victims of persecution at the hands of Jihadist powers is found in Southern Sudan. From the 1990s until now, more than a million and a half black Christians have been killed or expelled from southern Sudan or, in many cases, enslaved by the regime and its militias. Around the region, some 18 million non-Muslims are under various kinds of political and ethnic pressure, ranging from religious persecution to mass oppression at the hands of Jihadist and authoritarian regimes. Some governments do their best to extend protection to these communities, as in Jordan, Kuwait, Morocco, and Turkey. Nevertheless, extending international help to the suffering minorities and liberating them still involves a general confrontation with the forces of terror. The more that civil societies in the region are liberated, the more isolated the forces of radicalism will become.

"ELITE" CAUSES VERSUS "PEOPLE'S" CAUSES

In view of the massive abuses that have been taking place in the Greater Middle East for decades, one has to ask, Why was it that these issues weren't raised on the international stage long ago? Why was the Western public able to hear about the oppression of opposition movements by Latin American dictatorships, both military and Marxist, and not the suppression of liberties by Arab and Islamic regimes? Why was international public opinion well informed about the apartheid regime in South Africa but uninformed about the genocide in Darfur and Southern Sudan? Why did the world's journalists and television reporters focus intently and almost exclusively on the Israeli occupation of the West Bank and Gaza, but never acknowledge the Syrian occupation of an entire country, Lebanon (until 2005)? Why were the dissidents under Soviet totalitarianism able to explain their miseries to the Free World while dissidents in the Greater Middle East were shunted away from the media and diplomatic institutions for decades? Even more intriguing is the fact that Jihadists in the West have been raising the "issues" of Arab and Muslim émigrés as a "minority cause" within liberal democracies, while at the same time crushing minorities at home—Berbers, Kurds, Africans, Copts, and so on. It is perplexing that the Jihadists were swift to claim that Islamist women in the West are having a hard time wearing the *hijaab*, but almost no one in the West has seriously raised the issue of Saudi women being forbidden to drive cars. The answer to this inequality in "causes," or rather the marginalization of democratic and liberalization claims in the region, is found in the politics of obstruction practiced by the dominant political and ideological elites in the Greater Middle East. In short, in order to silence any mention of the mass injustices in the Arab and Muslim world, the regional establishment—ultranationalist and Jihadist alike—has overplayed their own list of causes, drowning out the claims of the popular majority and of national and ethnic minorities.

As mentioned above, the first claim promoted by the elites as of the 1950s was "Pan-Arabism." It had different variants: *Wihda* (Unity); *Uruba* (Arabism), *al Nidal* (the Struggle), and so on. These words were overused by leaders, dictators, commentators, and intellectuals—to the point that no other issue could be recognized.

The struggle to unify all Arabs under one *umma* (nation) crushed the struggles by Kurds, Berbers, Africans, Christians, and other minority groups to claim their own identities, let alone to call for national emancipation. Any attempt by these nationalities to raise their legitimate claims was met harshly by Pan-Arabists (and by Jihadists), who accused them of being *"in'ezalee"* (isolationists). The Arab ultranationalists demanded self-determination through the unification of all Arab countries into one mega-state, but they would smash nationalities living there if they dared to appeal to the same principles for themselves. The elites of the Arab world, indoctrinated by Pan-Arabism, were the first wave of authoritarians to eliminate all causes other than the Arabist cause. The ultranationalists also crushed the Arab liberals who wished to struggle for social and cultural causes other than the forced assimilation into one Pan-Arab state. Those ethnic Arabs who chose liberalism and democracy were dealt with in a way reminiscent of National Socialism; repeating word for word the Nazi slogan "Ein volk, ein Reich" in Arabic *"Shaab wahid umma wahida"* (One People, One Nation), the Arabists repressed every other voice and every other cause for decades.[10]

The second, narrower cause that was made an offshoot of the mother cause of Arabism was Palestine. Although the Palestinian Arabs have—like all other ethnic groups in the world—a legitimate right to develop a claim and struggle toward it, as was the case for the Jews, the Armenians, or even the Sudeten Germans, Cypriot Turks and other ethnic groups, it was the Arabist ideologues, Baathists or Nasserites, who loaded the concept with a much wider sense, linking Arab nationalism to the Palestinian cause and vice versa. In 1947, when British-mandated Palestine was partitioned by the United Nations, there were two ways for the Palestinian Arabs to address their dissatisfaction with the results: as an ethnic conflict with the state of Israel, or as part of the regional cause of Arabism. Unfortunately for the Palestinians at the time, it was the Arab League, mobilized by the dominant ideology of Pan-Arabism, that rejected the partition plan and forbade the Palestinians to erect their own independent nation-state with borders they did not accept as final, even though they could have asked for modification of borders later. Because the cause of Pan-Arabism was "higher" than the claim of local Arab populations in conflict with another national community, the Palestinian cause was absorbed—or maybe hijacked—by the mother cause, and thus left unresolved for decades.[11] After 1973, and thanks to the increase of oil power and its influence within the West, the cause of Palestine (as seen by the Arabists) became a central concern of the Western elites at the expense of all other crises and conflicts in the region. It became a cause célèbre for the Arabists, Jihadists, and their apologists, instead of being presented as a legitimate ethnic crisis that needed to be solved. Most of the region's authoritarian regimes had an interest in focusing world attention only on Palestine, so that all other significant issues related to human rights and democratization would be unaddressed. Once Palestine was branded as the sole meaningful issue in the Middle East, it rendered the other problems unsolvable.

The first to suffer were obviously the Palestinians themselves, who had to wait for the Arab nationalists and the Jihadists to decide when and how to end that war. It wasn't solved when Israelis and Palestinians found some common ground in 1993, because the real solution for Baathists and Islamists was to create the Pan-Arab state or the resurrected caliphate. The Palestinian cause was also seized upon by the apologists in the West and made into an almost political cult. No other cause was worthy of engagement—neither the genocide in Sudan nor the occupation of Lebanon, not the oppression of Kurds and Berbers nor the persecution of Copts and Assyrians. Palestine and nothing else, argued the mainstream Middle East studies and intellectual elites in North America and Western Europe. The cult of Palestinian struggle obliterated all the other issues, and they would come back to haunt the region and the international community years later as terrorism, dictatorships, social oppression, gender discrimination, underdevelopment, corruption, religious persecution, slavery, occupation, and ethnic cleansing.

And then, in the post-Soviet era, a new cause was advanced by a segment of the dominant elites: Jihad.

This ideological battle cry—often portrayed as a religious duty by some, and as a spiritual experience by others—had been transformed by mainstream academics in the 1990s into a legitimate tool of liberation. Although in reality a doctrine of conflict and war rejuvenated by the Salafists and the Khumeinists in the twentieth century, Jihad was projected not only by its own militants, but also by intellectuals in the West, as a valid cause superseding other concerns in the region. Meanwhile, Jihadism was causing human rights abuses, violations of security, and genocide. Yet in the 1990s, prominent scholars, mostly members of the Middle East Studies Association, advised Western governments to favor the Jihadi cause even as many segments of the populations were being victimized by its terror forces, as in Algeria, Sudan, Iran, Lebanon, and Indonesia. Here again, the elites promoted some causes to minimize others, particularly those that threatened to advance democracy, the liberation of women, the advancement of minorities, and a revolution in politics leading to change. Often Arab and Islamic regimes shut down democratic processes by claiming they were concentrating on Palestine, Pan-Arabism, or Jihad when they were actually using the country's resources to strengthen their own power. Hafez Assad invaded neighboring Lebanon to "rescue" the Palestinian cause. The PLO fought the Jordanians to "liberate Palestine." The Arab and Islamic regimes' picturesque use of the word "cause" at some point turned into tragedy. In 1981, I used to listen to Iraq's state radio air bulletins on the "brave Iraqi forces thrusting eastward to pave the way for the liberation of Palestine." And as I looked at the map, I saw that Saddam's tanks were deep inside Persia going farther away from the Jordan River, which lay to the west.

And to top off the mythical list, the intellectual elite of the region coined the famous expression "the Arab street." With *al shareh' al arabi*, propagandists, commentators and scholars can say anything they wish and impute it to the masses. For over a decade, experts, analysts, and the media have been fond of stating that the Arab street wants this or that, rejects this or that. Endless literature claiming to express what the masses of the Arab world want has stressed the subjects the elites wanted to raise and focus on. Any attempt to initiate an international investigation of a human rights abuse or terror activity in the region was met by a barrage of responses armed with the "Arab street" weapon. Such a game was possible, of course, precisely because the real street in the region's urban centers was suppressed. It would have been very difficult to assess what the masses really wanted when there was no political freedom, no free media, and no possibility for polling—but it was very easy to *claim* to know, for exactly the same reasons. The regimes spoke of their "streets" even as they oppressed their societies.[12]

Even more sophisticated users of the street slogan were the Jihadists and their supportive media, such as al Jazeera and Islamist Web sites. Modernized Jihadists were able to display pictures of "the people" angrily screaming and chanting. These militants were presented to the world as the voice of the Arab street, the real street, as opposed to the state-run streets. And for years the Western intelligentsia fell into this trap. At every opportunity al Jazeera, al Manar, or other radical media would rush to explain what those depicted in these pictures wanted to say, and the international media from BBC, CNN, France 2, CBC, *The New York Times*, *The Guardian*, *Newsweek*, and the rest ate it up. Some editorialists began creating substreets, calling them either "basements" or "palaces." However, gradually, after 2001, and after the removal of the Taliban and Saddam, and just before the Syrians left Beirut, the true voice of the streets in the region began to be heard. The masses that voted in Afghanistan and Iraq and demonstrated in Lebanon were the real thing. Then the pictures of hundreds of thousands and millions of people chanting against the traditional slogans of the regimes and the Jihadists finally appeared. The masses were indeed there, on these streets, but not as portrayed for decades by the Baathists, the Wahabis, al Jazeera, and the apologist intelligentsia in the West. Muslim women in Kabul were opposing the Taliban ideology, not supporting it, contrary to what the veiled Jihadists in the West had proclaimed. Young and old Iraqis, it turned out, wanted to vote, disliked Saddam, and loved debating politics—unlike the usual assessments of the classical Middle East studies overseas. Boys and girls in Beirut rejected Assad's armies, and an overwhelming majority among them didn't want to be recruited to the army of suicide bombers of Hassan Nasrallah in Lebanon. Just the opposite; a majority of Lebanese loves life not death.[13] On the Iranian street, the young particularly have been rising against the mullahs for years, only to be repressed by the Revolutionary Guard. Iran's majority, of women, students, and workers, and its minorities, both ethnic and religious, reject the *Vilayet e faqih* regime and wish to see it changed, when that is possible.[14]

Now, the fallacy of the elite's fictitious causes and imaginary Arab streets has been uncovered, at least by the dissidents in the region. But awkwardly, not to mention ironically, it still survives in the liberal West. The situation is almost identical to the crumbling of Bolshevik ideals in Eastern Europe and the former Soviet Union—a vanished ideology that survives only on the Berkeley and Sorbonne campuses. The next question then is, If the people wanted it, why wasn't the democratic revolution able to succeed in this region as it did on other continents?

FAILED REVOLTS

The reasons for this failure need a volume of research, and the answers would respond to the challenge of the worldwide confrontation triggered by the war with Jihadism. Indeed, how did it happen that Latin America, Eastern Europe, Russia, India, and South Africa were able to undergo revolutions that brought democracies of various sorts, whereas the Greater Middle East has failed to catch up with the rest of the world? There are certainly major reasons—historical, ideological, socioeconomic, ethnoreligious—that obstructed the transition from empire to modern nation-states, or at least from decolonization, fascism, and totalitarianism to liberation. Many have invoked Western colonialism as a chief reason. But comparative research shows that India, the single largest British colony, evolved straight to democracy, while Iraq, Egypt, and Sudan, for example, failed to match India's achievements. Israel and the Palestinian Arabs were part of the same British mandate, yet their societies evolved differently. Lebanon and Syria were under the same French mandate, yet they, too, evolved differently. One could even argue that the post-caliphate institutions in the Arab world that reflected constitutionalism and the separation of powers were inherited from the Europeans. Hence colonialism isn't the root cause.

Another theory argues that poverty and scanty resources hampered the ability of countries to move toward modernity and prosperity. Yet again, India (not especially wealthy in resources) moved toward democracy, while Saudi Arabia, extremely rich in petroleum reserves, couldn't produce a multiparty system. Cyprus, deprived of any natural resource and even lacking water, built a robust democratic system, while Libya, despite its titanic oil wealth, ended up with a dictatorship. Lebanon's cultural background created a multireligious democracy (till 1975) while Iraq's multiethnic society and oil wealth were subsumed under the brutality of Baathism. The list is very long but the results are simple: It is the ideologies behind the regimes that crushed the burgeoning of democracy, even at a primitive level. A few countries (such as Turkey, Jordan, and Lebanon) installed the basics of multiparty systems, but the dominant ideology in the region—ultranationalism and Jihadism—froze the natural evolution of its peoples toward transitional democracies.

But even though the regional ideology kept a lid on social evolution, there were many attempted uprisings. Egypt, Syria, Iraq, Iran, Pakistan, and other countries witnessed spasms of liberalism from decade to decade. Repression and counterrevolutions quickly crushed these risings of liberationist movements and intellectuals. Turkey moved brutally from Islamic empire (Ottoman Sultanate) in the 1920s through a secular but at the same time raw nationalist revolution. The reforms of Kemal Atatürk drastically shifted Turkish society from Islamic identity to a Turkish anticlerical republic. A part of the nation truly moved to secularism, but the pendulum had to swing back to Islamism with the rise of the Party of Justice, which seized power via elections in 2007. The French set Lebanon on the path to a moderate multiethnic republic in 1943. It survived a few decades before radicalism (Baathism, Pan-Arabism, and Khumeinism later) destroyed its foundations as of 1975. Other than Israel, a Western country in essence, the rest of the region has been fenced in by radicalism. At the center of the forces that suppressed democratic change are the totalitarian ideologies, the inescapable black hole of the region. But the continual failure of revolts, whatever the reasons, shouldn't condemn the region to be forever denied the benefits of liberalization and democracy.

THE "RIGHT" TO DEMOCRACY

One of the most significant parts of the War of Ideas waged against Western understanding of Middle Eastern political culture has been the change in arguments over democratization in the Arab and Muslim world. Before 9/11, the academic elites in the West argued that the reason democracy wasn't rising in the region was Western support for authoritarian regimes. Interestingly, none of the authoritarian oil producers funding Middle East studies programs were targeted, but others were: Egypt, Jordan, Lebanon, Morocco, Iran (before 1979), and so on. Hence the dominant line in this argument was that the United States wasn't supporting political change. However, what the academics meant by "change" was that the West should back the Jihadist forces and enable them to come to power; change, according to this understanding, was not characterized by support for liberal elements in order to unleash a real democratic revolution. Strangely, since 9/11 and particularly after the United States declared its intention to "spread democracy" and support dissidents, the regimes and the intellectual elites in America—and in Europe as well—lashed out against the new U.S. commitment. Their argument was puzzling: Washington was now openly intervening in the internal affairs of the Arab world and Iran. From being accused of not helping enough, America was accused of intervening too much. Evidently, the issue had to do with who the United States and the West were about to help and what kind of change was being sought.

Authoritarian regimes and apologists in the West exposed themselves on the issue of democratization when they attacked the United States, particularly the Bush administration (but also Congress) for extending support to opposition movements, ethnic minorities, women, and youth in their struggle for freedom and self-determination. The Jihadi Oil Empire and its long academic and media arm within the West realized that a bridge between the Free World and the democratic movements in the Greater Middle East could upset the status quo and, eventually, the dominant establishment. And as the voices of Middle Eastern dissidents got louder in the West, especially with the contribution of former slaves, militants, oppressed women, fleeing students, exiles, and bloggers, the Jihadists and the Jihadophiles made desperate attempts to stop the (weak) Western support for democratization in the region. This they did through a further ruse launched against public opinion. In waves of articles, books, and interviews, the army of apologists in Middle East studies branded Western-backed "democratization" unacceptable, because—they argued—the peoples of the Greater Middle East and the Arab and Muslim world rejected it! This simplistic argument ran against all natural trends in political sociology: The lobbies claimed that Arabs and Muslims do not *want* democracy and that their culture is incompatible with it. Al Jazeera, the Salafists, and the Khumeinists hurried after 2001 to convince their own constituencies that democracy is a Western value and the peoples of the region have different values. This essentially made the spreading of democracy a form of cultural imperialism—despite what the United Nations Charter and other instruments of international law say about self-determination and the rights of individuals and minority groups.

But soon dissident voices from the Middle East responded to this illogical ploy by accusing the regimes and the Jihadists of falsely claiming that the peoples of the Arab and Muslim world rejected freedom and democratic ideals. These responses to the authoritarian-Jihadi axis were rapidly vindicated: Elections in Afghanistan broke the Taliban taboo on women; elections in Iraq produced a multiparty system and millions voted; a million marchers in Lebanon shook off the Syrian occupation of the country and were followed by legislative elections bringing a new democratic majority. The flow of literature from the region reasserted in the face of world opinion the natural truth that, when conditions give them the opportunity, the masses will choose freedom and democracy. Hence a breakthrough—but not a revolutionary shift—has taken place. Welling up from below, a current is asserting that all nations, cultures, and individuals have a natural right and desire for freedom and democracy. Even against the mega powers of oil, ultranationalism, racism, and Jihadism, the right to choose and determine one's future will burst forth when opportunities arise.

REGIME CHANGE AND CHANGING CULTURES

As soon as the Taliban regime collapsed in Afghanistan, forces from the bottom strata of society, helped by the Coalition forces, began their difficult climb up the political ladders of the country. After years of Neo-Wahabi totalitarianism, gender and religious persecution, and systematic violence against dissidents and free expression, democracy activists in Afghanistan started to move forward. Obviously, the removal of the Taliban, a radical and very violent regime, opened the way for freedom to express itself. The link between regime change and the changing of political culture is clear. A similar situation occurred in Iraq as a result of the removal of Saddam by U. S. and Coalition forces. As will be shown in a later chapter, regardless of the debate leading to the intervention, the regime change allowed a gradual but real transformation in the political culture imposed by the Pan-Arabists and the Baathists for decades. After the ruling structures collapsed, hundreds of political parties, movements, newsletters, local media, and NGOs emerged. Terrorists rushed to lash out and maim these new movements, but proved incapable of stopping the cultural change. The transition will be long, probably proportional to the years of oppression, but a direction has been set, and the fight is now on between those trying to restore the past and those moving relentlessly toward the future. In a sense, what is happening in Afghanistan is comparable to revolutions happening in other parts of the world. Once an ancient regime is removed, the forces of totalitarianism will attempt to stop the change. They may trigger chaos, hesitations, and sometimes setbacks, but the impulse to change moves always forward. In Lebanon, the Cedars Revolution exploded as a result of an oppressive regime and Syrian occupation, but the popular movement there was possible because of events in Afghanistan and Iraq. The cascade of regimes collapsing or being removed can reach as far as the oppression itself, as was the case in Eastern Europe at the end of the Soviet era. The effects of changing one authoritarian regime have reached communities having the fewest resources and least outreach of any on earth: Consider Darfur. It is not only the peoples of that region who are seeking freedom; others, too, will rise as soon as they can see hope, even though the regimes oppressing them resist strongly.

REBELLION AGAINST THE IDEOLOGICAL ORDER:
THE SPREAD OF REJECTION

Despite Arabists', Jihadists', and their Western allies' restless efforts to block democratization, civil societies in the Greater Middle East have sent more and more signals about political change, at least since 2001. The widest forum of expression was and remains the Internet. The contest between Jihadists and democracy groups online began in the mid-1990s, with an advance by the Islamists, who had the advantage of being credited as the real opposition by Western academia. The region's underdogs, particularly Southern Sudanese, Darfurians, Lebanese, Syrian reformers, the Iraqi opposition (under Saddam), minorities such as Copts, Assyrians and Kurds, and the Iranian resistance to the mullahs, in addition to progressive circles, were marginalized in the real world of the media. But with the widening War on Terror and the Jihadi campaigns against democracy, the third current—dissidents and reformers—came to the fore in cyber warfare. Using the Internet as efficiently as the Islamists, the real underdogs of the Arab and Muslim world gradually put themselves on the map of world politics. While al Jazeera spread the Jihadi message, the dissidents managed to find a niche in the reformer site Elaph, other smaller projects such as CLIME, al Aafaq,[15] and a host of cyber media.

The genie of freedom has gotten out of the bottle and it is going to be difficult for the authoritarian and ideological order to suppress it. Afghan women—and especially the younger generations of graduates—will fight the returning Taliban. Iraqis are already fighting al Qaeda's attempts to create an emirate in the Sunni Triangle and Khumeinists' push to crush democracy. In Lebanon, although Hezbollah and their allies are moving to roll back the Cedars Revolution, the people will resist the return to a police state. In Sudan, the South and Darfur will be unlikely to accept the return of the Islamist regime to their areas and the slavery it brought before. In short, the inroads achieved by Arab, Middle Eastern, and Muslim societies over the last few years, especially in terms of democratization and liberalization, will be defended by the forces of civil society. The Jihadist and authoritarian powers will be met with a fierce resistance. The confrontation is unavoidable, with or without the West. For from Afghanistan to Mauritania, from Yemen to Lebanon, the rejection of tyranny and oppression is widening. While more Jihadists are being recruited from Salafist and Khumeinist pools of indoctrinated men and women, more liberated youth are joining the growing pool of reformers and democracy activists. In past decades the contest was between supporters of aging regimes and determined Islamists. Today, it is between aging Jihadi ideologies and determined civil society forces. The Islamists are (and will again) score political victories in a number of countries; these are the results of decades of organization and funding. But Muslim and non-Muslim liberationists are also coming together and will win political battles in the future. The victory of democracy will be decided within at least one generation from today. The years ahead will see three developments, one after the other: return to fundamentalism, reform of regimes, and revolution against Jihadism.

REFORM AND REVOLUTION

The road from authoritarianism and Jihadism to democracy and pluralism will certainly be rocky. The combined powers of totalitarian regimes and radical movements, backed by oil and ideological theology, are vast both in size and resilience.

The Ottoman Empire collapsed as an institution, but the imperialist design of the doctrines of Jihadism survived. The political culture of radicalism has managed to metamorphose since the mid-1920s and emerged strongly after the Soviet collapse. As mentioned earlier, a potential liberal elite generation was crushed between the Fascist regimes and the extremist movements, around the 1950s. A new democratic revolution in the Arab and Muslim world is due, but it may or may not be successful. All depends on the backing it gets from the international community and the solidity of its own leadership. This new revolution can develop in various ways. It may evolve as a reformist movement within regimes and governments, or it may explode as a revolt against tyrannies. The kingdoms and principalities of the region could accept the principle of reform and move gradually toward constitutional monarchies—some countries are already doing so. Morocco, Jordan, Kuwait, and the UAE are examples of possible modernization via political development. These are encouraging signs. The Saudi Kingdom faces a different and more difficult challenge: the self-proclaimed and state-promoted ideology of Wahabism. The Arabian oil-producing monarchy has a dilemma. As long as its establishment doesn't cross the line toward constitutionalism, any political change—gradual or abrupt—will bring more violent forms of Salafism to power. Wahabism has produced Neo-Wahabism, and the cycle continues. Unless a mass reform takes place from within, expectations are that the country may become even more pro-Salafi, and reformists will not be able to rise until the extremism of the Salafists shows its true colors. Iran and Syria are doomed to face revolts by their own societies, but the next forms of government are uncertain. Libya will witness its own revolution. And countries with oppressive regimes will also experience liberation movements, Jihadi spasms, and a future stage of radical political change, as in Sudan. In the final analysis, the democratic revolution in this region is bound to happen, but how it will unfold depends on the historical experience of each society, and, most important, on international support. The movement for change confronts massive forces wielding global resources. It will take proportionate energies from the outside to balance the forces of oppression. The peoples of the region may be able to fully complete these changes by themselves in half a century, or perhaps in twice that. But the magnitude of the dangers to humanity makes the option of waiting to see how this development turns out unacceptable. Hence the international community, the Free World, and the West must make the rational choice of assisting the peoples of the Middle East in their quest for freedom. The opposite scenario is simply too apocalyptic to accept.

PLATFORM FOR REVOLUTION

In view of these profound realities, shouldn't the Free World adopt a more humane policy toward the peoples of the Greater Middle East? Shouldn't the West apply to this unlucky region—plagued as it is with wars, genocides, and oppression—the policies it adopted for its own peoples and for others? Are Middle Easterners different from Latin Americans, whose struggle for independence and liberty was acknowledged by the international community, particularly by Europe and the United States? Are Eastern Europeans and Russians more deserving of freedom than the peoples east and south of the Mediterranean? Is South Africa an exception for that continent, or can the black Sudanese be supported in their dream of freeing themselves from similar racial and religious apartheid? And why should Arab and Muslim women have to wait for the Salafists and Khumeinists to "evolve" in order to gain equality with men? Is it fair for the overwhelming majority of the region's youth—not the graduates of Jihadi madrassas—to enjoy less freedom, hope, and resources than the other young people of the world? In sum, why should the masses of the Middle East remain in intellectual, legal, and political bondage to ideological and financial elites claiming divine or historical legitimacy?

As a matter of philosophy and history, humanity has a moral obligation—not just a political duty—to assist the peoples of the Arab and Muslim world in their quest for freedom and democracy. Obviously—to dismiss a propagandistic response before it is said—no one can force other people into freedom. The peoples of the Greater Middle East have a natural right to learn about it, choose it for themselves, experience it, and adopt it if they wish. But the forces of fascism in the region have come together to block freedom and isolate these civil societies from each other and from the outside world. Oddly, the authoritarians and Jihadists have built their defenses against Middle Eastern democracy inside the Free World, thanks to their petrodollars. Hence it is incumbent on the West and the rest of the international community to remove the cultural barriers imposed by the Jihadi lobbies and the apologists and help civil societies toward the enjoyment of their universal and natural rights. An international, legitimate platform for a democratic revolution in the Greater Middle East has to be developed, through the following:

1. *Intellectual:* The West must free itself from the ideologies and doctrines that oppose the natural right of Arabs, Muslims, and Middle Easterners to freedom and democracy.
2. *Ideological:* If a campaign to assist the region's societies in their quest for freedom is to succeed, it has first to identify the ideologies causing the oppression and the suffering.
3. *Media:* In this area, the Free World needs to support freedom of expression in the struggling democracy movements in the Arab and Muslim world.
4. *International solidarity:* Another fundamental step that will encourage the democratic revolution is to build an international solidarity with the reformist, liberal, and democratic currents in the Greater Middle East.

FUNDING FREEDOM

Over the past few years, the United States, and to a lesser degree the European Union, has launched a number of programs to fund education, NGOs, and other projects to advance civil society. Unfortunately, the billions of dollars and euros didn't irrigate the right soil in the region. Instead (although this is a metaphorical description), the hard currencies flowed into the hands of bureaucracies, into barren contracts, and never nourished the roots. Authentic dissident and democratic forces were left to wither for lack of even minimal support. Small and weak, they faced the oil-backed juggernaut. The reform movement toward freedom in the region must be accompanied by strategic, smart, and effective funding. Alternative educational programs must be first to receive; then support should be given to social and cultural activism. Human rights activities, which confront the oppressive machinery of regimes and terror organizations, should be directly and continuously supported, and not just by the United States. Europe should match North American efforts, and other nations, such as Japan, Russia, India, Australia, and Canada, must chip in too. But most important, those rich governments in the region who claim alliance with the Free World must spend as much themselves to promote freedom.[16]

FROM WITHIN

At the end of the day, any democratic revolution must come from within. No one can "force" democracy to "spread"; it has to be chosen and adopted. But for that to happen it has to be known and experienced. The forces of fascism in the Middle East are blocking the gates and controlling the microphones, the media, the schools, the courts, and more. The unleashing of the revolution in the region has to come from inside the walls; it has to be native and authentic.

CHAPTER 7

WAR OF IDEAS INTENSIFIED

IN ORDER TO TAKE THE POLITICAL BATTLE INSIDE THE CAMP OF THE radicals, so that the societies where the Jihadists and totalitarians thrive can be part of the confrontation, the rise of consciousness in the West must be complemented by a surge of dissidence in the East. The War of Ideas has to intensify and widen so that all social forces work together to reverse the tide. To shorten the global conflict that has now spread to all continents, strategists in the Free World need to pour all available energies into winning the battle for the minds not only of this generation, but of the next one—those now in schools or madrassas. The future depends critically on which message they absorb.

If the battlefields of Afghanistan, Iraq, Somalia, Palestine, Lebanon, and Darfur are to be stabilized; if the regimes in Iran, Syria, and Sudan are to be contained; if troublemaker authoritarian rulers in Venezuela and Bolivia and the dictatorship of Cuba are to be isolated before they destabilize their regions; and if unstable Marxist regimes—as in North Korea—have to be watched for future surprises, it is essential that the peoples of the countries oppressed by these dangerous regimes are enabled to seize control of their destinies. If even countries said to be friendly to Western concerns, such as Pakistan, Indonesia, Egypt, and Saudi Arabia, are witnessing the expansion of Jihadism, it is only logical that the single most important factor for the moderation and preemption of further radicalization is the public—or to be more correct, "the masses," for in nondemocratic or less democratic countries, public opinion is not a real factor because of a lack of press freedom, voting, and polling. The people make their presence felt in more activist terms. They are, in fact, the most precious vehicle used by the radicals, regimes, organizations, and ideological media to display their power and resistance to international pressure. By way of comparison, the Russian Communists tried hard to convince the proletariat (their reductionist term for the whole society) to adhere fully to the Marxist-Leninist doctrine and to defend the Soviet Union till the last man. However, as soon as the system began to crumble, from Berlin to Vladivostok, the supposed proletariat vanished, and there arose a great mass seeking prosperity and embracing middle-class, liberal values. From the five million members of the CPSU, only fifty thousand remained faithful to the "the tomorrows that sing,"[1] the Communist promise of a better future. Nowadays only a few thousand gather in Red Square every year to celebrate the anniversary of the October Revolution.

The Jihadists of today seem to have seized the political culture, the ideological rhetoric, and the vision of the future in the Arab and Muslim world. Very few moderates openly challenge the Islamist promise of the return of the caliphate—at least as an empire having earthly powers. This may be a significant difference between the Communist and Jihadist doctrines; the latter are deeply embedded in the region's political culture, which is produced and backed by the oil powers. And yet there is significant civil society opposition to the Salafi and Khumeinist doctrines, and particularly to the very extremist Takfiri school, which has the reestablishment of the caliphate or the imamate as an ultimate objective. But the anti-Jihadists are unable to rise up and reverse the radicalization as long as the radical regimes and organizations are able to force their vision on mainstream educational and cultural systems. From Algeria to Iran, from Lebanon to the monarchies of the Persian Gulf, a genuine movement of resistance to Jihadi fascism and Takfiri terrorism is gradually on the rise. Muslim liberals and social and ethnic minorities are pushing against totalitarianism. But the combination of terror, power, finances, freedom to act, and political space is overwhelmingly to the advantage of the Salafist and Khumeinist camps. The democracy camp is solidly embedded in the weakest segments of society, and it lacks the necessary tools for rapid or significant change. Left to their own devices, the liberals and the freedom movements may well achieve successes—in one or two generations, perhaps more. But the international community, and certainly the peoples of the region, cannot afford another century of terror, because the weapons that are being developed or acquired by the radicals and the totalitarians are more and more devastating, and could be catastrophic for all humanity, not just the Arab and Muslim world.

Hence, it falls to the international coalition against Jihadi terrorism to accelerate the pace of the War of Ideas so that civil societies in the Free World can mobilize the strategic resources needed for the confrontation. Democracy movements in Arab, Middle Eastern, and Muslim societies should be empowered to sustain the long struggle against radicalism and fascism in their midst. This alliance of an educated and alert international public and a movement within the region's civil society is a sine qua non for success in the War on Terror, which we could more accurately describe as the Democracy–Jihadi war. The acceleration of the War of Ideas should have two clear overarching goals: to spread awareness among the hundreds of millions in North America, Europe, Russia, India, Africa, and Latin America, and to enable millions of Arabs, Middle Easterners, and Muslims to oppose the Jihadists and the terror regimes. But to accelerate the flow of ideas and reach the widest circle possible in the shortest time, there are some crucial steps to follow. Leaders and diplomats have to support and improve their message by responding to the fallacies propagated by the Jihadists and their apologists, and directing a Muslim-originated rhetoric against Jihadism. In addition, new policies must concentrate on educating the West, identifying dissidents in the East, supporting pro-democracy NGOs, and developing educational strategies for the Greater Middle East. These issues are reviewed in greater detail below.

RESPOND TO FALLACIES

In the verbal jungle in which the West has been lost for years, the single most important task for world leaders, legislators, and experts is to respond to the fallacies produced by the apologist camp about the nature of the threat. Part of the role of the Wahabi-influenced Middle East studies establishment in North America and Europe has been to deflect understanding of Jihadism.[2] The lobbies have pressured leaders not to use crucial terms that would alert citizens to Jihadi intentions, and they have systematically camouflaged the meaning of these concepts so that even if they *were* used, the public would not understand them properly. For example, there were intense efforts to compel politicians not to use the terms "Jihad" or "Jihadism" when speaking of the terrorists; lobbies provided a false definition of Jihad that made it seem spiritual and unthreatening. Two opposed camps led these intellectual and verbal "offensives." On the one hand were the Islamists and their apologists in the West, and on the other a segment from the consultant community (contracted to provide advice and services to the government) who cater to oil interests but claim they are a part of the War on Terror.

The first camp, the Jihadi Salafists and Khumeinists, played the traditional *Taqiya* doctrine[3] by pretending—against the essence of their ideological beliefs—that Jihad doesn't mean conflict. In an incredibly deceptive ploy, Jihadi operatives in the West would on the one hand teach their followers the most aggressive methods of Jihad—violent urban warfare against the *Kuffar*—and, on the other hand, brazenly tell the media, government officials, and the public that Jihad is just a spiritual experience, an inner struggle. This deception stemmed partly from an awareness of the Jihadists' inferior technological power; the later the infidels found out they were under attack, the better, because by then it would be too late, if the Jihadists had reached a certain point in recruitment, mobilization, and armament. This lethal cultural strategy was initiated by the Muslim Brotherhood and Islamist intellectuals throughout the West. But more importantly, it was adopted by the academic and media elite, who are supported by the oil powers. The combination of Islamist militants and the giant intellectual establishment acting as their apologists has overwhelming force—very few politicians were able to escape the ideological fog that hid the true nature of Jihadism. Even using that term was said to be so incendiary it might provoke catastrophe. This extreme alarmism was aimed at creating a redline in the minds of decision and opinion makers: If they cut to the heart of the Jihadist ideologies, they would be touching on religion and thereby offending communities and insulting beliefs. In a stunning intellectual turnabout, those under attack by Islamic fundamentalists were terrified that if they mentioned that the terrorists were Islamic, Muslims might be offended! In addition to the do-not-mention taboo on the word "Jihad," the lobbies widened the ban to include all Jihadist foundational concepts: caliphate, Salafism, *kuffar, dar el harb*, and so on. The elephant was free to stroll about the room during the debate, unnoticed. While national leaders avoided addressing the core of the problem, they received kudos for their sensitivity. In reality, the political leadership of the Free World was manipulated skillfully by the Jihadi propaganda machine—until 9/11, when the public and the government were so shaken that public figures crossed the redline and spoke about the larger picture and the real actors in the drama.

THE HIRABA FALLACY

A new camp emerged as the War on Terror was evolving; intriguingly, it rose within the group supporting the war on al Qaeda and the campaign against the terrorists. A pressure group formed in Washington that attempted to convince the U.S. and allied military to drop the "Jihad" terminology from their statements. They suggested using instead "Islamic" terminology to blast the enemy. The thinking was that treating al Qaeda as "un-Islamic" would rally the true Islamists and Jihadists to fight the "false prophets" of Jihad! The suggestion made some inroads inside the defense apparatus before receding. After a careful review of the academic and ideological endorsers of this chimera, it was discovered that Jihadist ideologues, mostly the Wahabis and the Muslim Brotherhood, were the ones who actually invented this stratagem, which was nothing more than a Trojan horse. Their intention was to convince the U.S. leadership, particularly the military, that this was a "weapon of words" to be used against al Qaeda. Ironically, the Wahabis were offering the United States a tool to defeat terrorism that would in fact cause Washington to abandon learning about Jihadism as a strategic threat and instead view it theologically.

Military commanders were advised to use the term *"irhabi"* instead of Jihadi. In fact, this Arabic word translates as "terrorist." So the result was that U.S. officials were asked to drop the word that described both the actions *and* the motivations of the enemy ("Jihadist") and adopt another (the Arabic word for "terrorist") that merely described what they were doing. This was clearly a Jihadist victory in the War of Ideas. Another suggestion (coming indirectly from the overseas Wa-habis in Saudi Arabia) to U.S. defense officials was to use *mufsidoon* when referring to al Qaeda. This word can be translated as "evildoers." A more widespread lin-guistic fallacy introduced the word *hiraba*, a derivative of the word *harb*, which translates the English "war." The activists behind this trick wanted the United States and the West to believe that in Islamic theology there is such a thing as a "bad and evil war" that is condemned by Islamic law. They claimed it is called *hiraba*, and suggested that the word be used instead of Jihad when referring to Ji-hadists' actions so that Muslims would condemn al Qaeda for this bad war and join the United States in fighting it. This thesis was attractive to U.S. military authori-ties in Iraq as they were searching for any help, including linguistic help, in defeat-ing al Qaeda.[4]

However, a quick investigation of the term showed that it had almost never been used in Muslim history, and that when it was, it meant the "wrong war at the wrong time"—a war that is a strategic failure rather than a moral one. The Jihadist literature applies this term—though rarely—to hotheaded warriors who opened hostilities against infidels or moderate Muslims without official instruction from the caliphate or the proper military authorities! Hence, this school of thought was pressing American strategic thinking to "Islamize" itself and begin the use of so-called religious concepts that applied only to Muslims, particularly the fundamen-talists. The "Islamization" of language proposed by the consultants was perhaps the most advanced propaganda maneuver to persuade the United States govern-ment to stop its identification of the Jihadist movement. The American rhetoric resembled the Islamist rhetoric, and thus reflected an "Islamization" of the rheto-ric. Word by word, the consultants in the Trojan horses were pushing for the elim-ination of all terminology indicating the existence of a cohesive ideology, Jihadism, and advocating its replacement with a Saudi-like lexicon. But in reality, once you use the "language" of an opponent, you become the prisoner of his logic, and hence you are defeated. Stunningly, the farce was spreading and a host of officials were buying into it, until the experts began to expose it.[5]

THE "JIHAD" QUESTION REVISITED

In two previous books I briefly explained what Jihad was in history: a state policy to conquer territory and societies, and then to defend those conquests. It was a doc-trinal tool at the service of the caliphate, whose geography was mostly expanded by Jihadi wars (*al Hurub al Jihadiya*) from the seventh to the seventeenth century. For the sake of academic precision, it should be stated that Islam as a religion propa-gated far beyond the borders of the caliphate through nonmilitary means—for ex-ample, to Indonesia and East Africa. But the caliphate (Abbasid, Umayyad, and

Ottoman dynasties) was obviously a pure colonial and military enterprise, as were the Roman, Spanish, and European imperial expansions. If and when a movement develops geopolitical activity—even though it qualifies itself as religious or theological—it is and should be considered geopolitical. They all marched with armies that imposed their systems and values. The Islamic empires were not an exception to the rule, as they, too, invaded, conquered, and administered the occupied lands. The "historical" Jihad was at the heart of the caliphate's colonial designs and politics. It was to the Muslim empires what the Crusades were to the European Christians: the state-sanctioned use of force based in theology.

That historical Jihad was supposed to end with the crumbling of the Ottoman Empire, the last Islamic caliphate. But in the 1920s, and again in the 1970s, a new type of Jihad was resurrected by militants, the self-described Jihadists. The Islamists—from different schools and backgrounds—distinguish themselves clearly from other Muslims by openly stating that they haven't accepted the abolition of the caliphate and in fact are struggling to reconstitute it. Here is the central difference between those Muslims who have accepted the principles of modern international law and all its conventions, particularly the principle of a world society of nation-states, and those who have rejected the new state of international relations. The Islamists' fundamental reason to change modern international society is not their desire to see Sharia law implemented internally and in a personal way. It is Salafists'—and to a lesser degree Khumeinists'—rejection of the world as we know it. Their "caliphate" is a world society by itself, with little or no room for the rest, the infidels. So the "new Jihad," far from being what apologist academia presents as a "spiritual experience," is a comprehensive, totalitarian, and fascistic doctrine for resurrecting the caliphate by every possible means, including violence.[6] Therefore, the contemporary concept is, in the final analysis, ideological and geopolitical, and it is being practiced in the real world. It is as materially distinct from the old, historical Jihad as modern Western policies are distinct from those of the medieval world. The jihad of the empires was waged by the official heads of the Islamic states. This state-sanctioned Jihad ended with the collapse of the Caliphate in the 1920s. The new Muslim states were supposed to adhere to modern international law, which doesn't recognize religious wars—including Jihads—in modern times. Still, today's Jihadists link themselves to the historical Jihad of the seventh through fifteenth centuries; and they assert that their "work" today is a direct continuation of the old Caliphate. Hence they believe they are resuming the old Jihad. In international norms, including those regarding Muslim states, these "Jihad" wars aren't legal or accepted by the international community as such.

Contemporary Muslims must take as their primary commitment opposition to these claims of the current Jihadists. Just as enlightened Christians abandoned the idea of a religiously grounded (and even divinely sanctioned) war, post-caliphate

Muslims must reject the concept of a theologically mandated conflict with the "infidels" and thus reject the "Jihad" of the Jihadists. This is where the War of Ideas will make its central stand.

MUSLIM SPEECH AGAINST JIHADISM

What the majority of Muslims worldwide adopts as a discourse about Jihadism will be the single most important factor in the final stage of the War of Ideas. Even if a determined, antifascist, counter-Jihadist discourse within the Arab and Muslim communities worldwide begins with a numerical minority, it could turn the balance of power against the radicals and bridge the divide with the Free World. Against the assertions by many that criticizing Jihadism is automatically interpreted by most Muslims to be a critique of a religious tenet, I believe (as do many other analysts and researchers) that exposing what is totalitarian and oppressive in the Jihadi ideology will facilitate the rise of a Muslim discourse opposed to Salafism, Wahabism, Takfirism, and Khumeinism. This would not be a total innovation, for such rhetoric may be found throughout the course of Muslim civilization, beginning at least with the Muaatazila (a Muslim rationalist sect) of the Middle Ages.[7] As many dissidents are arguing, there are legitimate grounds for *ijtihad* (jurisprudence, a method of arguments), a mechanism obstructed since the thirteenth century by the partisans of Ibn Taymiya—no other than the doctrinaire father of Salafism. The global Salafists of the 1920s and the Khumeinists of the 1970s (that is, today's Jihadists) do not represent the majority of all Muslims and Islamic societies around the world. The fifty or so Muslim countries formed at different times, entered gradually into the international community and its organizations, and have a variety of tendencies, political parties, and local politics. The Muslim world is too vast, too diverse, and too complex to be identified as fundamentalist (or not) in black-and-white terms. True, it is profoundly impacted by religion, theology, and history—unifying traits—but presents endless differences as well. As in other civilizations, the struggle has been between the forces of progress and liberalization (in the general sense of the words) and the forces of reaction that favor the status quo. In the Muslim world, the equation includes the content of reforms and fundamentalism, but it is also about contemporaneity, with a sense of the period in Islamic history when these struggles first occurred. The Muslim world is fourteen centuries old and its experiment with modernity and the postcaliphate world is less than a century old. In other words, the struggle between fundamentalists and reformists is in its first stages. Hence, our expectations should consider the realities of the historical past and respect them. In such a massive challenge, the international community should act carefully along two tracks: One is to relate to the bulk of Muslim nation-states within the norms of international

consensus (international laws and the United Nations), and the second is to encourage and support Muslim efforts to merge with these norms.

In conclusion, when Muslims (or any other societies and individuals for that
matter) produce a political and social discourse based on the principles of international law and democracy, they have to be supported and protected. In view of the
precarious struggle inside the Muslim world, one major policy to be adopted by
leaders in the Free World is to systematically support and encourage Muslim discourse against Jihadism. The claim by one faction in the Muslim world that it represents the entire civilization at all times and can speak authoritatively on all things
must be rejected. Diversity is a right enshrined in international law and the United
Nations Charter; hence, just as the Jihadists should be denied the right to "seize"
the representation of the Muslim world, so the Islamists must be given their full
right to express their views, aspirations, and even their radical doctrines, but as
ideas, not as calls to action. The limit on any ideological agenda is the freedom of
other human beings. Any move by Jihadists or any other ideological (and even
nonideological) force, Islamic or not, to repress individuals, communities, or entire
nations cannot be accepted under international law and justice. A key question is
thus how to assist democracy-seeking Muslims when the political cultural of the
region has been dominated by Islamists for so long.

JIHADI DOMINATION OF MUSLIM POLITICS

One primordial reality the West must come to grips with is the Jihadi ideological
domination of Muslim politics and debates worldwide. Because Islamist ideolo-
gists in general—and the Wahabis, Muslim Brotherhood, and Khumeinists in
particular—are the best funded and have the widest support (by a number of
regimes), they haven't been challenged yet. Almost by default, the Islamists are
winning the regional debate against the rest. In the West, Jihadists' intellectual
facilitators are claiming that an overwhelming majority of Muslims around the
world are turning "naturally" to the Islamic fundamentalists because of Western
policies. In reality, the militants are seizing hold of the political culture just because the other disputants haven't been able to oppose them and develop their
own agendas, and above all because the opposition has been crushed by the
coalition of extremists and authoritarians. As I argued in previous chapters, following the collapse of the Ottoman Sultanate and immediately after the European withdrawal, the liberal, democratic, and reformist elites were pushed back
by authoritarian regimes—both left wing and conservative. Simultaneously,
these seekers of alternatives to the status quo were also intimidated by the Islamists. Across the Arab world, the two big forces remaining on the ground were

the governments in power and the Jihadists. In the latest round of the struggle, the Islamists have cornered rulers with theological agendas and forced them to back off ideologically. With Wahabis in power in Saudi Arabia, Salafists in Sudan, Khumeinists in Iran, populist Islamism promoted by Qadhafi in Libya, Taliban dominance in Afghanistan for a few years, and, recently, the influence of the Muslim Brotherhood on oil-rich Qatar, the political ideology of Islamism became irreversible, even though the movements were in jeopardy in many other countries. Oddly, the Muslim Brotherhood was suppressed in Egypt and Syria, but their concepts survived in both countries. Saddam's secular and socialist Baath marginalized the Sunni Islamists but espoused the symbolism of political Islam after its defeat in 1991. Even in Pakistan, where secular parties are omnipresent and the government claims a pro-Western posture, the Islamists have been setting the emotional agenda. Only Turkey leaped into the secular sphere in the 1920s and maintained itself there, at least until the coming to power of a political Islamist party in 2002. Turkey nowadays is among the few fully Muslim countries with a powerful balance between the two voices, fundamentalism and secularism. A similar balance exists in Indonesia, Bangladesh, and Pakistan, as well as in Central Asia. But even in the most secularized societies, the Islamists have been successful in shielding some of their principles—such as Jihad—from criticism. And with al Jazeera emerging in the 1990s, the struggling liberal movement saw their main slogan, political change, hijacked. For the Qatari-funded channel, rising to the top of regional popularity, claimed it was a revolutionary phenomenon "different from the broadcasts of the regimes," whereas in reality it dedicated most of its airtime to a sophisticated Islamist agenda using the most technologically advanced means. In short, the microphone has been grabbed by the antidemocracy axis in the region, leaving the potential reformist energies without any significant voice.

Here is why liberal democracies and the Free World need not only to support antiradical Muslims in their quest for change within their societies, but to consider them as partners—full partners—in the Free World. For the Muslim resistance to Jihadism (regardless of the debate about the possibility of a future spiritual Jihad) is a legitimate attitude deserving its place in the international solidarity against oppression. What this humanist Muslim movement is faced with is a superpower fed by oil royalties, security services, terrorist organizations, ideological cadres, and theological weapons. Muslim humanists comprise the weakest segments of Arab and Muslim societies—women, youth, students, labor, and a few intellectuals. An accelerated War of Ideas requires massive aid from the Free World to their networks, to NGOs, unions, and individuals, and even to courageous governments engaged in reforms.[8]

ACCELERATING THE EMPOWERMENT
OF MUSLIM HUMANISTS

The following are guidelines for accelerating the liberation of Muslim humanists worldwide in their confrontation with fascists and radicals.

First and foremost, there should be a campaign to educate and inform the public in the West not only about the dangers marching against its own societies but also about the real stakes inside the Muslim world. North Americans, Europeans, and others around the globe must realize that the political struggle should not be between the Muslim world and the rest of international society, as the radicals wish it to be, but within the Muslim world between the self-described Jihadists and the rest of the Muslims. Once the citizens of the Free World absorb this geostrategic reality, they can extend consistent support to their governments and to a coalition of countries and international organizations to empower humanist Muslims, a mostly silent (and muzzled) majority.

There should be a comprehensive response to the apologists in the West who for decades have blurred the vision of Western democracies. Profiting from aid from oil powers, the Jihadophiles have marginalized Muslim dissidents, reformers, and progressives, failing their own peoples by disconnecting them from the realities in the Arab and Muslim world and by obstructing humanist Muslims' attempts to reach out to the international community.

The Free World must identify the real forces of dissidence, change, and progress in the Greater Middle East and in the Arab and Muslim world everywhere. Encouraging those governments and officials who are putting effort into reforming their own laws, policies, and regulations is necessary. Enlightened executive leaders and open-minded legislators can help accelerate the process of openness. Supporting liberals and moderates at the grassroots level is important, but a change coming from the top of a country's institutions is also extremely helpful. Measures taken by rulers in Morocco, Jordan, Algeria, Kuwait, the UAE, Bahrain, Bangladesh, and Senegal should be appreciated. Turkey's historic experiment—in terms of secularization—should be valued and observed. But again, the hardest and perhaps the most important international effort is to reach out to the underdogs in the struggle for freedom and help them stand up. The so-called campaign for the minds and if possible the hearts of these nations is not really about persuading people to change their opinions; it is about finding those whose minds and hearts have been set on freedom for a while, but who have been denied access to their likeminded brothers and sisters around the world.

CHAPTER 8

ISOLATING JIHADISM

THE CONFRONTATION IN WHICH DEMOCRACIES ARE NOW INVOLVED has no parallel in history. True, in the twentieth century, the West had to face Fascism and Bolshevism, and both forces were lethal to liberty and human dignity. Fortunately, the Free World survived. It might seem then that the confrontation now is a similar struggle. But two differences exist between the current challenge to world peace and security from Jihadism and what went before: the first is about life and death, and the other is about the future.

Nazism was anticlerical and Stalinism was atheist. Both ideologies promised to create a paradise on earth, both called for gigantic sacrifices in lives and resources, but the ultimate goals were to be achieved here, on this planet, and possibly even in the lifetimes of their adherents. The Nazis and the Fascists called for mass efforts and violence to bring back the grandeur of national histories, so that this generation and future ones would enjoy geographical space, economic prosperity, and prominence in the so-called hierarchy of nations. The Soviets—and other Communists—were promising the proletariat a state of happiness with full equality and social freedom, with food supplies, sexual freedom, and technological advancement available to all. They were talking about corporeal, earthly life. Both ideologies were ready to use any level of violence to achieve their aims (even, in the case of the Soviets, if they had to use nuclear weapons). But the harshness of Bolshevism and the savagery of Nazism were aimed at enjoying life on their terms. Jihadism, at least in its Salafist, Takfiri, and Khumeinist forms, goes one step farther: It demands that followers give their lives. The teaching of ultimate Jihad requires the sacrifice of humans for the pleasure and the will of Allah. Death is not a limit to the Jihadists, as it was for the most fearsome twentieth-century ideologies (it would have negated their claim to produce "perfect" societies here and now, and the rewards promised to followers). Death is the beginning of the fulfillment of the promise, repeat Osama bin Laden, Khamenei, Sayed Nasrallah, and Sheikh Yusuf al Qaradawi. The master of al Qaeda has often declared that he loves death as much as the *kuffar* (infidels) love life. And here lies the gulf that separates the totalitarian doctrines of the past century from the challenge that confronts us in the present.

A belief in the life here and now has its consequences in action. Nazis tried to negotiate separate peace agreements with the Allies when they realized that annihilation of the Reich was imminent. The Soviets, too, came to understand that a mutually assured destruction would not bring about a proletarian paradise on Earth. The Communists were atheists and did not expect to celebrate the pleasures of socialist life after the disintegration of the body. But the Jihadists present a strong contrast to materialist philosophy. They aren't deterred by defeat, destruction, and physical death. Their ideology is lethal because it convinces them that their victories, when they win, are the divine will, and their deaths, if they die, are the will of Allah. Soon, they say, they will meet the Maker and be sent to *al-Janna* (paradise), where virgins will greet them and "earthly" pleasures will be available for eternity. Once convinced of this, nothing will deter a Jihadist, not even a nuclear holocaust. Thus, Jihadism emerges as an insatiable, undeterred, and unique phenomenon in modern history. And if no military, security, economic, or political deterrent can stop such a relentless, ruthless, and death-embracing movement, it is only rational to develop ways to isolate it. To build a global coalition with this end in mind, a first step is to determine and make clear just what Jihadism is costing the rest of the world.

JIHADI OBSTRUCTION OF ECONOMIC ADVANCEMENT

Few people realize that Jihadism obstructs the advance of humanity through its effect on the global economy. This was true in the past, and it is true now. In the decades following the decline of the Ottoman Empire and up until the present, the Salafist and Khumeinist ideologies have become a doctrinal resistance to modernity and to economic prosperity based on social justice. The key to understanding how Jihadism obstructs economic development is very simple: This ideology and its adepts put the so-called duty of Jihad (the form it takes in modern times, in spite of the contemporary system of international relations) above all other considerations, including socioeconomic growth and the equitable distribution of wealth. Take for example the oil-producing regimes in Saudi Arabia, Iran, Libya, Qatar, Iraq (under Saddam), and even Sudan. Their rulers control oil production and the benefits derived from this immense wealth—but instead of spending these billions of petrodollars on their own societies to end social disparities, they divert the revenues in other directions. They amass fortunes in international banks, build heavy security apparatuses, strengthen their regimes, buy disproportionate amounts of military equipment (destined for use in ideological wars), and when possible buy influence within other countries, particularly in democracies. The fortunes of oil regimes parked in world banks are legendary. These monies alone could seriously help fight poverty in their own countries—or at least in the most impoverished provinces of these countries, as, for example in Iran, Saudi Arabia, and Sudan. For example, in the latter, the South and Darfur suffered while the regime's leaders signed juicy contracts with Western, Chinese, and Indian companies. In Iran, the funds now socked away could ease the frustrations and brighten the futures of workers, young college graduates, and women. But petrodollars could have helped weaker societies, too, advance economically.

In an ideal strategic economic situation, Saudi oil wealth could by itself help the struggling economies of Yemen, Jordan, Palestine, Somalia, Eritrea, and even, as far away as it is, Bangladesh. These countries, mostly Sunni, could be helped tremendously by Riyadh's financial power. Libya's oil income could inject energy into the economy of neighboring Egypt, and Chad, too, as well as others. Algeria's gas riches could, in combination with Morocco's resources, create a dynamic Maghreb economy, in which Tunisia might also participate. To the East, Iraq's oil reserves could bolster Syria's precarious economy. Iran's petrodollars could be invested in Afghanistan, central Asia, and even in Pakistan. The Gulf's dizzying wealth could help boost the economies of Muslim countries in Africa and Asia. In short, the cash and reserves existing in the Middle East should be used to help the fragile economies of the Muslim world. Even a nonassertive petro-power such as Brunei is capable of shining a beneficial economic light across the islands surrounding it. A wiser distribution of resources and opportunities by the rich Muslim countries to the less-endowed Muslim countries south and east of the Mediterranean could be a formidable solution to the socioeconomic plight of millions of men and women in that part of the world.[1]

There are precedents for such cooperation. The stronger European economies, both after World War II and the Cold War, lifted up the weaker ones on the continent. The Asian tigers Hong Kong, Taiwan, South Korea, Japan, and Singapore stimulated their regional partners such as the Philippines and Thailand. This type of solidarity can even happen in Latin America, as it did when Brazil and Chile took off. But why don't the "rich uncles" of the Arab and Muslim world help their poorer cousins? Why is it that most oil-producing regimes in the region refrain from launching Arab Muslim Marshal Plans to assist the most deprived societies in the Greater Middle East? Arab oil could lift the minuscule Palestinian economy into a thriving and prominent financial position: Gaza doesn't have to be slums, and the West Bank could mirror Jordan's middle class. Egypt, with the largest Arab population, doesn't have to be at the mercy of the annual two billion dollars provided by American taxpayers. Libya, with barely two million citizens, and a couple of small principalities in the Gulf, should fund projects to double the size of arable land on both sides of the Nile River. Lebanon's once thriving banking system should be the depository of the region's cash overflow instead of Switzerland; were that so, credit (and microcredit) would be available to help the development of the region's poor. The list of possible exciting revolutions in the region's economies is very long and could have become a reality. But who has obstructed the rise of a harmonious regional economy?

The answer can be found in the last sixty years or so of Middle Eastern history. Thanks to extreme nationalism, such as Pan-Arabism, and ideologies such as Baathism, brothers didn't help brothers: Everything had to be geared to the greater battles—against "imperialism," "the enemies of the nation," and "Zionism." Even if millions had to live miserably in shantytowns for decades, the elites of the Baathist *Reich* had more important issues on their minds than social justice and an equitable distribution of wealth. Thanks to Salafism, Wahabism, and Khumeinism, oil royalties were used for Jihad, not for the expansion of the middle class, universal education, jobs, and women's emancipation. Wahabi petrodollars were spent on theological schools as far away as the Punjab, Afghanistan, and Gaza, but not on the socioeconomic needs of these areas. Arabian petrodollars were offered by the millions to buy influence on campuses in Europe and the United States instead of educating youth within their own borders. How ironic it is that the U.S. Congress is budgeting billions of dollars to provide education in the Middle East and North Africa while regimes of these regions are spending millions to indoctrinate students inside America![2]

The ironies abound. Iran's leadership is milking the oil industry to send military assistance and cash to Hezbollah in Lebanon—while workers inside the country are struggling to improve their lives. The Qatari petrol industry funds al Jazeera TV to support the spirit of Jihadism in the region rather than empowering reformists with economic incentives. The overconcentration on Jihadism instead of economic solidarity has also influenced populist governments overseas, as happened in Venezuela under Hugo Chavez. The authoritarian former army officer, who has seized control of the country's oil, has been reelected twice thanks to Venezuelan petrodollars. And as he linked up with Iran, Syria, and the Wahabis (together), Chavez applied ideological oil policies similar to theirs in his own hemisphere. Money is flying across the New World to support like-minded radical forces and tie them to the Jihadi Oil Empire across the ocean. Thus, in the end, the Jihadization of economics has had dramatic effects on the lives of millions of people throughout the region and far beyond.

In fact, Jihadism as an ideology, a movement, and a set of regimes not only refuses to engage in a mass redistribution of wealth in the region, but has been fueling theological wars that produce nothing but economic disasters and human tragedies. The Khartoum war on Southern Sudan and Darfur devastated those regions, carried out genocide, and destroyed the economies of African nations. Saddam's war with

Iran and invasion of Kuwait, Iran's support of Hezbollah and Hamas, Libyan's backing of radicals, the funding by oil powers of two decades of war in Lebanon, and other Jihadi-inspired aggressions have been at the core of Middle Eastern cataclysms. And now the region's horrors have led to the rise of extremism and suicidal terrorism and spread to other regions of the world, including Russia, other European countries, India, and the United States. If a general accounting of disasters can be calculated, the Jihadist phenomenon—in this large sense—has been the cause of many social and financial tragedies. Both through the explosive conflicts within the region—and responses from overseas (as has been the case since 9/11)—Jihad has caused losses to the world economy that can be measured in trillions of dollars, as well as enormous and unquantifiable human suffering. In short, a whole region of the world is lagging behind economically, mainly because of tragic adventures led by radical movements. Economic advancement is obstructed—among other reasons—by the determination of the Jihadi powers to

1. Maintain a social status quo under the domination of the oil elites.
2. Increase theological conflicts to deflect the public from economic liberation.
3. Feed the radical educational system as a way to block the rise of cultural alternatives.
4. Fund an apparatus within the West and the Free World so that economic globalization doesn't translate into cultural exchange with the region.
5. Keep the economies of the region in a state of dependence on the oil economy.

Thus, a large area of the modern world, stretching from Morocco to India, has its economies at the mercy of Jihadi wars and terror. Whether seen as single countries or as an entire region, an important part of the world's population is being denied the means to economic development as a direct result of the actions taken by regimes and movements linked to radical ideologies. And as a result of these economic and social tragedies, which affect literally hundreds of millions of men and women in dozens of countries, world economic progress has also been slowed.

JIHADI OBSTRUCTION OF SOCIAL AND SCIENTIFIC DEVELOPMENT

The doctrines, policies, and action of Jihadi terrorism have had tremendous negative consequences on social development in Arab and Muslim societies. Without going into the details of the numerous cases in which the radicals have damaged the abilities of these societies to grow and accelerate their emancipation, we can point to the attacks already mentioned in previous chapters on the rights of

women, youth, students, labor, artists, intellectuals, writers, and other active players in the civil societies of the Greater Middle East. One has to factor in the cur-
tailing of these freedoms in assessing the overarching loss of talent and innovation
crucial to social evolution. Segregating women, regardless of the extent or form,
affects and diminishes the general advance of society in all fields. The gender
apartheid in the region, from its most severe forms under the Taliban to less restrictive variants in Iran and Saudi Arabia to milder versions elsewhere, has obstructed a natural development of the workforce, the social psychological balance,
and, of course, a fair distribution of economic resources. Jihadism as an ideology
was and remains at the center of this gender suppression.

Oppressing youth and interfering with their liberation and emancipation has
played a similarly negative role. It has wasted energies inside societies that could
have developed democratically. The conditioning and indoctrination of youth have
led large segments to become antisocial and to take refuge in terrorism. Meanwhile other students or younger males and females have rejected theological radicalism and joined the social underground instead of experiencing normal
intellectual and cultural growth in a healthy environment. On a planetary scale, the
suppression of the region's youth has incalculable consequences for social development. Like marginalizing women, impeding the young in the Greater Middle East
deprives the world of the skills that the next generation might supply; these side-
tracked youth will not experience the interactions in this world necessary to imagine a future society. The ideologies of doom, by standing as a wall between billions
of younger men and women and obstructing the symbiosis that would result from
their free interaction, are breaking down the mechanism that leads to social
progress. Youth and women are a vital link in the progress of social conditions, as
well as in technological and scientific improvements.

Here is yet another often overlooked effect of ideological radicalization: It re-
tards the scientific progress of the world. At the core of the problem is the fundamental opposition of Salafism—and to a certain degree of Khumeinism—to free
scientific inquiry. The most fundamentalist of the elites are opposed to various aspects of technological innovations related to social advancement. These obstruc-
tions, often expressed in radical *fatwas,* touch upon medical, social, technological,
scientific, and related fields. The scientific community is often oppressed or constrained where Jihadis wield the power to do so. This was the case in Afghanistan
under the Taliban, but it is also true in a lesser degree throughout the region today.
Often Islamist regimes (as in Iran, Sudan, and Saudi Arabia) selectively fund or encourage scientific development in the field of armaments—including nuclear
weapons, as in the case of Iran, and biochemical warfare, as under Saddam. At the
same time, they keep a lid on the use of the Internet, limit access to satellites and
other technologies that open the society to non-Jihadi alternatives, and oppose improving science education and opportunities for women, minorities, and youth.

Thus, the normal evolution of scientific sectors has been derailed by radical forces. Marginalized and in many cases suppressed, talents who would participate in the region's global renaissance have been kept on the sidelines of social development. In most cases, only those scientists who worked on defense and security issues are backed by the regimes. And among the scientists who have focused on civil issues, a large number have had to emigrate to the West in search of recognition and financial advantages.

The region's scientific backwardness is a tragedy for its own peoples. As was the case with the Fascist powers of the 1930s and 1940s and with the Bolsheviks during the Cold War, scientific study has been redirected to the advantage of militarism. With the collapse of the Soviet Union, and especially since 2001, the radical regimes and movements attacked the democracies, the Free World, and international society. The latter diverted immense resources to respond to the challenge of terror. That subtracted gigantic amounts from the global effort to eradicate poverty, empower minorities and weaker elements of society, spread education, and improve human health. Although many may not see it, or wish not to admit it, there is a direct link between Jihadism (in its real-world form) and the failure of global science to achieve more in terms of serving humanity's growing needs. By dragging the international community into its Jihadi campaigns before 1990 and Jihadi wars after the Soviet era, Wahabis, Salafists, and Khumeinists, as well as Baathists and other radicals, have severely strained the world economy. They compelled the most advanced democracies to spend money and time on wars and war recovery—as well as to counter terrorist indoctrination, education, and acts—instead of focusing on major crises, such as environmental challenges, and medical discoveries and agrarian improvements worldwide. The emirs, radical clerics, and dictators of the region affected human history by causing the diversion of resources and energies that might have gone into achieving a breakthrough in the eradication of cancer, AIDS, diabetes, or other lethal diseases. The trillion dollars—perhaps more—spent on the wars against the Jihadists could have helped to alleviate many global problems, rather than exacerbate them.

Because of Jihadism's and authoritarianism's determined, extremely violent forces, the twenty-first century will likely see even more catastrophic setbacks for scientific and social improvement. Thus, it becomes even clearer that the leadership of the international community must put aside their endless disagreements and disputes, and come together to isolate the seeds of a century-long threat that could literally plunge humanity into the abyss.

ISOLATING JIHADISM DOMESTICALLY

The Free World's strategic response to Jihadism must come from the representative bodies within democracies. Islamists claim that the Arab public—if well informed—

is against the West and the other enemies of the Islamic fundamentalists. It is important to have the majorities in civil societies respond to this argument by rejecting Islamists' claim to a divine mandate and pointing out that Jihadism is promoted by radical clerics and ideologues and those profiting from and protecting their interests. The first and greatest rejection of Jihadism in all of its violent forms must come from these democratically elected bodies, for it is appropriate that the final target of fundamentalism—democracy—should become the principal means of its defeat.

The U.S. Congress must debate the phenomenon, identify it as akin to Nazism, racism, and apartheid and finally legislate against its terror dimension. Congress must come to the understanding that Jihadism is an ideology, even though its original concept is an unofficial part of religious tenets. Once that determination is achieved, Congress can identify the ideology—not the religious concept—as illegal, inasmuch as racial and theological discrimination and calls for violence are illegal under U.S. law. Passing such a law would be a significant step to isolate Jihadism by the most influential democracy on earth.

The rest will be an uphill battle, and difficult, but opposition to Jihadism will grow once Jihadism has been isolated in America. This will unleash both the agencies of government and the talents of the public to counter the threat in an educated and informed way. Only then will the United States solve the so-called conflict between civil liberties and antiterrorist actions. But this battle, resting on the shoulders of the Congress, and later on the executive and judicial branches as well, needs also to be taken up in all the other legislative assemblies in the world. This mobilization against terrorism has to be bottom-up, from a very aware and enlightened public to its representatives, and from there to the executive branches. The world confrontation with the radical Islamists and violent Jihadists has to be the expression of the concerns, the consciousness, and the determination of citizens-turned-fighters who wish to preserve their own freedoms and future. Past years have shown clearly that without popular awareness and agitation, governments can dodge their duties. Such irresponsibility leads to catastrophes, as was the case during the 1990s. And the War on Terror since 2001 has also shown that leaders waging wars without a full understanding by the masses can be exposed to lethal attacks by lobbies, other politicians, and the media, all of them influenced by the oil powers. Only a change in the thinking of the public can solidify the strategies of the leaders. Hence, after (or even as) the U.S. Congress has declared a War on Terrorism and identified it with the ideologies and the forces producing it, legislators everywhere, including especially those in the Muslim world, should also isolate the Jihadi threat. Each country has its own language, its own political culture, and its own norms of engagement. Many in the Arab and Muslim world may prefer to begin the counteroffensive on terror by denouncing Takfirism as the single most powerful weapon used by the Jihadists. Some governments in the region, including those in Jordan, Morocco, Kuwait, Egypt, and even realist circles in Saudi Arabia, have chosen counter-Takfirism as a means to defeat the Jihadists. Non-Muslim countries such as Spain, Russia, Britain, and France could ban Jihadism altogether as a movement similar to Nazism. The legislative march has to move forward in all countries that perceive themselves as part of the coalition against Jihadi terror.

Ironically, isolating Jihadism doesn't mean eliminating it as a historical and political phenomenon, but, rather, denying it the capacity to harm international society. As with other ideas and doctrines, Jihadism can always persist under the very same democratic system it wants to destroy. Like Neo-Nazis, Fascists, Bolsheviks, Trotskyites, Maoists, racists, anarchists, and other radicals, the Jihadists belong at the margins of society, isolated from the lives of most people and unable to affect their collective destinies. Until the strategy of the world focuses on isolating Jihadism, eliminating terrorism will not be possible.

CHAPTER 9

U.S. HOMELAND SURVIVAL

AL QAEDA'S ENEMY NUMBER ONE IS THE UNITED STATES OF AMERICA. IN all their speeches since 1996, Osama Bin laden, Ayman Zawahiri, and their deputies, emirs, and spokespersons have incited attacks against Americans and U.S. targets around the world.

The bombing of the World Trade Center in 1993 and the attacks in 2001 illustrate the ultimate wish of the Jihadists: to hit Americans at home, killing as many as possible and crippling the U.S. economy.[1] This determination by al Qaeda and the Combat Salafists to target the American mainland is at the heart of the Jihadi strategy. As I argued in *Future Jihad*, it is essential for those Islamists who have chosen the bin Laden option to wreak havoc inside the civil society of their main adversary. In fact, the long-term decision to attack the United States was adopted in the early 1990s, most likely after the Khartoum Jihadi conference, during which radicals assembled from all over the region under the sponsorship of the Islamist ideologue Hassan Turabi, but split on this issue. The "realist" Jihadists—Wahabis, Muslim Brotherhood, and their Iranian counterparts—preferred to focus on battles elsewhere in the world and not attack directly inside America. Their rationale was based on the assessment that with the current global balance of power the Jihadists cannot win—yet—against the United States. It was preferable to engage the infidels in India, Russia, the Philippines, the Balkans, Sudan, Lebanon, Israel, and even in some Arab countries, without inflaming Europe and North America.

Islamist strategists, some of whom revealed this analysis on al Jazeera and in other media after 9/11, have argued since the early 1990s that the West is an excellent source of funding, recruitment, and support for operations. But the realists didn't mind if hotheaded Jihadists struck U.S. targets abroad, as long as they didn't implicate regimes. Their lobbies would use these incidents to further condemn the West and the United States for their foreign policies, which their propaganda machine labeled the "root causes of these attacks." Hence, even if the realists disagreed with the strategy of the radical wing, they could still use the actions of al Qaeda or other Jihadists to score points inside the political system of the West. Meanwhile they continued with their War of Ideas and with the undermining of the Western capacity to respond. The famous manifesto of the Muslim Brotherhood clearly instructed its followers to follow the bottom-up approach of infiltration inside infidel nations. The Wahabi lobby also practiced the gradual penetration of the political and educational systems of America and the West. However, the Neo-Wahabis and the off-shoots of Muslim Brotherhood—those who would form al Qaeda—followed the path of *muwajaha mubashara* (direct confrontation) with the United States, both abroad and at home. Bin Laden's network as of the early 1990s had launched a series of attacks, issued declarations and fatwas, and assembled information on attacking American cities, targets, citizens, and military personnel. So, in sum, while the militant Islamic fundamentalists have been penetrating the society and government of the United States, the Combat Jihadists of al Qaeda have engaged in battle (that is, in terrorism) against the mainland. The attack against U.S. national security is driven by the central objective of the Jihadi strategic agenda worldwide: to force a retreat of U.S. forces and roll back the military presence in the region, eventually obliging Washington to cease all support of any country in the Greater Middle East. The reason is very simple: This withdrawal will make it possible for the Jihadists to pounce on these governments and bring them down, thereby gaining control of their resources, including the ability to levy armies, recruit terrorists, and acquire the weapons of mass destruction that might be needed for the next stage. The latter, of course, is the resumption of what they believe should be a *fatah*, resuming the old design of total conquest of the infidel world.

Hence the difference between the Jihadi militant penetration and the Jihadist terrorist infiltration of the United States is about timing and strategies, but the two thrusts are intertwined and feed each other. The political influence helps create pools of militants from which the terror organizations can recruit or from which individual Jihadists will emerge. The penetration of the system provides "cover" for recruitment, until the two paths can merge. The global aim is to defeat U.S. power by weakening the national resolve of Americans. The chilling conclusion is that the Jihadists from both trees want to destroy U.S. homeland security. It is a fundamental part of their global strategy, and the efforts and attacks will not stop as long as the Jihadist movement exists in its contemporary form.

WHY IS U.S. HOMELAND SECURITY
CENTRAL TO THE FREE WORLD?

Several factors make a threat to U.S. national security a strategic issue in the international confrontation with terrorist forces.

1. The United States, the largest, most powerful democracy, is leading the War on Terror against the Jihadists and their allies. If the latter can weaken American resolve, destroy its capabilities, or deter it from pursuing its campaign, they will win the conflict. In the current effort to fight al Qaeda, U.S. Armed Forces provide about 80 percent of all the resources in Afghanistan, Iraq, the Middle East, and beyond. In a potential containment of the Iranian and Syrian regimes (as well as Hezbollah), Washington would provide a similar percentage of military, logistical, and financial resources. Added to this is the fact that when a new battlefield opens with al Qaeda or its affiliates anywhere, the fastest and most reliable force to intervene and bring a decisive outcome is the one dispatched by the United States. This is not to say that other democracies or world powers do not have a similar capability to contribute to overseas antiterrorist activities, but in the present stage of geopolitics only the United States has the resources to sustain these kinds of efforts over a very long range, in multiple locations, and for a very long time. The Russian Federation, the United Kingdom, and France also possess powerful militaries and the capacity to deploy them worldwide; but each power alone cannot muster by itself resources comparable to those of the United States. The combined resources of these powers, had they been joined in a global strategy to counter Jihad, would have produced the most formidable antiterror power in history, much like that deployed during the World War II alliance against the Fascist forces in Europe and the imperial expansion in the Pacific.

2. By extension of the above argument, if the United States were taken out of the conflict, the other powers wouldn't be able to conduct a coordinated global resistance against the Jihadi forces. European democracies would be assaulted and their policies neutralized at home and abroad. This has already happened in Spain, the United Kingdom, Germany, France, and Italy. Russia alone cannot withstand a mass-terror intifada, which could be mounted using a combination of domestic separatist movements and overseas terrorism acts. Unable to withstand the global threat alone, these countries could then be picked off one by one by the Jihadists. The logical deduction is that the weight of the War on Terror rests on the Americans' ability—due to their global influence—to come to the defense of other countries attacked by terror forces. But the capacity of the United States to deliver deterrence anywhere in the world hinges on its own national security, meaning that it must retain its ability to function and produce the resources needed. Hence, the security of the U.S. homeland is at the core of American power, and thus at the core of the war with the terrorists.

3. From the above logic it follows that a race has been taking place between U.S. Homeland Security efforts (launched in the fall of 2001) and the Jihadi terrorists, who began their campaign as far back as 1991. Almost immediately after the collapse of the Soviet Union the Jihadists turned their attention to the United States. The decision to target the United States was made on the basis of a judgment by the Jihadists that they wouldn't have freedom to operate in the region, to seize power in Arab and Muslim countries, until America was taken down. The U.S. display of power during the Iraq-Kuwait war of 1990–1991 convinced veteran Afghan Islamists that hitting the American mainland was the only path to getting U.S. forces out of the region. Furthermore, the failure of Communists to regain power in August 1991 in Russia further convinced the internationalist Jihadists that America was the last remaining infidel power to be reckoned with. The first attacks against the Twin Towers came soon after, in 1993. Documents found later and literature that was already available, along with videos aired since 2001, certify that the call was sent out for the destruction of the security and the economy of the United States. The Jihadists, operating in the shadows, hastened their infiltration.

WHAT ARE THE THREATS?

The forces at work in this campaign are active simultaneously at all levels. I base this analysis on my observation of the evolution of the various Jihadi strategies and my ongoing analysis of their modus operandi over a decade (starting in the mid-1990s); on my participation in meetings, conferences, and seminars held by various U.S. governmental institutions that deal with national security, including Homeland Security, FBI, the Department of Defense, the National Security Council, and related agencies; and on years of interaction with top experts in the field. The threats are discussed below, beginning with those I deem the most strategic with the longest consequences:

a. *Infiltration of U.S. homeland security*
   Individual and organizational Jihadist activities' most frequently target is the collection, analysis, intelligence, and public policy segments of all agencies and departments dealing with U.S. homeland security. If and when the networks can place their operatives deep inside this body, the entire cohesiveness of national security will be compromised. The reasons are obvious, and are well understood by intelligence and insurgency experts. From inside the various agencies, the Jihadists can "see" the entire security map of the nation. They can find out who watches the terrorists,

and they can decipher how the machinery works. Jihadists can then relay strategic information to Jihadi regimes (or circles within these governments) in conflict with the United States. Second, they can divert the efforts of the U.S. government by providing bad advice, wrong data, and false analysis. By doing so, this counterintelligence Jihad can derail the national security assessment of the United States and thereby give more time to the terror groups to form and grow. Third, the infiltrators of the homeland security apparatus can embed a dangerous security and bureaucratic enclave, ready for future operations against the United States. This enclave, as the most lethal weapon of all, could threaten the national defense apparatus on national soil. After infiltrating the various military agencies, an attack launched on D-Day could disorganize the defense of United States territory from "behind enemy lines."[2]

b. *Infiltration of U.S. national defense*

Immediately after infiltrating homeland security, the Jihadists' most coveted achievement will be to insert their indoctrinated militants inside the multitudinous military institutions. Clearly, any Jihadist infiltration anywhere in the army, navy, air force, and marines, not to mention military intelligence agencies, will affect the national defense system. A defense penetration would have two main objectives: first, to warn the Jihadi regimes and movements about the U.S. defense plans, strategies, tactics, and types of weapons; and second, to subvert action from the inside. In future stages, if significant recruitment into these branches takes place, the end product would be an infiltration of units deployed overseas. With some imagination, one can project the devastating results in times of conflict abroad, as well as the chaos Jihadi-penetrated U.S. units could bring at home.[3]

c. *Penetration of the strategic weapons apparatus*

A third circle of threat against the U.S. homeland is undoubtedly a potential penetration of the country's strategic weapons apparatus, including nuclear, biological, and chemical arms. This menace is taken seriously by U.S. security and defense planners because of the fatal consequences of any success by the terrorists. Traditionally, U.S. concern has focused on the transfer of nuclear components or weapons, purchased overseas, into American cities or towns. While such a threat is real and continuing, as long as the Jihadi wars are going on around the world, another serious challenge would be a more patient and insidious insertion of Jihadists into the heart of the U.S. defense: the nuclear apparatus. Salafists or Khumeinists could either enlist operatives before they get recruited into the U.S. military or try to indoctrinate them after they have climbed the ladder of clearances and earned sensitive positions in upper echelons. The "nuclear

Jihad" is the ultimate offensive the terror forces could unleash inside the United States.

The atomic option as perceived by the Jihadists is still under study by the experts. I myself have given it a lot of thought, for the idea of America's nuclear destruction by the Jihadists raises questions about their ultimate goal: Do they want the United States to be annihilated, or do they want to vanquish it? Do Jihadists want genocide in the United States, or, as Islamists, do they ultimately wish to convert it and rule it themselves? These are crucial questions for which the final answers are still unclear. The Jihadists themselves are still mutating; at present they seem anxious to inflict massive casualties on their enemies, not just in America but around the world. Therefore, the penetration of the realm of strategic weapons inside the United States is to be taken seriously and in fact remains the highest issue on defense and security agendas, parallel to the capacity of Jihadi-inclined regimes to obtain and deploy these terrible arms elsewhere. What remains certain is that an infiltration of U.S. nuclear, biological, and chemical weapons facilities for terrorist purposes would be dangerously aided by any prior penetration of homeland security and defense institutions. These would provide a wedge, and Jihadists are willing to use any and all means to achieve their goals.[4]

d. *Influencing and deceiving the decision-making process*

The most sophisticated of Jihadi plans against the United States will be to insinuate themselves into positions where they can advise decision makers, deceive them, and provoke chaos in national security. Their expertise in diplomacy, public relations, counterterrorism, mobilization, alliances, dissidents, and other subjects could seriously erode the capacity of the government to perceive and act against the enemy. Well-placed Jihadi or Jihadophile operatives could weaken alliances and efforts with foreign governments to identify the terrorists, waste U.S. resources in the War of Ideas, deflect the concentration of counterterrorist forces from the real enemy to other targets, demobilize the public, block or pressure dissidents, and generally weaken homeland security and gain maximum time to widen the pool of radicalized elements for a future urban explosion.

e. *A systemic breach*

A country that cannot see, understand, and respond to a threat is weak and can be defeated. The final element in the Jihadi plan to defeat the United States turns on this fact. If the eyes of the country are blinded to terror in the making, the homeland will be strategically defenseless. If the court system is manipulated by Jihadophiles to block the prosecution and sentencing of terrorists, if the political mechanism actually strengthens the radicals, and if the media are made to promote the future insurgents, the United States will finally succumb. The scenarios in which defense capacities disintegrate are many and can multiply and evolve with time. Before 9/11, many Americans didn't realize that the country was falling into a systemic vulnerability and the Jihadists were making inroads. All the Jihadists needed was time, and their apparatus was patient—but the hotheaded wing, bin Laden and his ilk, abandoned the silent strategy and decided to strike head-on. The September 11 attacks shocked and awed the public and forced the top national leadership at the White House and on Capitol Hill to react. Since fall 2001, the national security structure has undergone significant changes. A Department of Homeland Security was created, the Patriot Act was passed, and a counterterrorism culture has developed. But still, in 2008, a systemic security breach is a possibility. Agencies have gotten better at searching for and detecting terrorists. In the past half-decade, the dismantling of cells, conviction of terrorists, and arrests in Oregon, Virginia, Florida, New York, Los Angeles, Seattle, Carolina, Georgia, and elsewhere have revealed past Jihadi infiltrations.[5] But the government hasn't mapped out the systemic breach yet. The country must undergo a cultural revolution and an informational and educational reform to energize the government's campaign against the Jihadists, dislodge the Jihadi network from the system, and build a defense against the looming threat.

WHAT ARE THE DANGERS?

Based on the above possibilities, what are the imminent dangers to the U.S. homeland? In my view, though the remainder of this decade and the next one will tell us more clearly, we can observe that there are two fundamental threats that could literally cripple American national security.

Nuclear Jihad

The first is a cataclysmic use of weapons of mass destruction, if the Jihadists—al Qaeda or others—acquire them in the next few years or have already done so. Contrary to popular belief, the worst possible danger, at its most extreme, is not about setting off one dirty bomb, or even one tactical nuke in one city. Such an event would indeed be catastrophic, but the United States would survive it and strike back. The more extreme scenario involves the terrorists (groups or regimes) detonating a number of weapons, of any kind, in many cities simultaneously. This indeed would produce an American holocaust. Obviously, the day after, the national cohesiveness of the American nation would evaporate. But again, such an enterprise—although attractive in the mind of mutant Jihadists—wouldn't be the first considered by "regimes" or even worldwide Islamist networks or powers. In such scenarios, because we have no historical events to serve as comparisons, no one can guarantee anything about the day after. This was precisely the foundation of the Cold War's doctrine of "mutually assured destruction" (MAD); it kept the Soviets—and the Americans, too—from even thinking of pulling the trigger. But while the Kremlin and the Pentagon knew exactly—or almost—how a second strike would follow, the international nebula of Jihadi decision makers cannot predict how a retaliatory U.S. military strike might work. Hence, while the ultimate scenario will always seem tempting among regimes' radical circles and to al Qaeda as well, the limited strike scenario is more likely. First, it is more achievable in the present stage of development to explode a single bomb of a great magnitude. Second, the day-after scenario is more manageable in terms of forcing the United States to capitulate, especially with a very weak leadership at the top of national decision making. But in the end, U.S. homeland security must factor in all scenarios and confront them at all levels.

Urban Jihad

The other danger imperiling the United States is the rise of what I have termed in my previous books "Urban Jihad." From various sources, including manuals and documents by Islamists based in the West and overseas (including the manifesto of Abu Musab al Suri, the al Qaeda strategist) and the Muslim Brotherhood's guidelines in North America,[6] as well as from a long observation online and in the media, it is clear that the ultimate objective of the Combat Jihadists in America (as in other countries outside the Arab Muslim world) is the creation of an urban army ready to engage in military, security, and sabotage activities. And from a review of most terror cases tried in the U.S. system of justice, whether the prosecution was successful or not, one can see a common trend: the effort to create urban cells, combat units, and terror networks. Even for individual terrorists who plotted alone to cause harm to infrastructure or to people, their ultimate ideological goal was to be carried out through urban violence.

The Jihadists inside America aim at creating as many groups of "fighters" in as many places as they can. From Virginia's "Paintball Jihadists" to the Fort Dix cell in New Jersey, from Miami's mutant terrorists to Oregon's training camps, one can read the emerging map: They are populating the U.S. homeland with brigades, ready for action. The radical indoctrination taking place in prisons, the formation of ideologically motivated groups in cities, and the infiltration of various social strata all indicate the rise of a nationwide urban force targeting the peace and security of the United States, as bin laden himself has warned. These militias would attack inside the country as long as American forces are deployed around the globe, not just in Iraq and Afghanistan. Furthermore, if Washington changed course and withdrew its forces from the region, the expectation would be that the Urban Jihadists would move to a second stage as soon as Jihadi powers reach a critical level overseas. That is to say, the "army" that is being created in the United States is here to stay, and will grow, simply because it is an ideological one. These are not the fictitious, issue-oriented Jihadists described by the apologist propaganda campaign; they will not stop committing violence if American policies change.

In 2005, I dedicated a section of my book *Future Jihad* to projecting a virtual scenario of a much wider 9/11 that might have taken place years after 2001 had bin Laden not attacked that year. I projected a hypothetical urban war that would have exceeded in violence what happened on September 11. The scenario was based on real terror cases, such as that of the Mohammed Atta cell, the Oregon group, the Virginia network, the D.C. sniper, the shoe bomber, and other conspiracies, in addition to projections drawn from literature and observation. To my astonishment, many of those scenarios actually materialized between 2005 and 2008. Almost all cases since 2005 reveal a Jihadist determination to create small cells aiming at specific targets: military bases and installations, biochemical sites, government buildings, military personnel, security agencies, as well as important civilian and economic buildings. In a way my chapter mapped what the Jihadists had on their minds; these evidences further convinced me and other analysts that the ultimate (and frighteningly, very achievable) goal of the Jihadis within the United States is to create and launch an urban Jihad. One can predict the grand plan of the Jihadists (of all backgrounds). Eventually, most of these urban cells—some have been dismantled—will reach a level of self-sufficiency. This means that the Jihadi "factories" within the country will produce waves of militants and won't have to rely on terrorists imported from overseas. This, to me, is the breaking point. When that level is reached, urban Jihad will explode across the country. Europe has gotten very close to that level, and some would even argue that urban Jihad is already there. With waves ready to take action and terror pockets in almost all major urban areas, network commanders would be able to choose their targets and design their rules of engagement. An army of ten thousand Jihadists could wreak havoc on the mainland. Backed by powerful lobbies and political pressure groups, supported by deep penetration within the layers of national defense, this army would be able to disrupt national security and affect the U.S. economy to the maximum. Then Osama bin Laden's vision would be realized: a shattered American society and a collapse of U.S. power.

Were this hypothetical—but not impossible—scenario to materialize, foreign Jihadi powers (regimes and movements) would advance within the Middle East region, changing geopolitical realities: Iran, Afghanistan, Iraq, Syria, Lebanon,

Sudan, Pakistan, and other areas of conflict would witness mass assaults by terror forces as U.S. cities struggled for their own survival. And in this dramatic context, choosing to use WMD could be considered by Jihadi decision makers. The rest I leave to the fertile imaginations of citizens, writers, and analysts. Unlike the 9/11 Commission, I believe Americans have a great deal of imagination, once their education is set on the right track. Once operatives secure basic grounds—easy borders to cross, a network on the inside, political lobbies to shield them, intellectual legitimization, indoctrination institutions producing homegrown Jihadists, training, legal aid, and freedom of action—it is not hard to imagine what they will do, given their ideology.

But even as the vital components of an urban Jihad are made clear, we can see the way to confront the threat.

HOW TO CONFRONT THEM

America is the most powerful nation on earth at this time, but the terrorist challenges it faces are enormous. As mentioned above, the Jihadists' thrusts into the layers of national defense and security are deep and wide and they continue, despite counterefforts deployed since 2001. For America to shield its homeland, it needs to confront and reverse the lethal advances of the Salafists and Khumeinists. Only then can its national security be fortified and readied for global conflict around the world. And to confront the Jihadi threat, the United States must take dramatic, quick, and long-term measures. Since the Jihadists began to engage America, overseas and at home, at least two decades ago, catching up will be hard and take longer than expected. Among the most important steps are the following:

1. *Protect the national security apparatus*

   Following a debate in the U.S. Congress on the identification of Jihadism as a threat to national security and assuming that anti-Jihadist laws are enacted to ban the terror ideology and fund a national program of awareness and de-Jihadization, the government will have to proceed with a strategic reform to ensure that the homeland security apparatus is not penetrated by active Salafists and Khumeinists. And in order to succeed in implementing this policy the national defense and security leadership must issue a central document clarifying the threat and organize a thorough and systematic campaign of information and education inside the various agencies dealing with the protection of the homeland. In addition to firming up the defense culture within these institutions, the leadership should base its future training and recruitment on the doctrine of counter-Jihadism, so that the intelligence and security community in the United States will be protected from ideological penetration. Once a de-Jihadization program is set forth, a system of counterespionage and counterintelligence would be able to detect attempts to infiltrate the core power of national security.

2. *Protect the defense apparatus*

In parallel with the cultural reform needed across the national security apparatus, a similar educational program should be launched throughout defense institutions so that all departments and agencies are duly informed about ideological penetration and are intellectually equipped to take countermeasures. The de-Jihadization program should be implemented at several layers so that infiltrators would be detected and new attempts to penetrate would be stopped. It would be effected from the inside out, in a top-down process, within the homeland at first and then overseas. Note that because of the time lost over the past two decades, a special effort will be needed to accelerate the educational process within the military. The two efforts, in the national security and military apparatuses, are the most pressing initiatives. From the commander in chief to the last policeman or policewoman, marine, sailor, and soldier, everyone involved in the protection of the nation must be informed and educated. Once that step is accomplished, the next stages can be engaged with a degree of security and psychological tranquility.

In sum, Jihadization is a political operation backed by ideological and financial resources, and hence de-Jihadization should follow a dual track: On the one hand, the government will have to choke off the funding of Jihadi enterprises in every possible legal way. On the other hand, it will have to assist the many NGOs, human rights organizations, and women and student groups that are engaged in educational campaigns to counter the Salafist and Iranian regime propaganda within the community. An equivalent of an "affirmative" counter-Jihadi action has to be legislated to ensure solid and consistent support for the humanist, secular, and moderate groups within the community. The Jihadi element will then be isolated inside the very environment it seeks to influence and control. As I have argued previously, a conspicuous Muslim, Arab, and Middle Eastern resistance to Jihadi terror in America would constitute the real front line against the threat.

WHAT ARE THE PRIORITIES?

As the new long-term defenses of the homeland are put in place, two priorities must be rapidly considered: First, we must find ways to shut down the flow of militants into the United States, which goes on unchecked. Hundreds of Jihadists are landing on American soil and joining the already growing "army," and they do it through illegal immigration, fake claims of a need for political asylum, and other stratagems. Legislators and decision makers must have a critical discussion on how to differentiate between Jihadists aiming at reinforcing the "project" and legitimate immigrants seeking a better life. The second priority is to train and educate the judicial body so that it can be a successful part of the new defense of the homeland. As discussed before, the Jihadi cultural propaganda has affected the bulk of the educated elite in the United States, thus also impacting the court system. In this regard, it is crucial to provide rapid and professional information about the threat to the judges, lawyers, and functionaries involved in the justice system and the tribunals that deal with immigration and security matters. One example is the eavesdropping program on terrorists, with the executive branch arguing that it needs to listen to communications between potential terror-involved individuals, and the critics insisting on having judges authorize these actions. Educating and training special antiterrorism judges would be one answer to the problem. If need be, for example, special judges could be sensitized to the depth and tactics of the Jihadists, so that in a short time, when consulted, they could authorize a search; or if the need arose, these counterterrorism judges could be recruited into the structure that conducts the operations.

WHAT ARE THE OBSTACLES?

One has to realize that immense obstacles will be put in the way of building an enlightened defense of the homeland. The resistance will naturally come from the already indoctrinated and influenced elements in the country and within the layers of institutions. The Jihadophiles will use all their political and academic power to protect the Jihadists, and the latter will use all their financial and diplomatic resources to protect Jihadism. Hence, even as America is in the seventh year of its campaign to vanquish terrorism, the forces of Jihadism are in their seventeenth year of penetrating the country. The capacity of the public to pressure their government to act strategically and hastily will determine whether the U.S. homeland is secured over the next few years in a manner that ensures its survival.

CHAPTER 10

A GREATER EUROPE TO CONFRONT JIHADISM

MANY IN EUROPE MARK MARCH 11, 2004, THE DAY AL QAEDA MASSACRED hundreds in Madrid, as the beginning of a new era: modern Jihad against Europe. One year later, suicide bombers killed dozens of people in London. The July 7, 2005, attacks further convinced analysts that the wave of Jihad was spreading across Western Europe and was linked to the war in Iraq. Indeed, Spain was among the main participants in the coalition during the invasion, and as soon as it was hit by the Jihadists, it pulled out. Britain was the second-ranked power in the coalition and thus, according to the classical view of Middle East studies, was targeted. In the fall of 2005, two hundred French cities witnessed urban uprisings, in which about ten thousand cars were burned. Despite mainstream media reports linking the violence to disenfranchisement and a youth crisis, the fingerprints of Salafi radical clerics were all over the French intifada. This could hardly have been a reaction to France's position on the Iraq war, because under President Jacques Chirac not only was the French government not standing by the United States, it was leading the international opposition against the war. Once again, the apologist theory that Jihad is caused by Western foreign policy was disproved by events. About a year later, violent demonstrations erupted in many European and Middle Eastern cities, again led by Islamic fundamentalists, who targeted Denmark's embassies and interests in response to the publication in a Danish newspaper in September 2006 of cartoons deemed offensive to Muslims. In January 2007, a vast coalition of Muslim Brotherhood, Salafists, Wahabis, and Khumeinists torched buildings and initiated street violence across the Mediterranean. Antiwar commentators said it was because of Iraq, but many of the countries involved in Iraq weren't attacked at this time.

Year by year, Europe is finding out more about the hidden Jihadi underground within its countries. Even in 2008, the European Union and its separate governments, mainstream media, and academia all still reject the harsh geopolitical reality of a surging European Jihadism. The official version remains that there is a problem with discrete radical groups and individuals, not with a transnational movement (i.e., Jihad). And the dominant theory articulated by the elite is about the "socioeconomic frustration of immigrants," instead of an ideological current spreading from Italy to Sweden. In short, Europe is still struggling, not with the question of the best way to win the War on Terror, but with the very idea of the existence of such a war. That is to say, it has not even turned the corner in the War of Ideas. One Europe (the official one, anyway) is trying to dodge the issue, while the people in the streets are witnessing the rise of Jihadism before their eyes. In between are two types of experts: the traditional scholarship of the self-blaming kind, which sees the West (and mostly the United States) as being responsible for the explosion of extremism, and at the other extreme the security and intelligence agencies, which paint a scary scene of terrorist activities, both ongoing and forthcoming. The latest arrests in Great Britain, in July 2007, and those in Denmark and Germany in September, as well as the Swedish cartoon crisis since then, all show clearly that Europe is actually in full confrontation with the Jihadists.[1] The issue at hand is (or should be) the grand designs of the Salafists and the Khumeinists, rather than all the other so-called root causes.

Between 2002 and 2008, I had the privilege of conducting fifteen research trips to Europe and spent months interacting with current and former ministers, legislators, diplomats, security and intelligence officials, prosecutors, police chiefs, NGO leaders, journalists and commentators, academics, and intellectuals. I met and worked with many officials at the European Commission and Parliament in Brussels and Strasbourg, as well as with European ambassadors at the UN Security Council and in Washington. These intense meetings and discussions, in addition to my constant study and monitoring of the Jihadi strategies regarding Europe, produced a global picture of where Europe stands in the confrontation with Islamist terrorism.[2] To investigate how Europe should reconfigure its position in this confrontation, one has to explore the attitudes on both sides: What moves are Europeans and Jihadists playing in this mortal game?

JIHADISM'S WAR ON EUROPE

Many historians, both European and Arab Muslim, have argued that the Mediterranean—unlike the Atlantic—has witnessed unending wars between the European north and the Islamic south and east. They view the last thirteen centuries as a constant back and forth between the Muslim powers in North Africa and the Levant and the Christian kingdoms and states between Greece and Spain. The first Islamic wave was the Umayyad *fatah* that overran the Fertile Crescent and was stopped at the Anatolian plateau controlled by the Byzantine Empire at the end of the seventh century A.D./C.E. Through an invasion of Berber North Africa, Arab

Muslim armies were able to land in Spain, a Christian land. This first wave was consolidated by the Abbasid Empire with a push toward France and the conquest of Sicily, Sardinia, Corsica, and Malta. In reaction, European Crusaders launched a counteroffensive against the Muslim-dominated Levant in the eleventh century, conquered Jerusalem, and held the Holy Land and other eastern Mediterranean coasts for a couple of centuries. The Muslim world countered with the Ottoman invasion of the Balkans, reaching as far as Vienna, threatening Rome, and dominating one-fourth of Christian Europe. On the western edge of the Mediterranean the Spaniards liberated their peninsula from Arab rule; between the fifteenth and the nineteenth centuries, European-Muslim warfare set the shores of both regions aflame and blocked the southern Europeans from sailing freely. Muslim historians see colonialism as a European enterprise intended to subdue their regions; to the European leaders of the time, the domination of North Africa came in response to the Ottoman-sponsored corsairs, and the later move into the Levant after WWI was a response to Turkey's conflict with the French and British occupation of the former Ottoman empire.[3]

Whatever the interpretations of centuries past, the modern age was supposed to abandon religious and imperial wars. Europe, after the tragedies of World War II and the Cold War, was heading toward economic integration and diplomatic union; the states of the Greater Middle East had obtained their independence. By the 1990s, the dialogue between European and Mediterranean nations had reached its apex, and despite the lack of democracy south of the sea, the European Union was nevertheless hoping it could engage in partnership with the oil-producing regimes and settle down for a long period in which northern democracies could profit economically and southern elites (though not the people) would be satisfied politically and financially. The reality was that, while the European north evolved into liberal democracy, the Middle East was left to suffer under authoritarian regimes and Jihadi ideologies. As soon as the Cold War ended, Western Europe began to witness spasms emanating from radical networks that had grown inside its own borders; networks with ideological roots in Salafism, Wahabism, and Khumeinism began operating across the continent, with a constant influx of fresh radicals from the region moving to Europe.

What the European elites missed during the Cold War and as it was ending—well explained by author Bat Yeor[4]—was the transformation of the Arab and Muslim world during those decades. By the end of World War II, European colonial elites had replaced their own direct presence in the region with local political and financial elites with whom they established a cordial economic entente. This new form of colonialism, termed neocolonialism, did not depend on ideological inclinations and strategic choices. Most of Western Europe's establishment formed financial bonds with the regimes ruling North Africa and the Levant in order to preserve their own advantage. The immense web of economic ties on both sides of the Mediterranean almost blinded the governments and interests groups in Europe to the extent that geopolitical transformations had shifted dramatically to the advantage of the radicals. The latter, both regimes and movements, through the use of European technologies, support, and diplomatic influence, had solidified their grip on their own civil societies while (much more dramatically than in the United States) simultaneously building a huge base of power and influence inside the prosperous capitals of Western Europe. By the mid-1990s, the Jihadi penetration of Western Europe was already profound. At the turn of the millennium, governments and experts realized that while Europe was politically sleeping, the Islamist movements had infiltrated most of its countries dramatically.[5]

The generation of Europeans now alive seems to have erased the old clash across the Mediterranean from memory. The assumption worldwide was that, with the rise of the League of Nations in the 1920s, and particularly since the founding of the United Nations in 1945 and the Universal Declaration of Human Rights in 1947, religiously motivated conflicts and claims were off the table as far as international relations were concerned. No crusades and no Jihads were to be accepted in the world political lexicon; instead, there was a vision of a mainstream discourse shaped by agreed international laws and values. But this isn't what the Jihadists have adhered to, to the surprise of the Europeans.

The Salafists (in all their varieties) perceived post–World War II Europe as the "Crusaders' old home" and thus as an enemy, regardless of European policies that were very conciliatory toward Arab and Muslim causes. The Khumeinists adhered to the same attitude, but with more realism: They worked on this premise but didn't publicize it as much as the al Qaeda type. The Jihadists took the path of conflict against European democracies as soon as the Soviets left the Afghan battlefield, and they increased it throughout the 1990s. But the Islamist strategists cautioned against awakening the Europeans until the right moment, when the balance of power would be ready to shift. Europe's geographical proximity put it within reach of the radical regimes of the region, and therefore made it more vulnerable. Initially, the mainstream Wahabis had planned a Europe-first strategy, but the bin Ladenists engaged the United States prematurely. Western Europe was more dependent on the oil economies, and thus on the petro-Jihadi exporting regimes. Since the end of the Cold War, oil finances and other interests managed by the petroleum economies and cash from the region developed an unprecedented influence in London, Paris, and the rest of Western Europe. Eastern Europe was emerging slowly from Communism, and was thus less attractive to the region's investors. But this is not an insurance policy forever. Its turn will come as European unification continues.

The influence of the oil regimes translated into an opening of the cultural realm on the continent to intellectual and eventually ideological penetration by the Wahabis and to a lesser degree by the Khumeinists: European Jihadophilia was born. Which meant that through its penetration of the politically correct realm of European politics, the Jihadi doctrines assumed the guise of acceptable ideas, ideologies, and policies; its terror-promoting dimensions went unchecked; the ideology thrived; and the militants snuck in. The European attitude toward Islamism was the window through which the networks moved. They developed roots, and extended their presence and cells across the land. With the ideology deemed acceptable and unquestioned by official Europe (governments and intellectuals), the Jihadi intellectual elite could further introduce it as culturally acceptable. The Europeans accepted both spiritual and militant jihad as long as it was perceived to be a legitimate response to past and present oppression rather than a basis for wanton terrorism. In a sense, intellectual elites argued that violent Jihad, when caused by frustration with Palestine's loss, had some legitimacy. They did not take the stand of labeling all Jihadi bloodshed as unwarranted terrorism, regardless of the possible motivations. And when the legitimization was achieved, the militants were able to organize, recruit, and form their own radicalized cells under that cover. So while government and union officials dodged the issue for years, academics favorable to the Islamists asserted that Jihadism is due to socioeconomics and not ideological beliefs. Hence the perception of the threat was hidden from public eyes in Europe.

The rise of Jihadism in Europe was an embarrassment to the ruling elites. If they had to confront it head on, they would have found themselves on a collision course with their Middle Eastern partners, which would be bad news for their interests in the region. So, playing the ostrich, they subcontracted the Jihadophile academic elite to deal with the matter; in other words, they camouflaged terrorism as an "explicable phenomenon" and so not worth worrying about.

In the 1980s and 1990s, when I visited government officials in Western Europe or met their diplomats around the world, they, with the exception of a very few, dismissed the concept of Jihadi threat as alarmist, and labeled it "American" or "Israeli." When confronted with the raw ideological statements of the Jihadists, most of my interlocutors said, "Europe has nothing to fear from the Islamists." And when I raised the persecution of civil societies at the hands of Jihadists or authoritarians, the answers varied between "This is the culture of the region" and "Perhaps time will fix it." After 9/11, the tone changed somewhat as European security officials—who knew better than the politicians—saw the images of New York and realized it could happen in their cities. That they were targets was clear from al Qaeda propaganda material found in various European locations. Indeed, in the fall of 2002, when I was asked by Dutch prosecutors to review and analyze documents captured from what they believed was a terrorist cell in Rotterdam,[6] I realized that the material submitted on DVDs, CDs, and in printed form showed a clear Combat Salafist indoctrination process. The writings were undeniable evidence that European infidels were next on the list. As I was reviewing documents in another terror case for the U.S. government in Detroit, I compared the literature and the sources: I found out that they were almost the same.[7] The Jihadists weren't singling out America, but rather were deploying their forces on different fronts.

THE TERROR CAMPAIGN BEGINS

During preliminary court proceedings in Rotterdam I told the judges, the prosecutors, and any on the defense side willing to hear that the Salafist movement in Europe and in the Netherlands was on the path of "Jihad." "But our expert told us Jihad is a spiritual journey," said one of the defense lawyers. I asked for the name of the scholar and checked his work. Indeed, he subscribed to the Jihadophile thesis: that Jihadism is only an expression of frustration, not an ideological teaching. The members of the alleged cell were released later on technical grounds. However, since then, the government has begun to see that the Jihadi phenomenon is widespread in the small country. As in other European countries, many plots were uncovered. Then in November 2004, filmmaker Theo Van Gogh was assassinated by a professed Jihadist militant.[8] The Dutch scholarly attitudes displayed during the Rotterdam trial weren't confined to the Netherlands, but were the mainstream thinking on campuses throughout the continent, from Oxford to the Sorbonne, from Louvain to Uppsala: The academic establishment was blinded by the massive influx of Jihadi apologism. Despite the attempts by authors in France, Switzerland, and other countries to warn abut the phenomenon, the general drive was to marginalize "alarmist" interpretations. This quarrel over an ideology was not a scholarly spat; governments within the European Union were relying on experts to determine the threat and assess the effectiveness of potential responses. As was the United States before 9/11, so was Western Europe blinded.

The Jihadi offensives began to have an impact on national policies with the Madrid attacks. Al Qaeda scored a master coup: It played Jihadism in Spanish politics and won. When the train attacks occurred on March 11, 2004, the leadership of both the government and the opposition coalition parties, instead of coming together—as did the public—to answer al Qaeda, permitted partisan politics manipulated by domestic politics to produce a policy change on Spanish participation in the War on Terror. Spanish forces were pulled out of Iraq. But did this stop the Salafists from targeting "infidel-occupied Andalusia"? Not at all. Since 2003, Spanish security services have uncovered more than one plot to engage in further terror against the country. By 2006 al Qaeda's threats had gotten bolder: Spain's government (the one that withdrew its forces from Iraq) was asked to hand over Ceuta and Melila (two Spanish enclaves on the North African coast) to the caliphate-to-be. Otherwise, a Jihad would be started against Madrid. In 2007, the Spanish forces serving in the UNIFIL in south Lebanon were attacked, and military personnel were killed. In 2008, most of Western Europe is bracing for terror strikes, Central Europe is discovering the early signs of Jihadist infiltration, and in the Balkans, the Wahabi and to a lesser degree Khumeinist presence is growing.

EUROPE'S JIHADI REGIONS

The Jihadist penetration of Europe has occurred over decades. As the European colonial powers such as Britain, France, Belgium, and the Netherlands gradually withdrew from Asia, Africa, and the Middle East in the late decades of the twentieth century, they opened their doors to large numbers of natives of these lands to gain citizenship in the Metropole. These new, mostly Muslim immigrants from the former colonies had many among them indoctrinated to Jihadism, either before their migration or recruited in Europe later. Another reason that Western Europe witnessed a faster rise of Islamism than Central and Eastern Europe was that under Communism there were no political liberties; ironically, the Salafists grew in larger numbers and much earlier in Western Europe than in the Soviet-controlled countries because of their greater freedoms. Then, in the 1990s, Wahabism spread in the Balkans during the ethnic conflicts there, particularly in Yugoslavia. After these conflicts stabilized, Wahabism remained strong, particularly in Bosnia, Kosovo, and Macedonia.

There are interesting differences in Jihadism within Europe. The claims advanced by the Jihadists in the south of Europe are mostly territorial, whereas in the center and the north they are mostly political. In Spain, al Qaeda aims to reconquer the land of the former caliphate. In Yugoslavia, the Wahabis are struggling for geographically separate states. But in the rest of Europe the Jihadists want a change in foreign policy and eventually the formation of enclaves. Hence, and without diving deeper into comparative analysis, the Jihadist war against—or in— Europe is segmented by particular regions and the various strategic and political goals in each. For this reason, policies to address the challenges will need to be similarly tailored.

WESTERN EUROPE

The main zones of operation for the Jihadists in Western Europe have been the United Kingdom, France, Benelux, Spain, Germany, and Italy. But all other countries in Western Europe, such as the Scandinavian lands, Austria, Switzerland,

Portugal, and Greece, are also areas of indoctrination, recruitment, infiltration, and action. Logically, European democracies that have the military capacity to intervene overseas have been targeted first, and at the top of that list are the United Kingdom, a strong U.S. ally, and France, which has its own strategic and historic ties to the Middle East. Both of these European powers are nuclear; hence their importance as pillars of *kuffar* strength in the West, as seen by al Qaeda and Iran. The Jihadist forces regarding Europe are of three types: (1) mainstream Wahabi, Muslim Brotherhood, and authoritarian regimes and lobbies; (2) al Qaeda and combat Salafi networks; (3) and Iranian intelligence and Hezbollah cells. Each of these forces operates with different strategic goals, timing, command-and-control structures, and decision-making processes.

The Wahabi and Muslim Brotherhood activities aim essentially at a grand design of weakening European resolve to intervene in the Arab and Muslim world, principally against the regimes in which the Islamists have interests, such as Saudi Arabia, Qatar, Sudan, and countries where Wahabism and the Muslim Brotherhood have increasing influence, as in Egypt, the Maghreb, the Gulf, and Libya. The aim is dual: to have Western Europe desist from supporting democracy and human rights, and at the same time protect the rise of Islamic fundamentalism in these countries. For example, Syria wants to keep Europeans from linking up with the Syrian opposition and promoting political change there. But the mainstream Islamist lobby in Europe, by far the most powerful and influential because of oil economics, also has an agenda for Europe: political Islamization and, in the long run, religious conversion. European democracies abandoned evangelism as a state policy centuries ago. Religious NGOs, mostly Christian, do operate in the Greater Middle East and in the Third World. But European governments have separated themselves both legally and politically from proselytism. Even the influential Christian Democrats of Germany and Italy do not advocate governmental policies of "spreading Christianity." This is the Europe of the twentieth and twenty-first centuries: fully secularized, almost to the point of anticlericalism and atheism. But across the Mediterranean there is a diametrically opposed agenda.

The Wahabi and Muslim Brotherhood circles, inside and outside regimes, are on a full-fledged state-sponsored campaign to spread religion and invite Europeans to convert. No violence is used, but significant sums of money have been spent. Since the 1970s, Middle Eastern governments have poured gigantic amounts of resources into this campaign; thousands of mosques, sociocultural centers, orphanages, medical centers, schools, and religious and academic programs have been funded. And to provide the necessary cadres to manage these urban centers, many governments have financed official clerics and envoys to satisfy what apparently was indeed a social and spiritual need for the millions of Muslims living in Europe. One could liken these religious leaders—drawn from Saudi Arabia, Algeria, Tunisia, Sudan, and even Turkey and sent to lead the new communities in Europe—to the missions of the Catholic Church and others that have sent priests, monks, and nuns to regions where eparchies and religious centers are in need of pastors. However, Muslim clerical authorities are under government auspices while Christian missionaries are not state sponsored. It is true that, under international law, the dispatch of religious leaders to counsel and minister to their citizens' international religious communities is normal and acceptable. Note, however, that as Middle Eastern regimes have promoted their religion, many voices in Europe, including the Vatican, have criticized the lack of reciprocity in this area.[9] Indeed, many of the Muslim governments that funded and supported religious communities in the West and Europe denied the same rights to European and other churches in their own countries. Saudi Arabia, Sudan, Afghanistan under the Taliban, Algeria, and even socialist regimes such as Syria and Iraq under Saddam froze missionary activities, and nationalized churches, schools, and religious institutions—and in the case of Saudi Arabia banned other religions altogether. The Taliban, Sudan, and Iran actively persecuted them.

Popes John Paul II and Benedict XVI demanded that these countries extend to Christian churches the same rights Europe grants Muslim religious communities. This debate is about laws and international relations, and perhaps in the future it will be addressed by the United Nations. But the issue at hand in the Jihadi penetration of Europe—although many in the West would argue otherwise—is the infiltration by the radicals of the religious web created and fed by the regimes, more than it is the efforts by Middle Eastern regimes to convert the majority of Europeans to Islam. And here comes the nuance difficult to discern: If governments spend money and exert diplomatic pressures to promote a religion, it is up to the host governments either to accept these efforts or to reject them. International law guarantees freedom of religion; but intervention by states in religious business overseas is also a matter of law, as well as diplomacy and international relations. Western governments, including those in Europe, do not fund Christian missions to non-Christian (and even Christian) nations. The West extends its legal protection to its citizens as they perform these missions, under the laws of the land, but it does not use public funds to propagate a particular religion. Arab and Islamic governments, while limiting and in some cases banning religious freedom within their own borders, use state funds to propagate their religion inside the West and particularly in Europe. The issue of terror is not specifically tied to these policies, but the channels created by the governments provide a vehicle for the infiltration of radical ideology into Europe. And here is where Jihadism emerges as a phenomenon produced directly or indirectly by these state-sponsored campaigns.

In short, the regimes and mainstream movements want to impact Europe's foreign policy, and gradually increase the number of converts so that they can exercise strategic influence. Perhaps, eventually, the Muslim Brotherhood and Wahabis, and to some extent the Khumeinists, will see an opportunity for a historic shift and a full conversion of the continent. This first current of Jihadism—nonviolent, but not necessarily in line with international law—has aimed at a long-term and gradual demographic shift. But its activities have profited from the second current: al Qaeda.

The hotheaded Jihadists of bin Laden and his cohort began readying themselves for a war against Europe in the 1990s. The Combat Salafists, although aiming at a final Islamization of the continent, and indeed the whole world, got impatient with the slow pace of the Saudi and Muslim Brotherhood program. The heroes of the Afghan Jihad, the victors over the Soviet Union, wanted things to happen faster. But America came first, according to Osama bin Laden; if the United States was defeated, why would the weaker European powers resist them anymore? Besides, in the underworld of militants and oil businesses, it was obvious in the Wahabi circles that gratified the *shabab* (guys) that their shops and social getaways were mostly in Europe. Ironically, many of the preparatory moves for 9/11 were implemented in Europe, in Germany, Spain, and the United Kingdom. And in the Jihadi mind, the European elites were corrupt and profiting immensely from oil revenues and investments. In a sense the continent's bourgeoisie was so steeped in moral and political decay that an emir from the Gulf could dictate instructions to the most powerful of Europe's prime ministers. The EU foreign policy toward the region had become so subservient to the oil regimes that it was called Eurabia by Swiss author Bat Yeor. Indeed, in the decade of the 1990s South Sudan's greatest horrors occurred, Lebanon's heaviest oppression by the Syrians took place, Saddam murdered the Shia and the Kurds, and the Taliban raped the rights of Afghan women. Brussels, meanwhile, kept silent on these tragedies and cut big deals for its petroleum and arms export companies. In such a modern Dark Age, the Jihadists didn't have to strike at Europe, but only to prepare for its fall.

The American reaction to the impetuous 9/11 strike was somewhat unexpected. Instead of retreating and calling its forces home, and rather than responding massively and incoherently, the United States answered strategically. Though the U.S. counterstrikes could have been better prepared and accompanied by more sophisticated political programs, nevertheless al Qaeda lost its stronghold in Afghanistan and the Jihadists witnessed an American offensive striking at the heart of the Middle East. Their priority from then on was to contain and ultimately reverse U.S. interventions in the region. And as we described earlier, the Salafist and Khumeinist strategies were to weaken the resolve inside America on the one hand and isolate the United States from the rest of the West on Iraq and Afghanistan. The ideal projection was to cut off ties between Europe's NATO partners and Washington at the onset of the war. But the overwhelming worldwide support for the Afghan campaign set the stage for the punishment to be inflicted later by al

Qaeda. Bin Laden and his spokespersons began threatening the European allies of the United States; Jihadist websites issued threats against the United Kingdom, the Netherlands, Denmark, Spain, Italy, and many other coalition partners. The escalation grew more violent with the invasion of Iraq: Every European country involved in any of the two battlefields was put on a list, often cited by Ayman Zawahiri. The Iranian regime, in more subtle ways, sent the appropriate messages to the Europeans. If not hit directly by Iranians, their people would be hit by local Jihadists, many of whom had been smuggled by the Syrians into Iraq. In 2004, al Qaeda attacked Spain and got it to leave Iraq. In 2005, it attacked London, but failed to push it out. However, the al Qaeda (and Jihadist) war on Europe signaled to local groups, cells, and individual terrorists, that the hatchet had been dug up: It became a free-for-all. Omar Bakri and the British Islamist leaders, supporters of al Qaeda, declared that the *mu'ahada*, "treaty," with London was over. Zawahiri offered a last truce to Europe as a whole.[10] The Jihadists were trying to bully NATO into abandoning Washington, and in fact during the Iraq campaign France and Germany led the opposition to the war. Some of their leaders thought this would avoid punishment by the terrorists. But soon enough, both Paris and Berlin would witness the rise of local Jihadist activities: In the fall of 2005, France felt the ire of what could become an urban intifada—ten thousand cars were burned, police officers were hit, and entire suburbs slipped beyond the authority of the government. One year later, Germany would discover plot after plot targeting its installations and allied bases. By 2008, a continent-wide Jihad was mushrooming. Whatever the arguments, false or relevant; whether they concerned "offensive cartoons" or the *hijaab* for women, they were a part of a European Jihad ravaging the most prosperous part of the continent. This Jihad marched forward as follows:

1. *Great Britain.* The 7/7 attacks, the foiled plot of the summer of 2006 targeting airliners over the Atlantic, the subsequent arrests of medical doctors in 2007 following the airport conspiracies, and the activation of cells in Birmingham, Manchester, Leeds, Brighton, Edinburgh, and London, show that an army is already in place. British security sources estimate its number at about 1,500 suspects.[11] Experts believe it is much higher and its capacities and intentions more lethal. With the resignation of Tony Blair and the installation of Gordon Brown as prime minister, the naïve hoped the British Jihad would cease. But as Brown was moving to 10 Downing Street, forty-five Jihadi doctors were planning on blowing up British citizens across the country. The United Kingdom is targeted, no matter the number of soldiers it has deployed in the region. The Jihadists want Britain to abandon its foreign policy, not just to redeploy its soldiers. Hence, the projection is that the confrontation between the Jihadist army and Britain will continue.

2. *France.* President Jacques Chirac took his country as far as he could away from U.S. involvement in Iraq and distanced France from the so-called U.S. War on Terror. In a desperate move to satisfy French oil interests and preserve arms exports to the Middle East, the Gaullist leader insisted on resuming *la Politique Arabe de la France* (France's Arab policy) after 9/11. In short, juicy contracts with the Gulf (and previously with Saddam) were more highly valued than was solidarity with the United States and the civil societies of the region. Chirac's extreme stance on avoiding a confrontation with the Pan Arabist and Islamist regimes and militants on terrorism survived as long as he could maintain it, but soon the terrorist forces menaced French interests as well. By 2004, many Salafi attempts to cause security breaches were being stopped by French security. The North African networks weren't gratified by Paris's stance on Iraq. The suburbs were slipping away from state control, and in the summer of that year, Syria and Iran pushed a dear ally and friend of Chirac, Rafik Hariri, out of power, thereby damaging the economic relationship between the two countries. Chirac responded by co-introducing UN Security Council Resolution 1559 with the United States; it asked Syria to withdraw from Lebanon and Hezbollah to disarm. War broke out between the Tehran-Damascus axis and Paris; it was joined by the Salafi Jihadists, who were already mobilized in France. On February 14, 2005, Hariri was assassinated by the Syrians (and their allies) in Beirut. Chirac was furious, and along with Bush (with whom he disagreed on Iraq) threatened Assad with action if he didn't withdraw from Lebanon, which he did in one month. But the proxy war continued in Lebanon with more assassinations. During that fall, the suburban uprising that struck France created a new reality. Tens of thousands of youth, mobilized by radical clerics, formed an urban army. In the view of many French experts, thousands of Salafists are preparing for a confrontation, which may become—if the current administration of President Nicolas Sarkozy doesn't take appropriate strategic steps—the largest and widest in Europe in terms of numbers and geographical extent. France has troops deployed with UNIFIL; its leaders are pressing Iran to halt construction of nuclear weapons; and it is facing an army of Salafists on its own soil. Like Britain, France is a nuclear power and a catastrophic target for potential Jihadi missions.

3. *Benelux.* The Netherlands, Belgium, and Luxembourg as a trio face the same terrorist threat, each in its own national setting. Holland and Belgium have large numbers of Salafi militants and a significant presence of Hezbollah sympathizers. The Jihadists have already engaged Amsterdam in confrontation, and the Dutch authorities have begun their campaign to

contain the various networks of radical Islamists. In the Netherlands, the assassination of film maker Theo Van Gogh, was a watershed event because the attacker didn't target a military leader, a politician, or a media newscaster, but an artist, whose only crime was to have produced a documentary about persecuted Muslim women. The murder showed that the Jihadism in Benelux—and Europe in general—is connected to deeper agendas, bypassing foreign policy. The Jihadist outlook envisions a forceful transformation of Europe's political culture and violent attacks on the fundamental freedoms of secularism in Europe. The Jihadists have shown that they will administer their own form of ideological justice to opponents, as did the National Socialists and Fascists in the 1930s with assassinations and terror.

In Brussels the Islamist pressure groups are very influential. In September 2007 they were able—thanks to their clout with city officials—to stop a demonstration by local activists (though on the right) who were rejecting what they called the Islamization of Europe. Ironically, the Jihadists, the far left, and the Neo-Nazis were able to take to the streets when demonstrating against the West, but not the demonstrators who opposed the agenda of Jihadism. Belgium, as a headquarters of the European Parliament and Commission, has gotten the attention of oil-backed lobby groups, still very powerful in the capital of Europe. Holland and Belgium can expect to be sites for future confrontation between the radical Islamists and their opponents; but at the same time, Benelux has witnessed the development of anti-Jihadist Muslim immigrants, such as Ayaan Hirsi Ali, a member of the Dutch parliament and a critic of the Jihadists who sought refuge in the United States. Other dissidents from Morocco, Algeria, and sub-Saharan Africa are attempting to reach out to the public to warn about the fascist attitudes of the Jihadists.[12]

4. *Germany.* Germany's wrestling with terrorism is decades old. As soon as Nazism was removed after World War II and West Germany established, another type of ideological terror emerged: the Marxist Baader-Meinhof gang and other Communist groups, mostly manipulated by East Germany and the KGB. And when the Berlin wall crumbled, and with it the Bolshevik subversion, yet other terrorist players emerged: the Neo-Nazis on the one hand and the Jihadists on the other. Unified Germany, a member of NATO, is home to millions of Middle Eastern immigrants from Turkey and the Levant. As in the United Kingdom, France, and Benelux, traditional tensions related to social integration exist across the various émigré communities.[13] But the German Jihadists, as elsewhere, aren't interested in fixing the socioeconomic conditions of the neighborhoods, nor are they

frustrated because of these conditions. They have been patiently selected by Islamist cadres operating within the communities, gradually indoctrinated, and selected for action when needed. Self-declared Jihadis follow a parallel path. They are touched by the ideology, indoctrinated through its literature, and eventually seek to ally themselves with the major terror networks.[14] Once in the Jihadi pool, they are drawn to the appropriate organizations, depending on whether they are Salafist or Khumeinist types. Hence Germany is facing off with al Qaeda on the one hand and with Hezbollah on the other.[15] The two networks have a convergent agenda: to strike at German national security. But al Qaeda has it as a standing order, when possible, whereas Hezbollah has it as a measure to use should a confrontation occur with Iran, Syria, or Hezbollah in Lebanon. Over the past few years, Berlin's counterterrorism units have often arrested terrorists claiming to be Jihadis, but the most significant catch—up to the beginning of 2008—was the arrest on September 6, 2007 of a cell preparing for a massive attack on U.S. military installations and air bases.[16] Earlier that year, a Hezbollah supporter was caught plotting to attack trains.[17] The German government now realizes that two armies are active within their homeland and, despite having different outlooks, they share a strategic goal of engaging in confrontation.

5. *Austria and Switzerland.* Across these Alpine nations the Jihadists have attempted to create cells. Despite more restrictions on immigration and citizenship than the rest of Western Europe, the two countries nevertheless aren't immune to terrorists. Austria began to experience the syndrome of violence related to the Israeli-Palestinian conflict in the 1970s. The terrorist Carlos the Jackal attacked OPEC headquarters in Vienna in 1975. In 1979, a social democratic politician was murdered by the Abu Nidal group. In 1985 an attack by the PLO targeted the Vienna airport. In 2007, three third-generation Muslim youths, two males and a female, were arrested before they could undertake Jihadi activities. Another group, the Global Islamist Media Front, operates between Germany and Austria. Austria is bracing for the development of more cells within the country.[18] Switzerland, the unassailable fortress at the roof of Europe, with its restrictive immigration laws and police scrutiny, was projected as the last bastion of resistance to Jihadi penetration. But even Helvetia has been infiltrated, not only by émigrés turned terrorist, but by Swiss citizens converted to Jihadism.[19] Interestingly, according to analysts, the mountainous country has attracted not only militants, but also Islamist intellectuals, who are often influential in Europe. In Austria, the Jihadists have the advantage of a more open system they can use to infiltrate the country, and the prospect

of using the fact that Vienna is a seat of important international organizations, including OPEC and the Atomic Energy Agency. In Switzerland, the Jihadists have a harder time penetrating the system, since it is difficult to obtain Swiss citizenship. The way around it is to convert Swiss-born citizens to Islam in the first stage, then indoctrinate them in a second stage. These native Swiss Jihadists have the advantage of being free to roam the country, penetrate its systems, and rise to sensitive positions. Ultimately, a long-range Jihadi objective in Switzerland is to impact the banking system at some point, creating reverberations across frontiers and using the country for military purchase transactions.[20]

6. *Scandinavia*. The north, although remote geographically, is not insulated from terrorism by distance and weather. Three out of its five countries are already ideologically infected. Over the past five years, Denmark, Norway, and Sweden have shown signs of Jihadist activities, while Finland and Iceland have shown signs of Islamist indoctrination. Norway was mentioned several times by Ayman Zawahiri and other al Qaeda officials as a country on the "target list." Its affiliation with NATO and the presence of its military among the coalition was the stated reason, but the strategic reality is that Norway has its own oil reserves, a dangerous fact for the global Jihadists. An infidel nation not relying on the region's oil is basically free in its action. Such a nation can eventually become a supplier for other infidel powers in case of a heightened confrontation, a new oil boycott, or if the flow of Middle East oil is choked off. Hence, Salafist or Khumeinist war rooms perceive Norway as an enemy reservoir that has to be dealt with. Oslo has been the host city for a number of radical Islamists, including Mullah Krekar, leader of the Ansar al Islam, previously based in Northern Iraq and allied to al Qaeda. Also active in Norway are supporters of Hamas, the Islamic League, involved in fund-raising for the Gaza-based group.[21] Denmark, another NATO member, also appeared on al Qaeda's hit list, mainly for ideological reasons. Traditionally, the Danes have a strong resistance to persecution in their national character, a trait boldly manifested during the Nazi occupation. Along with the Dutch, they were among the few in occupied Europe who stood up to their Germanic kin to protect Jews and other minorities from Nazism. And as in Scandinavia and northern Europe in general, Danish political culture is deeply and humanistically liberal. In the cartoon crisis of 2006, Denmark was targeted by Islamist militant violence across the world. Since then, Copenhagen's crisis with the Jihadists has grown. In long conversations I had during the spring of 2007 with the editor of *Jyllands-Posten*, Flemming Rose, I realized that the Jihadist wave has hit a nerve in Danish society. For regardless of the offensive

character of the cartoons—which could be qualified as being in bad taste—
the issue was perceived by the Danish liberals as a question of freedom of
expression. This is a fault line between liberal democracies and Jihadism
which may widen as radical Islamists and liberals discover each others' limitations.[22] But while Norway and Denmark are active members of the Atlantic alliance and have dispatched military personnel to serve in the War
against Terrorism, their neighbor, the very neutral Sweden, discovered the
reality of not-so-neutral Jihadism only in 2007. After preserving its neutrality throughout the twentieth century, Stockholm entered the fray with al
Qaeda six years after 9/11 when a second cartoon crisis hit. One of its publications, the *Nerikes Allehanda*, published another cartoon deemed offensive to the Islamic faith. Omar al Baghdadi, the al Qaeda commander in
Iraq, said Lars Vilks, the artist who "dared insult the Prophet," should be
killed for a reward of $100,000, and if he was "slaughtered like a lamb," the
killer would receive another $50,000. In addition, he offered a Jihadi finan-
cial reward of $50,000 for the murder of Ulf Johansson, the editor of the
Swedish paper that printed Vilks's cartoon on August 19, 2007.[23] Indica-
tions based on an observation of Jihadi activities within the Nordic kingdom are that violent and militant activities will increase there. Finland has
already been infiltrated by radical Islamist cells and will follow the fate of its
Scandinavian neighbors, leaving Iceland and Greenland as the last to be
reached by the ire of Jihadism.

7. *Southern Europe.* The warmer parts of Western Europe are perhaps the
   most geographically sought after because of Jihadi historical claims.
   Salafist literature and Neo-Wahabi chatter have signaled a future historical
   claim to Sicily and Sardinia (both autonomous regions of Italy) and Malta
   (an independent republic). Libyan bravado in the 1970s (when Qadhafi
   was still leading international Jihadis) and post-9/11 rhetoric by Jihadists
   online assert that all lands once covered by a legitimate authority of the
   caliphate should revert to Islamic sovereignty.[24] Although contested by
   modern scholars of Islam, these visions are validated by powerful mass
   movements to reclaim the caliphate, such as Hizb al Tahrir.[25] This thinking would mean that southern France would also revert to the caliph. The
   greatest reclamation project for the Salafists is Spain—not only Andalusia
   in the sunny south, but the real historical al Andalus, the once Arab-occu-
   pied peninsula that would include today's Spain and Portugal together.
   There is an ideological ground for the Jihadists' appetite for the European
   nations on the Mediterranean. Jihadi networks have already penetrated
   Spain and Italy and are on their way to infiltrating Portugal. Undoubtedly
   the Madrid attacks in March 2004 revealed to the world, and to the Euro-

peans, how determined al Qaeda is to strike Spain. But most important strategically is what happened after the attack: vigorous Spanish antiterrorist judges and services apprehended a number of cells building for new attacks. Hence, the issue wasn't only the Iraq War, as Jihadi apologists were quick to claim; it was really about Spain itself. Literature I reviewed independently and my interviews with former prime minister José María Aznar, his national security adviser, Rafael Bardaji, experts at the think tank FAES,[26] and the European Socialist MP from Portugal, Paulo Casaca, clarified two important matters: One is that al Qaeda and its branches in the Maghreb, beyond the classical terror culture, were and still are on a campaign to bring Jihad and *fatah* to Spain and Portugal, a matter that the rest of the European elite can't perhaps fathom yet. But even though an Islamic reconquest seems like geopolitical nonsense at this time, the effects of the attackers' determination, doctrinal mobilization, and projected violence will be strongly felt. The next generation of al Qaeda will fight for al Andalus, not just some foreign policy. To the east of the Iberian peninsula, the Italians have also come to realize that Salafist North African networks and al Qaeda supporters are already on their soil. A number of plots have been foiled, but, as in Spain, the army is already inside the gates. And if Jihadism expands farther into the Balkans, Italy will receive even more pressure from east and south.[27]

CENTRAL AND EASTERN EUROPE

As noted earlier, during the Cold War, while the Islamists were penetrating most of Western Europe under NATO, sometimes encouraged because they were seen as an ally against Communism, Eastern Europe was shielded by its own authoritarianism. Nevertheless, thousands of students and members of progressive organizations from the Greater Middle East were hosted by the Communist governments in Europe and by the Soviet Union. Not all guests were necessarily secular Arab nationalists, socialists, or Marxist-Leninists. Many were simply seeking education and jobs, but some had been indoctrinated by the Muslim Brotherhood in the Arab world. Most graduates of Eastern Europe returned to their home countries, primarily Egypt, Syria, Iraq, Algeria, Sudan, Southern Yemen, and Libya, but scores stayed back. Among them were those who, faithful to the Islamist ideology, would wait out the Cold War, and thus form the nucleus of the Jihadi presence in Central and Eastern Europe in the 1990s. As the European Union expanded eastward, they linked up with the Jihadi movement in the Western democracies. Traces of Islamist literature and Jihadi propaganda can be detected now throughout the old Soviet Bloc. In the Baltic States, the Jihadi influence is traveling from Scandinavia, along with the general socioeconomic ties between the two regions. Repeating the strategies implemented in Western Europe decades ago, Wahabi and Khumeinist interests are progressing with the help of investments in Central Europe, allegedly tending only to the interests of émigrés in these countries, and invitations to the region's new companies to partner with Gulf and Iranian sister corporations. Qatar, Saudi Arabia, and Iran, among others, are competing to attract the newly freed parts of Europe into a fatal financial association, the tried and true method for facilitating ideological penetration. Hard currency can do miracles in countries that have recently emerged from poverty and deprivation. However, unlike the countries of Western Europe, those in the East are less anti-American. Because of their collective experience under repressive Communism, Eastern European citizens have preserved a resentment of dictators and developed a strong attraction to freedom and the fight to spread democracy. This explains why, during the War on Terror, Eastern European countries have sent troops to Afghanistan and Iraq and, diplomatically, sided unashamedly with the United States during the difficult hours of intra-Western tensions. In 2003 Poland stood up to French president Chirac, who had treated it as one of the small and "inexperienced nations" and asked them not to intervene in Iraq. (Ironically, two years later France realized that it was confronted by a Jihadi army on its own soil. The flames of 10,000 cars finally illuminated its fate in the global confrontation.) Between 1991 and 1993, Estonia stood up to Russia, which had railed against the little country. Eastern Europe, if it is not deeply impacted by Wahabi and Khumeini oil imperialism over the next few years, could become a model for resistance against totalitarianism, ironically assisting its big sisters to the West and East in the War of Ideas.

During my visits to Eastern Europe, I have seen how the younger generation of intellectuals and politicians surpass their colleagues at the European Parliament in their ability to identify the threat of totalitarianism, including Salafism. During my participation in European seminars, one of the highlights came during the Prague international conference on peace and security in June 2007. As a speaker on the United Nations and democratization, I shared panels with former dissidents, human rights activists, and legislators from across Europe and from Russia and the Middle East. Inspired by leaders such as Vaclav Havel of the Czech Republic—whom I had the chance to meet—Lech Walesa of Poland, former Soviet dissident Natan Sharansky, Gary Kasparov, and others, the exiles and speakers from the Greater Middle East testified to the persecution they had suffered under a different form of totalitarianism. Ironically, the Arab and Muslim dissidents were better received in Eastern Europe than in the West, for a simple reason: Those who have lived under oppression can better identify with those who are still suffering from it.[28]

THE BALKAN CONFRONTATION

If most of Europe is dealing with fluid Jihadist movements, the Balkans is a region where the Salafists and Wahabis could push for an actual takeover of governments, in Bosnia, Albania, and Kosovo. The region has experienced bloody wars reflecting unsolved historical conflicts. As one studies the roots of the wars in Bosnia and Kosovo as well as the tensions in Macedonia, one sees that the claims to territory by Serbs, Croatians, Bosnian Muslims (now identifying as Bosniacs), Albanians, and Macedonians are all related to historical events that took place during the Ottoman conquest of the Balkans four centuries ago. As in Iberia, a *fatah* invasion led by the Turkish sultans pushed northward from Anatolia into Slavic and Germanic areas, reaching the walls of Vienna. Historians have thoroughly documented the wars between the Ottoman armies and the indigenous population, which at the time was mostly Christian, both Orthodox and Roman Catholic. Under the Ottoman occupation of more than three hundred years, a shift in religious identity occurred. In several spots Islam became the faith of entire populations, including Slav regions, as in parts of Serbia, and many areas in Albania.

This tangled situation exploded after the fall of Communism in Eastern Europe. With the collapse of Yugoslavia as a federal system, Slovenia and Croatia seceded at once, with Serbian minorities contesting the latter's move and seceding from the Croatian Republic. That opened an armed conflict. Muslim-dominated Bosnia, a multiethnic society with Croats, Serbs, and Muslim Slavs, also seceded, triggering a countersecession by the two other ethnic groups. The early 1990s ethnic conflict devolved into a bloody multidimensional war; European and U.S. troops soon entered to stabilize the region and force a UN-sponsored peace settlement. Toward the end of the decade, a similar scenario was repeated in Kosovo, a province of Serbia inhabited by an ethnic Albanian (Muslim) majority. The Albanian forces fought against the Serbian government and the violence produced masses of refugees, mostly Muslim. A settlement was forced on both sides by NATO, but the question of independence for Kosovo remains open in 2008.

The Yugoslav conflicts opened the way for Jihadi infiltration. In Bosnia, groups of Wahabi fighters with an al Qaeda core participated in combat against the Bosnian Serbs. Since the end of the war, many Jihadists have stayed in the country and can ultimately provide bases in the Balkans for al Qaeda. Sarajevo authorities and U.S. agencies have spotted activities supportive of al Qaeda and Iranian infiltration. Also, after the Kosovo settlement, Islamist groups emerged in the area and began agitating for the establishment of an emirate when independence is achieved. Now, in 2008, the Jihadist presence in the Balkans has developed two main streams, almost mirroring the dual approach across Europe. On the one hand, Middle Eastern oil-producing regimes with an interest in spreading Islamism among Muslims and

Islam in Europe, as a stated policy, are heavily investing in Bosnia, and they are planning to do so in Kosovo. Saudi, Qatari, and Iranian investments are intended to help raise three Islamic states in the region: Albania, Bosnia, and Kosovo. A fourth possible entity is projected in the parts of Macedonia inhabited by ethnic Albanians, where tensions have already begun. At the same time, al Qaeda–type Salafi activities are being undertaken by groups not under the direct control of the oil regimes; so-called Jihadi settlements have spread from Bosnia and Kosovo into Albania and Macedonia. As in other cases worldwide, the Jihadists follow in the ideological wake of the oil regimes. Al Qaeda and its kind do not operate in a vacuum; they follow the madrassas and the Wahabi centers.[29]

In the logic of the Salafi Jihadists, the Balkans will become a staging ground for a future *fatah* in Europe. The Jihadists believe that they will make out of these small emerging Muslim countries "advanced positions" in the West, aiming at Western Europe and Russia simultaneously, just as they perceive the early Arab conquest faced off with Byzantium and Persia. The bin Laden view of the Balkan emirates, if they can be developed, is to repeat the experience of the Taliban in that part of Europe, but in more adaptable ways. Indeed, the local Muslim population in the Balkans is not attracted by the Wahabi model, having lived for decades in somewhat modernized societies. But the European lifestyle of Bosnia's Muslims could change—so the Salafist ideologues hope. The experience of Western Europe is instructive: If the Islamists were able to establish fundamentalist enclaves in ultraliberal Sweden and Holland, surely the experiment can also be tried in Sarajevo. Given the strategic interest of the Jihadists in the Balkans, material support by oil powers, the unachieved peace in the area, ethnic tensions, and Western noncomprehension of the stakes, it is most likely that Jihadism will develop significant resources in the Balkans and drag the area into future violent conflicts.

Neighboring Greece is already seeing its national security slowly changing after decades of fortunate peace. The most imminent concerns stem from the advances the Jihadists have been scoring to the north, in Macedonia and Albania. The Greek community within southern Albania is already signaling the rise of an Islamist presence in the country. While the government in Tirana, despite its instability, remains attached to an alliance with the United States, it is not able to contain the growth of the Salafi ideologies. Another basis for concern in Athens is the penetration by Wahabis of Macedonia, with which Greece has identity tensions. Wahabi activities in southern Bulgaria are creating tensions as well, not to mention the rise of soft Islamism in Turkey. Greeks and Turks, after decades of sour relationships, have managed to coexist and ameliorate their relationship as members of NATO. But the rise of the AKP (the Justice and Development Party) portends a change from the secularist state of Atatürk to a fundamentalist government (which the Turkish military openly opposes as the heritors of Kemalism).

Athens is well aware of the threat this poses. If Turkey goes fully Islamist, a new Ottoman Empire will be formed with Wahabi enclaves omnipresent north of the Hellenic state. Such a dramatic change in Turkey, if the secular Turks lose the cultural and constitutional battle that looms, will also affect Cyprus, the European island-nation closest to the Levant. In this part of the northeastern Mediterranean, the spread of Jihadism could bring about a crisis not only in the region but also in Europe as a whole.

NEW EUROPEAN POLICIES

Like the United States and the rest of the Free World, Europeans must undertake a cultural revolution and implement economic reforms and a diplomatic reconfiguration to handle the crisis of Jihadism. But one has to admit that there are tremendous difficulties awaiting the Europeans in this endeavor—far more than those faced by the United States, Australia, New Zealand, and Canada. First, there are the political and contextual differences between the various regions and subregions of Europe in terms of their perceptions of the Jihadi threat and their abilities to make strategic changes, as well as the political and economic prices to be paid. The first distinction is between the countries that are members of the European Union and those countries not yet members. The unified governments can coordinate and legislate together regarding the rise of militant Islamism through the Parliament and Commission in Brussels and Strasbourg, while the nonmember governments will have to come to national decisions in isolation from the rest. And this applies to stable and economically advanced governments such as Switzerland as well as to countries moving toward stability yet heavily involved in ethnic conflict and Jihadism, for example, Serbia, Bosnia, Macedonia, and Bulgaria.

Another issue is membership in NATO. Defense against the threat will work best if integrated within the Atlantic alliance, but countries such as Sweden, Switzerland, and Serbia lie outside it, and could be targeted for that reason. Within the European Union, the older Western democracies have different attitudes toward the Islamists then the newer countries of Central Europe. The southern countries such as Spain, Portugal, and Italy are the focus of the geopolitical ambitions of the Jihadists, while the north is being targeted more for urban insurgencies than outright political takeover. France's Jihadi demography is extremely serious, more so than any other country's, but French realignment on NATO strategies can reinforce the alliance tremendously.

Another difficulty arises through the various degrees of reliance on oil. Germany and France are very dependent on Middle East petroleum, as are Holland, Belgium, and Italy. Britain imports large quantities of oil, and its companies are intertwined with multinational corporations operating in the Gulf. Other countries have diversified their oil resources from different regions. In sum, there are two economic problems that limit European resistance to Jihadism: the reliance on these resources, and the reliance of the companies on the revenues generated by the gigantic oil contracts and also by defense and construction contracts, running to billions of euros. These financial ties are a major impediment to a change of policy.

In addition, the fact that Europe has multiple homeland security systems, because of national sovereignties, demands negotiation between the various state security agencies over the type of counterterrorism tactics to be pursued. Although the European Union has developed top advisory boards on terrorism, it has no equivalent of the American FBI or CIA, which are capable of operating on a continental scale. The multiplicity of national policies also reflects various readings of the Jihadist threat assessment. French, British, Scandinavian, and East European analysis of the root causes and aims of Salafists and Khumeinists are diverse and sometimes contradictory. Are the Salafists who are infiltrating Western Europe the only threat? While this is true for some countries, other countries host the Muslim Brotherhood and even consider them to be partners. Is Hezbollah part of the threat? European politicians in Brussels have recognized the political dimension of the organization, lending it legitimacy. Are the Wahabis in the Balkans a threat to Europe, or only to the Slav populations? Many differences still exist.

Last but not least, Europe's ability to coordinate with outside superpowers also has to be addressed. The opposition of Germany under Chancellor Gerhard Schroeder and France under President Chirac to the U.S. invasion of Iraq was widely referred to by the Jihadists as legitimating their strikes against the West. Weak European support to Russia as it battles the Wahabis in Chechnya and the Caucasus reverberates into Jihadi escalation against Western Europe. The tragedy of European policy in the War on Terror is that the European Union didn't ally itself critically with its transatlantic partners (perhaps one can now see emerging change on that score), nor did it have a clear strategy of its own. It was managing the counterterrorism efforts instead of confronting the threat as a bloc.

Through my many meetings with European leaders (both intellectual and political) over the past decades, and particularly since 2001, I have come to realize that the issues discussed here amount to a series of strategic impediments to European action and that have prevented the nations from acting as a cohesive unit in the confrontation with the forces of terror. In the 1980s the general feeling in Europe was that Communism posed the greatest menace. After the collapse of the Soviets I thought the European elite would begin reflecting on the rise of Jihadism, particularly with the genocide in Sudan, the Syrian occupation of Lebanon, Iran's suppression of its opposition, Hezbollah's attacks in Argentina, and the ravaging civil war in Algeria. But I found very little interest among my European interlocutors in exploring the ideology behind these massive human rights abuses and terrorist acts. In 1997, the head of the Near East[30] office at the Ministry of Foreign Affairs in Stockholm lectured me on how Hezbollah is a liberation movement, not so different in its operations from a social democratic party! Europe's awakening to Jihadism was hopelessly distant in those lost years.

But immediately after 9/11 (and certainly after 3/11 and 7/7) I noted a change of tone across the continent. The terror issue was finally taken seriously, but its root causes, ideology, and movements weren't fully addressed. In the expert community, there were two schools: the sharp and the naïve. Some security experts and private analysts saw the issues clearly. But in the Brussels bureaucracy, the so-called politically correct lexicon was still in use. Actually, I was told that the European Commission, on the advice of Islamic experts (these included Professor Tareq Ramadan[31] and others), had created a "linguistic lexicon" in which words such as "Islamic terrorism," "Jihad," and "the War on Terror" were banned from use by officials. This is clear evidence that the War of Ideas is still being won by the Islamists on the EU level. In international security bodies, however, awareness is making inroads. For example, in a meeting I conducted at the headquarters of Interpol, I heard excellent analysis regarding Jihadism, but also learned that some officials there considered the Iranian police force—which operates under the intelligence branches of the regime—"helpful in exchanging information." I was wondering in what part of the sentence the Iranians were scoring points for their side? Probably by obtaining information about exiles and opposition individuals whom they could then accuse of every possible crime. But meanwhile dozens of think tanks—as in the United States—have emerged in most European countries and are focusing on the threat. Also, likeminded public figures from different parties have been attempting to educate the public as to the real challenges facing the continent and the world. European legislators and politicians such as Jaime Mayor Oreja in Spain, Paulo Casaca in Portugal, and James Elles in Great Britain do understand the problem. Elles and Mayor Oreja, of the conservative camp, have already engaged in the battle of ideas through a regional think tank and called for reforming European policies against Salafi Jihadism. From the socialist camp, Casaca, the former chair of the European delegation to NATO, has been leading efforts to counter Khumeinist Jihadism.

STRATEGIC SUGGESTIONS FOR EUROPE

European policies against Jihadi terrorism, like American policies, need reform. First and foremost is the need for unity: It is strongly advised that the rising movement among European leaders, politicians, legislators, and intellectuals who understand Jihadism and its ideological menace join in a vast push for reform. The

gathering together of all energies, across boundaries and points of view, is a necessity if Europe is to reverse the lethargy of European politics regarding Jihadi terrorism, radical Islamism, oil imperialism, and the oppression of civil societies in
the Greater Middle East. Across the benches and party aisles, a European movement for the defense of democracy must have a single theme and agenda: confronting Jihadism.

The second step is to engage in a full-fledged educational campaign on a national and continental scale so that all appropriate policies will have consistent
popular support, unaffected by the War of Ideas and the heavy propaganda machine of the Jihadists and Jihadophiles. The defense of democracy must galvanize
legislatures, executives, and the private sector to form political coalitions with full
awareness of the problem, backed by corresponding popular majorities. It is up to
the national governments and the multiple institutions of the European Union to
launch public reeducation programs on the grounds of preventing terrorism and
identifying the enemy. It is my estimate, very like that voiced by Prime Minister
Tony Blair before he stepped down in 2007 and hopefully Nicolas Sarkozy and An-
gela Merkle, that the most difficult part of the European reformation in the War
on Terror will be intra-European, meaning it must take place against the powerful
political and propaganda machinery of the oil, armaments, and media industries,
which are already submissive to the diktat of the Wahabi and Khumeinist international interests. This will be a decisive battle in the European War of Ideas.

Like the United States, Europe needs to pass legislation at the supranational
and national levels that equates Jihadism (as an ideology) with racism, on the
ground that it calls for a forcible sectoral division of existing democratic societies,
and identifies Salafi and Khumeini Jihadism with terrorism on the ground that it
calls for violence against segments of these societies—the non-Muslim *kuffar* and
the Muslim apostates. These new laws would allow the European Union, the national governments, and nongovernmental organizations to counter the ideological penetration by Jihadists of the continent in general, and their infiltration of
Muslim communities in particular. Anti-Jihadism laws can become the basis upon
which executives, bureaucracies, courts, and public education lay bare the fascistic
nature of these doctrines and protect the youth from brainwashing by radical ideologues. A very clear line must separate freedom of thought—including Islamism as
a worldview—from the very specific zone of indoctrination and compulsion that
force Jihadi adherents to become violent. Such a distinction would deny the Jihadists a legal loophole and a means to excuse their violence by claiming it as a free
speech issue.

Once Europe has an alert and mobilized public, appropriate laws, and informed governments, it should be able to wage a counter-Jihadist campaign across
the continent. When the leaders of the European Union are on track in the cam-

paign and the national leaders see the conflict clearly, the resources that Europe can bring to bear are simply monumental. If the capacities of France, Britain, and Germany are combined with all other Western democracies and complemented by those of the East European and Balkan governments, the Jihadists will lose the battle on the continent.

Perhaps one of the most important steps is the establishment of a European agency against terrorism—a counterpart to the U.S. Department of Homeland Security—which at present does not exist. It could revolutionize the fight against the Salafists and the Khumeinists. While national governments should address their ethnically motivated terror crises domestically (as they have in Northern Ireland, the Basque region, Corsica, and so on), the continental European political apparatus also needs to be brought in when it is needed. The struggle against international Jihadism has to be truly trans-European.

A master stroke of the new European policy against Jihadism would be to identify and recognize the anti-Jihadism dissidents and democratic forces within the Arab and Muslim world, starting with those who are in exile on European soil. The European Union and the Council for Europe must extend their support to the fragile and vulnerable Muslim, Arab, and Middle Eastern individuals, groups, and communities that have been targeted by terrorists, radicals, and authoritarian forces in the region and in Europe as well. Aid must be given to these important witnesses, who can better inform the peoples of Europe of the dramatic situation within their communities and in the Greater Middle East. European expertise on the Jihadi threat should also be drawn from the lived experiences of these dissidents.

Strategic alliances will also need adjustment to meet the surging Jihadi threat on the continent and around the world. A European-American alliance is a must, to repair and restore the antitotalitarian alliance that existed during the Cold War. It would meet the new threat and benefit both sides of the Atlantic and would further attract other powers, convincing them that the core of the Free World is set on fighting and winning this battle. It would also dishearten the Jihadists to see that their divide and conquer strategy hasn't worked, and that European anti-Americanism is no longer a lever for weakening opposition to Jihad. At the same time, a European-Russian understanding on resisting terrorism not only is logical but would deny the radicals another card they have always dreamt of playing: A Russian-Western divide on Middle Eastern affairs. The children massacred in Beslan and those citizens killed in London and Madrid were all savagely executed by followers of the same ideology. The response to this terror cannot be dispersed and diluted with political bickering. Europe can play a tremendous role in bridging the gaps between Russia and the United States so that the Free World's determination to combat Jihadist terrorism can't be undone by any power, including the Oil Empire.

Freed from the pressures by the Jihadi lobbies and economic arm twisting by oil regimes and pressures groups, a new European policy in foreign affairs should engage in a revolutionary approach to issues related to international terrorism, the War of Ideas, and human rights. European diplomats and politicians have often claimed they were at the cutting edge of these issues, but in fact the European Union and many of its member states were just the opposite. For too long, Europe ignored the plight of the Southern Sudanese and those in Darfur. Only in 2004 did it begin to change. Since 1976, Europeans, including the French and British, have accepted the idea that the Syrian occupation was beneficial to Lebanon. A quarter of a century later, France, followed by other EU partners, joined with the United States in asking the Assad regime to pull out. And while it was massacring its own population, the Saddam regime benefited from fat contracts with German, French, and other Europeans. Human rights have been abused across the Arab and Muslim world, and minorities, intellectuals, women, and youth have been brutalized while European state officials celebrated the "advanced" European method of addressing abuse in the region. Unfortunately, Brussels' dialogue has been with the oppressors about their relations with Europe, and has not addressed what they were doing to their citizens in their own lands. In short, the entire European policy vis-à-vis the region has to change, and radically. In the last few years, the European agenda has been slightly modified in a positive way by the United Kingdom on some issues (Iraq, Iran, and Sudan) and by France on others (Lebanon, Syria, and Darfur); but a general, concerted overhaul has yet to be performed. Great change must happen if the European revolution is to be successful.[32]

CHAPTER 11

RUSSIA'S WAR ON JIHADISM

IN THE ONGOING CONFRONTATION BETWEEN THE FREE WORLD AND the terrorist forces, observers tend to forget that the second most powerful democracy on earth is Russia. The Federation, successor to the totalitarian USSR, has inherited the USSR's armed forces, most of its enormous landmass, its industrial complex, and the majority of its citizens. Crucially, Russia today is as advanced, in terms of nuclear and military capability, as it was during the Cold War. The immediate question we have to ask is, What is Russia's perception of its own national security? The answer will be important in identifying Moscow's role in the War on Terror. Since the collapse of the Communist state in 1991 and the separation of thirteen of the fourteen republics, what force is the potential strategic foe of the Federation? Does Moscow in fact have an enemy at this time?

Russia is certainly strong militarily. The country of Yeltsin and Putin still has thousands of nuclear warheads, tens of thousands of tanks, hundreds of divisions, an impressive air force, and a large navy. The world is still a dangerous place and nations need to defend themselves from potential threats, large and small. Russian national defense naturally sees the mounting power of China as one reason to arm itself, the advancing influence of NATO as another, the capacity of American interventionism as a third, and, as some economists suggest, the ever-important military export market as yet another. This reasoning could apply also to France and Great Britain, which, unlike India and China, have no immediate geopolitical worries (or so they think). But Russian defense thinking has been affected by the rise of a threat that never existed in the country's modern history, and it has already hit: Jihadism.

Russia has long been involved in military, political, and urban conflicts with Wahabi and Salafist Jihadists. From Afghanistan to Chechnya, mujahideen and Russian soldiers faced off in tough battles. As Hezbollah was blowing up the U.S. Marine barracks in Beirut in 1983, the Jihad-inspired insurgents were blowing up Soviet tanks in Kandahar. And while Jihadists were shooting down a Blackhawk helicopter in Mogadishu in 1993, blowing up U.S. embassies in 1998, and hitting the USS *Cole* in 2000, Russian Mil Mi–24 Hind helicopters were being shot down in Grozny and soldiers were being beheaded in Chechnya. And after thousands of civilians were massacred in Manhattan, hundreds of Russian adults and children were killed in a theater and a school in post-9/11 Russia. Both America and Russia are targeted by forces claiming the same ideology. Al Qaeda has endorsed the terror attacks on both countries and put both on notice that they are on Jihad's international hit list; the two former foes are combined in the Jihadi standard of "death to the infidels."[1]

In the post–Cold War era, one might have expected that Washington and Moscow (and perhaps the European Union as well) would have initiated a rapid entente against terrorism in general and the Jihadi menace in particular. However, no Russian-American or Russian-Western cooperation against the web of Jihadism has materialized. Just the opposite: Western democracies often criticized "Russian brutality" in Chechnya—indeed it often was brutal—but Americans and Europeans looked away from Jihadi brutality there. Few in the West noted the advances of Wahabism in the Caucasus and in Chechnya. After the 9/11 attacks on America, the Russians firmly condemned al Qaeda—but again, that didn't open the way to meaningful cooperation with the United States. The enigma grew as both countries clashed with the Salafi Jihadists around the world and in their homelands. America was hit by al Qaeda in New York and Washington, bringing an American response in the Middle East. Russia was struck in Moscow and Beslan, triggering a Russian commitment to fight the Jihadists everywhere. The Chechen Wahabis have declared war not only on Russia but also on the Americans and their allies as well.[2] The two powers have been engaging the same foe everywhere but lack a common vision. Moscow opposed the war in Iraq and provided support to the Iranian and Syrian regimes, despite the terrorist acts the latter endorsed in Iraq, Lebanon, and Palestine. Hence, determining Russia's place in the war with Jihadism is key. Does a Russian war on Jihadism exist, is it strategic, is it selective, and has it been impacted by a War of Ideas in such a way that a wedge separates Moscow from Washington in their respective efforts against a common enemy? In order to answer these questions, one has first to review the Jihadi perception of Russia. How do the various Islamist regimes and movements see Russia, and what are the strategies they developed for use against Moscow, both under the defunct Soviet Union and the new Russian democratic state? Only with answers to these questions can one envision the possibilities for a change in perception in Russia and the United States that could lead to a repositioning of the giant Slavic nation to the center of the collective confrontation with world terrorism.

JIHADI HISTORICAL PERCEPTION OF RUSSIA

In their fundamental teachings, the radical Islamists view Russia as a *kuffar* nation, an infidel entity that they describe as "at war with Islam." The global Salafists base this view on their division of the world into two zones, the *dar el Islam* (house of Islam) and the *dar el harb* (house of war): Russia, from Saint Petersburg to Vladivostok, falls into the second category. The Jihadists condemn Russia on historical grounds as well. In their vision of the world—a perception not necessarily shared by all Muslim politicians and intellectuals—the Russian tsars from the fifteenth century on wanted to inherit the Byzantine Empire, and as Constantinople fell into the hands of the advancing Ottoman *fatah*, the Christian Orthodox power moved forward to fill the vacuum in the Balkans and around the Black Sea. In short, the deeply rooted Jihadi vision of Russia claims that Saint Petersburg's imperial regime and later the Russian Empire contested the caliphate's "opening" of the vast lands of Ukraine and the Caucasus. And that alone is an act of enmity, in their eyes; just as the Iberian and Frankish forces met the advancing Arab Muslim armies in their territories, the Russians are accused of the same "sin": resisting a "caliphatic" mission. In that sense, in the eyes of modern Wahabis and the Muslim Brotherhood, the Russians, even before their expansion southward and east, were guilty of resistance to the initial conquests. In the following centuries, the tsar's armies marched toward the central Asian plains and pushed their borders farther south and east, incorporating large areas previously conquered by the Umayyad and Abbasid Dynasties (and also dominated a number of khanates that had converted to Islam under the Mongols).[3] Contemporary Salafist ideologues interpret these expansions into Asia as an invasion of Muslim lands, even though the same lands had been invaded a few centuries before by Arab armies moving east. Furthermore, they portray the pushing back of the occupying Ottoman armies in the Caucasus toward Asia Minor in the eighteenth century as a colonialist drive against the caliphate. Hence, with their dream of rebuilding the world Islamic state, they see it as the duty of the Jihadists to "liberate" these lands (like the Iberian Peninsula, Sicily, etc.) and restore them to the caliphate.[4]

Thus, the Salafist reading of Russian expansion (in the pre-Soviet Empire and in the contemporary Russian state) is that the expansion was illegitimate and it should be reversed. In short, the Jihadists of today wish to dismember Russia and reduce it to a country bordered by the Baltic states and the Ural Mountains. Until the Bolshevik Revolution of October 1917, such a reduction of Russian territory was supposed to have been the responsibility of the Ottoman Sultanate, then in charge of Islamic world affairs. But the outcome of World War I was catastrophic for Jihadists; bin Laden and his spokespersons have often stated that the "humiliation that struck the Muslim world is eighty years old."[5] He means that with the collapse of the caliphate in the early 1920s, the various geopolitical Jihadist duties—including pushing the Russians northward—were suspended. Hence, in the mind of the emerging post-Ottoman Islamist movements, including the Wahabis and Muslim Brotherhood, the duty of taking back territories from the Russian state and reattaching them to a new caliphate is incumbent on a reinvigorated and revived global Jihad. The Jihadi attitude toward Russia contains therefore not just its original ideological component—fighting the *kuffar* wherever and whenever possible—but also some very tangible strategic objectives: reach out within the Russian territories and support separatist movements in the provinces inhabited by a Muslim ethnic majority.

"Noble" this may seem, but the Jihadis are far from granting every ethnic minority or nationality its right to self-determination. The Salafi-Wahabi agenda focuses only on the Muslim causes for separation, as in Dagestan, Chechnya, Azerbaijan, Turkmenistan, Tajikistan, Kazakhstan, Kyrgyzstan, the lands of the Tatars and other Muslim minorities within Russia, and not Armenia, Georgia, Ukraine, Moldova, and so on. This selectiveness reveals a wider agenda; in the final analysis, the Islamists want separatism only as a prelude to another reunification, meaning that they seek to dismember Russia so that they can use the separated entities to reconstitute the caliphate. This is not self-determination, of course. This historical logic was applied immediately after the collapse of the Ottoman Empire, but the Wahabi power and the Muslim Brotherhood of the time were too weak before the 1930s to confront the iron fist of Stalin's regime. The Communists suppressed all religious manifestations, including the Muslim tradition, inside the Soviet Union.

When Nazi Germany invaded Russia in 1941, Hitler had already forged alliances with Arab Islamic leaders in Iraq, such as Abdel Hamid Kilani, with Muslim Brotherhood cadres in Egypt, and, most importantly, with Mufti Ali Haj Husseini of Palestine. The latter sought an axis with Berlin to defeat Britain and Free France.[6] But when the panzers rolled into Ukraine, a whole new perspective opened up: a defeat of the Soviet Union by the Nazis would open the path to dismembering Russia and separating the Muslim regions. The bet was strategic, but the allies won the war and the project collapsed. However, the post–World War II phase was viewed by the Wahabis and the other fundamentalists as opening up new possibilities.

ANTI-SOVIET JIHAD

The Cold War was viewed by the Salafists as a huge opportunity to weaken the world *kuffar* powers, particularly the Soviet Union. Once the United States and its NATO allies mobilized against the Warsaw Pact, Wahabi circles and the Muslim Brotherhood joined the fray against the Communists, but they meant to do so only until the Soviets were defeated. Hence the Salafist war against Russia inscribed itself within the wider anti-Soviet alliance; Jihadists hoped the West and the Islamists together would bring down the USSR—after which a long-term oil-backed effort by the fundamentalists would take care of the West, too.

The years of the Cold War were spent on two major tracks: One was to penetrate as many Arab and Muslim countries as possible under the label of Islamist efforts against Communism—and so with implicit Western approval—and the second was to prepare for the seizure of as many pieces of the Soviet Union as possible after it fell. The confrontation between the global Islamist web and the Communist bloc raged across two continents: Asia and Africa. The Wahabis since the 1950s, followed by the Khumeinists after 1979, had faced off with the Marxist-Leninists and also with their Arab and Muslim allies, such as the left-wing Arab nationalists (Nasser of Egypt, Nimeiri of Sudan, and the Baath parties of Syria and Iraq). And beyond the Middle East per se, Wahabi and Deobandi[7] influence clashed with the "atheist" enemy along the borders of the Soviet Union. The Iranian Shia fundamentalists crushed the Tudeh Communist Party in a few years, preempting any domestic alliance with the Soviets, while militants backed by the Saudis and Pakistanis fought the Afghan Marxists for control of the country. And it was precisely in that central Asian plateau that the decisive battle between Sunni Islamists and Soviets took place; this explains why Wahabi and Muslim Brotherhood offshoots headed to the great "battlefield of Jihad" backed by the Gulf states and the Pakistani intelligence service.

In 1979, two major events inflamed the Jihadis. In Iran, the Shia Islamists seized power under Khumeini, and next door the Soviets invaded Afghanistan. The Sunni Islamists rushed to fight the invading Russians, an ideal context for their Jihad. Indeed, this was the opening they needed to engage the Soviets with the backing of the Free World. The mujahideen were the Afghan Islamic fighters, but in their midst foreign Jihadists planted the seed of a new generation of transnational Salafists. The Afghan Jihad opened the path for the rise of the Taliban, who were backed by the Saudis and Pakistanis. But it was through that door that those who would become al Qaeda later encountered the Russian forces on the ground for the first time since the collapse of the Ottoman Empire. The international Jihadists, among them Osama bin Laden, Abdallah Azzam, and fighters coming from around the world, including the Soviet Union itself, formed the beachhead for the anti-Soviet push. In 1989, the Soviets withdrew from the country as their regime was about to collapse. The Soviet defeat in Afghanistan, followed by the crumbling of the USSR, was transformed into a divine victory by the Salafist ideologues: It was the relentless sacrifices of the mujahideen and Allah's intervention that did away with the great infidel enemy, they concluded. But from that moment on, the Jihadists were bent on defeating the successor of the Soviets, the Russian Federation.

ANTI-RUSSIAN "JIHAD"

With the dissolution of the Soviet Union, the fourteen republics recognized by the Soviet Constitution became fully independent states and joined the United Nations as sovereign countries. While the Baltic states refused any alliance with

Moscow as they moved toward the European Union, most former republics, including the Muslim ones, remained part of the Russia-centered Commonwealth of Independent States (CIS). The Wahabi-Salafi position was that the five Muslim republics of Central Asia (and Azerbaijan) should quit the CIS and gradually join the core of Islamic countries. The new Muslim republics, still mostly ruled by secular elites, naturally joined the Organization of Muslim States but remained distant from the radical Islamist attitude. But the Jihadist movements, already emboldened by their victory in Afghanistan and celebrating the rise of the Taliban in 1996, began infiltrating the republics and planting the seeds of Algeria-like scenarios. The Russians came south to help their associates in Central Asia, while the fundamentalists moved north from Asia and the Middle East to incite their brothers in arms in Tajikistan, Kyrgyzstan, Turkmenistan, and even Kazakhstan to rise against the "former Communist elites," as they termed Muslim leaders not abiding by Salafism. But the Taliban's blockage in northern Afghanistan by the Northern Alliance of Ahmad Massoud Shah impeded a massive influx of support across the borders. And while the central Asian Jihad started to catch fire in various areas, the removal of the Taliban from Kabul and the forcing of al Qaeda's leaders to retreat to Waziristan (inside Pakistan) weakened the Jihadi thrust into Central Asia—but only for a time. The international Jihadists opened another front against the Russians: Chechnya.[8]

As in other, similar conflicts in the Balkans, Cyprus, and Kashmir, the Chechen crisis was originally about ethno-territorial separatism. A Chechen nationalist movement demanded independence from Moscow after the disbanding of the USSR. A confrontation ensued as a result of Russian refusal to further dismember the Federation and the Chechen rebels' rejection of any degree of autonomy short of complete secession. And as in any other comparable crisis, the Chechens were divided on their own agenda while the Russian parties were advancing different solutions. Enter the Wahabis: Penetrating the separatists, the Salafi Islamists transformed the ethnic cause into a Jihad. Chechnya had to quit Russia so that it could join a future caliphate, they claimed. With this ideological dimension added to the conflict, terrorism became one of the tools used by insurgents. Far from the battlefields around Grozny and the surrounding mountains, suicide bombers and terrorist groups struck in Moscow and remote Russian lands.

The Jihadi war against Russia reached very violent levels in the 1990s, and after 2001 especially. On October 23, 2002, about forty armed Chechen Special Purpose Islamic Regiment (SPIR) militants who claimed allegiance to the separatist movement in Chechnya seized a crowded Moscow theater. They took 850 hostages and demanded the withdrawal of Russian forces from the province. The crisis ended in a massacre. Then, on September 1, 2004, Wahabi terrorists took more than 1,200 schoolchildren and adults hostages at School Number One in the town of Beslan, North Ossetia–Alania. On the third day of the standoff, 334 civilians were killed, including 186 children.[9] Jihadist leader Shamil Basayev took responsibility for the hostage-taking.[10]

As of 2008, the Jihadist campaign has not abated. In multiple videotapes, Osama bin Laden and Ayman Zawahiri described Russia as a major infidel enemy and called for the support of their "brothers" in Chechnya. And to underline the Pan-Islamist dimension of the cause, it should be noted that Chechen militants are often found, killed, or apprehended on battlefields as far away as Waziristan, Afghanistan, Kashmir, and Iraq, and they are active in the Salafist networks worldwide. In return, Arab and Asian Jihadists have fought on Russian soil for the sake of the Chechen Jihad. Abu Abdul Rahman al Hattab, a prominent terror figure well known on Islamist websites, headed the Arab legion in the Chechen war until he was killed by the Russians. The goals of the international Jihadists from al Qaeda and its allies in the Caucasus are to reignite the war in Chechnya, enflame similar intifadas in Dagestan and other provinces inside the Russian Federation, strike deep inside the country and its cities, and link up with the Jihadi pockets in central Asia. This agenda, second to the Middle East, is the largest Jihadi war plan in terms of land area involved; such a war could stretch for another twenty years, or a whole generation, if the global conflict with Jihadism is not ended soon.[11]

POST-RUSSIAN VISION

The Jihadist vision of a post-Russian phase has been sometimes debated in chat rooms and online. I have had the opportunity to take part in live discussion of the question with Islamists both before and after 9/11. Their long-term objective is to bring down the governments of the five Central Asian republics and erect emirates in their place (à la the Taliban), before merging them into a regional Central Asian *wilaya*. The latter would subsequently include a re-Talibanized Afghanistan and more land in Siberia. Additionally, a Jihadi war with China is supposed to detach the whole province of Sin Kiang from the Northeast and attach it to the *wilaya* as well. Chechnya, Dagestan, and other Muslim districts south of Moscow and north of Azerbaijan would form another *wilaya* of the Qafqaz (governorate of the Caucasus). These two large federations of emirates would eventually adhere to the caliphate, to be installed worldwide.

But the Jihadists have other strategies to achieve their aims against Russia. The most pressing would be to seize the nuclear weapons and military equipment found on the soil of the former Soviet republics. Islamists could obtain additional nukes and other weapons of mass destruction on top of those in Pakistan, which they see as destined to fall into Jihadi hands at some point. Another choice target eyed by the Salafists is the former Soviet aerospace program, currently Russian and based inside Kazakhstan, in Baikonur. In many cyberchats about the future world caliphate, the moderators—ideological commissars—often promise that the Jihadists will catch up with the West militarily and technologically. By acquiring Pakistani and former Russian strategic weapons, and by sending Jihadi cosmonauts into orbit, America and its allies wouldn't be able to hide anymore, they fantasize.

RUSSIA'S "AXIS" POLICIES

Post-Soviet policymakers have responded to the Jihadist threat with the expected counterterrorism measures, both in Chechnya and in Central Asia. The harshness of ethnic conflicts is borne out in the Russian-Islamist confrontation. Since the Russian democratic revolution of 1991, both the Yeltsin and Putin governments have committed to a fierce fight with terror and followed up with action. In the 1990s, the Russian counterterrorism efforts relentlessly pursued the terrorist forces across the country. After 9/11, President Putin was the first world leader to openly name the caliphate as the ultimate objective of the Jihadists. But while the Russian resistance to the Salafist menace was clear-cut, its policy toward the other tree of Jihadism was disappointing. Indeed, and despite the vanishing of the Soviet Union and the rise of a new Russian Federation seeking pluralism and democracy, the Russian diplomatic ties to authoritarian regimes such as Iran's and Syria's contradicted its tough antiterrorist actions. Throughout the 1990s, Moscow maintained military and other ties to Syria, despite its occupation of Lebanon; to Iran, despite its support of terrorism; and to Saddam's regime, against the UN sanctions. These policies were a relic of the Soviet era and were totally at variance with Moscow's counter-Jihadi stances elsewhere. The fight against the Jihadists in Chechnya and Central Asia looked incongruous, with Russian diplomats shuttling to Tehran, Baghdad, and Damascus. These three regimes were, combined, the most oppressive bloc in the world.[12]

The enigma of this Russian anomaly has been explained from two angles. One has to do with axis games: Iran's Islamism is Shia, while al Qaeda's Islamism is Sunni. Playing one against the other seemed to be a strategic choice—but Tehran was supporting Hamas and Islamic Jihad, both of them Sunni Salafi, and is connected to the Jihadi international web, including al Qaeda. A second explanation had to do with cash: The Kremlin needed to market its industrial products, including its weapons, in a very competitive area and wanted to gain hard currency. But this enterprise could come at the expense of Russian national security. Enabling and arming one tree of Jihadism could get out of control, as we see in Iranian and Syrian support for Hezbollah, other Jihadists, and Hamas. The Islamist underworld could erupt in Moscow's public places or in the embattled enclaves. Yet another explanation of Russia's contradictory behavior is diplomatic competition with the United States, an unnecessary sequel of the Cold War. Logically, relations between Moscow and Washington should be like those between France and America, with ups and downs, but both parties still members of the Free World with common interests and concern for the remaining threats to civilization.

A RUSSIAN POLICY REVOLUTION

Russia's young democracy but old statehood has to undergo, like the United States and Europe, a further democratic revolution. Russia has moved from the obsolete Soviet system to a modern, pluralistic, and progressive Federation. Throughout the twentieth century, the Russians endured extreme oppression by totalitarian rule and survived two devastating wars that destroyed its cities and its economy. Its citizens have suffered through Nazi occupation and Stalinist purges and terror; tens of millions perished in horrific conditions. While the United States has fortunately not been invaded by a totalitarian power destroying its cities, Russia went through this ordeal during World War II. And while Western European democracies survived the Cold War, the peoples of the Soviet Union weren't spared by their Communist rulers, and Russians paid a dear price, particularly under Josef Stalin. These historic realities should be the background for the new political leaders of the country to devise post–Cold War policies and revolutionize their participation in international relations. In short, a nation such as Russia should be at the forefront of the War on Terror, for the Russians more then Western Europeans and North Americans combined have felt the ire of terror, dictatorship, and genocide for almost a century, and thus their decision makers should be among the most opposed to similar regimes in other regions of the world.

But instead, since the mid-1990s, Moscow has resumed many of the alliances established by the old Soviet regime—not only with Syria, Iraq, and Sudan, but even with Iran, a state implicated in domestic oppression and foreign support for terrorism. These alliances simply go against the nature of a newly emerging, large democracy like Russia. Supplying the authoritarian Assad regime with advanced weapons is in fact enabling the Syrian intelligence forces to resume assassinations in neighboring Lebanon while oppressing its own population. Wasn't it in a show against similar Communist and KGB behavior that Boris Yeltsin climbed onto that tank in August 1991? Equipping the Sudanese regime with Ilyushin bombers to devastate the black villages in the south and in Darfur doesn't accord well with Russia's historical rejection of the Stalinist massacres. And last but not least, supporting the mullahs' regime in Tehran doesn't accord with an evolving democracy that empowers Russia's men and women. Something is utterly wrong in the mismatch between the new pluralist Russian culture and foreign policy decisions that favor oppressive regimes in the Greater Middle East. More important, pragmatically, is the dangerous results these policies could have on Russia's national security and its civil society. Backing Iran and Syria means supporting Hezbollah, Hamas, and Islamic Jihad, three renowned terror groups. By backing the latter, Moscow would be allowing them to channel support to the Jihadist web around the world, including to those who have killed Russian adults and children in the last few years. Any support Russia gives to totalitarian and Jihadi forces in the region will backfire and harm its own people. Hence, whatever the calculations in Russian foreign policy circles, these policies are lethal and self-defeating and should be changed.

NEW RUSSIAN POLICIES

Just as there must be changes in the West, so must the East—Russia and India—also change, rearticulating their role in the War on Terror. And, as should be the case for Western liberal democracies, including the United States, a redefinition of the conflict, an identification of the foe, and a subsequent redrawing of strategies and alliances must follow.

First, Russia's legislature, followed by its executive, should debate and define the conflict. President Putin has stated that the enemy wants to force the establishment of a caliphate by terror. A Russian debate can develop from there, and should agree on the definition of the clash between Jihadi forces and democracies. Russian policy could then accommodate international tensions, including those with other democracies, over many issues—including security—but still maintain the national focus on containing, reversing, and defeating terrorism. This stage should lead to the next: identifying the main forces, such as militant Jihadi regimes and organizations, that menace international law and institutions and obstruct the democratic evolution of many civil societies. Short of this identification, Moscow will be confronting a terrorist power that has the advantage of being strategically invisible, and, what is worse, an ability to actually gain favors from Russia, as has the Syrian-Iranian axis and their Jihadist emanations. In short, a new Russian policy must continue to focus on al Qaeda and the other Wahabi and Salafist groups, but also radically change its approach to the Iranian and Syrian regimes and their offshoots by cutting off their supply of arms and diplomatic support. It may take another generation of younger and better informed politicians in Russia to absorb the dangers of the contradiction of fighting one wing of terror while backing another. Ultimately—through reason and not as a result of greater tragedies unfolding—that change will happen.

As with Western democracies, the new Russian policy will also have to rework alliances. A U.S.-Russian entente—if not an outright alliance—is the core of a global shift to win the War on Terror. While the Russian elites may want to reposition their country and power as another pole in international relations—a legitimate goal—reconfiguring their antiterrorist strategy should unite them first with Washington and second with the rest of the Free World in opposition to Jihadism. As we have seen, the Islamist war planners want to take down their enemies one by one, the ancient divide-and-conquer strategy. The Wahabis wish to create an emirate in Chechnya—and have the West clash with Russia over that same objective. And the Iranian regime wants to obtain Russian weapons to use them against the West, but ultimately also against Russians. In the end, the room for strategic maneuvering by the international Jihadists is narrow, and Russia's swift convergence with the West on an antiterror campaign would upset this maneuver.

Reshaping the alliances won't be an easy task in view of past outcomes and current tensions. NATO members, especially the former Eastern European and Baltic states, feel (at least psychologically) threatened by their Russian neighbor almost as much as by the terrorists. And the Russian military sees the advance of NATO to their European border as menacing. In addition, tensions related to the Balkans are still high as the West has—from the Russian point of view—stood by two Muslim entities that can generate Wahabism in the region. The West in turn resents Moscow's backing of the Syrian-Iranian axis and, by extension, Hezbollah. Thus, what is crucially needed is a Western-Russian dialogue, and eventually a historic entente on the common foe, the Jihadi terror forces. That would bring the overwhelming majority of the Free World under one global strategic umbrella. Based on this anti-Jihadist alliance (which would also include Muslim and Arab countries and civil societies), the equation would turn dramatically against the terrorist forces. Practically, the West and Russia should bring in Bosniacs and the Kosovars to work with the Serbs against a common enemy, terrorism. And in Chechnya, Russia should commit to a far greater autonomy and respect for human rights, a moderation that would allow the alliance to undermine and even cut off the Wahabi influence from that province and the whole Caucasus.[13]

NEW MIDDLE EAST POLICIES

In the Middle East, the Western-Russian alliance could oppose Tehran's drive to acquire nuclear weapons; support the democratization of Iran, Syria, and Palestine; and protect Lebanon from terrorism. Russian backing of Central Asian containment of Salafism is essential, and, along with American cooperation, it would make containment of Jihadism a possibility in this generation. Russian cooperation with the West could turn the tide in many other battlefields as well. In South Asia, a Russian-American joint diplomatic effort could convince India and Pakistan to limit their nuclear arsenals, and so lessen the risk of conflict between them or of seizure of the weapons by the terrorists. In Iraq, a Russian military participation—even symbolically, and under a UN banner—could have an important effect. The mere presence of Russians next to American deployments would by itself have a greater deterrence to the radicals. Moreover, a Russian abandonment of the Syrian regime would hasten change and lead to a crumbling of the war party in that country, with resultant wide-ranging beneficial effects on the region. Moscow's diplomats could be very helpful in consolidating a Palestinian-Israeli peace and isolating Hamas and its allies. Furthermore, Russian personnel and diplomats in blue helmets could help pacify Lebanon. The Russians could also have an impact on Sudan, if Russian units were to join a UN force (if one is ever deployed), and on Somalia, through backing of the Somali moderate government against the Mahakem Islamiya.[14] The image of U.S.-Russian cooperation against the world threat could be the basis of future stability and international security in the twenty-first century.

A JOINT ANTITERRORIST DEFENSE

President Putin's government opposed the deployment of antimissile defenses by the United States in Eastern Europe during 2007 and 2008 on the ground that it threatened Russia strategically. That argument is Cold War reasoning. It assumes that NATO is still Russia's foe. But since 1991, the East-West strategic confrontation is over, and, instead, the West and the East are confronted by the Jihadi powers. The Bush administration and U.S. allies in Eastern Europe told Moscow that the defense system was aimed at potential Iranian and other Jihadi missiles launched from the Middle East toward Europe. Russia should consider any shield deployed in Europe as a defense structure covering the Russian populations as well, for the Jihadists have it in mind to strike Russian, as well as Western European, cities when and if they have capacity to do so. Barbaric terrorist attacks on Russian populations throughout the 1990s and until the present have demonstrated this intention. Hence, Russia and NATO, instead of becoming mired in obsolete Cold War bickering, should move quickly to deploy antimissile shields, not only across Europe but also throughout Russia and the Caucasus. Better, a joint missile defense—with radar and antimissile batteries—maintained by Russia and NATO is the most appropriate response to the Jihadist threat. In fact, a global joint antiterrorism defense would be a major shift in world resistance to terrorism in general and to Salafi (al Qaeda and others) and Khumeinist Jihadism especially. The effects of a common NATO-Russia defense would be enormous, as would be the combined resources.

Russian and NATO units, under a higher command (and ultimately joined by other democracies), would be deployed when needed in the Middle East, in Iraq, Central Asia, the Caucasus, the Balkans, and even in Africa. Both navies would coordinate the containment of the Jihadi forces and cells internationally. The cooperation would also cover surveillance, space activities, and special operations. Such an era would see the beginning of the end of Jihadists' astute manipulations designed to drive a wedge between the two blocs. The emergence of the Russian-Western alliance would also encourage Arab and Muslim governments to align with the international coalition because it would provide a feeling of true security and remove the sense of being squeezed by a lingering post–Cold War competition. Last but not least, with a landmass including North America, Europe, and much of Asia, the new antiterror global alliance would convince rogue powers such as North Korea that the game is strategically over. The most recent developments have shown that Pyongyang's best containment occurs when all its neighbors and the United States and Japan come together to contain its regime's extremism. And as the world community progresses toward security, relations with a developing China would be grounded in reassurances that all nuclear powers are in agreement that the planet cannot afford "nuclear Jihadists."[15]

THE PRICE OF CHANGE

From a realist perspective, the next question would be: What is the price for such a massive change in Russian policy? I argue first that such a global reconfiguration of Western-Russian strategies against Jihadism is not a matter of choice; there is no serious alternative. Only in this way can the international community gain time, maximize efforts and resources, and reduce sacrifices and losses. In the real world of Western and Russian societies, the popular culture, youth trends, and psychological aspirations are heading in the same directions. From Saint Petersburg to New York, a global humanist culture is emerging, and it has to do with lifestyle (rock and roll, jobs, dating, debating, personal freedoms) and with politics (environment, laws, values). In the general view, freer is better. The trend extends to Japan, Latin America, India, and emerging democracies everywhere. The governments managing these societies must realize that future generations will ultimately see the world in a similar way, while yet keeping their specific local and national traditions alive. What threatens this future oneness is the ideological totalitarians, whatever their backgrounds, but most particularly the Jihadi terrorist forces. A rereading of bin Laden's and Khumeini's speeches is a chilling reminder of this gruesome reality. Thus, Russia's merging of its resources with the Western alliance to protect the future of its youth is not even a matter of choice—it is a must. If this generation of leaders (who lived through the Cold War) can't move in that direction, the next one will have to, and without hesitation. And the price of making such a move too late ought seriously to be considered.

If in the next few years Russia's policies aren't changed, urban warfare, terrorism, and Jihadism are going to devastate the Russian homeland, with Chechnya as a mere prelude. The recent rise of Jihadi terror activities in neighboring Dagestan is a clear indication of what is to come.[16]

If Moscow doesn't let go of its commitment to the current Iranian, Syrian, and Sudanese regimes, the boomerang effect of that misguided support will hit Russia and also harm Europe significantly. For Europeans and Russians are in the crosshairs of future Jihads, more urban and lethal than ever. The United States and its Western European allies must also reassess their policies toward Russia as the War on Terror is evolving; they, too, must free themselves from Cold War mistrust and open their arms to the tens of millions of Russian survivors of Bolshevism. Washington and Brussels should direct NATO to engage in a historic dialogue with Russia on a variety of issues, including the Balkans, missile defense systems, economic issues, the Caucasus, the Middle East, and Central Asia. To put it bluntly, the West cannot cover all these territories and meet all these challenges alone. It needs all the allies it can muster. Russia is perhaps the crucial ally. Think only of the oil agreements the West and Russia could reach, and how that would change the current equation to the disadvantage of the petro-Jihadists. Russian oil fields can play a substantial role in supplying the democratic industrialized bloc.

In the final analysis, Russia has a crucial role to play in defeating the emerging terror threats, and the West needs to understand this. There would be grave dangers for Russia's future if such a global reconfiguration is not accomplished in less than a decade; Moscow needs to absorb this. The West and Russia will share the same fate, and they need to work together accordingly. One could ask why, if the United States and Russia, though basically enemies, were able to cooperate to defeat the Nazi threat, they can't cooperate to defeat Jihadism at this moment in history, when there is no longer an ideological gulf or fundamental distrust.

CHAPTER 12

CONFRONTATIONS IN THE GREATER MIDDLE EAST

THE CURRENT WORLD CONFRONTATION THAT HAS BEEN DISCUSSED IN this book originates in the region of the Greater Middle East; stretching from the Atlantic shores of Morocco to the Afghan borders with China, it is so dense in ideological challenges and so critical to the future of the world that I have termed it "Middle Earth," after the famous imaginary world of J. R. R. Tolkien's *Lord of the Rings* series. It is where the first and final scores are being settled and where the War with Terror will be won or lost.

Middle Earth has been the locus of historic battles between empires and great powers, rulers and insurrections, shifting majorities and minorities for millennia. While commentators often credit this region for having been the birthplace of the three monotheistic religions, Judaism, Christianity, and Islam, the most violent religious wars have sprung from here as well, producing seemingly endless conflicts. But whatever the philosophical debate about its past and future, it remains a fact that today's War on Terror is happening mostly in this region, and that the passions generated by the ideologues inspiring these struggles play out here.

Is there a link between the terrorist attacks on the United States, Europe, Russia, India, and Africa, and the enflamed battlefields of the Greater Middle East? Obviously, yes. The Jihadis not only often come from Middle Eastern countries, but are guided by ideologies sprung from and seeking radical transformations in the Arab and Muslim world. This is an inescapable reality. The earth-shattering events since 2001 in Afghanistan, Iraq, Lebanon, Gaza, and Sudan, as well as the escalating crisis with Iran, are the regional manifestations of the rise of Jihadism and expansion of the totalitarian elites in the region. The U.S. Marines battling al Qaeda in Fallujah; American and NATO units chasing the Taliban in Tora Bora; Hezbollah launching missiles south of Haifa, in Israel; Antonov bombers dropping napalm on African tribes in Sudan; al Zarqawi beheading civilians; and Khumeinist and Jihadist terrorist bombers blowing up minarets in Iraq . . . This is the chaotic landscape of the first decade of the twenty-first century. What lies behind these awful scenes, and will the peoples of the region be doomed to witness them forever?

STARGATE JIHAD

The Jihadist message, and that of Pan-Arabists and other ultranationalists, in essence is a call for Muslims to return to a way from which, in the radicals' minds, they have wrongly deviated. The reference points for all the varieties of Islamists and all those who are generating violent radicalism in and beyond the Greater Middle East come from past historical events. The messages reverberate through children's classrooms, are transformed by radical clerics, and are further transmuted by ideologues and political leaders into marching orders. In short, an ideological elite representing the interests of a dominant political establishment in the region has been indoctrinating the masses with the belief that no peace, no stability, and no hope are possible before the complete realization of their ideals. In the case of Pan-Arabists, the future is deferred until *Uruba* (Arabism) becomes the exclusive identity of the region and all its peoples are united under one Pan-Arab state. In the Islamist version, it is not until all Muslim peoples are united under a caliphate and infidels are defeated in the region and beyond. In both, there is no room for democracy— deemed Western—or for human rights. Women are not allowed to challenge the "righteous" male rule of these societies, nor are minorities such as Copts, Kurds, Berbers, Africans, or the Aramaic people allowed to challenge the leaders. Obviously, there is no space for anyone to challenge the dominant order, whether they be powerful, like the Jews of Israel, or weak, like the oppressed blacks of Sudan. A multitude of ideologies at the service of elites want to see a uniform empire stretching from the Indian Ocean to the Atlantic. In this nation the elites would dominate civil societies and suppress both the various ethnicities and the individual. Baathists and Jihadists, leading the forces of the past, look like an army from previous centuries somehow displaced into the present.[1]

As mentioned in earlier chapters, the Jihadists have been indoctrinated to reject the end of Islamic history caused by the fall of the caliphate. Everything that happened after the mid-1920s is unacceptable and illegitimate. Everything that rose—other than Islamism—has to be brought down: twenty-three Arab countries and fifty-two Muslim governments, secular constitutions, modernization, Western influence, globalization, women's rights, minority recognition, non-Muslim states, and more. Hence the global struggle is between the Islamists and all the rest. But the rest encompasses everyone else, including other fascist and totalitarian ideologies, authoritarian regimes, democratic forces, civil societies, and Western influence. In the Greater Middle East each surging force seems to clash with all other forces, with some convergence into alliances from time to time.

In the current evolution of the War on Terror and the Jihadist campaign, it is important to understand how the Islamists—although using cutting-edge modern technologies—are indeed seeking a transhistorical Jihad to accomplish the *muhimma* (mission). They resurrect the past with the promise of reconstituting the caliphate, and ignore the present, evolving world and its current realities, such as international law, the rise of the modern state, and modern Muslims' rejection of the caliphate. The Jihadists operate from a reference period beginning in the seventh century A.D./C.E. till about the golden age of the Ottoman conquests in the seventeenth century. That is the period they wish the Muslim world to return to, but with contemporary technologies. These very same Jihadists praise the scientific achievements that advance their goals, though not the ideals of their adversaries. Al Qaeda uses Internet warfare intelligently. The Iranian regime, particularly under Ahmedinijad, is looking forward to obtaining a nuclear weapon. The contemporary Jihadists want to use twenty-first-century military and defense technology to achieve seventh-century goals—a terrifying proposition for the Free World. For their part, the Islamist regimes, in Iran, Saudi Arabia, Qatar, Gaza, and Sudan, heavily use the image of past "Islamic glory" and future "Islamic prominence" to mobilize the people. Even secular and socialist powers such as Syria's Baath, the Saddam regime, Libya, the Palestinian Marxists, and their supporters speak of the need to achieve "historical goals." Arab governments that clash with the Islamists and the radicals—Egypt, Algeria, the current Iraqi government, and the Palestinian Authority—while not openly pursuing the same goals, foster similar narratives, fearing a backlash by the Islamists.

Given these ideological readings of history, the region's crisis will prove very difficult to resolve. For when the Jihadi position regarding Israel is to not recognize the "Zionist entity" at all, there can be very little room for negotiation or agreement on a peace. These maximalist positions reject all forms of conflict resolution when it comes to other ethnic identities (for example, radical Arab nationalism rejects non-Arab nationalities; Islamic fundamentalism rejects non-Muslim identities and non-Islamist forms of government). The authoritarian systems refuse to open up any political space for the opposition and instead mobilize national resources against outside enemies, real or imagined, in order to freeze reforms and obstruct change. In almost all cases of radicalization and oppression, "history" and "theological" invocations are invoked. With these two powerful reference systems, the peoples of the Greater Middle East are kept in check. The forces of ideological terrorism skillfully craft identity and religiously grounded ideologies to confront both the civil resistance and the international community. Jihadists and the authoritarians may dress their conflicts in the colors of nationalism, culture, and religious dignity, but these battles are in reality about sheer, nonsharable power, whether held by sitting regimes or sought by Islamists and radicals.[2]

MIDDLE EARTH IN THE MODERN PERIOD

The two branches of Jihadi Salafism rose in the mid-1920s—the Wahabis in Saudi Arabia and the Muslim Brotherhood in Egypt. The Wahabis spent the decades until the Cold War consolidating their teaching inside the Arabian kingdom. The Muslim Brotherhood gradually spread through the Arab world, creating in each emerging country affiliates of what would become the Arab League. The Salafist hopes for a victory by the Nazi-Fascist Axis (which they supported) against the British and French *kuffar* and the expulsion of the latter from the region faded in 1945. During the Cold War, the Brotherhood patiently infiltrated the Arab states; using a bottom-up approach, they reached a point where they dominated the region's political culture, even though they had never actually seized governments. The Muslim Brotherhood occupied the cultural space of all Sunni Arab countries in the Middle East, making themselves guardians of the so-called Arab street's ideological voice—though such a street never existed because of repression and lack of free speech. During the same period, the Wahabis saw a cascade of oil revenues, which were used to spread Wahabism.

With the onset of the Cold War, the Salafist powers, regimes, and movements profited from Western alignment against the Communists and used the resources of the United States against the Soviet advance into the region.

The Arab nationalists, mostly on the left, sided with Moscow against the West. Nasser, the Baath, and the PLO, as well as a host of other regimes, as in Libya, Sudan, and Yemen—all claiming Pan-Arabism—transformed what was an ethnic conflict between Jews and Arabs in Palestine into a full-fledged historical war with Zionism and the state of Israel. Four major wars—in 1948, 1956, 1967, and 1973— failed to create a breakthrough in the Arab/Israeli conflict until Anwar Sadat of Egypt broke ranks and signed a separate peace treaty in 1977. Another decade and a half of warfare involving Lebanon, Israel, and later Hezbollah led to the Oslo Accords in 1993, but only because the Pan-Arabists of the PLO realized that the Soviet Union was gone, as Yassir Arafat told CNN the night prior to the signing.

This began a new era, as the 1973 oil shock proved that oil Jihad could impact Western economies. From then on, the rise of Islamist state ideologies became more powerful and penetrating in the West as well. In 1975, a war exploded in Lebanon between a camp including the PLO, Arab Nationalists, Lebanese Muslims, and Syria, on the one hand, and, on the other, the Lebanese Christians, distantly and occasionally backed by the Israelis. This was the last battlefield of the Arab-Israeli war. In 1979, Iran's revolution installed in Tehran a tyrannical Khumeinist regime with a global Jihadi agenda. It created Hezbollah in Lebanon. As of the early 1980s three major ideological currents were competing for the dominance of the region: the classical Salafists, Wahabis, and Muslim Brotherhood; the

Khumeinists of Iran; and the radical Pan-Arabists and Baathists. Facing them (putting Israel aside for the moment) were the moderate Arab governments and Turkey. Crushed between the two were democracy groups and ethnic minorities.

Several major developments in the last decade of the Cold War acted to shape the 1990s. The Soviet invasion of Afghanistan in 1979 gave the Salafi Jihadists the opportunity to coalesce on a geographical battlefield, and later led to the creation of al Qaeda. In 1981 the Jihadists assassinated Sadat, signaling the beginning of a rupture between the Jihadists and most Arab regimes. An Israeli invasion of Lebanon in 1982 first gave the opportunity for a Lebanese victory over their PLO and Syrian foes before the Lebanese Christians were defeated. A Sudanese Islamist offensive on the southern provinces in 1983 generated a human disaster developing into genocide as of 1989. The Iran-Iraq war erupted in 1980, killing millions on both sides. As a consequence of Saddam's 1990 invasion of Kuwait, the United States and its allies developed a constant military presence in the region from 1991; and on October 13 of 1990, the Syrian army invaded the last free enclave of Lebanon, bringing Iranian influence to the Mediterranean's shores. In August 1991, after the last spasm by the Communists failed to bring back the USSR, the Soviet giant crumbled for good, opening a new page in modern history.

MIDDLE EARTH IN THE 1990S

The East-West confrontation was not good for democracy in the Arab and Muslim world. The West was busy containing the East, and the East wasn't keen to support freedom in the Middle East. This state of affairs helped the oligarchies of the region to keep the status quo and crush the liberal element. But when images appeared of Ceausescu tried by rioters, a Lenin statue falling, Czechs ringing their bells in Prague, East Germans rushing to West Berlin's supermarkets, Polish workers defeating the Communist militiamen with flowers, and masses roaming in the streets of Eastern Europe chanting for freedom, a chill hit the dictators, absolute monarchs, and mullahs: They knew this could happen to them. Accordingly, the main three antidemocracy powers of the region rushed to consolidate their grip on whatever power they had. The Global Salafists stepped up their campaign, the oil-rich Wahabis speeded up their penetration of Western decisionmaking and media centers, and the Muslim Brotherhood espoused a parallel track in the West by infiltrating educational, defense, and political milieus (and began guiding the broadcasts of the newly formed al Jazeera TV).[3]

Nor were these uncoordinated actions all. In a historic and successful move, the National Islamic Front of Hassan Turabi, then under the auspices of President Omar Bashir, gathered Jihadist forces from around the world, including those who would form al Qaeda, Hamas, Islamic Jihad, Algeria's Salafists, and other Jihadi organizations, in Khartoum (1992–1993) to launch a Jihadist Internationale. Second, in Sudan Jihadists waged massive ethnic cleansing operations against the tribal African south, which had been resisting the onslaught since 1983. Turabi and his Islamist comrades had already predicted, after the end of the Cold War, that at some point, the West would intervene on human rights grounds. Hence, the terror escalation against the south and eventually against Darfur was a preemptive offensive—a decade before the international community woke up to the tragedy. The Salafist powers in the region used the 1990s efficiently to pervert the local political culture and direct it toward Jihadism, while weakening the Western response. Hamas and Islamic Jihad similarly tried to destroy the Palestinian-Israeli peace process that began in 1993. As soon as both sides signed the declaration of principles opening the path for a peaceful resolution with two states living side by side, the Palestinian Jihadists struck hard with suicide bombings, wounding the process and delaying it for another decade. In the mind of the Islamists, any peace process with the infidels would bring about open borders, trade, and, even worse, interaction with a democratic culture. That would be lethal to the Islamist agenda.

Khumeinism followed a similar trajectory, both inside Iran and abroad, with the help of its axis partners Syria and Hezbollah, who consolidated its regional space. Across Persia, students and women were brutalized, especially in the years leading up to 9/11. The Iranian regime spent hundreds of millions of dollars in Lebanon to keep the anti-Syrian opposition at bay, penetrate Lebanese institutions, defeat the Israelis in the south, and dismantle the last remaining force outside Syrian-Iranian control, the South Lebanon Army. In addition, Tehran's Pasdaran (Revolutionary Guards) perfected their weapons, readied cells, and engaged in training Iraqi militias and Lebanese operatives while waiting for the right moment to act.

The authoritarian regimes also scrambled to secure their defenses before the ineluctable spread of democracy after the liberation of Eastern and Central Europe. Competing with the Islamists, and fearing the liberals, each regime tailored its policies to suit local conditions. Egypt, a recipient of massive U.S. aid, balanced its responses between playing cat and mouse with the Muslim Brotherhood and other Jihadists and upsetting the already powerful Islamist influence. Liberals and Copts paid the price—repression and political intolerance. The Egyptian state rationale was that any opening of the system to empower the secular opposition and the Christian minority would also open the gates for the Islamists to overwhelm the regime. Similar situations developed in Tunisia and Yemen. In non-Arab Turkey, with its solid secularist roots in Kemalism, a milder form of Islamism was expanding through the Fadila (Virtue) Party of Najmedine Erbakan as of mid-1996 (although it would not reach the highest offices of the land until 2007). In Iraq, Saddam's regime, despite its defeat in Kuwait by the U.S.-led coalition, was slowly reemerging and forming alliances with non-Baathist radicals, including Islamists, to escape the UN-imposed sanctions, lift the no-fly zones, and eventually build an anti-American bloc with the other rogue states, principally Iran and Syria.

But the most extreme of all Jihadist forces, al Qaeda, was moving faster than any of the others. While the gradualists moved ahead with their strategies, bin Laden suddenly took the region into direct confrontation with the United States. This opened the new post-9/11 era. A new Middle East would begin to emerge from the ashes of ground zero in New York.

MIDDLE EARTH FROM 9/11 ONWARD

When al Qaeda's planes hit the Twin Towers and the Pentagon, I felt that a new era began instantly. Long before the B-52s pounded Tora Bora in Afghanistan, Zarqawi was beheading his victims in Iraq, and the girls of Beirut were challenging Syrian tanks, the die was cast. Despite the radical elite's decades of violence, including wars, terror, massacres of their own populations, assassination of opponents, and rule by the sheer power of fear in the Greater Middle East, they had never openly attacked the American homeland. They knew by instinct what it meant to engage America head-on. Nibbling at the enemy and penetrating its defense are one thing, but violently awakening its people and inviting its forces into the region was something else. Osama bin Laden and his band, however, didn't abide by the conventional Jihadist wisdom. He decided to strike hard at what he believed was the "head of the snake," on his own timing, believing firmly that Allah loves the "daring."[4]

The collapse of the Soviet Union had convinced the Neo-Wahabis and the Muslim Brotherhood offshoots that the Creator had entered the battle directly on the side of the Jihadists. That is why the hotheaded al Qaeda followers at the Khartoum meetings in the early 1990s departed from the realist Islamists' line. The bin Ladenists felt that they could kill two birds with one stone: bleed the West from the outside and terminally wound the Arab and Muslim regimes from the inside. Massacring Americans on American soil would either collapse the American government or drag it to its doom in the Middle East. The end result would be that the apostate regimes would fall. Allah had shown the way with the Soviets, and he would continue to crumble the Western *kuffar,* so they thought. But for the lords of Middle Earth, this came too soon; their peoples might seize the historical opportunity to rise against them. If al Qaeda vanquished America, the apostates were doomed; and if the United States established the beginnings of democracy in the region, they were also doomed.

On September 10, 2001, the Taliban were strong enough in Afghanistan to spread Jihadism in Central Asia, tend to terrorist forces in Somalia and southern

Asia, and provide a training ground for Jihadists from around the world. In addition, the men of Mullah Omar and al Qaeda were able to influence Pakistan's tribes, infiltrate Pakistan's services, and eventually attempt to reach its nukes; Saddam was rearming, weakening the Kurds, making links with the Jihadists, and getting ready to reemerge; the Assad regime had secured Lebanon and Hezbollah had reached its international border; Tehran and Damascus had armed Hamas in Gaza; Khartoum was pushing the Janjaweed inside Darfur; North Korea was shipping missiles to the rogue regimes; the Islamists were burrowing deep inside the West; Russia's resistance to the Jihadists had been successfully framed as an anomaly; Jihadism was considered a form of yoga by the Western elite; the August 2001 Durban conference had signaled the all-out demonization of America; and Middle Eastern dissidents were at the nadir of their persecution.[5] And then came the attacks.

As soon as President George Bush addressed both houses of Congress in October 2001 on the American determination to wage a War on Terror, everything changed. With approval from both parties, an overwhelming majority of Americans, and European leaders, the power of the American military was unleashed. Al Qaeda, busy with saber rattling, failed to understand what was to come. But the rest of the authoritarian web in the region observed the assault on Afghanistan with alarm. Finishing off in a few weeks what the heavy armor of the Soviet wasn't able to deal with in a decade, U.S. and NATO forces removed the Taliban with the help of the Northern Alliance militias and pushed the remnants of the Jihadists into Pakistan. The first lesson wasn't only about the miscalculation of American psychological reactions to massacres at home, but also about how quickly alliances could be made with local antiterrorist forces. A new equation was established: The United States would find local allies. Another lesson would follow: Don't replace a hostile tyranny with a friendly one. Stunningly, the region's elites—across their divides—understood that a myth had been shattered. From al Jazeera to al Manar, the regimes' media warned of an apocalypse. The entire Jihadi-authoritarian aggregation of forces attempted to deter the U.S. and other Western forces from intervening beyond Tora Bora. They urged Washington to stop there. Taking down the Taliban was authorized by the United Nations and accepted by the region's leaders as justified revenge for Manhattan's towers and American humiliation. The oil and political establishments thought this would calm the wounded eagle and put it back to sleep. It was not to be. Decades of indoctrination and radicalization had ended badly: An out-of-control element, willing to provoke the wrath of Allah, had triggered a clash of titans. The winds of change had begun blowing across Middle Earth. The war on the infidels had provoked a War on Terror that mutated into a war by the region's totalitarians against forces advancing the cause of freedom. The confrontation has no boundaries except the reversal (or not) of the recent achievements of democracy. And to hasten one or the other outcome, a War

of Ideas has been waged relentlessly by the Jihadi powers to intimidate their opponents—but it has also been resisted with determination by those who have tasted
democracy in Afghanistan, Iraq, Lebanon, Darfur, and beyond. These resistant regions have become the war's battlefronts.

THE BATTLEFRONTS

Afghanistan

Since the fall of the Taliban in 2001, the struggle in Afghanistan has been to consolidate a freshly emerging government headed by President Hamid Karzai. A
local army has been created, and civil society is supported by the international
community. Coalition forces, led by NATO, have pacified the rugged country and
fought to find and eliminate Taliban remnants. The latter, from their bases in
Waziristan, a rebel province inside the neighboring Pakistan, have engaged in
guerrilla warfare against the democratically elected Afghan government. But coalition forces should be reinforced with more international forces, including Europeans, Arabs, and Muslims, under United Nations auspices, and aid to these
democratic forces should be increased until three goals are achieved: the defeat of
terrorist forces inside Pakistan, the rise of democratic forces in Iran, and the development of a new generation of young Afghans—produced by a new schooling system, educated in and willing to fight for the basic, internationally recognized
freedoms (rather than Jihad).

Iraq

With the invasion of the country by U.S.-led coalition forces in 2003, a war of at-
trition was begun by Jihadi forces, many of whom were helped into Iraq by Syria
and Iran. The extreme violence of al Qaeda and other Jihadists in the center and
the expanding pro-Iranian militias in the south have slowed the political process
and inflamed sectarian violence. The Kurds have tenuously reached a high level of
autonomy in the north; the Sunnis are divided between political parties and
movements willing to join the process and a radical minority pushing for the return of an Arab nationalist power reminiscent of Baathism. In the Sunni Triangle,
the Jihadists continue to attempt, but have failed as of early 2008, to create vast
enclaves leading to the establishment of a Taliban-like emirate. The Shia community, the largest in the country, resents the radical Sunni elements; a majority of
its younger members wish to build a new Iraq without radicalism of any kind.
However, a large component of Shia radicals have ties to Iran, and among them
are forces allied with Tehran, such as the Mahdi Army and Badr Brigade. The
coalition forces, the largest deployed in the Middle East, have worked toward na-

tional stabilization to deny the radicals, both Salafists and Khumeinists, the ability to create enclaves or develop large paramilitaries. The struggle is over the future of the country: The United States wants to leave behind an ally in the War on Terror, while al Qaeda and the Iranian-Syrian axis aim to cripple the current political process, push the United States and coalition out, and gain control of large areas of Iraq. Al Qaeda's strategic goals are to establish an emirate in the Sunni Triangle, and the axis wants to control the Shia areas and establish a land bridge between the two regimes through Iraq.

If a withdrawal is imposed on Washington and its allies, the forces of Jihadism—al Qaeda and Iran—will provoke a landslide that could transform the battlefields across the whole region. Iran's forces, local Iraqi militias and Iranian Pasdaran, would be able to reach the Saudi, Jordanian, and Syrian borders, as well as the Kuwaiti frontiers. In this new situation, the Syrians would be able to join the axis from their end. Such a cataclysmic change would put those countries at the crosshairs of the powerful military of Iran's mullah regime. Furthermore, a large share of Iraqi oil would fall to the axis, and U.S. deployment in the Gulf would be endangered strategically. In addition, the corridor between Iran and Syria would bring strategic pressure to bear on Lebanon, where Hezbollah would enjoy tremendous backing—allowing it to seize power and open the path for Iranian influence and military presence in the Mediterranean. The Iraq battlefield deserves a massive reevaluation in light of its centrality to both the terrorist forces and the Western coalition. It is also important to note that Iraq's civil society experiment since its liberation from the Baath dictatorship is perhaps the single most important factor for future change.[6]

The strategies needed are like those of Afghanistan, but on a far larger scale. The first need is for the rapid (yet patient) development of a modern and well-educated Iraqi army. These forces would be deployed gradually in urban areas and across the country to replace U.S. and coalition forces. But the latter would then be redeployed on the Iranian and Syrian borders to deter the axis from future action and send a strong message to the opposition in those two countries that democracy in Iraq is here to stay, and that Iranian and Syrian civil societies must increase their pressure to reform the authoritarian regimes under which they live. The United States and the coalition should also invite the United Nations, the Europeans, the Russians, and moderate Arab and Muslim countries to participate in an Iraqi renaissance. The international community must help the various Iraqi currents develop a constitutional and political system that reflects the country's multiethnic society and the desires of its various national communities. Ideally, a federal system, allowing significant autonomy to non-Arab minorities, including the Kurds and the smaller Assyrian-Chaldean, Mandean, and Turkoman communities, should be established. The larger Arab communities, Shia and Sunni, could decide upon their regional status within Iraq. But the new Iraq strategy, inasmuch as it is crucial to win the confrontation against the terrorist camp in Iraq, will need to be integrated into a regional set of strategies to defeat the global forces of Jihadism and totalitarianism and enlist the support of vast and untapped civil society resources in the region. Hence, for the new plan to work, a counteraxis plan is needed, based on the principle of a generalized democratic revolution in the Levant and a firm containment of the Iranian-Syrian alliance.

Lebanon

As already shown, Lebanon has suffered from the Syrian invasion and the Iranian-backed rise of Hezbollah. The Lebanese resistance to the Baathists, composed mainly of Christians at the time, fractured and collapsed. In 1990, a final Syrian invasion seized the government and sent the Iranian-sponsored militia to confront the last enclave in the south (supported by Israel). In ten years, the Syrian-Iranian plan was successful in forcing Israeli forces to abandon their local allies and leave the country. In May 2000, the Syrians and Hezbollah secured full control and suppressed all opposition. But as of 2003, exiled and émigré pressure groups convinced the United States and France to ask for a Syrian withdrawal. In 2004, the United Nations Security Council issued resolution 1559, ordering Damascus to pull out and Hezbollah to disarm. The Assad regime and its allies responded by assassinating a Sunni former prime minister, Rafik Hariri, who was critical of their behavior. A popular uprising, nicknamed the Cedars Revolution, ensued; international pressure increased; and Syria by April 2005 had withdrawn its units.

But since then, an axis-organized terrorist campaign has targeted elected legislators, journalists, politicians, and ordinary civilians in an effort to destroy the anti-Syrian Fuad Seniora government. Opposed to the Syria-Hezbollah alliance, a majority of Christians, Druse, and Sunnis and a growing number of anti-Khumeinist Shia have resisted the terrorists. In July 2006, Hezbollah triggered a limited war with the Israelis, preceding an axis comeback against the Lebanese government with urban subversion and more assassinations. In 2007, the Syrian-Iranian services began to use a number of small Jihadist (Salafist) groups to unleash terror on the Lebanese army and the Cedars Revolution. Among them was the Fatah al Islam, based in Nahr al Bared refugee camp.

The most important element in the confrontation is the Lebanese-Syrian border. Whoever has control of the frontier can basically win the conflict. If Hezbollah and its allies control the border, a land bridge will be opened between the Bekaa Valley, Syria, and Iran. But if a multinational force and the Lebanese should seize the area, Hezbollah will be isolated from the Syrian and Iranian hinterland. In addition, the battle for the election of a new president will also determine the direction the country will take. A pro-Syrian head of state would bring back the anti-Western forces and aid Iran in its effort to become a Mediterranean power, while an independent president would hold the line against the terror forces until the international community decides to lend the country significant support.[7]

Syria

The regime in Damascus has been a strategic ally of the Khumeinists in Tehran since the early 1980s, when Hafez Assad struck a military, security, and financial deal with the ayatollahs. When the coalition removed the Baath from Baghdad in 2003, its sister Baath Party in Syria—although a competitor—feared its time was coming, too. The ominous signs since 2001 were seen as signals for a change, and revived opposition inside the country. The Bashar Assad elite reacted by sending Jihadi suicide bombers across the Iraq border to kill U.S. military personnel. It also resumed its backing of Hamas and Palestinian Islamic Jihad (PIJ) in their suicide operations in Israel, attempting to shift attention back to the Palestinian-Israeli issue. Syrian strikes against its opponents in Lebanon were among the preemptive thrusts by Damascus to protect against what was seen as a growing threat against the oppressive regime. But Syria miscalculated, and Washington and Paris were able to come together on Lebanon. As noted above, they got the UN Security Council to pass resolution 1559. Hariri's assassination followed, and Syria resumed the terrorist attacks in Iraq and Palestine. Even after withdrawing its forces, the Syrian regime maintained a "second army" inside the Lebanese borders to bleed the new democratically elected government. Meanwhile, the United Nations formed a special tribunal to try the assassins of Hariri, which could implicate the Syrian regime and bring it to its knees. The only choice for Assad was to destroy the Lebanese government so that no proceedings threatening his rule would take place.

Syria is the bridge between Iran (via air or through Iraq) and Hezbollah. Damascus is the center of a web reaching the Sunni Triangle to the east, Beirut to the west, and Gaza to the south. The Assad regime has blocked all attempts to finalize a peace settlement between Palestinians and Israelis and obstructed the return of democracy in Lebanon and Iraq. On these grounds alone, the U.S.-led efforts in the region and the international coalition must move forward with a campaign to thwart the actions of the Assad regime:

1. The borders between Lebanon and Syria should be controlled by UN and Lebanese army units, severing the bridge and isolating Hezbollah from the Syrian hinterland.
2. The Iraqi-Syrian borders should be sealed off to Jihadist activities.

3. The Palestinian Authority should contain Syrian-backed activities in the West Bank.

4. The International Criminal Court must take its course and bring to justice those who killed Rafik Hariri and other Lebanese legislators, politicians, and journalists.

5. Serious support should be extended to the democratic opposition inside and outside Syria.

6. Diplomatically, when circumstances allow, Europe and the Russian Federation—as noted in an earlier chapter—should put greater pressure on Damascus to stop its support of terrorism. The European Union can shift the balance, and Russian pressure can stop Syria's maneuvers in the region.

The Palestinian Territories

The emergence of Mahmoud Abbas as Yassir Arafat's replacement in November 2004 promised a change in the Palestinian Authority attitude toward a durable Palestinian-Israeli conflict settlement. But in the following year, after the Syrians withdrew from Lebanon and Ahmedinijad came to power in Tehran, axis-allied Palestinian forces, particularly Hamas, went on the offensive to sink any rapprochement between the Palestinian Authority and Israel. A series of suicide bombings was meant to halt the negotiations; then, with endless funding from Iran, Hamas got a majority in the legislative elections in January 2006, snatching the cabinet from Fatah, which was loyal to the Palestinian president. The Jihadists spent a whole year disarming the forces under Abbas and preparing for a full takeover of the Palestinian territories. By mid-June 2007, Hamas forces had seized control of Gaza, after sanguinary attacks on Fatah, ensuring a victory by the axis. Thus, by early 2008, the Syrian-Iranian power had secured a second access to the Mediterranean via a Hamas enclave on the beaches south of Tel Aviv.

The readiness to reinvade the Gaza strip is one of the options that Israel has constantly asserted as Hamas continues its campaign of bombings. But since Hamas has conducted a coup d'état against a sitting Palestinian president, it would be more advisable that the international coalition against terrorism, along with moderate Arab governments, lend their support to the Palestinian government based in the West Bank so that it can regain control of the Gaza enclave. It should be up to the Palestinians first to regain their territories under their legitimate government. The tactic of Hamas is to draw Israel into military engagement as part of a greater plan to invite Hezbollah, Syria, and eventually Iran into a new conflict with Israel. A better strategic option is to have the United States sponsor Arab and Middle Eastern governments to support the Palestinian Authority against Hamas while it engages in a peace process with Israel. The peace agreement would bring economic support, while the regional coalition would balance axis intervention; reforms inside the Palestinian entity would shift popular support back to a more democratic, and, hopefully, noncorrupt government.

Iran

Next to al Qaeda's worldwide web, Iran's Khumeinist regime is the greatest menace to the region's peace, progress, and democracy. Using oil revenues to equip its forces with advanced weapons systems, to assert the dominance of its central militia, and to finance Hezbollah and other groups (such as Hamas and Islamic Jihad), the Iranian elite has established a Jihadist version of the Stalinist USSR. The mullah regime has dominated all public offices through the ruthless grip of the Pasdaran—comparable to an armed Bolshevik Party or the Khmer Rouge. The Basij (popular militias) keep order on the streets of Iran's cities. The ruling elite, topped by the office of Ayatollah Khamenei, the successor to the founder of the Islamic Republic, Khumeini, has full control of the system and decides national security and foreign policy. A "president" of this republic, currently Mahmoud Ahmedinijad, represents the entity to the world, while the mentor, a grand ayatollah, represents Allah on earth. The Iranian regime struck an alliance with Syria's ruling Alawites in 1980[8] and founded Hezbollah in Lebanon to lengthen the reach of the Khumeinist revolution.

Since the late 1980s, the regime has followed a path to acquire nuclear weapons. As with other totalitarian regimes in the world, possessing the ultimate weapon provides the elite in power with a protective shield from international interference with their own oppressed civil societies. But until 2001, the Tehran ruling establishment wasn't in a great rush to complete nuclear development, and its path to expansion wasn't significantly checked by the West or the Russian Federation. Till the U.S. campaign in Afghanistan, the mullahs of Iran were unconcerned about a possible marriage between the Iranian opposition and the international community. Like other oppressive regimes in the region, they had good reason to believe that oil power would obstruct any such outreach to the people. Iran's petro-regime, although not the most influential in the West, benefited from Saudi and other Arab shields. The Iranian contribution to the project of numbing the Free World was filtered through other Western parties, including the massive French, German, and other European interests in Iran's resources and markets. And it was effective. For example, the level of human rights abuse in Iran exceeded by far the incidents in Haiti or even the authoritarianism in Egypt, but the human rights organizations, including the prestigious UN Commission on Human Rights, kept silent. In 1998–1999, student uprisings spread across Iran, and thousands of youths were arrested and tortured without a significant response from liberal democracies around the world. Hezbollah, a terrorist organization, was described by European and even American diplomats as a "legitimate resistance movement."

Iran's regime was on its way to international prominence, a formidable concentration of power, and possession of the bomb. But Osama bin Laden—whose spokespersons once said al Qaeda was inspired by Hezbollah's suicide operations—ruined the mullahs' ultimate fantasy. Since 9/11 their world has changed. The deployment of U.S. and NATO forces in Afghanistan had an effect on the strategists in Tehran: America, it turned out, was not the weak-minded giant who had been intimidated in Beirut in 1983 and in Mogadishu in 1993. The fiery Jihadist speeches by bin Laden and Sleiman Abu Ghais (his spokesperson) during the fall of 2001 showed the average U.S. citizen what was really on the minds of the Salafi Islamists: genocide of Americans, including adults, the elderly, women, and children. Iranians and Hezbollahis have constantly chanted "Death to America"—*Al maout li amreeka*. Hussein Fadlallah, the mentor of the Party of Allah, constantly repeated in his sermons *Amreeka sharrun mutlaq*—"America is evil at heart." In fact, the Khumeinist rhetoric was more violent even than al Qaeda's, which accused America of "crimes" and thus ordered "reprisals." But the Iranian ideologues say that America is "evil in essence," meaning there is nothing that can be done to fix it. The Jihadists of al Qaeda want to kill millions of Americans, but the Khumeinist regime chants "Death to America"—the whole nation.

As noted above, after the collapse of the Taliban in Tora Bora, the Iranian regime—and all other totalitarians in the region—hoped the matter would end there. But to the unpleasant surprise of the Pasdaran commanders and their superiors, it did not. Even as U.S. leaders were mobilizing to thrust into another location in the region, and as many American politicians and a number of Europeans were desperately opposing the move, the Khumeinist strategists in Tehran and their Salafist counterparts in the region saw what was to come. The battle would be in Iraq, but not about Iraq; indeed, as Westerners were still debating if the war in Iraq was really about "spreading democracy" or not, the region's Islamists—including the Ayatollahs—and its authoritarian regimes—including Syria, Sudan, and Libya—knew that a democracy movement would shatter the old regime altogether. Hence the most threatened center of power after Afghanistan and Iraq was Iran. Therefore (and though it was missed by the media and academia till very recently) the Iranian strategy to counterattack the United States was set months before the American and coalition forces landed in Iraq. As soon as the Americans arrived and Saddam was taken down, Tehran and Syria unleashed their forces. Thus, by early May 2003, the first suicide bombers were exploding themselves against the American convoys. The battle for Tehran and Damascus had begun—deep inside Iraq.

The Iranian strategy is to bleed the United States until it withdraws from Iraq, as in Vietnam, leaving the country open for the Pasdaran to move in. But Syria's excesses in opening the borders wide for the terrorists to cross over and Assad's miscalculations in Lebanon angered Tehran. Now that Syria has been made to leave Lebanon, the ayatollahs have to fight on two fronts. Worse, Hezbollah was quickly isolated politically by a coalition of former foes: Sunnis, Druse, and Christians. In 2005, as these spasms were occurring, the ultimate leadership in Iran brought their most lethal man to power: Mahmoud Ahmedinijad. A former Islamic revolutionary student, Pasdaran, and protector of the Tehran elite, he reshuffled the cards and launched offensives in all possible directions: escalating terror in Iraq, increasing terrorism in Lebanon, widening suppression in Iran, and accelerating the race toward the bomb. These moves were designed to stun the enemy and force him to leave the area. By 2008, Ahmedinijad was still playing hardball with the democratic forces in the region, both the Western coalition and local reformist movements in Lebanon, Syria, Iraq, and Iran. The two main battlefields of Middle Earth are now Mesopotamia and Lebanon; there the Iranian regime will either crush the political processes or face the consequences at home. Thus, strategically speaking, the main geopolitical center of the Jihadi forces in the region is Tehran, and its center is the Pasdaran. With al Qaeda, it comprises the two towers of terror of Middle Earth.[9]

The Arab Brothers

The Arab League was formed in 1945 to prepare the Arabs for a future of unity and progress. Obviously, as most Arab reformers and liberals admit, it has failed. Among the most salient reasons for the failure are the following:

1. Putting Pan-Arabism ahead of Arab democracy and forcing entire societies to struggle for outside causes instead of domestic freedom;
2. Adopting an irredentist attitude toward non-Arabs regardless of the justness of ethnic claims: Kurds, Sudanese, Berbers, Copts, Assyrians, Aramaeans, and other minorities have been forced to assimilate through violence and ethnic cleansing;
3. Focusing on the Arab-Israeli conflict and on the sole solution of dismantling one party to the conflict, Israel, as a condition to finding a solution for the other party, meaning a Palestinian state; and
4. Allowing Jihadism to spread freely, leading the region and the world to catastrophes, such as the war on democracies.

Arab governments varied in their complicity. Egypt's influence in the Arab world could have been crucial. Unfortunately, Pan-Arabist fever under Nasser crushed liberalism, Sadat's hurry to conclude a separate peace with Israel led to unleashing the Muslim Brotherhood, and President Mubarak's tenure didn't strengthen the liberals or contain the Jihadists—it allowed the latter to persecute the Copts. Jordan, Kuwait, and Morocco, constitutional monarchies, aren't copycats of Sweden, Norway, and Holland yet, but have made significant advances in containing terrorism and its ideologies. The Kingdom of Saudi Arabia remains a complex and contradictory phenomenon. As Saudi Arabia's state policy has been to fund the spread of the Wahabi doctrine and teachings inside the country and globally, it bears responsibility for the indoctrination process of radical Islamism. Yet, since 2001, the Saudi authorities have waged multiple campaigns against al Qaeda. But, even though the latter put the al Saud on their target list, the antiterrorist campaign inside the peninsula didn't go beyond the country. Evidently, a new international policy will be needed to pressure the kingdom to make inside reforms to eradicate extremist teachings and follow the examples of Jordan, Morocco, and Kuwait's reeducation campaigns. Such a task will be gigantic, as a significant segment of the Saudi establishment has committed to Wahabism. But hard choices have to be made by the government, and particularly by enlightened royalty and princes. Short of that, the factories of indoctrination worldwide will continue to be fed by oil revenues. Next to Iran, as a pillar of Khumeinism, the Wahabi Kingdom stands as a major maker or breaker of the next generation of Jihadists. But now that al Qaeda has branched out into second-generation Salafism, or technically a Neo-Wahabi current, reforms by Saudis of their own country's political culture may well create the conditions to gradually contain, and perhaps reverse, the doctrines of Takfirism, the hard core of Salafi Jihadism.

Turkey

For seven decades a solid secular tradition, protected by the constitution and at times by the armed forces, has ruled Turkey. Ironically, the country that held the Ottoman Sultanate for centuries was the society that abolished the caliphate after thirteen hundred years. In 1949, the Turkish republic, whose population is 98 percent Muslim, joined NATO to protect itself from the Soviet threat. Faithful to the Western alliance, Turkey's rulers got involved in a limited invasion of northern Cyprus, ensuring a separate state for the Turkish minority there in 1974. Interestingly, while Ankara was severely secular and almost anticlerical, two of the most conservative Islamic countries recognized the tiny Muslim entity. But as of the mid-1990s, a wave of Islamic fundamentalism affected Turkish elections, bringing an Islamist prime minister, Najmedine Erbakan, to power. As soon as the latter manifested Islamist inclinations in foreign policy and domestically, the Turkish armed forces staged a bureaucratic coup to push him out of power. But in 2002, a second wave of Islamism, led by Tayyep Recip Erdogan and Abdullah Gül got a majority in the Parliament. After an election made Gül president of the very secular Republic of Turkey in 2007, the future of the country has to be decided again. Either the Islamic government will reform the educational system so that in one generation a re-Islamization of Turkey becomes reality, or the secular forces will bring the country back to the status quo. Some say a balance will be established; others discount that possibility, as both forces are adamant about their vision of the national identity. But in any event, a NATO country with an Islamic fundamentalist regime is hard to imagine, for in the years to come, NATO and the Jihadists will be increasingly at odds. Where would the Turkish armed forces stand? In 2003, under the present Islamic government, came an ominous first sign: The United States was refused the right of passage to enter Iraq, Turkey's sister state. In 2007, the Islamic Party won legislative and presidential elections in Turkey and is bracing for major changes in the secular institutions amidst secular opposition and the army's apprehension. The future is wide open.[10]

MIDDLE EARTH AND THE CONFRONTATION

In the end, the world confrontation between the Free World and the forces of Jihadism will be decided in the Greater Middle East. The outcome will depend on two factors: a determination by democracies worldwide to stay the course and adopt a strategy of liberation; and a determination by the leaders of the oppressed civil societies to rise in this generation, not a future one. It all hinges on the capacity of the Free World to understand the nature of the region's deeper struggles and choose the appropriate policies. At present there are two major battlefields, Iraq and Afghanistan; two open conflicts, Syria-Lebanon and Palestine-Israel; and two grand Jihadi powers, the Khumeinists of Iran and the Salafists of the region. Other countries, such as Egypt, Saudi Arabia, the Gulf states, and, by association, the surrounding regions of North Africa, the Horn, central and southern Asia, and beyond, will be affected by who wins in the Sunni Triangle, the Bekaa Valley, and Gaza. The geopolitics of the Greater Middle East would be impacted by a hasty withdrawal from Iraq, a rapid thrust by Iran, and a comeback by Syria in Lebanon. The world and the War on Terror would be shaped by a victory of al Qaeda in the Triangle and a Salafi insurgency in Saudi Arabia.

This decade, more than any previous one, will witness either the rise of Jihadism and totalitarianism in the Middle East or the rapid growth of freedom and democracy. How the confrontation evolves will depend very much on choices made in many places, including Washington and Brussels, but also in Beirut, Baghdad, and Kabul.

CHAPTER 13

THE SOUTHERN BATTLEFIELDS

LONG BEFORE THE COLD WAR ENDED, THE CONFRONTATION BETWEEN the Free World and the Jihadist forces had spread beyond the Greater Middle East into all other continents. Although Western Europe and North America were targeted, the main goal was to capture the political cultures of as many countries as possible in the Third World. These thrusts into Asia, Africa, and Latin America—into what I term the southern battlefields—by the Wahabis, the Muslim Brotherhood, the international Salafists, and the Khumeinists have been funded, politically and diplomatically, to spread the influence of Islamism as far as possible. The Free World witnessed a number of Jihadist activities as early as the 1970s in the Philippines and Nigeria; in the 1980s in Sudan and Kashmir; in the 1990s in Algeria and Indonesia; and since 9/11 in the triborder zone of South America, in Venezuela, and in South Africa.[1] The strategic objectives are familiar: to plant the seeds of emirates on the one hand and to insert Jihadi enclaves inside infidel lands on the other. To do this, the Jihadists have created a multitude of scenarios for struggle and subversion.

ASIAN BATTLEFIELDS

The Asian battlefields of Jihadism are Central Asia, the Indian subcontinent, Indonesia, and the Philippines. From a comparison of literature, tactics, and strategies, it appears that most of the Asian Jihadi wars are under the ideological control of the Salafists. Many among the madrassas dedicated to indoctrinating and producing pools of Islamists are or were originally funded by Wahabi resources, though Deobandi influence naturally is present in most of the Indian region. A separate study could establish the history of the expansion of Islamism from the edges of the Middle East in Arabia, Iran, and Afghanistan to the extremities of the Indonesian archipelago and as far as the Chinese steppes. As in other areas of the world, the Jihadist trail was blazed by oil-producing regimes, militant cadres, and organizations.

The Greater Central Asian Open Field

In the north, Salafi Jihadism spread from Afghanistan into Central Asia's Muslim republics, and from there it penetrated into northwestern China. All told, Salafi Jihadism eyes a total of seven new emirates: the five Muslim republics of the former Soviet Union (Kazakhstan, Turkmenistan, Tajikistan, Uzbekistan, and Kyrgyzstan), Afghanistan, and the Sinkiang province inside China. The former USSR republics are all ruled by either former Communist bureaucracies or by secular elites. The various Islamist parties operating in these newly independent countries, as well as the Jihadist movements clashing with the governments, are becoming copycats of the Taliban, although with different outlooks and their own ethnic and national identities. Most prevalent in Tajikistan, Uzbekistan, and Kyrgyzstan, the Jihadists intend to overthrow the local authorities and multiply what was the Taliban-like emirate. The grand plan is to seize control of these countries, transform them into emirates, and merge them into a regional governorate or sultanate. A strategic goal would be to gain control over nuclear weapons in Kazakhstan and the Russian space program. If these plans are executed, the space conquered by the Islamists would be close to India and a major threat to that nation. But the five "stans" aren't the last frontier sought by the Jihadists in their Asian confrontation. As mentioned earlier, and as cited by al Qaeda commanders and Jihadi chat rooms, the Uighur "Muslim" nation inside China is also cultivated by the Jihadists as an eventual part of a growing caliphate. Sinkiang province is very important to Beijing. For in addition to important natural resources, it is the site of strategic space and military programs. China would shrink significantly with the loss of the province, for this would lead to a separatism domino effect in Tibet and lower Mongolia. But projecting even farther, even though not touched by serious analytical studies, the rise of a nuclear caliphate on the western border of Communist China could be a prelude to a lethal conflict between the Jihadi powers of Central Asia and a Marxist-Leninist—but industrialized—great power. It is expected that a growing al Qaeda power (maybe a mutant form of Central Asian Jihadism) will start a devastating campaign against the Chinese. The last Communist great power in the world, while preparing for a competition with liberal democracies, could find itself targeted by even greater terrorism than that faced by the West. Al Qaeda has already recruited Uighurs into its ranks, and China's Jihadism has already begun. It will be some time before Chinese cities feel the wrath of the same menace that hit New York, London, and Moscow. That is, unless they fail to develop counterterrorist strategies before the end of this decade.

On the western frontiers of Central Asia, one has to factor in the role of Iran—though limited because of Khumeinism's Shia background and its conflict with the Salafists and Wahabis, who can recruit heavily in a larger Sunni environment. Tehran has already attempted to penetrate the Hazara ethnicity inside Afghanistan, though this group is mainly of Mongol ancestry and of moderate tendencies.[2] But the Islamic republic of Iran will redouble efforts to create a Hezbollah-like organization within that community, even though it won't be very popular. In addition, the Khumeinist regime has been trying to make inroads with the Tadjik republic on the ground of common bonds, because of the linguistic and ethnic links between the Persians and the Tadjiks.

The initial game plan of the Taliban and their al Qaeda protégés was to spill over into Pakistan—since 1999, the shortest road to the so-called Islamic nuclear bomb. In some of his speeches bin Laden has mentioned "our weapons" in Pakistan. All Mullah Omar and his guests had to do before 2001 was to increase their infiltration across the borders; instead of Pakistani penetration of the Taliban, it was to be the other way around—Jihadi infiltration of the Pakistani secret services and armed forces. Had al Qaeda been patient, had it not attacked the United States in 2001, it might have already secured the doomsday device through an uprising or a coup in Islamabad. Perhaps to assert his authority among the world's Jihadists and to become a hero to sympathizers around the Muslim world, the commander of al Qaeda had to strike deep into infidel lands. But the price was high: The Taliban and al Qaeda were displaced from the only emirate they had built. After the battle of Tora Bora in December 2001, the main remnant of the Jihadi command moved into Pakistan, into the most pro-Taliban sector of the country, Waziristan. Oddly, bin Laden and Mullah Omar are now closer than ever to the center of ultimate power in Pakistan. With their influence over the large fundamentalist tribes stretching over several provinces and with an unknown number of supporters in the armed forces, the game is still not over—and it has become more dangerous.

From the above summary, one can see that the Central Asian Jihadi movement can impact several fronts. To the north it penetrates the former Soviet republics and eventually Russia, and aims at the strategic assets in that area. To the east, it aims at penetrating western China and controlling strategic resources. To the south, it eyes Pakistan's tremendously important location, large population, and critical defense systems. Central Asia's Jihadist plans could thus link up with the Jihadi operations in the Indian subcontinent.[3]

The Indian Subcontinent's Jihads

Since the Taliban's defeat in Tora Bora in December 2001, signaling the collapse of the purest model of Salafi Jihadism, the next main focus of Western attention in the War on Terror has been the fate of Osama bin Laden, especially his whereabouts. The overstress on this topic is naturally related to the psychological shock of 9/11: How could a man lead an attack on America, kill thousands, and not be found and apprehended or eliminated? As the U.S. public was poorly prepared for the existence of such a war and the ideology behind it, it was left with one sentiment: find the mastermind.

What was neglected in this collective rush to take revenge was the fact that bin Laden, although a leader of the terrorist organization behind the massacre, was merely a soldier in the struggle. He was a product of a much bigger killing machine, a gigantic body stretching across many countries and over many years. When the remnants of al Qaeda crossed into Pakistan (and some fled to Iran), the world, while following the traces of the ailing Osama, began to realize that his hideout is in the midst of a much gloomier environment. Indeed, the Taliban of Afghanistan do not compare in numbers to the scores of Jihadists dispersed in the densely tribal areas of Pakistan's outlaw border regions. The men of Mullah Omar were in fact a fraction of a larger Pakistani whole. The spread of the Deobandi version of Islamism inside Pakistan and its intertwining with comrades across the western border has created one of the largest Jihadi zones in the world. That explains why the head of al Qaeda and his band could vanish deep inside the Waziristan no-go land. He and Mullah Omar are at home among the greater Taliban force sitting inside the country that owns what bin Laden and many other Jihadists describe as the "bomb of the Muslims." Now that the Taliban leadership is in exile inside Pakistan, it is inciting their allies to bring down the government by all means and extend the influence of the Islamists. In the 1980s, Pakistan's intelligence service (ISI) backed the Jamaat-e-Islami (JI) in connection with the Musjahidin of Afghanistan as a state policy to thwart Soviet influence. Later, more prominence was given to Jamiat-e-Ulema-e-Islam (JUI), the more fundamentalist and sectarian of Pakistan's Islamist parties, which subscribes to the Deobandi-Wahabi doctrine. In recent years a unified front has grown, a six-party conglomerate called Muttahida Majlis-e-Amal (MMA), or United Action Forum, which entered the elections in 2001 by capitalizing on the upsurge of anti-American sentiment and benefiting also from the ban on mainstream political parties. In these conditions, the MMA alliance gained 58 out of 342 parliament seats, making it the third largest block in a house where no party was able to win a clear majority. Furthermore, the Jihadist core is protected politically by a larger bloc that has become a pillar of Gen. Pervaiz Musharraf's government. Oddly, while al Qaeda and the hard-core Taliban have declared war on Musharraf, their Islamist allies are still sitting on the fence, awaiting a strategic moment for the final assault. The real question is, What is the grand plan of the Jihadists in Pakistan?

Regardless of bin Laden, the deeper goal of the Wahabi-Deobandi forces in Pakistan is threefold. First, they want to penetrate the state and its defense apparatus until they acquire the ability to control or paralyze the military capacities of this large and powerful Islamic nation. Second, they want to continue to engage the

Afghan government and coalition forces to weaken them, until they seize greater power in Islamabad; then they can transform Pakistan into a sort of Jihadist North Vietnam, meaning they would seize power, declare an emirate, and begin supporting Jihadi guerillas in such places as Afghanistan and Bangladesh. Such a new Jihadi power—under a nuclear umbrella—would be capable of stirring intifadas in multiple Jihadi South Vietnams, including the Indian part of Kashmir. Which brings us to the third pillar of radical Deobandi strategy: the establishment of a super-emirate—or even sultanate—from northern Afghanistan to the Sind and Kashmir provinces inside present-day India. For the Wahabi-Deobandi vision of the return of regional Jihad encompasses Pakistan deep inside India, and eventually—a long-range goal—the establishment of a land bridge to Bangladesh.

India has been declared a prime enemy of the world Jihadist movement in various video statements by Osama bin Laden and Ayman Zawahiri. In the Jihadi vision of the caliphate's history, the Hindus are perceived as mortal enemies. In a way, the reestablishment of a post-Islamic Indian federal state is seen by the Salafists as parallel to the Reconquest of Iberia by the Spaniards and the Portuguese. The Islamists read the history of the Indian subcontinent in terms of the east-bound Fatah (Islamic Conquests), in which the ancient Hindu and Buddhist civilizations south of the Himalayas were *kuffar* in nature and thus open to invasion and suppression. Thus, after the conquest of Persia by the Umayyads and Abbasids, the Arab armies clashed with the Indian forces along the Indus River in Sind. The Indian resistance to the Fatah gave the subcontinent a few more centuries before other dynasties, including mainly the converted Moguls, carried the conquests into the Hindu territories. The *fatah* invasion of India eventually led to Muslim domination of almost two-thirds of the country. Hindu sovereignty was pushed all the way south to the end of the cone. The Islamic domination of India persisted almost until the British conquest in the nineteenth century. Hence, in the eyes of the Salafists, India was subdued by the advancing forces of the caliphate and was ruled under a legitimate Islamic state, and thereby became a part of the *dar al salaam* or *dar al Islam*. Inescapably, it should return to the caliphate. The withdrawal of the British was a signal for that return to Islamic legitimacy, but the emergence of an Indian secular state under Gandhi prevented that; in the eyes of the Jihadists, the partition of the subcontinent was the first step toward a reversal of that restoration. Hence, after the partition in 1948 (into Pakistan and India), the Islamist project then became to slice off the mostly Muslim Indian province of Kashmir. This conflict has brought the two countries to the brink of all-out war several times. But the splitting off of Bangladesh (formerly East Pakistan) from Pakistan delayed the dismembering of India. With the end of the Cold War, however, the Jihadi campaigns against India reignited. The Kashmir ethnic conflict became an Islamist cause. As in Afghanistan and Chechnya, so-called volunteers joined the fight from countries as remote as North Africa and the United States. Thus, though commonly presented in the Western media as a border dispute, the Kashmir battle has been reshaped by the Islamists as part of international Jihad.

Pakistan's governments backed the local Kashmir Jihadists. Attacks were staged from inside Pakistan's borders not only into the province but also against Indian targets faraway in the south. As of 2001, the Jihadist warfare boldly aimed at Indian centers, including the parliament on December 13, 2001, Mumbai on August 28, 2003, and Indian trains on July 11, 2006. As the War on Terror evolved, the attacks involved more and more Indian Jihadists recruited in India, thereby achieving another strategic goal: Not only would Jihadists "liberate" lands inside India, but they would use the hands of Indian citizens to do so. The Jihadists wished to incite as many sectarian clashes as possible inside the Hindu nuclear power, using Pakistani-based organizations in the first phase, massively mobilizing militants from Kashmir in the second stage, and recruiting Indian Muslims to Jihadism in the final stage. A massive Hindu-Muslim unrest inside the giant democracy's civil society could collapse its defenses. In Jihadist Machiavellian calculations numbers can overwhelm. Fueling Deobandism and Wahabism within a population of one hundred million Indian Muslims could produce hundreds of thousands of Jihadists; in turn, Jihadists calculate that out of the one billion Hindus, millions of ultranationalists would respond to a sectarian conflict. The ultimate strategic goal of a Talibanization inside India would be to devastate the country's rising economy and eventually to hit its military, including (worrisomely) its nuclear weapons. Hence, the Jihadist global plan for the subcontinent on the nonconventional level is to seize the nukes of Pakistan and partially destroy those of India, provoking a holocaust-driven demographic change. For the Hindus, unlike the Jews and the Christians, are not *dhimmis, people of the book*, and so—according to Salafi Jihadists—actions against them as infidels are permissible outside the *dhimmi* conditions.[4]

This apocalyptic Jihadi campaign in the subcontinent factors in Bangladesh as well. The Islamists have engaged in a series of threats, assassinations, and bombing campaigns in the past two years, showing their strength. A takeover by Taliban-like forces would parallel a takeover in Pakistan. Ironically, if the Jihadists win in both countries, it is to be expected that they will engage in a unification of resources, including mutual support for terrorism inside India and a deployment of Pakistani nuclear weapons in Bangladesh. If Dhaka falls to the Jihadists, this will enflame the Indian subcontinent and lead to very dangerous consequences. And from Bangladesh, a strategic bridge would be established with the Jihadists of South Asia.[5]

The South Asian Emirates

In the eyes of the international Jihadists, the areas between the Indian and Pacific Oceans are the "lebensraum"[6] of the future world caliphate: This vital space between China, Australia, and the Americas can make an empire a planetary one. To Salafists and Khumeinists, breaking the hold of Western and non-Muslim Asian powers in that part of the world will ensure that the world power they seek to establish is well rooted in almost all parts of the globe. Indeed, an arc of Jihadi activities and organizations stretches from the Bay of Bengal to the shores of the southern Philippines. In it there has been established a conglomeration of radical and Islamist groups, at the center of which surges Jemaat Islamiya, the powerful transnational Taliban of South Asia. Urban and rural Jihadism are omnipresent in southern Thailand, Malaysia, and Indonesia—indeed, all the way to the Philippines. These Jihadi forces have been in existence since long before the end of the Cold War but have surfaced as allies to al Qaeda prominently since 9/11.

In Thailand, the Jihadi efforts concentrate in the south, as the Wahabis attempt to infiltrate the Muslim populations and incite their political forces to organize an insurgency against the Thai government. The Jihadi model repeats itself: At first, the Islamists' claims on central authorities are local and deal with political participation, application of Sharia law, and related demands. Soon after, claims for separatism surface. As incitements by the Islamists are successful, the "struggle" is hijacked by the Jihadists and becomes about the establishment of an emirate in southern Thailand, to be united at a later stage with other emirates to further the reemergence of the caliphate.[7]

The next entity marked for "Talibanization" is Malaysia, a successful and, initially (in the 1950s–1970s), secular Muslim country. The plan of the Wahabi-Salafists is to bring an emirate form of government to Kuala Lumpur. Geostrategically, such a victory could reshuffle the forces in South Asia, as it would create a continuum between southern Thailand and Indonesia.[8]

Indonesia

Indonesia is the nation with the largest Muslim population in the world, and it has significant Christian and Chinese minorities. Although historically not conquered by a *fatah*, this immense archipelago, with thousands of islands and over two hundred million inhabitants, was settled by Arabian traders while the caliphate was in power in the Middle East. The settlers propagated the religion of Islam by economic incentives and conversions. For many centuries it was a collection of many local sultanates and principalities. It was colonized by the Dutch in the seventeenth century. After the Japanese occupation between 1940 and 1945, Indonesia joined the community of independent nations and adhered to the United Nations under President Sukarno. Its second president, Suharto, was a cofounder of the Non-Aligned Movement.[9] He ruled until 1998. The Wahabis penetrated Indonesia early on in the twentieth century, and many groups were influenced by their Islamist ideology.[10] During the Cold War, the focus of the political establishment swung between global neutrality and local containment of Communism. The elite's main focus was to preserve the unity of the large but multiethnic and multireligious country. Many separatist movements, Muslim and non-Muslim alike, were seeking independence and statehood, endangering the fragile unity of the country. The most visible nationalist struggle was in East Timor, a former Dutch and Portuguese colony, invaded by Indonesia in 1975 upon the pullout by the Portuguese. The East Timorese, mostly Catholics, argued that they were not part of any Indonesian sultanate or emirate to begin with, but Jakarta's establishment across the political spectrum insisted that East Timor was an integral part of Indonesia. The confrontation persisted throughout the Cold War and beyond. East Timor obtained UN-recognized independence in 1999 as Timor-Leste.

To the Islamists, this self-determination process was deemed an affront to the *umma*. Both Laskar Jihad inside Indonesia and al Qaeda opposed it and accused the United Nations, the United States, and Australia of detaching a Muslim land from the caliphate-to-be.[11] Bin Laden personally attacked the East Timorese independence movement, confirming that international Jihadism is not an anti-Western movement as much as it is an anti-infidel trend. Opposing self-determination for a small country like East Timor on the grounds of defending the "lands of Islam"— despite the fact that the area isn't inhabited by Muslims and was never part of the Islamic nation—shows that Salafism is indeed a form of imperialism that emerges from Jihadi fascism. There are many other cases of islands that want to separate from Indonesia, both Muslim and Christian; the Jihadi response to all these movements and to the secular trend is the same: repression. Accepting the separation of entities that break away from a Muslim country means a regression from the ultimate goal, the caliphate. Hence, Jihadi antiseparatists in Indonesia linked their position to the mainstream nationalist position, and thus allowed the Laskar Jihad militia to thrive and expand. It was backed by circles within the Indonesian army. This attitude emboldened more extreme Islamists, such as Jemaa Islamiya, which linked up with al Qaeda regionally and internationally and began conducting terrorist attacks against Christians, Hindus, Buddhists, and moderate Muslims. In 2004, they attacked Western businesses in Bali. The Indonesian government began to react against the most extreme Salafi Jihadists, but is still in a bind in regard to the mainstream Wahabi movements and the Laskar Jihad. Too many political factors prevent the government and the armed forces from launching a genuine anti-Jihadist campaign; for example, the Islamists have penetrated the main centers of political culture of the country, an end product of decades of Wahabi influence. As in Saudi Arabia and Pakistan, the government wages war against al Qaeda's affiliates, but not its ideology.[12]

Regardless of the domestic political situation, the Jihadi agenda of dominating Indonesia and imposing strict Sharia law has significant geopolitical dimensions. By eventually seizing control of the immense archipelago, the Jihadists could claim the most populous Muslim country in the world, and with Jakarta as a major South Asian center, a Taliban-like regime could strike against Australia and New Zealand and overturn other governments in the region. As in the case of Afghanistan-Pakistan, a Jihadi regime in Indonesia could reinvade East Timor, overrun Singapore, export its militants to Borneo and the Sultanate of Brunei; and if Malaysia hadn't already fallen, it could bring Kuala Lumpur under its aegis as well. A Talibanized Indonesia would change the strategic landscape of two continents, Asia and Oceania. The Jihadists could raise a very large army, mobilize Pasdaran-like militias through Laskar Jihad, and create a very powerful South Asian sultanate stretching from southern Thailand to the southern Philippines. And by combining the oil reserves of Indonesia and Brunei, this transnational Salafi power would be a massive anti-Western and antide-mocratic force in the world, shifting the attitudes inside OPEC and the Organiza-tion of Islamic countries (OIC) toward Jihadism. A more apocalyptic scenario is that a Laskar Jihad domination of Indonesia would be able to project nuclear and other weapons of mass destruction across the area, a strategic development that would put India, Vietnam, Australia, New Zealand, China, Japan, and Hawaii under the threat of a first strike. Though far from achievable at this stage because of the presence of secular and moderating forces in Indonesia, these doomsday scenarios could be real-ized if the Jihadists have their way in the early stages of the confrontation.[13]

The Philippines: The Eastern Door to the Pacific

The easternmost front in the southern Asian battlefield is the Philippines. For the global Jihadists, the southern provinces of this mostly Catholic country are the ex-treme oriental tip of the caliphate to come. As in many similar cases, the local struggle started with a separatist claim, on behalf of the Moro Islamic Liberation Front, which sought statehood for the mostly Muslim southern islands of the ar-chipelago. Historically, the spread of Islam came through Indonesia and converted the populations of Mindanao and other nearby islands. The separatist movement since the 1960s has been based on Muslim leaders' claims that the Muslim popula-tion formed a distinct national group and was seeking full independence. That move was opposed by the Philippine government. The separatist movement was supported by many Muslim governments, including Libya's and Saudi Arabia's. But in the early 1990s, in a move parallelling global Jihadist trends, a Salafi-Wa-habi current took control and transformed the independence movement into an Is-lamist one. The main claim remained a separation of Mindanao and the southern Muslim islands from the rest of the country—but now on the ground of forming an emirate, which would ultimately join a future world caliphate. The Jihadist stream produced a number of terror groups, including the most notorious, Abu

Sayyaf, which became infamous for kidnappings, beheadings, and mass killings. The Salafist Jihadi organization soon joined the al Qaeda network and became its franchise in Southeast Asia.

The first objective of a Jihadi emirate in Mindanao would be in effect to surround Oceania's infidel powers, Australia and New Zealand, from the north, in concert with a potential emirate in Indonesia next door. These two future *"wilayas"* (governorates) would put the two democracies (staunch allies in the War on Terror) in the line of fire of long-range missiles—provided by Iran, Pakistan, or other sources. From Indonesia and Mindanao, the waters could carry terrorist infiltrators into Australia and New Zealand. The tactic would be to indoctrinate immigrants from the northern islands into the Oceanian cities. By Jihadizing the areas from which immigrants would eventually come, the radicals inside Australia and New Zealand would be pre-indoctrinated at the source.[14]

Aside from waging war against the infidels south of the Jihadi archipelagos, a launchpad in Mindanao would open the last frontier for the Islamists: the hundreds of islands in the South and Central Pacific. Indeed, the international Jihadists often incite their supporters to take Jihad *Ila aqsa al ard*, "To the end of the world." This goes beyond the reestablishment of the old, historical caliphate and sets the agenda of the new resurrected caliphate: world domination. Settling the far islands of the Pacific, both the island-nations and the colonies of Western powers, is not a farfetched enterprise. Abu Sayyaf has already shown its ability to conduct raids across the waters. If it is backed by a full-fledged Talibanist regime that has control of the southern Philippines, and has aid from much larger and wealthy Jihadi regimes in South Asia or the Middle East, the power of such an emirate would be capable of reaching the Fiji Islands and French Polynesia.

THE AFRICAN BATTLEFIELDS

Africa, the unachieved Jihad *wajib* (a neglected duty), has an Islamist leader in Hassan Turabi of Sudan, who has asserted Jihadist ideology in his many travels around the Muslim world and the West. Indeed, the Jihadists of all Salafi backgrounds have looked at the so-called black continent as a prize owed to Jihadism but never fully brought under the rule of the caliphate, although the doors were wide open for centuries. The Islamic fundamentalist "story" in Africa is somewhat comparable to their clashes with civilizations in Europe, Russia, and Asia: a narrative of the "liberation" of nonbeliever populations. But the African continent has a special place in the perception of the Jihadists. Historically, the wide southern littoral of the Mediterranean provided a route between the Levant and Europe. It was conquered in just a few years after Egypt fell into the hands of Arab general Amr Ibn al Aas in 648 A.D./C.E. and the caliphate spread over three continents. The forces commanded by Tariq bin Ziad crossed into Spain in 715 and never stopped their march northward until they were defeated by Charles Martel at Poitiers, France. This vision of swift conquests stretching across North Africa and into the heart of Europe is still revived in the accounts of recruiters of present-day Jihadists. But as usual in Islamist narratives, Africa is portrayed as having been liberated by the early *fatahs*, not invaded. Today this vast and rich continent is seen by Jihadists such as Hassan Turabi as the breadbasket of the future caliphate. The natural resources, riches, and location of the continent make it in the eyes of the international Salafists the greatest prize of all, an untapped region easier to dominate and control than the powerful West, a rising Asia, or a remote Latin America. Another ideological incentive in the Jihadi attention to Africa is the theological competition. While most of the world has come under the influence of one of the world religions or atheism, large parts of Africa's populations have not yet converted to Christianity or Islam, yet are very spiritual. This religious "emerging market" is a prime target of all religious groups seeking as many converts as possible. But to fundamentalists in general and the Jihadists in particular, religious conversion aims at provoking real-world events, some through divine intervention, others by more practical means. The Jihadist sees Africa as an incomplete Jihad. In their view, the first Arab dynasties, the Umayyads and the Abbasids, took Egypt and the regions that became Libya, Tunisia, Algeria, and Morocco, before they invaded Spain. A second Ottoman Caliphate pushed farther south along the Nile River into what is today the Sudan. A third wave of Islamic conversion spread through the Sahara, engulfing large parts of Africa from Sudan to Senegal, and pushed south along the east coast without major military conquests. The Jihadists of the twentieth and twenty-first centuries plan to resume the march and refuse to acknowledge the current multireligious identity of the continent. The National Islamic Front of Sudan, the Islamic Salvation Front of Algeria, and the various other Salafist groups of North Africa and those who support them from the Levant believe a global Jihad should carry Islamism from the Arab north to the Cape of Good Hope. Turabi, one of the leading ideologues of the Jihadist movement in Africa, has often advocated a push from Sudan to South Africa to eliminate the vestiges of colonialism, as he puts it, though in fact he aims to replace native African cultures and religions with Salafism and Pan-Arabism.[15]

The pursuit of Jihadism in Africa, especially since the end of the Cold War, is taking place in five major areas.

Sudan

"The land of the blacks"—this is the name of Sudan in the Arabic language. It was described as the land of the black people of Africa when Arab armies and tribes moved along the Nile River, conquering the old Nubian kingdoms between the Red Sea and the sub-Saharan lands some thousand years ago. The borders between the northern Arab and Arabized populations and the southern tribes fell across the middle of Sudan, along a frontier running from the Nuba Mountains all the way to the mouth of the Senegal River on the Atlantic Ocean. The northern tier of Sudan has become Arabized; the central tier is mostly African Muslim; and the southern tier is black African. After Sudan gained its independence from British rule in 1956, it entered abruptly into civil war. The north rejected the federal system and imposed the Arab identity as well as Islamization on the south, and the latter rebelled. The first war ended in 1972, but a second, more lethal conflict rekindled in 1983 when Khartoum's regime attempted to enforce Sharia laws in the mostly Christian and animist south. The war brought by the Islamist regime of Gen. Omar al Bashir and Dr. Hassan al Turabi devastated the southern provinces: genocide killed more than one million civilians and the northern militias, the Difaa al Shaabi, took up to 750,000 African slaves. By 2002 the Jihadi war was also directed against a Muslim black population in the Darfur region. A regime-backed militia, the Janjaweed, a local form of Taliban, has perpetrated genocide against the African tribes of western Sudan. The battle of Sudan has become the heart of the Jihad for Africa in the mind of the Salafists, who want to subdue the two African resistance movements (the south and Darfur) that are obstructing the advance of the Jihadist machine. The National Islamic Front (NIF) logic was that after defeating the southern rebellion and, later, the Darfur uprising, nothing could stop the forces of Jihadism from thrusting into black Africa—Chad, Ethiopia, Zaire—all the way to South Africa.

From the mid-1980s, the South Sudan Liberation Movement, under the leadership of Col. John Garang (and other leaders such as Riek Machar and Lam Akol), waged a fierce resistance to the Jihadist offensives. The balance of power was overwhelmingly to the advantage of the Islamists in Khartoum, as the Arab League stood by them. Ironically, though they had clashed against one another during the Cold War, Arab regimes from opposing ideologies came together against the black resistance in the south. Saudi Arabia's Wahabis on the one hand and socialist Pan-Arabists of Iraq, Syria, and Libya on the other lent their unconditional support to the Jihadists of Sudan to crush the southern rebellion. Years later, when the black Muslim revolt exploded in Darfur, the Arab bloc remained associated with their ethnic brethren in Sudan. The black Muslims in Africa realized that Islamic solidarity wasn't stronger than Pan-Arabism. Arab elites would stand by Arab oppressors, even against black Muslim victims. Salafi Jihadism in Sudan thereby exposed itself as a racist movement that wants Arab interests placed above all other Muslim rights, particularly in the case of black Africans. But despite the extreme toll in human casualties occurring in the south and regardless of the practice of slavery, the international community (and the West in particular) didn't intervene to stop the genocide. In the 1980s, the rationale could have been Cold War priorities, but no logical impediment was obstructing United States and European intervention on humanitarian grounds in the following decade. Curiously, most Western nations suddenly expressed concern for Darfur's population after 2004. The Save Darfur campaign in America, UN resolutions regarding Khartoum's regime, and European campaigns mobilized public opinion and triggered vast diplomatic initiatives with the African Union and other international organizations to protect the population of Darfur—to the great surprise of the Sudanese regime and its backers in the region. How was that possible in a very short span of time?

In the 1990s, the Oil Empire was in solidarity with the Sudanese regime, which was itself a developing producer. The Wahabis and the Muslim Brotherhood stood by Turabi and Bashir as they crushed the black Christian and animist south. As long as the Jihadi regime was backed by the combined powers of oil and Pan-Arabist and Islamist ideologies, it would have been impossible for Western governments, including the United States, to mount an international offensive to rescue the non-Muslim African populations. The influence of Wahabism and the political bloc it controlled, from Washington to Brussels, was too strong. The veto power exercised by the empire was visible in the treatment of various crises. For example, while the West intervened massively to stop ethnic cleansing in the former Yugoslavia in the 1990s, and went to war twice against Serbia, just a thousand miles south, it did not put pressure on Sudan as it was massacring one million black Africans. Some argue that the identity of the victims was central to Wahabi lobbying. For in the 1990s, the victims in Sudan were non-Muslims, whereas the victims in Yugoslavia were Muslim, so that the West felt free to unleash military interventions north of the Mediterranean but not south of it. As of 2004, when the victims were still blacks but now Muslims, too, the pressure against intervention coming from the Muslim states was lessened. Besides, other African Muslim countries were protesting the ill treatment of their kin inside Sudan. That, too, weakened Arab-Wahabi clout internationally. Finally, the shock of September 11, 2001 allowed the pro-Darfur campaign to gain ground with the American public, and later more broadly within the West. For the battle for human rights in the Arab and Muslim world is possible because of the public's awareness of the violations committed by the Jihadist and totalitarian forces. Thus, by 2008 Western policies regarding Darfur, and ultimately the south, had changed dramatically. But these policies will change again if a new direction is taken in Washington and Brussels to end the War on Terror. The Islamist regime in Sudan has signified its commitment to fight any serious intervention in Darfur or in support of the African south. Jihadist forces, including al Qaeda and Iran, but also authoritarian regimes in the region, have declared their solidarity with Khartoum. Sudan is and will continue to

be a principal battlefield in the confrontation between the Free World and the Jihadists and their allies; but it won't be the only battlefield in Africa.[16]

Jihadism in the Horn

The second most important Jihadi battlefield in Africa is centered on the Horn of
Africa region, that is, Somalia, Ethiopia, Eritrea, Kenya, and Djibouti. Traditionally, the main adversary of the Jihadists in this region is Ethiopia; the grounds are
ideological differences and religion. Ethiopia's main religion is Orthodox Christianity and thus falls into the category of *kuffar*. But more relevant is the geopolitical
position of that country, across the waters from the Arabian peninsula. In religious
tradition, the ancient king of the Abyssinians hosted early Muslim exiles fleeing
Meccan oppression. But in later centuries, during the expansion of the caliphate,
by remaining true to their faith and refusing to Arabize and Islamize, the Ethiopians kept their kingdom independent from the expanding Islamic areas around
them in Sudan, Eritrea, and Somalia. Ethiopia became a sort of an enclave that obstructed the expansion of the caliphate deeper into East Africa.

These historical tensions were supposed to recede with the rise of the modern
nation-states in the region and their acceptance of United Nations membership and
international law. Whatever the old enmities, which related to civilizational clashes,
international law had become the new guarantor of borders and national choices.
But not to the Jihadists, of course. In their eyes, infidels are infidels. While in the
1970s and 1980s the Arab regimes supported Khartoum in its campaign against the
southern provinces, Addis Ababa backed the African rebels inside Sudan. But the
Ethiopians, both under Emperor Haile Selassie and Communist leader Haile
Mariam, were responding to Sudanese support for a separatist movement in Eritrea.
In the early 1990s, with the end of the Cold War, mostly Arab-speaking Eritrea obtained its independence from a post-Communist Ethiopia; but Southern Sudan still
struggled against the Islamist regime of Khartoum. Then the Jihadists found a new
battlefront in the region, allowing them to spread further south: Somalia.

At the time of the U.S. humanitarian intervention in Mogadishu in 1993, the
Jihadists had already established influence in the Horn of Africa. The returnees
from Afghanistan's war against the Soviets, who would ultimately form al Qaeda,
had chosen Somalia as a base for future operations due to the collapse of the state.
In one decade, al Qaeda set up local organizational structures in Somalia, the Mahakem Islamiya, or Islamic Courts. By 2007, these Taliban-like militias had seized
the capital but receded quickly thanks to an Ethiopian intervention at the request
of the Interim Somali government, backed by the United States and moderate
Arab countries. But the Mahakem, like the Neo-Taliban in Pakistan's border areas,
continued to carry out attacks inside Somalia. Around the region, from the Horn

to most of East Africa, the Jihadists have established cells and influence in Eritrea, Kenya, and Uganda. Throughout the 1990s these countries were containing the Sudanese regime, particularly when bin Laden was working on an al Qaeda regional base outside of Khartoum, and they initially sided with the international campaign against terror. Uganda and Kenya have been, till 2008, among the staunchest resistors to the Jihadi expansion, while Eritrea, because of the fluctuating Wahabi influence in its midst, swings between forces sympathetic and opposed to the Islamists.

The Jihadists' plans for the Horn are strategically daring: solidifying Mahakem control in Somalia, establishing new al Qaeda bases in the country, and then destroying Eritrea's antiterrorist forces to link up with Sudan along the Red Sea. With such a regional sultanate, the Jihadi forces can join with the Salafists based in Saudi Arabia and ensure financial and diplomatic support. Their next target would be to thrust west and south toward equatorial and southern Africa. But these offensives from the Horn and Sudan toward the heart of sub-Saharan Africa cannot happen without the help of the powerful bases of Salafism in North Africa.[17]

North Africa

The Jihadist movement from Egypt's Western Desert to the Atlantic Ocean has a solid history, both organizationally and militarily. For decades the Muslim Brotherhood grew powerful branches from the Nile Valley in North Africa, but was not able to control a single regime. In the early 1970s, Libyan dictator Muammar Qadhafi launched an Islamist campaign for Jihadism, a mixture of populist Arab nationalism, Islamism, and socialism, presented in his book, the *Kitaab al akhdar*.[18] Its main objective was to Islamize Arab socialism. Although his movement impacted many cadres inside Libya and in the region, he wasn't able to create a zone of influence. The offshoots of the Muslim Brotherhood developed stronger bases in Algeria, Morocco, and, to a lesser degree, Tunisia: the Maghreb Jihadists. Many among the Salafists from these countries joined the struggles in Afghanistan, Chechnya, and Lebanon. With the end of the Cold War the Islamists rose in the Maghreb. The most powerful among these movements, the Front Islamique de Salut (FIS), in Arabic Jabhat al Khalaas al Islamiya, was based in Algeria. After a quarrel with government over the general elections in 1992, the Front and its allies mounted an insurgency throughout the 1990s. An offshoot of the FIS, the GIA (Algerian Islamic Group), massacred civilians who refused to cooperate. And later in the decade, yet another offshoot, the Salafi Group for Religious Call and Combat, took the violence to unprecedented levels: women, children, the elderly, journalists, intellectuals, and musicians were slaughtered. The Algerian civil war took the lives of more than 140,000 among Arab and Berber ethnics, all Sunnis.

This Jihadi war against a Muslim civil society inclined to follow the path of modernization is perhaps the clearest example of what awaits the majority of Muslims who have chosen secularism, modernity, and humanism. The Salafists of Algeria along with the al Qaeda in Iraq and the Wahabis in Chechnya have shown the international community the level of violence these movements are capable of when their ideologues and commanders move them.

Jihadist groups also developed in Tunisia and Morocco, all influenced by the North African Salafist movement. After 9/11 the Maghreb Jihadists, recruited in the Maghreb and infiltrating Western Europe, were behind many attacks in Spain, Algeria, Morocco, and the Netherlands, and assassination attempts in Germany, Denmark, Sweden, Great Britain, and Italy. North African Salafists are overwhelmingly predominant among the Jihadists in France and are thought to be the real force behind the urban insurgency in the fall of 2005. In 2007, in a revealing move, the Salafi Group for Religious Call and Combat declared it was merging with the "mother ship" and changed its name to Al Qaeda in the Maghreb. Since then it has conducted terror operations in Algeria and mobilized and recruited on both sides of the Mediterranean. Ultimately, these al Qaeda cells aim to destroy the governments of Morocco, Algeria, and Tunisia and install emirates as part of a future caliphate. These North African future *wilayas* on a much larger scale—as sultanates—would develop strategic assets aimed at Western Europe. But one of the most worrisome moves is a southward-directed sub-Saharan Jihad.[19]

Sub-Saharan Jihad

Sub-Saharan Africa is the weak link that could allow Jihadism to make advances in Africa and perhaps in the world. This region encompasses the traditional desert states of Mauritania, Mali, Niger, and Chad, but also in the large geographical continuum, the coastal nations located between Nigeria and Senegal. Since the 1980s, the regimes of Libya and Saudi Arabia (and to a lesser extent Iraq) have invested heavily in the sociocultural infrastructure of these newly independent countries to gain political influence. Similar militant activities were performed by the Muslim Brotherhood. In the mid-1980s Iran and Hezbollah began their own support networks in the region. The main objective of these investments was to exert diplomatic influence over the mostly Muslim governments in order to draw on their support at the United Nations, and—in the case of the Wahabis and the Khumeinists—push for further Islamization of those countries. During the Nigerian civil war in 1968, the Arab League stood by the Hausa, of Muslim ethnicity, in the north, and against the Ibo, of Christian ethnicity, in the south. But beyond the "religious solidarity" was a politico-economic calculation, because Biafra, the secessionist province of the Catholic Ibo, has most of Nigeria's oil reserves. The Oil

Empire wanted to ensure full control over this natural resource as a way to force the West into political submission. Nigerian oil in the hands of the Catholic Ibo could have subverted this strategy. However, since 9/11, the United States has developed an interest in buying oil from Nigeria as a way to diversify its imports.

For decades after the conclusion of the civil war, the Nigerian political establishment wanted to use the oil revenues to improve the country's economy and society. The multiethnic establishment wished to distance itself from Islamism. But since 2001, the Salafists have increased their intervention among the local Islamic fundamentalists, particularly in the north of the country. A race is now on between the Islamists from the north and the moderates in the rest of the country; whoever gains control of Nigeria will basically dominate the geopolitics of the sub-Saharan region. The international Salafists, Wahabis, and Muslim Brotherhood know all too well that Nigeria could become the black Saudi Arabia of Africa, and they are intensifying their efforts to prevent it from becoming a rich African state outside of Wahabi control.

To the East of Nigeria, Chad has become another target of the Jihadists. Like Sudan, the country is ethnically multilayered. To the far north there is the Arabized Muslim population; in the large central area a majority of black Muslims; and in the south, African Christians. In 1975, at the instigation of Libya, a civil war took place between the Muslim center and north against the Christian south. But one decade later, African Chadians from both religions united to push back a Libyan occupation of the north of the country. The Libyan Jihad was defeated. But since 2004, another Jihadi offensive has been triggered as a result of the Darfur genocide. As soon as Chad started to support the Darfur movement and assist the refugees, a Wahabi-inspired movement began guerrilla warfare against Njamena. Chad's government, stunningly, accused Saudi Arabia of backing the Jihadist movement inside the country, a charge very few countries ever dared to level against Riyadh.

Chad's location is strategic. It stands between the Jihadi forces in Sudan and the Horn of Africa and the vast Sahara, and provides a connection to West Africa and the Maghreb. Hence, expectations are that the Jihadists may redouble their efforts to destabilize Chad in the future. The Jihadists also desire to break the unity of black Christians and Muslims, so that the Salafists can recruit among the re-Islamized Muslims. This follows the same pattern as in Sudan, where the Islamists have focused on dividing the country on the basis of religion to obtain a majority of black Muslims and Arabs against black Christians, and to prevent a majority of Africans of all religions struggling against the northern Arabized population, which might be seen as being like the European colonialists. If successful, the Jihadists could continue their westward spread through Niger, Mali, and Mauritania, and on to coastal West Africa, from Senegal to Togo.

In Mauritania, the Islamists have already developed political bases in the north, profiting from the ethnic struggle between the Arabized northerners and the blacks of the south. Siding with the slavers in the north, the Salafists find themselves at odds with the black Muslims of the south, who are still suffering from slavery and cultural oppression at the hands of Nouakchott's ruling elites.

In northern Nigeria, where they've established influence and militias, the Salafists plan to seize control of the southern provinces with Yoruba and Ibo majorities and capture the oil fields. The more centralized al Qaeda and Wahabi elements may engage in attacks against petroleum refineries, industries, and export infrastructure to limit the ability of the United States and other Western democracies to import from outside the Arab Middle East, thus maintaining Washington's economic dependence on the Arabian peninsula's resources.

Jihadist influence has already reached the coastal countries of West Africa, particularly the Ivory Coast, as the Salafist element has been organizing the insurgency that is spreading in the northern part of the once prosperous country. Abidjan, once the Paris of Africa, has been paying the price for its long friendship with France and the West and for using its strong diplomatic influence throughout the continent to support African Unity Organization initiatives against terrorism. Beginning in 2004, Islamist militias in the mostly Muslim north marched south to destroy the multiethnic government. Demarcation lines were drawn between the two zones of the country, under the surveillance of French troops. But as predicted by Islamist militants, including those who appear on al Jazeera, the Jihadists will resume their offensive to bring down the government and ultimately declare a local emirate. As one can guess, the whole Sahara is a zone of combat and maneuvering among various brands of Jihadism. The Iranian and Hezbollah networks are extremely active in West Africa. Operating among Lebanese émigré communities, Hezbollah and Amal[20] movement cells have been set up in Sierra Leone, Liberia, Togo, Benin, Burkina Faso, and other neighboring countries. Hezbollah's financial operations in these areas are important to its infrastructure in southern Lebanon and as a part of the overall Iranian network in the region. Projecting an increasing need by the West for natural resources, including oil from Nigeria and the coastal nations, Tehran's deployment of cells is a logical part of its future terrorist strategy if the regime itself is put under pressure. Because of these linkages, one can project that dramatic developments in the Levant, for example in Iraq and in Saudi Arabia, would ripple all the way across the northern part of the African continent. But the southern part of Africa, though at present less touched by Jihadi terror, won't be safe for long.

The terror attacks in Kenya and Tanzania in 1998 showed how vulnerable sub-Saharan Africa is to al Qaeda and other networks. These may be only a prelude. If the Jihadists consolidate their bases in the Horn and the Sahara regions, equatorial Africa will be wide open. Weak security systems can be circumvented by very sophisticated cells and movements that seek to strike against the West—and threats can cause these governments to distance themselves from the Free World. Congo, Zimbabwe, Angola, Mozambique, and Namibia fall into this category. In a sense the Turabi doctrine may well become a reality if Sudan and Somalia become regional launchpads for Jihadi activities. South Africa, evidently, is the prize to be won in a massive undertaking by the Jihadi forces. The historical symbolism of the black struggle, the fall of apartheid, and the rise of a working African democracy incorporating ethnic European communities within a black majority are powerful achievements that have created a model for success among young African nations. Indeed, its self-liberation by Africans, maintenance of a pluralist democracy, and advances in infrastructure and development provide an example to other countries—a dangerous one if you are a Jihadist pushing a totalitarian, mono-ethnic, and theological ideology.[21]

South Africa and the Liberation Struggle

In the 1970s and 1980s, Pan-Arabists and Marxists sought to form a united front with the African liberation movements in an attempt to flank the West via an alliance between the Communist world and the Third World, particularly in Africa. Many of the nationalist movements either sided with Moscow or were infiltrated and made to identify with the front. These alliances developed fully in Angola and Mozambique, where Communists took over the leadership of the liberation movements, and partially in Zimbabwe, Namibia, and South Africa, where Marxist elements penetrated the movement apparatus. Historians now debate whether the nationalist groups were actually Communists faking a national cause or nationalists using Communist support. Nevertheless, the Pan-Arabist strategy, using its influence in traditional Muslim countries, succeeded in appearing supportive of African issues, gaining the moral support of leaders such as South African symbol Nelson Mandela. Using the podium of the African Union, Muammar Qadhafi, the Sudanese regime under Nimeiri and Bashir, the Algerian FLN, and before them Nasser of Egypt all affirmed their full support for the African struggle against Western imperialism.

In reality, these positions were coordinated with the Soviets in order to cut off Western Europe and North America from the African continent altogether. But the Pan-Arabist diplomatic propaganda exposed itself at several occasions during the Cold War, as when the Arab League and its African members sided openly with the northern Muslim faction during the Nigerian civil war against the non-Muslim faction in the south; also when the Arab League stood firmly by the Khartoum Arab brothers against the black enemies in the south. Other African leaders struggling against European domination, however, dismissed the Arab League fraternization with Arab ethnics against black ethnics throughout the continent. The African National Congress, struggling against white power in Johannesburg, didn't see the blackness of those massacred in Juba, Southern Sudan. And as soon as the Soviet Union collapsed and the white apartheid was isolated by the international community, Jihadi apartheid became starkly visible. By the mid-1990s, the struggle of the black South Sudanese in defense of their Africanism versus the imposed Arabization and ethnic cleansing drew the attention of equatorial and southern African countries. The Eritrean president, although his country is a member of the Arab League, nevertheless said, "We are facing terrorism and an Arab imperialism." This was the position of the leaders of Uganda, Kenya, and Ethiopia in their resistance to Sudan's campaigns. The Jihadists ideologues and strategists realized that the Southern Sudan Jihad would hurt their image in Africa and the Third World. Hence they unleashed a massive campaign using PR companies in the West to discredit Sudanese rebel leader John Garang and foment divisions with his allies. Furthermore, a Jihadist alliance with the extreme left wing—formed after the orthodox Communists of Moscow lost power—waged a relentless campaign to demonize the United States everywhere in advance of the terrorist strikes on America. Ironically, the apex of this campaign materialized during the UN-sponsored international convention on racism, held in Durban, South Africa, during August 2001. One month before the 9/11 attacks, the largest gathering of anti-Western movements in the world assembled in South Africa; they sought to build on the symbolism of the antiapartheid movement to transform it into an anti-American phenomenon. But the real, disguised agenda was to preempt and obstruct the rise of an anti-Jihadism movement linked to the slavery and ethnic cleansing carried out by the National Islamic Front in Khartoum. The news about black people enslaved by Arab tribes and the Difaa al Shaabi militia was about to break the alliance between the Islamists and the African liberation movements. Durban was staged to prevent that, but only one month later, bin Laden launched the attacks in America. As a result, U.S. leaders began speaking to the oppressed peoples of the Greater Middle East and Africa, and this breached the Jihadi propaganda shield, bringing more witnesses from Africa to the Free World to denounce the horrors of the slavery and massacres.

This belated discovery validated the cause in the West and the United Nations, European Union, and nongovernmental organizations rushed to the rescue. Black Muslims were now seen as the victims of Jihadists; this reality was also discovered in Mauritania, where the poorest among black Muslims were slaves of Arab masters. Jihadi racism was revealed for what it was. When Chad revolted against Sudanese incursions and Wahabi support for terrorism on its own territory, the continent began to understand that Africanism had been used by the Islamists to manipulate a noble cause for the sake of building a new Taliban empire, in which *abeed* (slavery) would be tolerated, if not widely practiced. South Africa and the other giants of black Africa such as Nigeria and Ethiopia may reject the claims of the Arab League, many of whose members are supporters of the racist regime in Khartoum. The next decade may witness a surge of Africanism—Muslim, Christian, traditionalist, and humanist—opposed to Jihadism. But the path will be difficult as the Salafists and the Khumeinists are extremely powerful, wealthy, and have deeply infiltrated many African nations.

Jihadists, having realized the awareness spreading in the continent, have developed cutting-edge strategies to preempt the rise of this new liberation movement by subverting the three main black powers that oppose them: Nigeria, Ethiopia, and South Africa. The Islamists intend to break Nigeria apart by inciting sectarian violence in the north while the terrorists strike at the oil industry in the south. The Jihadists are spending significant energies to surround Ethiopia with menacing battlefronts: Somalia, Eritrea, and Sudan. Last but not least, the Jihadists, including al Qaeda, have already infiltrated South Africa and have formed terror cells there. It is only recently that Africans have realized that, long after colonialism receded, one major threat still imperils the continent: a terror campaign whose ultimate goal is to replace the old European colonial enterprise with a new imperialism called the caliphate.[22]

THE LATIN AMERICAN BATTLEFIELDS

Latin America, along with Australia, is the continent farthest from the centers of Jihadism in the Greater Middle East. But although remote from the Arab and Muslim world geographically, Latin America is strategically important to the Salafists and the Khumeinists because it is in the backyard of their major enemy; it borders the continental United States, both by land and sea. In Jihadist thinking, there are two ways to penetrate and strike the North American mainland: through Europe and Latin America. Assuming that the European Union—although infiltrated and waging its own war on Jihadi terrorism—is now conscientious about the use of its soil to attack U.S. interests and blocks travel to America for those on terrorist missions, the Jihadi machine has to develop alternatives, and so it is reaching deep into the Latin American region. And unlike European-American tight cooperation on counterterrorism, the north-south hemispheric relationships aren't yet at their best in countering Jihadist penetration. Hence this Jihadist strategy is extremely dangerous for the U.S. homeland and also for the future of the transitional democracies in the region.

Historically, the relations between Latin American and the Arab Muslim world depended on three major streams. The first stream of ties was between the various countries of the region and those regimes in the Middle East interested in acquiring credibility in international relations, such as Saudi Arabia, Egypt, and Morocco. A second stream of relationships was established by left-wing regimes on both sides of the Atlantic. Cuba's Communists—via the Soviet Union—had ties to the Communist parties in the Arab world. Iraq under Saddam used its oil revenues to cultivate Pan-Arabist supporters among Arab émigrés. Libya's Qadhafi also used his petrodollars in the 1970s and the 1980s to build Islamic bases of support, particularly in Surinam and Caribbean nations. More recently, as we will note later, Venezuelan leader Hugo Chavez has established more strategic relations with powerful Jihadists.

However, the third, and potentially most important, stream of relationships between Latin America and the Greater Middle East is undoubtedly the ties among the millions of émigrés and their descendants who have arrived from the Greater Middle East, and from Lebanon in particular. Lebanon (and to a lesser extent Syria), enjoyed a much wider web of relationships, altogether disproportional to its size when compared to other countries of the Middle East, but proportional to its very large diaspora in Latin America. There are about 15 million Latin Americans of Lebanese descent, including about 5 million in Brazil alone; another three million from Syrian descent, half a million of Palestinian ancestry, in addition to another million of Arab, Assyro-Chaldeans, Turkish, and Iranian origin. This huge number of citizens of Middle Eastern descent, in addition to large Jewish communities, is of great demographic importance to radical organizations and regimes aiming to penetrate the southern hemisphere.[23]

Regime Influences

The objectives of the Middle Eastern regimes in the Americas are of long standing. The Syrian regime, for example, has been the most engaged in Latin America, using its own émigrés to recruit supporters. Since 1976, and increasingly as of 1990, the Baath Party in Damascus has been able to mobilize Lebanese emigrants who were pro-Syrian. Iraq under Saddam attempted to compete with Syria by using large amounts of cash to enlist Arab emigrants in general. Libya also spent significant amounts trying to create Arab-Islamic supporters in South America and the Caribbean during the 1980s. But it was the Saudi Wahabis who were the most generous in funding institutions and religious and cultural centers dedicated to the spread of Wahabism. The Saudi drive was conducted openly and solicited support from sitting governments. As of the late 1990s, another competitor for Jihadi indoctrination showed up in the area: the Iranian regime. Counting initially on the Syrian influence with Arab émigrés, Tehran's overseas networks soon developed their own, thanks to Hezbollah. Indeed, the Iranian-funded Lebanese-based organization successfully used patience and petrodollars to create bases across South America; they opened a wide path for Iranian influence and future strike capabilities. In addition to turning to émigrés, a number of Middle Eastern regimes employed economic advantages. On the one hand, and thanks to their unlimited revenues, regimes such as those in Iraq, Iran, and Saudi Arabia are able to purchase weapons from countries such as Brazil, Chile, and Argentina. They also can cut favorable deals in trade and oil commerce.[24]

Regime Alliances

The Latin American strategies of the Jihadists rest first on acquiring open and solid relations with influential elites. Until the end of the Cold War, only Cuba was seen as anti-American enough to be perceived as an ally—but an orthodox Marxist regime was too insulated to allow a vast back-and-forth stream of activity outside the relationship with the Soviet Union. With the collapse of the latter, it was also too risky for Havana to openly host American enemies without protection. It took the Jihadi powers of the Middle East almost a decade to find their new Fidel, a leader who would espouse Jihadism as a real strategic ally. That populist militaristic leader is Hugo Chavez. For as soon as he grabbed power and began consolidating it, a web of Islamists rushed to embrace him. The Venezuelan populist president was interviewed several times by al Jazeera in 2006 and was thus introduced to the Arab and Muslim world as a viable, credible ally against the United States. Soon afterward, Caracas was visited by top Iranian leaders, and Chavez was invited to Tehran and other capitals in the region. Iran and Venezuela are now building a strategic alliance, which most likely will develop four tracks of collaboration: a joint oil strategy; joint military cooperation, including the potential installation on Venezuelan soil of Iranian missiles capable of reaching the United States, Canada, and Latin America; the training of units destined to intervene overseas, as Cuban units did in Africa during the Cold War; and last, the sharing of nuclear military technologies when Iran completes its strategic weapons system. Such a military alliance between Chavez and the ayatollahs would bring Iran directly into the Caribbean, a shift that would put the U.S. homeland in peril. Other Middle Eastern regimes that could also develop such strategic relations with a hardened Chavez regime include Syria, Sudan, Libya (if it reverses its policies), and potentially the Saudi Arabian and Qatari governments if they fall under Salafi influence in the future. Note that Chavez's expanding alliances are not only the result of his theories but the product of a long-term buildup by Levantine-descent Venezuelans with ties to radical movements, particularly in Lebanon. This web of interests could expand to Bolivia to create similar cooperation with Evo Morales's regime. Wherever radical populist regimes rise, the Jihadist regimes will follow.[25]

Jihadi Movements

The Jihadist movements, both Salafist and Khumeinist, have more flexibility in infiltrating and expanding their operations than the radical regimes. They can take advantage of cooperation between Iran, Syria, and the Wahabi circles of Arabia with Chavez and Morales, and also profit from the space provided by Latin American governments trading heavily with the Middle East, such as Brazil, Argentina, Chile, and Uruguay. Also, al Qaeda and Hezbollah will create their own bases independent of all sponsors, when and where they can. Experts believe that the pro-Iranian organization has already established networks in a number of countries, with two main hubs: One is situated in the so-called triborder area between Brazil, Argentina, and Paraguay. A lawless land at the crossroads of traditional routes of smuggling and other illegal activities, the area has become a Hezbollah center for training and networking. The terror attacks in Argentina in the early 1990s, linked by the Argentine authorities to Hezbollah and Iran, are an example of the Khumeinist reach in South America. The northern bases of Hezbollah are allegedly found in Venezuela, including on Margarita Island. Further analysis shows that Hezbollah has a wider presence in Guyana, the Caribbean, and Mexico.

Al Qaeda is present in many more Latin American countries than Hezbollah is, and is more fluid and decentralized and counts on the support of a great many Salafist supporters. Also present in the triborder area, the bin Laden organization grows around pools of indoctrinated Wahabis, themselves funded by Gulf grants. As in any other region in the world, the Wahabis fund, the Muslim Brotherhood indoctrinates, and al Qaeda recruits.[26] The Salafi Jihadists are present in Venezuela as well, alongside the Iranian networks. Al Qaeda has been growing in influence all across the Caribbean, from Grenada to Santo Domingo and Jamaica, developing a presence aimed at the United States. Profiting from poor socioeconomic conditions, such as those in Haiti, the cells can establish their logistical capacity unchecked.

Central America and Mexico are also staging areas for both al Qaeda and Hezbollah, which could ultimately allow them to reach the final target: America. The crumbling U.S.-Mexican border is an ideal crossing point for the Jihadists, especially Spanish-speaking ones. Once on U.S. soil they can vanish into a huge Hispanic population, and emerge on D-day for their final mission. A sound analysis should not dismiss the more dangerous development, which according to experts is already happening: the alliance between Jihadists and Latin American terrorists, gangs, and radicals. This is a lethal combination, and it is spreading along American frontiers and even inside American borders.

CHAPTER 14

THE STATE OF THE CONFRONTATION

Si vis pacem para bellum

THE ROMAN ADAGE "IF YOU WANT PEACE, PREPARE FOR WAR" MAY BEST describe the state of the confrontation that has existed for almost two decades and which continues to define international relations and the so-called global war on terror. The natural inclination of nations, public opinion, and the forces of civil society is to end wars, all wars. From the diplomatic arrangements in post-Napoleonic Europe to the Kellogg-Briand Pact after World War I to the founding of the United Nations after World War II, humanity has tried over and over to put an end to its violent history. Hopes rose again after the Cold War, but the 1990s showed that the scourges of ethnic conflicts and ethnic cleansing were still alive; that some dictatorships—as in Cuba, China, and Myanmar—were committed to staying outside the acceptable norms charted after the fall of the Berlin Wall; and that some states sought to destabilize the balance of nuclear power, for example, Iran and North Korea.

But these were exceptions—albeit large and very bloody in some cases—to the trend of history. By the last decade of the twentieth century, China was modernizing too fast to remain as rigidly Communist as it was, and was morphing into a new type of corporate Marxist-business power minus pluralism. There will be many major events in China that will move it in the direction of a more open society and a freer economy. Latin America's transitional democracies are also mutating, and their democratic processes have gone much faster in the 1990s, despite the surge of populism in Venezuela and Bolivia. Cuba after Castro will be different from the "Give me socialism or give me death" fanaticism of the 1960s. It will take some time, but younger Cubans will seek social democracy. Even Vietnam and Cambodia are tasting little doses of entrepreneurship and personal freedom. Myanmar's

Buddhist monks are pushing the military regime for change, heedless of repression. The south of the African continent is enmeshed in great difficulties, and the consequences of tribal ethnocide are still looming in Rwanda and Burundi—but only as spasms from historically unresolved legacies. In the Northern Hemisphere, Central and Eastern Europe are racing toward economic development and modernization. And regardless of how Russian governments behave, Russian youth know what type of society they want to live in—certainly not in the shadow of Stalinism. Of course, in world politics some will continue to resist idealism, but in this age of modernization and globalization the younger generation may not respond to the war cries of the ruling elites; thus, many conflicts could die for lack of fighters. The future—outside the current War on Terror—may really be what Francis Fukuyama thought it would be immediately after the Soviet collapse—an end to history as we have known it. But his vision discounted one detail: the persistence of retrograde forces.

The Jihadist hurricane is pushing international society backward. These forces aren't looking to ameliorate the future by struggling against oppression; they are pushing for a future that would look like the past, with their own version of oppression. While modern society moves toward enhancement and advancement, the forces of Salafism and Khumeinism are breaking this energy and using all methods to reverse it.[1]

The end of the first decade of an undecided century is fraught with complexities. Where are we in the global confrontation that has been the subject of this book? Is there a single measurement? Which decisions, strategies, and directions are the correct, possible, and necessary ones, for now and for the future? In conclusion, what is it that the international community should and can do to be able to win this confrontation?

WINNING THE WAR OF KNOWLEDGE

From a comprehensive review of the nature of the conflict, the goals of the Jihadists, their strategies, the responses of democracies, and the public's current understanding of the root causes of the confrontation, the essential conclusion is clear: A war of knowledge has to be won first. The sine qua non of surviving a challenge is to understand it.

A War, Not Incidents

First, we have to admit that this confrontation is a war, or a series of wars, clashes, tensions, and hostilities, and part of a global conflict, and thus we have to plan and act accordingly. The Free World has to plan on winning this war and thus reaching peace. But there is a difference between attaining peace and merely stopping a war. The Jihadists and their allies understood this part of the game early on. They prepared for a war and launched it; then, as they made progress on the ground, they induced their opponents into believing that it is the other—the democracies—not the Jihadists, that began the conflict. Cleverly, they trigger—and sometimes support—the rise of a "stop-the-war" movement inside infidel lands. But if the West and the Free World, along with the oppressed in the Middle East, unilaterally adopt this antiwar attitude (while their opponents don't), this will lead to further wars and ultimately the democracies' defeat. Therefore, the initial definition of the confrontation is essential: This is not a series of incidents to be dealt with separately, but rather a war to be managed globally and comprehensively. Last but not least, it is a war of the Jihadists' ideology and actions and it affects many nations.[2]

A War with a Known Entity

Despite the way it is portrayed by many apologists, this war is against a known party; it isn't a war with terrorism as a concept or a method of war—just as there is no war against Special Forces, suicide bombing, or carpet bombings. Hence, the thesis that this is a war on or with terror is neither accurate nor logical; but neither is its antithesis, which is that the violence we're witnessing around the world consists of dispersed events that we cannot connect until we have the names and serial numbers of all the attackers and a declaration of war from them. Politicians on both sides of the Atlantic, including those in the European Parliament and the U.S. Congress, have demanded the abandonment of the concept of a War on Terror—but they do no wish to replace it with a better term, such as a conflict with the Jihadists. They propose instead to deal with terror on a case-by-case basis, ignoring the planned and concerted nature of Jihadist violence. This is an absurdity, given that there are two huge world forces, the Iran-Syria axis and the al Qaeda web of organizations, engaged in more than twenty battlefields around the world, having caused hundreds of thousands casualties, and having issued dozens of declarations of war and hundreds of fatwas openly stating that they are waging war. And yet some in the Free World still mislead the public and themselves as to the nature of the confrontation. Without a change, this illogic could lead to losing the so-called war on terror.[3]

A War Declared Unilaterally and Preemptively

The propaganda machines of the Salafists, Wahabis, Takfiris, Khumeinists, dictators, and authoritarians have pounded international public opinion with the assertion that the West has initiated aggressions against the "peoples of the region" in order to pillage, dominate, and (in the rhetoric of the Jihadists) "attack Islam." These arguments, relentlessly used by the spokespersons of the antidemocracy forces and their allies within the West, accuse the United States principally, then every country they are confronting, of being the first to begin hostilities. The chief target of their criticism has been the so-called preemptive wars waged by the United States, and particularly the Bush administration, against innocent governments. This fraud has to be reversed and the full picture drawn so that national and international public opinion will recognize, not necessarily the justness of Western policies, but the unfairness of the allegations made by the terror propagandists. Western policies have been error-prone in past decades; but the West did not initiate a war with Jihadism. The Jihadists initiated war; the Salafists and the Khumeinists follow different strategies, but both mounted terror campaigns. The attacks of the 1990s, as well as the 9/11 attacks, were all unilateral aggressions. The 1996 and 1998 declarations of war by al Qaeda were also one-way statements. And at the planetary scale, Islamist preparations for the greater geopolitical Jihad are too obvious to be treated as mere reactions. Their goal is to establish a worldwide caliphate on the ashes of fifty-two Muslim states.[4]

The Jihadists Are Ahead

This is a disturbing but necessary fact to absorb: The Jihadists began their war long before their opponents counterattacked, and al Qaeda, the other Salafists, the Iranian and Syrian regimes, and Hezbollah gained an advantage in time. The Muslim Brotherhood and the Wahabis rose in the mid-1920s, giving them an eighty-year head start on the United States and the West, which took many decades to understand their ideology, project their strategies, and respond to their actions. Even as of 2008, the Free World is slow to recognize the progress made by the Jihadists, both inside the Muslim world and in other regions. The Islamist movements set the cultural agenda in the Greater Middle East and successfully penetrated Western political systems. They have been taking the initiative since the early 1990s in many battlefields and have been able to further infiltrate the West as well. This reality has significant consequences. For example, in Iraq, the Salafi Jihadists have been building for decades, not only under Saddam's rule but before he was even in power. The claim that the Islamists came to Iraq after the United States invaded is wrong. It fuels the notion (equally incorrect) that there is a causal relation between the American move and the Jihadist reaction. But it is true that the U.S. and Western war planners prior to Iraq did not project the existence of a hard-core Islamist movement, below the Baathist layer, and worse, still haven't devised a strategy to counter them. Another analytical mistake was the failure to understand the Jihadists'

time advantage in the region. The pro-Iranian Iraqi Shiites have been in cahoots with Tehran at least since the late 1980s, and certainly since the early
1990s. The Khumeinists had a plan for Iraq long before the United States developed one. The critics who argued that Iranian involvement in Iraq is due to
the American invasion are mistaken: The Iranian Islamists had prepared their
infiltration of Iraq long before the marines moved in. And the war planners who
boasted about the expected Shiite rallying were also proven wrong. The Jihadi
preeminence and time advantage are also unfortunately the case on other battlefields around the world. Compared to this cataclysmic reality, the programs
and policies set by the West in general and the United States in particular to
counter this violence and the ideologies behind it are almost a joke. The coun-
terstrategies shaped to deal with these challenges must study the deeper layers
of Islamist propaganda and the number of ideological generations already built
by the early waves of radicalization. Compared to the depth and sophistication
of Jihadi indoctrination and propaganda, Western understanding of the war—
though improving—is still ridiculously primitive.[5]

A Long War

Another crucial realization for the confrontation is its projected duration. The
War on Terror may be shorter or longer depending on who holds power in the
major capitals, which elites are in charge of the theorization, and what doctrines
determine the prosecution of the conflict. Spain's contribution to the post 9/11
Western offensive began in 2001 and ended in 2004 with the Madrid attacks and
the subsequent decision by the Spanish government to pull its troops out of Iraq.
Britain's deployment of troops alongside those of the United States peaked in
2007. France's participation in the pressures on the Iranian regime to stop the
nuclear buildup began only after the election of President Nicolas Sarkozy (also
in 2007). So far, Russia has not engaged the dangerous regimes in the region.
What is often missed is that al Qaeda didn't relinquish its claim on Spain after
2004, and its cells are still engaging in terror activities in Iberia and against
Ceuta and Melilla. The UK withdrawal from Iraq is not causing a dismantling of
the Jihadi networks targeting Britain. Despite the Sarkozy awakening, the
Salafist forces in France continue to take advantage of the Gaullist decades-long
"Arab policy." Russia's Middle East policies of sustaining Iran's and Syria's military powers will not reduce Wahabi growth in the Caucuses and in the trans-
Ural regions. In short, the Free World is acting as if the War on Terror is a
manageable conflict that can be ended abruptly if the national interests of the
moment are served fully. This is a grave mistake. For the Jihadist war on democracies—and more pointedly, on the infidels—will not be stopped by dispersed

and contradictory efforts on behalf of the Free World. The Jihadi agenda is comprehensive, long-term, and systematic. They have waged a patient and irredentist campaign over eight decades, based on a historical vision going back thirteen centuries. They aren't stopping at the request of a UN Security Council resolution, a U.S. congressional vote, or a Kremlin executive order. The Jihadists are in for a long war. The Free World has no choice but to prepare for a long confrontation, one that is dictated by the many years the Salafists, Khumeinists, and other terror forces have spent preparing. By way of comparison—even an imperfect one—it took the Nazis about twelve years to seize power and conduct their blitzkrieg in Europe and North Africa. It took the Allies—after being attacked, forming an alliance, and engaging fully in the conflict—six years to bring down Nazism. By the same proportion, it would take the Free World thirty years to accomplish the same victory over the Jihadi terror. It took the West about sixty years to defeat Bolshevism. The Salafi Islamists rose in the 1920s, and they've struggled for decades to build their power with a combination of regimes, vast pools of indoctrinated cadres and partisans, economic empire, and organizations. The Khumeinist elite has been preparing for the confrontation since 1979, using its oil revenues and moving one step at a time. How, then, can Free World strategists calculate the factor of time in their War on Terror?

No American, European, Russian, or Indian leader has quantified the length of time needed for the confrontation, nor even provided an estimate. We haven't heard from Arab and Muslim leaders—those who are on the side of freedom—make statements on the duration of the crisis. To be fair, top leaders such as President George Bush, Vice President Dick Cheney, former Prime Minister Tony Blair, and legislators on both sides of the Atlantic have stated that this is or could be a long war. But even though they uttered these words, their advisors and spokespersons haven't explained why it is going to be a long conflict. Hence the public has received three conflicting versions from their leaders: (1) This is a conflict initiated by the West and thus can be stopped as soon as the West ceases its so-called War on Terror; (2) This is a war with terrorists but it can still be ended quickly if the Free World responds with massive force; (3) This is a War on Terror, it will be a long one, but we don't know how long. What has not been shared with the public is a fourth explanation, perhaps the most dramatic: This is a war begun by the Jihadists a long time ago against the Free World, and because of the Jihadist camp's penetration and preparations, it is going to be a long war—especially if the Free World doesn't accept the principle that there *is* a long struggle ahead. By extension, the earlier the international community accepts the concept of a long war and acts upon it, the shorter the conflict will last. The Free World can only shorten the confrontation if it prepares for a long conflict. This is the secret equation of this so-called War on Terror.[6]

THE PAST COMMANDS THE FUTURE
OF THE CONFRONTATION

The outcome of this ongoing confrontation will also be determined by the events that took place in the past in terms of Jihadi actions and planning. It won't suffice for governments, a coalition of countries, or civil society in the Free World to decide on a particular course of action unless a very precise and strategic understanding of the Islamist apparatus and Jihadi deployment is achieved. As noted earlier, a U.S.-led invasion of Iraq with sheer force wasn't enough to bring the conflict to an end in a limited period of time, despite the shock and awe of American military might. Miscalculations about Salafi influence and Iranian clout with many Iraqis and failure to analyze the history of the Syrian-Iranian axis blurred analysis and expectations. In the post-Taliban Afghanistan, the depth of the Islamist penetration of Pakistan's northwestern provinces was the root cause of not only the difficulties in stabilizing the country, but also of the menace of a radical takeover of nuclear-armed Pakistan. France's struggle with the urban intifada was determined by years of Salafi expansion in the country's suburbs and the consequences of the French "Arab policy," which paralyzed Paris for years. Every unchecked move by the Jihadists in the past will come back to haunt democracies and moderate Arab governments; it is not only the previous actions of the Islamic fundamentalists that will count in the future, but also the past and present inaction of the countries of the Free World. To begin with, the United States has made foreign policy errors, for example: failing to assist civil societies endangered by the Jihadists (Lebanon, Iran, Afghanistan, Sudan, Algeria) and by authoritarians (Syria, Lebanon, Iraq); and even failing to support human rights enhancement in allied countries (Egypt, Saudi Arabia, Pakistan). These mistakes were transformed into democratic debacles. Not helping the needy in the past led to the rise of the radicals, the further weakening of the weak, and the radicalization of political cultures. No wonder that, after 2001, to the astonishment of many in America (and in the West for that matter), "spreading democracy" has been so difficult.

Critics of the bipartisan policies of countering terrorism (as per the 9/11 Commission findings) based their opposition on the fact that peoples and cultures in the region were not ready to join the community of free nations. In reality, their ability to move at the desired pace was impeded by Western and American lost opportunities since 1945, and more intensely after 1990. For if these societies, including their minorities and democratic forces, had been assisted earlier, they would have been marching shoulder to shoulder with the international coalition against terrorism. But thanks to past mistaken (or nonexistent) policies, the Free World is now faced with a much greater task. Saudi Arabia's governments have spent billions of petrodollars over five decades to grow Wahabi influence around the Muslim world, and also within the West. The acknowledgment of this reality alone would have an impact on the deradicalization process. As we will note later, those who contributed to world instability and directly or indirectly caused harm must reinvest in the corrective processes. The Saudis will have to address the consequences of their past financing of indoctrination. The United States, France, and Europe must support the societies they abandoned, and Russia will have to cut the link to the rogue regimes it has been supplying. Israel's abandonment of the South Lebanon Army to Hezbollah in 2000 ignited the al Aqsa intifada and brought the Iranian-backed terrorist group to Israel's northern border.[7] Past false analysis and wrong policies in the domestic realm also have played a role. For example, U.S. government endorsement of Islamist organizations to officially represent the "Muslim American community" and its laissez-faire attitude toward Wahabi funding of Middle East studies programs have crucially contributed to the rising national security threat. Western Europe's domestic, decades-long acceptance of the Jihadophile agenda as legitimate has been responsible for its precarious security. In short, a global mea culpa has to be made before an essential change in the course of geopolitics can even be possible.

Mayhem and Genocide Loom

Policies and strategies to counter Jihadism should have priority on national and international agendas now because of the apocalyptic vision of Salafi and Khumeinist doctrinaires. Since the 1920s the Jihadists have propagated the legitimization of mass killings, mass destruction, and mass civilization disruption, and their efforts should not be underestimated. While academics debate, the Jihadists acknowledge no real limitations on the means to reach their goals. Indeed, the Islamists—whom many scholars in the West still claim can develop a purely political branch and integrate into pluralist society—have a grand plan, a grand design, and a grand goal in sight, and intend to have it with or without force. If the world falls on its knees before them and gives them the keys to its cities, they will gladly ask those cities to convert and join the caliphate-to-be. That, naturally, would be their preference; but if they encounter an obstacle, they will reduce it. And pluralism is such because it negates the idea of a worldwide caliphate. The Islamist propagandists claim that the "Muslim laws of war" apply. But who legislates these laws? The Jihadists, of course. All means are permissible in Jihadi wars, including actions illegal under international law. The modern fighters for Allah abide by the norms of their emirs and their supreme commanders such as Osama bin Laden, Hassan Turabi, Hassan Nasrallah, and Ayatollah Khamenei. If achieving the divinely sanctioned aims requires beheading innocent civilians, so be it; if babies and rock stars have to be savagely killed, then they will be (as the Salafi Group of Combat in Algeria has done). If foreigners have to be kidnapped, tortured, and killed, diplomats blown up in their embassies, community centers bombed, it must be done, according to the Jihadist mandate that this is Allah's will. Even massacres and genocide are acceptable to Jihadism; one need only recall Iran's elimination of its opposition by the thousands, Assad's mass killing of the Sunnis in Hama in 1982, the Syrian bombardments of Beirut in the 1970s and 1980s, Saddam's gassing of the Kurds, the mass graves of Shiites in Iraq, and even now, the ethnic cleansing and murder of the black people of Southern Sudan and Darfur by the Islamist regime in Khartoum. The lesson here is that, if left to roam freely on the planet, the Jihadists have no self-restraint; there is nothing they will not do to achieve their aims. Bin Laden has called for the massacre of 4 million Americans. And Ahmedinijad and his acolyte in Lebanon, Hassan Nasrallah, openly call for "death to America." In their literature, and sometimes on al Jazeera, the Salafists have no shame in legitimizing the elimination of the *kuffar*.[8]

The term "infidel" as used by the modern Jihadists permits any action to be taken against those thus branded. For as they follow what they believe is a divine order, they offer the *kuffar* three choices: converting, paying a war tax, or dying. One cannot but admit that Jihadism is genocidal. Hence, the confrontation from a Western perspective isn't about foreign policy issues or violence that can be stopped by negotiations or by addressing demands. The followers of al Qaeda and similar forms of radicalism are set on destroying whatever obstructs their march. As has already happened in Sudan, Lebanon, Iraq, Syria, and Iran, cities in Europe, Russia, India, and North America will witness mass casualties if the confrontation with Jihadism is not won. And time is a crucial factor, as things will go worse if Jihadists and authoritarians acquire weapons of mass destruction. Such weapons, for example chemical weapons, have already been used by regimes such as Saddam's on their own and other peoples; that fact should send a chilling message to those who backpedal in the face of rising challenges instead of changing the course of the conflict toward faster resolution.

Not Foreign Policy but Radical Ideologies

As noted, one of the most misleading assertions made during the two decades preceding 9/11 and thereafter is that terrorism is a reaction to U.S. and Western foreign policy. This argument is made on campuses by academic elites critical of their own government's handling of aspects of international relations. The specific assertion that Jihadism is only a reaction to American policies is, however, a component of the agendas of the Wahabis, Muslim Brotherhood and Khumeinists and is aimed at deflecting Western attention from the real root of terrorism—the ideological vision and strategic objectives of the Islamists. In other words, the argument was concocted by the Islamist lobbies to cripple the Western ability to intervene or even respond. "You have created terrorism by siding with Israel, with oppressive Arab regimes, and with your capitalism," the Arabists and Jihadophiles assert. In reality the argument should be turned upside down: "The Jihadists are pre-emptively attacking the West by claiming it is responsible for triggering terrorism, whereas in fact it is Jihadism that legitimized terror in order to gain its objectives."

Another aspect of the confrontation that is difficult to understand—both in the West and in the Arab Muslim world—is religion. Ironically, the stipulation that the issue is about a religion, Islam, has been advanced on both sides of the clash. In fact, though the Islamists (and Jihadists in particular) do refer to what they believe are Islamic injunctions, and while there is an ongoing debate among Muslims and non-Muslims about the doctrines of war and peace in Islamic theology, the conflict per se isn't about articles of faith so much as it is about radical movements' (Salafists' and Khumeinists') political interpretations of Islam's theological texts. So, if religion is involved, it is because militant groups have been invoking verses of the Koran and texts from the Hadith, and because radical clerics have been issuing fatwas and forming opinions favorable to Jihadism—and, last but not least, because political leaders have endorsed such theological claims. But whatever the sources used (or misused) by militants, the body of their production is an ideology: Jihadism. The latter can be loaded with as much theological content as the ideologues wish, but in the eyes of scholars, courts, and legislatures, "Islamism" is a political philosophy, like Marxism or other isms. Jihadism is a doctrine, like Trotskyite Communism or National-Socialism. The Islamists are claiming that they represent Islam, and that they are the only ones who can do so, but to accept the Jihadists' argument that they represent Muslims everywhere, or even a Muslim reaction to world politics, is to accept the fact that the Islamists-Jihadists have seized the exclusive representation of one billion believers by using force and intimidation. Their claim would be the equivalent of the Communist parties' claiming to represent all Russians, Eastern Europeans, Central Asians, and Mongolians during the Cold War. The Communists could do so, but the reality was otherwise, and as soon as the USSR began crumbling, it was revealed that the Communists represented just 4 percent of the population.

The Islamists nowadays claim they represent a growing segment of Muslim societies. That remains to be seen, and it will be seen when full democracy takes root in the Greater Middle East. The Jihadists aren't relying on numbers to back up their claim, however; it is the power of Allah that justifies their ideology. Unfortunately, many in the Western elite confuse expressing a self-constructed representation of Islam with representing Muslims. The international community, Muslim and non-Muslim alike, shouldn't accept the Jihadists' claim that they represent the majority of Muslims around the world, nor that they represent the religion of Islam (as long as the proper religious authorities haven't expressly mandated them). Hence, short of an international and political statement by the Organization of the Islamic Conference (OIC) and the Arab League mandating the Jihadists as legitimate leaders and spokespersons, the Islamists represent only themselves.

The Salafists and the Khumeinists wrongly promote the idea that the West in general and the United States in particular are waging a war against Islam. From al Jazeera's rhetoric to Iran's propaganda machine, the conflict is a *"Harb ala el Islam"* (a war on Islam). It is fundamental that democracies and the entire Free World must address the Muslim world directly (and in its own languages) to refute this Islamist campaign slogan. It is important that the West inform the peoples of the Greater Middle East that its campaign—or its War on Terror—is not a war on Islam. Critics argue that it is ludicrous for the West to claim that it is not waging such a war so long as its forces are deployed on Muslim lands and its policies target mostly countries with a Muslim majority, but their critique can stand only if the West is silent about its real agenda or if it dodges the whole raison d'être of its mobilization. The Free World should clarify the aim of its campaign by naming its foe, very specifically, as the movement of the Jihadists. A "campaign against Jihadism" is the most accurate term for use worldwide. It can be refined further in Arab and Muslim countries as being directed "against Takfiris" or "Salafi Jihadists" or "Khumeinists," and so on. Once the Free World brands the ideology as Jihadist, the majority of Muslims will realize that the target is not Islam as a religion, but an ideological movement that represents a small minority: "It is about Jihadism, not Islam" should be the slogan of the campaign.

Such a clarification would also affect the debate within the Free World, particularly in the West. For, as a result of the Jihadist's frantic campaign to "speak on behalf" of Islam as a whole and for all Muslims, a wave of commentary in the West has begun equating terrorism with all things Islamic. The cultural response to the Jihadists in many Western quarters—particularly after 9/11—is rooted not only in the highly radical discourse of the Combat Salafists (such as al Qaeda) and of the Khumeinist leaders (such as Ahmedinijad), but also in the extreme apologist discourse that left no space for debate on the issue, thereby practically negating the existence of an ideology named Jihadism. In response, many writers, historians, and commentators in Europe and North America began researching the theology of Islam in quest of the religious motivations for the Jihadi terrorists. But since, ironically, the socioeconomic arguments of the apologists were also rejected by the Islamists themselves, many Western critics followed the only option available—to find the sources of terrorism in theology, which was precisely where the Jihadists claimed they drew their inspiration. Hence, oddly, it was the Salafists and the Khumeinists themselves—by referring to verses and suras when calling for action—who invited many of their victims' intellectuals or opponents to research these very texts. In a few years, some intellectuals broke away from the apologist mainstream and produced a large body of research touching on the actual texts of Islamic theology and attempting to link the actions of Jihadi terrorist groups and regimes to religious injunctions. This new wave—nourished intellectually and factually by Muslim dissidents and intellectuals from non-Muslim minorities—has led to a political clash on theological grounds. As a result, the arguments are now about the nature of religion, the Prophet, past theological debates, and Islam's history, instead of limiting the issues to international law and current geopolitics. The debate on the current confrontation must be about the geopolitics of terror, not its theological claims. In this particular case, the issue is about the right (or illegality) of waging a war based on divine injunction. A historical study of the caliphate can produce many academic conclusions, but a caliphate established in the twenty-first century (per the Jihadi vision) would destroy the world order. In the final analysis, although Jihadists use Islamic concepts, words, and references, regardless of the intellectual debate it generates in reaction, the confrontation per se is about self-defense for democratic countries, preservation for internationally acquired freedoms, and assistance for civil societies (including Muslim societies) under duress. If the Jihadists bring in "religion" it is the responsibility of the appropriate religious and political authorities to rebuff them. Jihadism, like all other isms, is a political ideology and a global movement bearing responsibility for its acts and their consequences, and hence falls within the purview of international law.

Inner Readiness Is Low

The inner readiness of most nations that are part of the coalition against terror is dangerously low. Because of the realities noted above, the level of mobilization in most democracies doesn't match the required strength for the challenges to come. Americans, Europeans, other Westerners, Indians, and Russians were not prepared by their governments to sustain the type of sacrifices and efforts they have already incurred and will most likely have to reorganize in order to stop the forces of Jihadism. In the United States, the leading defender of the Free World, public education on the danger has barely begun. We are short of strategically driven leaders to hold the top positions in the next half decade and move the nation forward in homeland security and revolutionary strategies. America may stagnate— or worse; it could weaken its resolve in the face of an escalation in urban terrorist activities. Its court system, the center of its legal defense, has not been enabled to understand and respond to the new challenges. More worrisome is the capacity of the Jihadi lobbies to use the justice system to paralyze or slow a national response. In short, as described in previous chapters, still in 2008 the American public is not endowed with all the elements of national readiness for a long war. Eventually, the state of mind of most Americans—in one way or another—will have to change for

America to meet the challenges; that is inescapable, but the question will be, At what price? As has been shown, the inner readiness in other democracies is also critically low.

In Russia, the public readiness is even lower than it is in the United States. In India, paradoxically, the public seems to understand the challenge, but the official rhetoric hasn't pinpointed ideology as a prime root of Jihadism. In both of these countries the stakes are different than they are in the West, as the Islamists can have a much larger influence on the native segments of the societies and hence the treatment of doctrinal and political matters is more sensitive. Tens of millions in the Russian Federation belong to Muslim communities, and more than one ethnicity is entirely Muslim. The country is facing a separatist movement in Chechnya with great Wahabi influences. India, too, has a very large Muslim community, and the government is facing a secessionist movement in Kashmir that is basically Jihadist. Both powers are nuclear and facing political challenges. Hence, it is understandable that a national mobilization—if not well clarified and smartly designed—would risk provoking civil unrest among their minorities. A crucial element in the national strategies of Russia and India in their resistance to Jihadi terrorism is support for a strong antiterrorist movement within these communities, lending them all the backing they need.

The Importance of Enlightened Leaders

In my general approach to conflict analysis, I put more emphasis on the evolution of ideas, historical developments, and strategic choices than on the leaders who have to carry out these decisions. Perhaps I have been counterbalancing the overemphasis that the majority of American and Western analysts give to the personality of politicians, leaders, and decision makers. The massive literature that followed 9/11, particularly in the United States, focused on the men and women who play a role in the War on Terror, to the detriment of historical and strategic issues. This overemphasis was found on both sides. An immense interest was generated in the person of Osama bin Laden, and very little attention was given to the analysis of the ideology. I often call it "the looking for Waldo" syndrome. The emphasis on personalities in the conflict spread to lower players in the drama. Former terrorists and escapees from the hell of terror became celebrities. In American political culture, it seems, the teller's story is more important than the story he or she is telling. Which helps explain why the Jihadi lobbies didn't have much difficulty derailing national analysis in the United States. They blurred Americans' vision of the substance of the history and ideology of the radical movements involved in the war, and the pop culture of the country did the rest. This explains not only the disproportionate space given by the media to trivial matters about the players in the war (such as the appearance of bin Laden or Saddam) but also the inexplicable zooming in on the personality of the president during the war. "Bushomania" struck the media. There was more information about the minutiae of presidential politics—and George W. Bush—than basic information about the enemy that attacked the United States. As the Jihadi machine naturally manipulated the "Bushophobia" of the president's critics, the stunning choice presented by the media was either to support President Bush, and thus "his" War on Terror, or oppose the War on Terror because it was led by Bush. This illogical equation shows that many haven't understood the challenge—or, more accurately, that many were led, misinformed, and miseducated about the nature of the confrontation. The al Qaeda attack "happened" during the first year of the Bush administration, which prompted the White House to respond—as would any president. Other attacks occurred during the Reagan administration (1983, Beirut), the first Bush Administration (1992, Somalia), and the Clinton administration (1993, Somalia; 1998, New York; 2000, East Africa and the USS *Cole*). The Jihadi War has been waged "on" the United States, not "by" America. Thus, even after President Bush leaves the White House in January 2009, the Jihadi warfare will continue. Therefore, what counts are not the personalities of the leaders but the decisions and measures taken by the chief executive regarding the campaign.

Obviously, the first measure is to analyze the leader's vision of the conflict. If the U.S. president or a prime minister acknowledges that the confrontation is indeed a war, not an incident, he or she will have passed the crucial test. The second test concerns the leader's understanding of the identity and the long-term objectives of the adversary. Not only must a leader know this is a war, but he or she should realize against whom and for what purposes. A third test should assess the ability of these leaders to educate their nations and mobilize them for a full engagement—political, economic, and, when need be, defensive—so that the war will be made as short as possible. Further massive developments in this global confrontation or major terrorist strikes on American soil would lead the public to demand a leadership capable of educating the bureaucracy, inspiring a cultural revolution, and winning the war. Eventually, enlightened leaders will emerge. The question is, After how much trial and loss?

If a majority of voters in the United States elect a president who changes the direction of the conflict by withdrawing from this War on Terror, the Jihadists and their allies will advance their program to establish much greater power and further infiltrate the United States, with cataclysmic results. A change of direction in the U.S. presidency will have ripple effects everywhere, and certainly at home. A president who would continue in the direction we are going without any improvement would prolong the conflict and incur gigantic spending on the prosecution of the war. The options are two: withdrawing from the conflict and awaiting the greater confrontation to follow, or changing course by thrusting forward and preempting the long-range goals of the terrorist forces. The choice will affect world events. The same assessment holds for the leaders of Great Britain, France, Russia, and other world powers. But the catch here is to offer a clear vision to the voting public so that the people can select the right leader. In democracies, chief executives educate the public as to the challenges ahead. But who will educate the voters as to the best leader to face these challenges? In a relentless War of Ideas, the radical forces have managed to keep the national audiences in a state of ignorance. If the public isn't informed about Jihadism's history and substance, how can voters weigh the knowledge candidates have of the threat? Note that when leaders have attempted to educate their constituencies as to the nature of the threat, as Bush, Blair, Sarkozy, and Putin have tried to do at different times, the propaganda machinery of worldwide Jihadism has slammed them viciously. This indicates clearly that the ideological forces behind the terrorist movements have an edge in this confrontation.

Alliances or Failures

In the years after the Iraq campaign began, critics targeted the White House for not forming the right alliances beforehand. The Bush administration was faulted for not having brought on board President Chirac, Chancellor Schroeder, and President Putin to endorse the move into Iraq. Washington was also criticized for not having secured the support of most Arab countries before toppling the Saddam regime. This debate had three dimensions: In principle the widest alliance to accomplish a massive change in international relations should always be the first option, but if the alliance is limited to a number of countries because not all governments join, there are two possible courses of action: not to engage in the confrontation, and run the risk of the foe becoming much stronger, or to engage in the confrontation on the ground of widening the alliance as progress is made on the ground and as change is implemented. The campaign for Iraq was a central example of how past failures in the international system could lead to unpreparedness. Most of the West had somewhat allowed the Saddam regime to roam unchecked, causing massive human rights abuses and finally invading Kuwait. The 1991 international coalition was wide indeed, as France and many Arab countries joined the liberation campaign. But the conclusion of that first war with Saddam was truncated because oil influences refused a regime change at the time, and a botched ending of that conflict led to a weaker alliance in 2003. Alliances aren't always the widest when they form. In 1940, the United States wasn't at the side of France when it was invaded by the Nazis or Britain when it was bombed by the Luftwaffe. The USSR was at the side of Hitler when his forces were invading

Czechoslovakia and Poland. At the end of the war, not only were U.S. forces in Germany shaking hands with their future foes, the Soviets, but a myriad of small and new countries had declared war on the Axis, some just a few days before its surrender. Hence, from a brief review of the history of alliances—including those of the modern era—what is important is the direction of the conflict, not the number of countries adhering to it at first.

In the War on Terror (or, more precisely, the Jihadi campaigns to establish a caliphate), antiterror coalitions aren't easy to build, and vast international alliances or unanimity even less so. But when bin Laden delivered his strikes to New York and Washington, a very wide de facto alliance formed. America's traditional allies, such as Britain, Australia, Canada, New Zealand, France, even Russia, and scores of other governments immediately sided with the United States, the victim. The pictures of the fallen towers spoke to the world. The Jihadists isolated themselves quickly. The fate of the Taliban regime was sealed, no questions asked. The "world"—minus the classical rogues (the regimes in Iran, Iraq, Sudan, and North Korea, for example)—more or less licensed America to strike back and take out the sponsoring regime. Strangely, the radical groups had just wrapped up their anti-American, UN-sponsored conference in Durban a few weeks before. Support for the United States was overwhelming and international forces coalesced to bring down the hyper-Salafists of Kabul.

That universal alliance had two key elements: One, it was seen as righteous self-defense, and two, it wasn't seen as a global campaign against the international Jihadist movement that had produced al Qaeda and the Taliban in the first place. America had crossed into the new era of post-9/11, but not every government made that leap. From then on, two visions developed among world leaders: those who endorsed Washington's view of a war against the terrorists, particularly in a preemptive mode (United Kingdom, Spain, Poland, Italy, etc.); and those who didn't accept the premise of a War on Terror, let alone a conflict with Jihadism (France, Germany, Russia, etc.). Therefore, when the United States (with a growing opposition) headed toward Iraq in 2003, it had a coalition of the willing instead of a universal alliance. Again, the decision to invade Iraq and remove Saddam had to take into consideration a choice between a smaller alliance that would produce a geopolitical change in the region or a larger consensus that would better preserve the status quo. In reality, the choice was between change and status quo, not between the types of alliances.

Was a change needed? Was time a factor? Were those who planned the regime change in possession of a vision from the beginning of the campaign? These are crucial questions yet to be addressed. But in considering the future of the confrontation, it is well to remember that a better order of priorities in strategic planning is to have the vision before the action, not after an action has been undertaken. Then leaders have to rally their constituencies to adopt the global vision, not just permit the immediate steps. It is peculiar to see today a strong opposition to the change in Iraq developing in the United States and other allied countries; it is based on a misunderstanding of the conflict, that is, a misperception of the big picture. Any strategic move toward confronting the powers that constitute the long-term threat has to be inscribed in a global doctrine clarified to the public and in harmony with homeland security. Alliances that are built around one project—say, bringing the Baath regime in Iraq down—cannot handle the greater picture, and thus when the foes counterattack globally, they make the U.S.-backed efforts greater, costlier, and longer. This is what has caused allies like Spain to drop away. From Iraq on, the game has to change. It is crucial that future coalitions should be built on solid bases. Obviously, such success necessitates a clear vision, strong leadership, and revolutionary thinking.

Wars against the Ability to Respond

So where is the coalition of democracies in the confrontation with its adversaries? Do the United States and the Free World have the ability to respond to the offensives launched a decade ago? If we assume that al Qaeda and the Salafists have engaged in battle against the West and other countries since the early 1990s, this means that their first strikes have been delivered already, and that the sum of all efforts exerted by the international coalition are a counterstrike. But the real question is this: Did the Jihadists paralyze the coalition's ability to strike back? Are the United States and its allies really using all their resources in this confrontation? Are all talents at the service of the resistance? Are courts, educational institutions, the arts, legislatures, executive powers, national security departments, military planning, and the War of Ideas really engaged and headed in the right direction? Hundreds of billions of dollars have been spent since 2001, but have they been used to implement the appropriate plans and back the right forces? Did the combined efforts of the foes block the most efficient paths, channeling the energies into more difficult strategies? As can be seen from the foregoing analysis of the evolution of the conflict, the Free World may well be somewhere in between; having risen to meet the challenge, but not yet seeing clearly how to win the war, let alone shorten it.

CONCLUSION

PAST CHOICES AND NEW DIRECTIONS

IT SHOULD BE CLEAR BY NOW THAT REVOLUTIONARY CHANGES ARE necessary if the Free World is to win the current war—and the first change needed is to clear up the misunderstanding of the war. That misunderstanding is encoded in the mislabeling of the war as a "war on terror." Changes in outlook, in strategy, and in perception of the timeframe of action are all necessary, not to mention coordination among the various targets of the international Jihadi network. Some of those targets are Western democracies, and others are not. As the menace is global, so must be the response; if the Jihadists are for the most part united in their ideology and global strategy (which can be seen in their successes since the early 1990s), so the anti-Jihadi and pro-democracy side must stop seeing the conflict as less a war than a series of incidents or independent issues. Thus, in conclusion, I would like to summarize the changes I think are necessary, and who should make them. However, the listing of individual recommendations keyed to specific country situations should not obscure the overriding need for the whole Free World to act together—the older democracies with emerging ones and pro-democracy forces in the Middle East itself.

THE WAR'S STRATEGIC CHOICES

The leading force at this point is undoubtedly the United States of America; it can and should play the role of strategic backbone in the response. This role, however, as has been shown, needs to include a web of other powers, countries, and international organizations. The United States is in the center, but it cannot be alone in the struggle. Even as necessary coalitions are built, America still is in a position to lead the efforts. This is actually how al Qaeda and the other Jihadists have perceived the American role, and from the Beirut attack of 1983 to the September 11, 2001, attacks and beyond, they have treated the United States as the main threat to their agenda. In their view, it is on U.S. soil that the world confrontation can be effected.

Indeed, by striking deep inside America, the global Jihadists hope to stun, weaken, and eventually erode American will and resources.[1] The idea is to provoke a change in the balance of power in the world: a U.S. withdrawal of forces and a change of foreign policy. It is therefore logical to expect that al Qaeda and the American Jihadists will relentlessly expand their assaults on the United States. One can also expect that Iranian-led Jihadists will join the battlefield inside America. But these direct actions will be accompanied by further Jihadi infiltration and penetration of the entire spectrum of U.S. national security, from cultural and legal institutions to the defense and security levels. Hence, the strategic decision to create a homeland security program was essential. Three guidelines need to be followed thoroughly:

1. The Homeland Security Department exists in the United States because the country is at war. In reality, this is the Department of the War on Terror, though it may address natural disasters, emigration, and policing duties. Perhaps future presidents and legislators should consider changing its name or restructuring it to fit its real role. We suggest that all issues related to non-war emergencies be addressed by appropriate executive entities while the institution dedicated to prosecute the conflict remain especially focused on the confrontation. This recognition (and full support for the mission) may be the key to defeating Jihadism inside America. The Department of Homeland Security must confront the mobilizing and recruiting force within Jihadism; short of that it will fail in its mission, and America will have to fight urban unrest just as European and Middle Eastern countries have.[2]

2. The foe has to be defined ideologically, politically, and organizationally. The perception of the threat—despite some good achievements—until 2008 has been critically missing. Despite the reality that America is facing a threat doctrine, Jihadism, the national security institutions haven't yet made that fact clear or translated it into guidelines to follow. More concerning is Jihadophiles' success in penetrating many layers of the homeland security apparatus.

3. National priority must be given to the role of Middle Eastern, Arab, and Muslim communities in America as they resist and confront radical ideologies, including Salafism and Khumeinism. Both the government and the private sector must support the counter-Jihadist segments of these communities in an effort to contain and reverse the processes of indoctrination, recruitment, and strategic penetration of the country. Until 2008, most U.S. policies regarding domestic countering of extremism have failed, principally because of the co-optation of groups advocating Jihadophilia and rejection of the real antiterrorism elements. This trend in the U.S. government must be reversed so that true anti-Jihadist Muslim

groups, as well as Americans from Middle Eastern descent, will be recognized and supported and those who apologize for and support Jihadism will not be offered opportunities to acquire and use political influence to spread Jihadism in the Muslim communities.[3]

AFGHANISTAN

Removing the Taliban from power in Afghanistan was the logical response to the attacks of September 11, 2001. As the sponsor and host of al Qaeda, they had to be brought down and a democratic alternative established by the international community. However, the Taliban episode should teach the public and policymakers that the nature of these regimes is bound to produce terror and violate international law and human rights. Similar ideological regimes and movements have committed atrocities in Arab and Muslim countries and exported bloodshed to Russia, Europe, and North America. The battle of Afghanistan is, in fact, a battle against "Talibanization" elsewhere. The development of society and raising of a generation of young Afghans freed from radicalization is one of the most strategic responses to Jihadism. For the Afghan emirate model has played a central role in the Jihadist project. Bringing the country back from extreme Islamism to solid Muslim humanism would shatter one of the main pillars of Jihadi terror.

Several steps are needed to accomplish this important task. The coalition should

1. Maintain the U.S. and NATO presence and increase international participation—including that of Muslim moderate governments—to enable a new Afghan military to assume its strategic responsibility, supported by an Afghan democratic renaissance at the hands of civil society forces.

2. Engage in a mass effort for reform and education so that within one decade, the younger generation of Afghans will have the intellectual and political freedom to face the Jihadists with a democratic response that will isolate radicalism in their society. Encouraging a revolution in education is crucial to winning the long-term battle of ideas in that country.

3. Direct international aid to civil society and nongovernmental organizations that commit to pluralist democracy and counter-Jihadism. The focus should be on empowering the weakest segments of Afghan society, those targeted by the ex-Taliban regime, instead of on general reconstruction efforts. The battlefield is between those who will change the political culture and those who want to reimpose Talibanization.

4. Help the Afghans and the Pakistanis who share democratic values to come together. A transnational alliance of pro-democracy Afghans and Pakistanis

would help to contain and isolate the radicals in both countries. Effecting this by using nonviolent, educational means is perhaps the best response to the radicalization of the region. (Only an alliance between the two governments for defense and security that would confront and defeat the common terror threat could do more.)

INTERNATIONAL ALLIANCES

Soon after the collapse of Tora Bora and the end of the Taliban as the ruling power in Afghanistan, the United States found itself in a quandary. Two strategic options were considered: One was to return to the pre-9/11 status quo in the fight against terror but with a vigorous international cooperation "on terrorism." This would have been a return to bilateral or multilateral cooperation among governments, at the level of regional and international organizations, so that terrorists would be found and brought to justice. But this option avoided recognizing that there was a "war" on terror; there was an international campaign to reverse Jihadism, to extirpate its most visible and violent manifestations. In other words, this first option was a crime-fighting model of international cooperation, in which terrorism was seen primarily as a criminal activity and not as a political ideology employing and advocating criminal means. Many countries, including most European and some Arab governments, preferred this policy. The second option was to mobilize for an actual proactive "war" on terrorism, unleashing vast resources to preempt the battlefield and stop the further expansion of Jihadi terror. In 2002, President George Bush named three terrorist organizations, al Qaeda, Hamas, and Hezbollah, and three regimes, Iraq, Iran, and North Korea, as members of an "axis of evil." This declaration basically broke with the traditional policy of "wait and see" and initiated an alternative posture of "don't wait any longer." The Bush doctrine wasn't (as initially portrayed) a classic preemptive strike. In fact it was a "choose your camp" doctrine. It put pressure on regimes on the list to find a way out of the category. Moreover, the list wasn't even comprehensive, for diplomatic reasons: Syria, Sudan, and Libya had terror issues to address, but their rulers were given a last chance to begin changing. This new policy in Washington leaped far ahead of the consensus established in the 1990s in world politics, but not as far as was needed to complete a full revolution in international relations.

The Wahabi and Khumeinist powers, the oil Jihadists and their allies and clients in the Greater Middle East and around the world, had established two no-go lines for the West: no regime change and no spread of democracy. Apart from this, the United States and Europe could cooperate with the appropriate regional authorities and regimes to achieve limited goals. If Saddam was a problem, it was to be solved with the "family's" blessing and intervention through the Kuwait war, but the coalition had to stop short of changing his regime and encouraging a democracy. It was allowed to pressure Syria, Sudan, Iran, and the rest of the regimes on human rights and political pluralism. But the limits stood. Hence, it was only natural that the political establishment in the region opted for the "police" approach against proven terrorists and not for a War on Terror, which could lead to regime change throughout the entire region.

The Bush administration, under the pressure of 9/11, leaped beyond the established norms—understandably, because its analysis didn't show a guarantee that other attacks would not take place if the same policies continued. So acting to provoke a change in the region was seen as better than maintaining the status quo. At this theoretical stage, Washington was right in seeking change, and its opponents were wrong in maintaining business as usual. The reason was simple: It was an oil-imposed status quo—which meant in practice there would be no democratization—that opened the path for Jihadization and radicalization. Hence it became necessary to help societies struggling against authoritarians so that the Jihadists and radicals could be stopped. Indeed, the Salafists and the Khumeinists were creeping under the protection of the authoritarian regimes' regional system. The Islamists were expanding and the Jihadists were infiltrating the institutions of the oppressive regimes; they were striking at the free world while the Arab League and the OIC obstructed democratic change. The expected result was that within one decade or so the region would change toward radicalization. Conclusion: The world was changing anyway, so the questions were, Who would make deliberate moves to change it, and who would benefit from them?

Bin Laden's 9/11 strikes on America impelled the United States to react strategically. Al Qaeda's unleashing of its agenda on al Jazeera compelled the United States to respond with the "spreading democracy" doctrine to counter the "spreading death" slogan. Thus, as of early 2002, an international alliance of those willing to fight terror was forming around U.S. efforts, while the unwilling formed islands of resistance, awaiting better times. The international coalition against terror was born under U.S. leadership, but this alliance, though determined and willing to take action, lacked clarity about the enemy and its political grand design. The coalition was firm in its determination to "chase out" the terrorists and "bring them to justice," but it wasn't clear on the ideology and on the stages of the campaign against it. The public saw only what was next to happen, not the big picture. This was a defect. In the future, any coalition will need to explain to the people who the foes are and how the conflict will be concluded, knowing fully that being clear about the problem will influence the scope of the alliance.

THE WAR IN IRAQ

It may take years before historians can evaluate whether the invasion of Iraq and the removal of Saddam in that particular year was a right step in the War on Terror. As

I argued in 2006, the move by itself shifted the balance against the strategic interests of the Iranian and Syrian regimes and had an impact on Lebanon and the region, but the final outcome will depend on how the Iraq campaign develops in the future.[4] The essential question at this stage is whether or not that war is part of the global confrontation between the Free World and the Jihadist-totalitarian axis, and if the order of battle was logical in the context of the post-9/11 era. Many criticisms have been leveled against the war, including unilateralism and alleged secret U.S. goals. But the authors of these arguments do not recognize the state of terror under which the Iraqis were living, particularly those who were not Baathists. Hence, since the regime was indeed genocidal toward its own population, a better criticism is that the West was late in removing Saddam. But as has been shown, intervening on behalf of the oppressed in the region was long forbidden, as it was in Sudan, Lebanon, Afghanistan, and Iraq, to name some of the most extreme cases. Since 1945 the regional system has placed over the area a shield that blocks humanitarian and human rights interventions. Opposed to this, at the core of U.S., European, and international policies, there should have been the principle that an extremely destructive regime can be removed by an international (UN-sponsored or not) initiative. Now, by leaping forward and removing the oppressive regime, the new American policy was correcting decades of servitude to the oil regimes and the status quo. But the subsequent strategic questions are what will make the Iraq war a factor (or not) in the bigger picture of the confrontation.

1.   First question: Was the invasion of Iraq and the (legitimate) removal of Saddam opportune strategically in 2003? In the grand scale of the confrontation with Jihadism, not the relativist scales of arguments and counterarguments that followed the move, was the regime change a move in the right direction? Only historians will be able to tell whether the efforts led to a defeat of the Jihadi axis in the region. But the larger question is, Had the United States not intervened at that stage, what would the opposing forces have done? One theory says, nothing more than before. But the Jihadists were expanding, Saddam was rearming, the Iranians were developing strategic weaponry, the Syrians were following them, and Hezbollah, too. The Sudanese regime was pursuing a policy of genocide and the Islamists were gaining across the region. Had an intervention not taken place after 9/11, these forces would have moved in two directions: further oppression of their peoples, and further support for expansionism, with terrorism as one of the tools. One major development would have been the crumbling of Kabul's government and the rise of a vast regional conglomeration of regimes and movements irreversibly committed to oppressing their peoples and shattering democracy.

2. A second question remains, even if removing Saddam was a step in the right direction: Was the campaign appropriately prepared, the projections carefully analyzed, and the foes' strengths and reactions strategically appraised? The short answer is no. The military prosecution of the war was admirably swift and on target. But the political and administrative management after liberation didn't match the grand objectives of the global campaign. For it took a greater length of time to redirect energies and reshape plans; the balance of power inside the country began to shift only in 2008. The military efforts since the fall of the dictator dramatically contrasted with the political achievements. The reasons behind that dichotomy were rooted in a grand design not well clarified to the American public or even to the peoples of the region. The Iraq war was part of a larger Middle East campaign; it was not just a local war intended to unseat a dictator and change public life in one particular country. Only when analyzed in those terms can the efforts and sacrifices be properly evaluated.

3. Third: Did the Iraq campaign accomplish a strategic shift in the War on Terror? Did the removal of Saddam and the establishment of representative government move the antiterrorist struggle forward? The answers are not to be found in sterile debate about how many attacks are still occurring in one particular zone in the country. Terrorist operations will continue for a long time, not just in Iraq but in the entire region, until a generational victory over the ideology of terror is obtained. Although victory against the Baathist military machine was accomplished in the first month of the conflict, denying the formation of Jihadi enclaves was accomplished two years into the campaign. Reducing the influence of the terrorists among the Sunnis began to be achieved four years after the intervention, and the containment of Khumeinist elements is dependent on the rise of liberal elements in Iraq. But as long as the strategic configuration of a geopolitical shift in the region doesn't materialize, the gains made till 2008 will be in jeopardy.

4. Fourth, what would happen if the United States and the coalition were to withdraw abruptly from Iraq? If the war is abandoned before new anti-Jihadi forces are empowered and before a dual containment of the Iranian and Syrian regimes is achieved, the result is predictable: Iran's power will be projected across the Shia areas. Its forces—Pasdaran and Iraqi allies—will reach the borders with Kuwait, Saudi Arabia, and Jordan. They could link up with Syrian security elements westbound. The Kurds would be isolated. Al Qaeda would seize power in the Sunni Triangle, and a land bridge would open between Tehran and Damascus. If the coalition initiative is not successful in Iraq—in smarter and faster ways—an Iranian Khumeinist

power would emerge between Afghanistan and the Mediterranean Sea. This is the context in which the Iraq campaign belongs strategically.

5. The fifth question is, What strategic moves can enhance the situation in Iraq in light of the global confrontation with the terrorist forces? At first, the coalition must redeploy its forces along the Iraqi borders with Iran and Syria. Strategically, this would deny the emergence of the Iranian Khumeinist axis and its threat against the region and the Free World. Iraqi forces should be trained rapidly and deployed inside the country and a robust federal system established to provide communal rights to Arab Shia and Sunni, Kurds, and other minorities such as Assyro-Chaldeans, Turkomans, and Mandeans. These steps would defend the new Iraq from regional threats. But to assure the success of democracy in Iraq in the long term, further steps to confront the terrorist forces in the region will be needed. This new configuration in the Iraqi battlefield also happens to be what is needed to win the next battles for democracy in the region; they are intertwined.

LIBERATING LEBANON

After Iraq, the United States and its allies acted to remove the Syrian occupiers from Lebanon by issuing UN Security Council Resolution 1559 asking the Syrian regime to withdraw its troops. Was it the right decision in the War on Terror? Yes, it was a strategic move in the campaign to roll back the Jihadi and totalitarian forces in that country.

The axis is on the counterattack: By early 2008 seven legislators and politicians had been assassinated, dozens of civilians and security officers killed by terrorist attacks, and the democratically elected government besieged by Hezbollah and the pro-Syrian militias. A war triggered by Hezbollah against Israel in July 2006 ended with the deployment of United Nations forces in the south. But the campaign against the Cedars Revolution continues relentlessly. Another set of steps by the antiterrorist coalition is warranted: Controlling the Lebanese-Syrian borders by sending a multinational force to the country; reorganizing and supporting the Lebanese Army; protecting the democratically elected leaders of the country; and, last but not least, beginning the process of preparing for the disarming of Hezbollah and the other militias. However, to proceed in that direction the international efforts have to address the two major foes of the democratic process in the region: the Syrian and Iranian regimes. As for Afghanistan and Iraq, securing the national borders is a strategic priority. In the case of Lebanon, controlling the borders with Syria is vital. For through these frontiers stretching from the northern borders to the southern Bekaa Valley, a vast space is still open whereby Syrian intelligence is providing logistical support to Hezbollah and other Jihadist organizations. The battle between Lebanese Army units and an al Qaeda–linked group (which made Syrian-aided infiltrations), the Fatah al Islam, in the summer of 2007 shows how permeable are the borders. Iran's military equipment and support can be exported to Lebanon via Syria in a matter of hours. Seizing these borders would cut off Hezbollah's supply lines from the axis. Once that is achieved, the coalition would be able to support the Lebanese institutions, its army, and the Cedars Revolution. The main question is how to stop Syrian intervention inside Lebanon.

A STRATEGY FOR SYRIA

After his coup d'état in 1970, President Hafez Assad developed a long-term strategy for the Syrian Baath in the region. It included the annexation of neighboring Lebanon, an alliance with Iran, developing terrorist organizations, and resisting the peace process between Arabs and Israelis—all to shield his oppressive Alawite regime from a popular uprising that was opening the door for democratization. Hafez died at the apex of his success, and Bashar succeeded him. Damascus got nervous after the 9/11 attacks as the United States was declaring war "against terror," and Syria was a hub for a great many terrorist organizations. The downfall of the Taliban was a first warning. And as soon as Washington declared its intention to remove Saddam, Bashar's regime rushed to defend his father's old enemy. Syria's Mukhabarat began a war against the coalition preemptively; first by diplomacy and intelligence warfare and then as soon as the marines reached Baghdad, by opening its borders to the first Jihadi suicide bombers. The Syrian-backed campaign in Iraq was as intense as al Qaeda's. As noted earlier, the Syrian plan is to meet up with an Iranian advance and to open a path between the two regimes via an Iraqi radical partner.

The United States began responding by the end of 2003. The U.S. Congress, in a bipartisan manner, voted the famous Syria Accountability Act, which called on Damascus to withdraw from Lebanon and as we noted earlier the United States and France introduced UNSCR 1559 in 2004. By April 2005, after Syrian troops evacuated Lebanon, Assad left behind a "second army" consisting of Hezbollah and the pro-Syrian militias. Since the summer of that year, the Assad regime has escalated on three axes: assassinations and terror in Lebanon, backing for Hamas and Islamic Jihad in Palestine, and relentless support for terrorist operations in Iraq. Domestically, a mass suppression has silenced the rising dissident movement.

In response, what can the coalition do? It can

1. Deploy a multinational force on Lebanon's border with Syria. This would cut off Damascus's strategic lines into Lebanon and with Hezbollah and other

terrorist groups. The regime would lose influence, control of organizations, and immense revenues produced by secret drug-trafficking networks.

2. Deploy U.S.-led coalition forces on Syria's Iraqi borders. This would stop Assad's meddling in Iraq and cut off potential land bridges into Iran.

3. Support the Palestinian Authority against Hamas, which would reduce Syrian control over terrorist operations in Palestine.

4. Most important, generate strategic support for the Syrian opposition to Bashar. Ultimately, antiterrorist forces around the world must back up the Syrian people in changing the Assad regime and establishing a pluralist democracy in Damascus.

IRAN'S KHUMEINIST EMPIRE

The Islamist government of Iran is eying ways to export its influence to eastern Arabia, central Iraq, and Central Asia, as well as consolidating its power in Lebanon. Domestically the regime eliminated the left, including Tudeh, the Communist Party, and all other forms of opposition in the country, among them the left-wing Islamic movement People's Mujahideen Army (MEK, Mujahidin-e-Khalq). Since 2001, Tehran has feared the spread of democracy, and hence began counterattacks on the United States and coalition activities in the region as well as against Arab Sunni and moderate countries along multiple fronts: supporting Neo-Taliban groups in Afghanistan, organizing and sponsoring radical Shia movements in Iraq, backing Hezbollah in Lebanon, reinforcing the axis with the Syrian regime, threatening the moderate principalities in the Gulf, inciting radical Islamists in the Eastern Arabian peninsula, and widening the oppression of Iran's own domestic opposition.

Iran's regime and its regional ambitions exemplify state-centered Jihadi power. Tehran has at its disposal revenues from oil, the muscle of the Pasdaran, the brutality of the Syrian regime, and the terrorist cadres of Hezbollah in Lebanon. The efforts to acquire a nuclear weapon will transform the Iranian regime into an even more dangerous power having control over lethal terrorist networks. A success by the Khumeinists to establish a land bridge to Syria and the Mediterranean would create an empire extending from inside Afghanistan to northern Israel. As of 2008, the Iranian regime was successful in obtaining from the Russian president statements shielding the regime and its nuclear program from Western and UN pressures, a move that would jeopardize international cooperation against terror. In view of these challenges, U.S. and coalition strategies should seek to contain the expansionism of Tehran's regime before gradually reversing its offensives, including, as already mentioned, deploying coalition forces on the Iraqi-Iranian border to cut off the strategic thrust toward the Eastern Mediterranean.

The coalition must also control the Afghan-Iranian border to stop Khumein-ist support for the Neo-Taliban and future arming of radical elements in the Shia Hazara community inside Afghanistan. In Lebanon, the Pasdaran contingent must be isolated to cut off the supply line with Hezbollah. The U.S. naval task forces in the Persian Gulf must be maintained in order to deter the potential production of an atomic weapon and delivery systems. More important, pro-democracy powers must launch the widest possible campaign in support of the Iranian opposition. They can do this by reviewing past policies toward the various democratic move-ments struggling against the Khumeinist regime, funding civil society NGOs, and improving a powerful and efficient broadcast in Farsi aimed at Iran. Last but not least, moral and political support should be extended to the minorities inside Iran—the Kurds, Ahwaz Arabs, Baluchis, and Azeris, as well as to civil society movements for women, students, labor, and artists.

But even though the international community needs to confront the oppres-sive regimes in Damascus and Tehran, it nevertheless has to help solve the crisis used by all radicals in the region to further their "struggle." Addressing the Pales-tinian problem is a must, not only from a humanitarian and moral perspective, but also as a way to reduce the extremists' capacity for manipulation.

PALESTINE

The fate of the Palestinians has been hijacked for half a century by the Arab-Israeli conflict. The rise of a Palestinian state has been jeopardized several times since the UN partition plan of 1947, mainly because the radical regimes and movements claiming to represent Arab nationalism rejected it and, later on, through Jihadist interference. The ethnic conflict between Israelis and Arab Palestinians, like all other similar conflicts, has been bloody and filled with injustices and lost opportu-nities. But in 1993 a window for a solution opened: a mutual recognition between the state of Israel and a Palestinian Authority. Unfortunately, while Egypt, Jordan, and other Arab moderates entered the peace process, rogue regimes including Iran, Iraq (under Saddam), and Syria used their influence over radicals to sink all initiatives aimed at solving the crisis. After 2001 the United States and its allies in the West began to develop a new policy toward the Palestinian question: the estab-lishment of a Palestinian state living in peace next to Israel. But the Iranian and Syrian regimes in association with their radical allies among the Palestinians un-leashed violence to block the peace process. After the death of Yassir Arafat in 2004, his successor, Mahmoud Abbas, moved closer to accepting the two-state so-lution. But in 2007 Hamas sprang a coup d'état in Gaza and took over the terri-tory, transforming it into a Taliban-like entity on the Mediterranean shore. The Hamas coup was engineered by Tehran and Damascus to stop the peace process and block the Palestinian Authority from normalizing relations with Israel. In military interpretation, the full control by Hamas of Gaza and the attempts by Hezbollah to regain control over South Lebanon is aimed at putting much of urban Israel under their fire, literally, undermining the Palestinian Authority's security and offering the Iranian regime military access to a front with Israel.

The post 9/11 policies of the U.S. and the West toward the Palestinians have been to recognize their right for a state and to extend support to the more moderates among them, in this case the Palestinian Authority. But since Hamas has declared its own Jihadi regime in Gaza, the coalition against terror, which in this case must include Arab moderates and the Palestinians opposed to Syrian-Iranian influence, must undertake the following actions:

1. Help Israelis and Palestinians move faster toward a final Peace Agreement that would address most of the vital issues: borders, principles for solving the refugee question, security cooperation, and so on.

2. Empower the Palestinian Authority, which with Arab moderate support should take back Gaza from Hamas and engage in a massive reform and a comprehensive social justice program.

3. And, to make the above moves possible, secure the democratic government of Lebanon's control over its own territories and hence cut off Hezbollah's strategic ability to mount terrorist operations in the Palestinian territories. Controlling the Lebanese-Syrian borders would diminish, if not entirely halt, Syrian-Iranian support for Hamas.

PAKISTAN

Undoubtedly, Pakistan is the ultimate base for the Jihadists' international struggle. Its location, size, military, and nuclear weapons (and delivery systems) bring it to the fore. Salafi control of Pakistan would transform the world movement into a great (and lethal) power. Hence, it is vital for the international coalition—including moderate Muslim forces—to deny al Qaeda, the Neo-Taliban, Jaish-e-Muhammad, (JEM), Harakat-ul-Mujahideen (HUM), and Anjuman Sipah-e-Sahaba (SSP), as well as the Muttahida Majlis-e-Amal (MMA) control over the power and military-security apparatus of the country. To that end, Pakistan's main political parties must decide on an agenda that promotes democracy and nuclear stability. The secular and moderate Muslim currents, whether in the government or in the opposition, have to shield Pakistan's national security from the Jihadists. And to help the mainstream moderate parties of the country to ensure this internal consensus, the international coalition has to address the external factors that favor Talibanization. Among these steps is control of the Afghan-Pakistani border by the coalition on one side and the Pakistani army on the other, by which the Neo-Taliban influence could be contained significantly. Two, a rapprochement between Islamabad and New Delhi must be brought forward under international sponsorship, on the grounds that stabilization and counterterrorism would ease the tensions on the Indian-Pakistani borders, and thus allow Pakistan's armed forces to pacify the Jihadi-dominated areas on both borders, including Waziristan. The radical Islamist movement in Pakistan has to be cleansed of its terrorist elements and allowed to become a part of the political spectrum of the country on the same basis of pluralism among political parties. The assassination of Benazir Bhutto in 2007 was a benchmark showing the determination of the influential Jihadist web in Pakistan to stop all attempts to promote pluralism, democracy, and secular values. A response must come in the form of an alliance of all government and civil society antiterrorist forces in the country against the Jihadist web. This reality can only develop when the forces of pluralism unite against terrorism while playing by the norms of the democratic process.

SOUTH ASIA'S NEW STRATEGIES

Progress in Pakistan can reverberate through the whole of South Asia, including Bangladesh, Malaysia, and Indonesia. The ultimate strategic aim of Asian Jihadism is to become a nuclear and world-class power. Thus, denying Combat Jihadism control of a nuclear Pakistan would hamper their spread into the rest of the continent, though it would not necessarily affect them ideologically. In the latter regard, the international coalition against terrorism needs to encourage moderate political forces to find a center of gravity whereby they can isolate the terrorist forces but continue to interact with them in a pluralist democracy. The objective of the coalition in most Muslim states targeted by Jihadists must be to neutralize and isolate the radical Islamist phenomenon, thereby preventing it from seizing security assets or building terrorist bases. However, the classical Islamist movement can adapt to pluralism and be part of the political system. The international coalition should encourage Indonesia, Malaysia, and Bangladesh to create their own security arrangements in cooperation against terror and to reach out to countries targeted by the Jihadists, such as Thailand, the Philippines, and even Timor-Leste.

AFRICA'S COUNTERCAMPAIGNS

As has been documented, the Horn of Africa has become a theater of major operations for al Qaeda and other local groups. The central battlefield of the Horn is Somalia. Were the Jihadists who are pushing the Islamic Courts (Mahakem Islamiya) to take over Mogadishu and install a regime, it would be able to link with the Jihadist forces in Sudan, Eritrea, East Africa, and Chad. Hence it is strategically important to assist a national unity government in Somalia to interdict the Mahakem and form a strategic alliance with democratic governments in Eritrea and Djibouti. This trio of countries should then coordinate efforts with Ethiopia, Kenya, and Uganda to contain the radicals in the Horn.

The even larger battlefield of Sudan needs direct intervention by the international community to solve the crisis. The initiatives required are summarized below:

1. A UN initiative must enable the people of Darfur to express their aspirations through a series of referenda determining the future of their area. To bring that about, there must be a UN-sponsored intervention in Darfur with a multinational force placed between the province and the forces of the regime, and throughout the province to protect the population from the murderous Janjaweed.

2. Another UN intervention is required for Southern Sudan to oversee the referendum already agreed on with Khartoum in the peace agreement of 2005. If the Jihadi regime of Sudan resumes its offensives using the armed forces or the *Difaa al Shaabi*, a multinational force could be deployed between the south and the north and on the southern international border.

3. A third international force, with African participation, should be placed on the border between Sudan and Chad to interdict the Sudanese-backed Jihadists crossing into Chad and backing the Wahabi movement inside that country.

Similar measures need to be implemented in other spots in sub-Saharan Africa to contain the Jihadi threat, such as Côte d'Ivoire. The United Nations must increasingly empower the African Union to take responsibility for the strategies and measures essential across the continent. The great powers should assist the African governments in training their armed forces to participate in these missions and to implement peace and stability in the face of the escalating radical menace. Both the United Nations and the international community opposing terrorism should help countries threatened by Jihadism to form national coalitions capable of resistance and of fostering pluralism and democracy.

North Africa's domestic struggle with Combat Salafism must also be supported by the world campaign against terrorism and by various international organizations, such as the Arab League, the African Union, and the Organization of the Islamic Conference. Algeria should be assisted in particular, but Morocco and Tunisia also need assistance in implementing counterterrorism efforts and political reforms. Libya, which has agreed to give up its nuclear capability, must be helped to rapidly reform and allow greater pluralism.

REGIONAL ORGANIZATIONS

As mentioned in earlier chapters, a political and cultural revolution must be initiated in international relations in order to isolate the threat of terror and to use the existing regional organizations in the campaign against it. The European Union should integrate its policies into one global campaign against Jihadi terrorism, and NATO, in conjunction with the United States and Canada, should become a leader of the alliance, so that other regional alliances can rely on it in their containment of terror. The Commonwealth of Independent states (CIS), led by a new (and yet to be constructed) Russian policy, could influence the Central Asian countries and China to contain Jihadism there. NATO and the CIS must coordinate with India and the African Union against the international threat on a global scale. But the most important moves of all have to be a series of reforms in the Greater Middle East leading to the rise of enlightened governments able to redirect the policies of the Arab League and the Organization of the Islamic Conference. In the end, Arab and Muslim state organizations should be the ultimate powers to contain and reverse Jihadi terrorism. Such massive moves will necessitate radical cultural reforms over many years; but at least both the Free World and the democracy movements in the Muslim world would have an agenda to follow and the necessary energy and resources.

THE NEW DIRECTIONS

In the final analysis the world confrontation with the terrorist forces needs new directions. But this should not mean collapsing efforts now under way, retreating from the battlefields, cutting deals with the terrorists and their sponsors, talking to the radicals even as they are mounting offensives, abandoning the forces of democracy, or opening the gates to radicalization in the Arab and Muslim world—actions that would permit the Jihadi penetration of the West and the Free World to deepen. New directions, instead, should correct flaws in the current world campaign against terror, provide a better definition of the conflict, and redirect resources and efforts in an integrated way so that allies against the radicals will receive more recognition and support. Such new directions would require:

1. Better-informed debate in the Free World, and better public education to generate popular support for needed action.
2. Better execution of the War of Ideas, with better identification of the conflict and outreach to appropriate allies, in order to generate genuine support within the Arab and Muslim world.
3. Strategic legislative decisions to render Jihadism illegal and illegitimate in all nations and internationally.

4. Interdiction of the establishment of al Qaeda–Taliban type emirates as a way to prevent the creation of bases for international terrorism.

5. Formation of regional coalitions to isolate terrorist networks in Africa, Latin America, and Asia.

6. Containment of the Syrian-Iranian axis in the Middle East and opposition to the production and deployment of nuclear weapons by Khumeinists.

7. Reformation of UN policies on counterterrorism, to direct a campaign of international education, deradicalization, and coordination against terrorism and its ideologies.

8. Battlefield containment of terrorist activities in Iraq, Lebanon, Afghanistan, Gaza, Darfur, Southern Sudan, the Philippines, and all other spots where terrorist forces threaten democracy, pluralism, and international law.

9. A shift away from exclusive reliance on oil regimes to explore new sources and ultimately new types of energy.

10. Engagement in a global campaign to support moderate and humanist Muslims' efforts, both inside the West and around the world, to reduce the influence of Jihadism and other radical ideologies and to promote pluralism and democracy.

These actions list the how and what of a new direction. In the end, the Free World does not need to decide whether or not to have this confrontation with Jihadi forces worldwide: Those forces have been developing strategies for decades, and have been on the offensive since before the Cold War and 9/11. The Jihadis have decided, irrefutably and irreversibly, to have this conflict. Democracies and global modern society have only two, linked questions to answer: First, to see or not to see, and second, when to act.

First, will the Free World "see" these offensives as part of a global campaign and will it decide to fight back, or will it be blinded by its enemy and its own corrupt elites and walk away? Thus there is the battle I've described between those who want to educate and inform their societies about this threat and those who wish to camouflage, dismiss, or minimize it. Ironically and amazingly, both in the West and the East, the confrontation with this twenty-first century totalitarian plague is centrally linked to knowledge. Never before has the adage "the truth will set you free" been so central to determining the future of humanity.

If the understanding of the threat is acquired—if the threat is seen clearly—acting against it is the logical next step. Then the second question is as dramatic as its predecessor: When should the Free World act? The time to respond is now. Today, the forces of counterterrorism face the results of decades of preparation and mutation by the forces of radicalism. Tomorrow the Free World will have to fight what its foes achieved today. Thus, those who call for postponing this sour engagement do a disservice to today's societies, and worse for future generations. All our lives will be impacted—that too is inescapable. Yet with knowledge and urgency we can prevail.

In the final analysis this struggle is intimately and internationally intertwined. The more educated Westerners are about the threat, the more able they will be to help Easterners free themselves; and the more liberated Easterners are, the more secure the Free World will be. This is the new direction for the future.

NOTES

PROLOGUE

1. *Future Jihad: Terrorist Strategies against the West* (New York: Palgrave Macmillan, 2005).
2. On the great post-9/11 debate—on which war against what terror—see, for example, opinions asserting the War on Terror being not necessary: Ian Lustick, *Trapped in the War on Terror* (Philadelphia: University of Pennsylvania Press, 2006); or the opposite views with Mark Steyn, *America Alone: The End of the World as We Know It* (Washington, D.C.: Regnery Publishing, Inc., 2006), or Jean Bethke Elshtain, *Just War against Terror: The Burden of American Power in a Violent World* (New York: Basic Books, 2004). And a multitude of clashing directions in James F. Hoge, Jr., and Gideon Rose, eds., *Understanding the War on Terror* (New York: A Foreign Affairs Book, 2005).
3. The Salafists are the Islamists (Islamic Fundamentalists) who rose from a Sunni environment. As it will be explained later, Salafists constitute an ideological "tree" including Wahabis, Muslim Brotherhood, and Deobandis. Khumeinists, another "tree," are the followers of the Islamic Revolution of Iran, from a Shia background. For further information on Salafism and Khumeinism see Gilles Kepel, *The Roots of Radical Islam* (London: Saqi, 2005) and *Jihad: The Trail of Political Islam* (London: I.B. Tauris, 2004); Robert Rabil, "Salafists vs. Liberals: The Struggle for Islam," *The National Interest*, January 2005; and Amir Taheri, "The Iranian Heresy," *New York Post*, June 1, 2004.
4. *Al Taadudiya Fi al Aalam* [Pluralism in the World], vol. 2 in author's series *Al Taadudiya Fi Lubnan* [Pluralism in Lebanon] (Juniah: Kasleek University Press, 1979).
5. *Khalifiyat al Thawra al Khumeiniya al Islamiya* (Beirut: Dar el Mashreq, 1987).
6. Dr. Jean Aucagne, SJ, "Preface," in Walid Phares, *Treize Siècles de Lutte* [Thirteen Centuries of Struggle] (Beirut: Dar al Mashreq Publications, 1982).
7. *Mashreq International*, 1984–1987.
8. Articles appeared in several daily newspapers such as *al Liwaa, al Safir, al Ahrar, al Amal,* as well as in the periodical *Haliyyat* between 1981 and 1983.
9. Walid Phares, *Radical Islam and the Middle East* (Miami: IRP Press, 1993).
10. Toward the end of 1992 and early 1993, Islamist leader Hassan Turabi held a worldwide Pan Islamist conference in Khartoum on the future of Jihadism. The conference was attended by almost all Jihadi forces, including Muslim Brotherhood, Wahabis, Hezbollah, radical Pan-Arabists, Iran, and others. Highly reported in the Arab media at that time, particularly in *al Hayat*. See Robert Satloff, *War on Terror: The Middle East Dimension* (Washington, D.C.: Washington Institute for Near East Policy, 2002), p. 103.
11. *The War of Ideas: Jihadism against Democracy* (New York: Palgrave Macmillan, 2007).
12. *Kafir* or *kafir billah* in Arabic language means "sinner against Allah." In European languages it was equated with "infidel." The translation is not accurate, but is accepted for general use. The plural of *kafir* is *kuffar*. In Jihadi rhetoric, *kafir* and *kuffar* are specific categories classified as theological enemies. In contemporary Jihadi literature by Salafists and Khumeinists, geopolitical enemies such as the United States, Europe, Russia, India, and some Arab and Muslim governments are described as *kuffar*.
13. Samuel Huntington, "The Clash of Civilizations," *Foreign Affairs* 72, no. 3 (Summer 1993).

14. Including France, the United States, Great Britain, Switzerland, Italy, Spain, Greece, Cyprus, West Germany, Sweden, the Netherlands, Belgium, Portugal, the Soviet Union, Poland, Romania, Bulgaria, Austria, Mexico, Canada, Venezuela, Colombia, Ecuador, Brazil, Argentina, Uruguay, Peru, Chile, Australia, Surinam, Turkey, Syria, Egypt, Algeria, Israel, Palestine, Iraq, Iran, Saudi Arabia, Kuwait, Oman, India, Senegal, Morocco, Chad, Sudan, Ivory Coast, Nigeria, China, and many others.

15. Among the boards I was cofounder of and adviser for were the American Anti-Slavery Group (AASG), the Coalition on Human Rights in the Islamic World, the Florida Society of Middle East Studies, and others.

16. These outlets include NBC, Fox News, MSNBC, CNN, C-SPAN, The Discovery Channel, PBS, CBN, *Oprah*, Canadian CBC, CTV, Global TV, British BBC and Sky News, French TF1, Channel 24, RFI, and Russian TV, as well as Portuguese, Spanish, and Belgian media, among others.

17. www.walidphares.com; www.futurejihad.com; www.thewarofideas.net.

INTRODUCTION

1. See, for example, Francis Fukuyama, *The End of History and the Last Man* (New York: Free Press, 2006).

2. See the various projections in Michael J. Hogan, ed., *The End of the Cold War: Its Meaning and Implications* (Cambridge: Cambridge University Press, 1992).

3. *Future Jihad: Terrorist Strategies against America* (New York: Palgrave Macmillan, 2005).

4. *The War of Ideas: Jihadism against Democracy* (New York: Palgrave Macmillan, 2007).

CHAPTER 1

1. On the Salafist propaganda see Douglas Farah, "Al Qaeda's Propaganda Machine Kicks Into High Gear," *The Counterterrorism Blog*, February 16, 2007; the author's article "The Continued Misunderstanding of the Salafi Jihad Threat," *World Defense Review*, October 2006; on the Khumeinist propaganda, see Tashbih Sayyed, "Wahhabis and Khomeinists: The Death Is At Our Doorsteps," *Muslim World Today*, November 4, 2005.

2. Sheikh Yussuf al Qaradawi's comments have been broadcast as part of a weekly TV show on al Jazeera under the title *al Sharia wal Hayat* [The Sharia Law and Life], airing on Sundays.

3. On the Leftist Trotskyte alliance see Hossam el-Hamalawy, "Youssef Darwish Passes Away," *The Arabist*, http://arabist.net; Amir Taheri, "Europe's Islamist Alliance," *Jerusalem Post*, July 12, 2004; for background on the alliance see David J. Jonsson, *Islamic Economics and the Final Jihad: The Muslim Brotherhood to the Leftist/Marxist–Islamist Alliance* (Salem Communications, 2006) and also his article "Global Threats Leading to the Leftist/Marxist–Islamist Takeover," *The Global Politician*, April 4, 2007.

4. See Doug Farah, "U.S. Muslim Brotherhood Groups Called 'Threat Organization' in DOD Memo," *The Counterterrorism Blog*, September 12, 2007. According to Farah, he received the memo from Joseph Myers, senior Army advisor. On the Huraba campaign, see Patrick Poole, "What's in a Name? 'Jihad' vs. 'Huraba,'" *The American Thinker*, September 18, 2007. According to Poole, the author of the DoD memo is Stephen Coughlin, Pentagon joint staff analyst. See also Jeffrey Imm, "Why The New York Times Can Legally Help The Enemy in The War on Terror," *The Counterterrorism Blog*, September 10, 2007; William McCants "Problems with the Arabic Name Game," Combating Terrorism Center at West Point, paper, May 22, 2006; Walid Phares, "Preventing the West from Understanding Jihad," *American Thinker*, July 16, 2007.

5. See "Islam, America and Europe," *The Economist*, June 22, 2006; Alan Cowell, "A 'Dangerous Moment' for Europe and Islam," *International Herald Tribune*, February 7, 2006; for a background see Walter Laqueur, *The Last Days of Europe: Epitaph for an Old Continent* (New York: Thomas Dunne Books, 2007).

6. See David Rennie, "America to Withdraw Troops from Saudi Arabia," *The Telegraph*, April 30, 2003; Syed Saleem Shahzad, "The Two Faces of Saudi Arabia," *Asia Times*, May 23, 2002; Nawaf Obaid, "A Defense of the Saudis," *The National Review*, May 10, 2002; for background see Bernard Lewis, "License to Kill: Usama bin Ladin's Declaration of Jihad," *Foreign Affairs*, November/December 1998.

CHAPTER 2

1. Alexander Ritzmann, "The Myth about Terrorists," paper presented at the American Institute for Contemporary German Studies (AICGS), The Johns Hopkins University, July 26, 2007; also see M. K. Bhadrakumar, "The Roots of Muslim Anger in India," *Asia Times*, July 15, 2006.
2. See Dan Ackman, "The Cost Of Being Osama Bin Laden," *Forbes Magazine*, September 14, 2001; also Paul Klebnikov, "Millionaire Mullahs," *Forbes Magazine*, July 21, 2003.
3. The Eastern mostly Shiite province of Ihsaa was conquered from the Ottoman Empire by the al Saud in 1913. The Western province of Hijaz, including Mecca and Medina, was seized by the Saudis and Wahabis between 1924 and 1925.
4. See Desmond Butler, "Probe: Oil Funds Paid for Bombers," Associated Press, November 17, 2004; also Richard Murphy (Council on Foreign Relations) and Bill O'Reilly, "Are Saudis Supporting Suicide Bomber Families?" transcript, Fox News, April 11, 2002.
5. See Haidar Ibrahim Ali, "Juzur al Istibdaad Fil Alam al Arabi" [The Roots of Authoritarianism in the Arab World], in *Awraaq Dimuqratiya* [Democracy Papers] (Baghdad: Markaz al Iraq Li Maalumat al Dimocratoya [Iraqi Center for Democratic Information], 2005), vol. 1.
6. On the theory of terrorism as a reaction to colonialism, see Howard Zinn, *Terrorism and War* (New York: Seven Stories Press, 2002); also, "Chomsky on 'Terrorism,'" interview with Noam Chomsky, in *Information Clearing House*, October 26, 2006. On rebuttal of the theory see Samir Khalil Samir, "Islamic Terrorism, a Disease within the Muslim World," *Asia News*, April 17, 2007.
7. During the Durban final declaration of the UN World Conference against Racism in August 2001, the European Union agreed to an apology for colonialism. See "EU Agrees to Apology for Slavery," Associated Press, September 7, 2001; critique of this position in David Horowitz, "Europe's Tradition of Appeasement," *Front Page Magazine*, September 10, 2001. See also Teresa Malcolm, "Priests Demand Apology for Aiding of Colonialism," *National Catholic Reporter*, November 20, 1998; and criticism in Shelby Steele, "War of the Worlds: The West Must Stop Apologizing for the Greatness of Our Civilization," *New Criterion*, September 17, 2001.
8. See Bernard Lewis, "The Roots of Muslim Rage," *The Atlantic Monthly*, September 1990; Lee Kuan Yew, "Muslim Anger on the Rise," *Forbes*, October 9, 2006; Bassem Mroue, "Are Mideast Governments Exploiting Muslim Anger," *Chicago Sun Tribune*, February 6, 2006; and Philip Yancey, "It's Not about the Crusades: The Clash with Islam Is Over New Global Realities," *Christian Science Monitor*, July 19, 2007.
9. *Stargate* is a science fiction movie—also developed into a television series—in which modern powers can visit the past and the future via a "passage," encountering forces and peoples from different ages.
10. On the Jihadi goal of reversing the "Reconquista" see Rafael L. Bardají, "La Espana Vulnerable," *Papeles FAES* no. 15, September 11, 2005.
11. *Dhimmi*, from Arabic *ahl al dhimma*, are the non-Muslim populations living under the Islamic state or the Caliphate since the seventh century. On the subject, see Bat Ye'or and David Maisel, *The Dhimmi: Jews & Christians under Islam* (Madison, NJ: Fairleigh Dickinson University Press, 1994); and Antoine Najm, *Lan Naeesha Dhummeyeen* [We Won't Live As Dhimmis] (Beirut: Dar al Ilaam, 1980). See also an Islamic perspective with Mohammed Salim al Awwa, "Natham Ahl al Dhimma: Ruya Islamiya Muassira" [The Dhimma Status: A Contemporary Islamic Vision], *Islam Online*, July 2005.
12. For examples of the use of the term *al harb ala al-islam* [the War on Islam] see Safwat al Shawadfi, "Al Harb Ala al Islam" [The War on Islam], audio lecture, *Majallat al Asr* Internet magazine, August 7, 2007; also Abdel Salaam, "Awlamat al Harb ala Islam" [The Globalization of the War on Islam], Almahdi.net, October 16, 2007. The term is constantly used by commentators on al Jazeera and particularly by Sheikh Yussuf al Qaradawi on the weekly forum *al Sharia Wal Hayat* [The Sharia Law and Life].
13. Paul Marshall, "Four Million: The Number to Keep in Mind This November," *The National Review*, August 27, 2004; also Stewart Stogel, "Bin Laden's Goal: Kill 4 Million Americans," NewsMax.com, July 14, 2004.
14. The Islamic Groupings are an offshoot from the Muslim Brotherhood in Egypt. See Muntasir al Zayat, "al Jamaat al Islamiya Wal U'nf" [The Islamic Groupings and Violence], al Jazeera, April 8, 2002.

15. Bernard Lewis, "Bring Them Freedom, or They Destroy Us," *Real Clear Politics*, from the national speech digest of Hillsdale College, July 16, 2006.
16. Janjaweed militias supported by the Islamist regime of Khartoum are persecuting the black African population of Darfur, who are also Muslim.
17. For example, the State Department division dealing with the War of Ideas was advised by Professor John Esposito, whose academic program at Georgetown University receives funds from Saudi emirs, the last of whom was Walid Ibn Talal.

CHAPTER 3

1. See the findings of the 9/11 Commission Report.
2. Jeffrey Imm, "2007: Strategic Thinking Needed in Fighting Global Jihad," *The Counter-terrorism Blog*, December 31, 2006.
3. See Katherine Kersten, "Shariah in Minnesota: Radical Muslim Activists Go Fishing in Troubled Waters?" *Wall Street Journal*, March 27, 2007; Homa Arjomand, "International Campaign against Sharia Court in Canada," nosharia.com, July 30, 2007; also Baradan Kuppusamy, "Malaysia's Minorities Unite against Sharia," *Asia Times*, January 14, 2006.
4. See Walid Phares, "Preventing the West from Understanding Jihad," *American Thinker*, July 2007, available at www.americanthinker.com.
5. See Martin Kramer, *Ivory Towers on Sand: The Failure of Middle Eastern Studies in America* (Washington, D.C.: Washington Institute for Near East Policy, October 2001); see also Walid Phares, "Education and Jihad," *Journal of Homeland Security Today*, November 2006.
6. See Gilbert Sewall, "Honesty In Textbooks—In U.S. Classrooms Jihad is Defanged or Oversimplified," *The Social Contract Press* 15, no. 2 (Winter 2004–2005).
7. See Clifford May, "The Enemy's Ideology," *Scripps Howard*, September 14, 2006; see also the various documents and files on the war of media at The Foundation for the Defense of Democracies, www.defenddemocracy.org.
8. *The Glenn Beck* show on CNN.
9. See Stew Magnuson, "When It Comes to The Battle of Ideas, The U.S. Has No General," *National Defense*, July 2007; and Vince Crawley, "'Battle for Ideas' Critical in Fighting Terrorism," *The Washington File*, The United States Department of State, April 6, 2006, available at http://usinfo.state.gov/.

CHAPTER 4

1. See Ralph Peters, "Blood Borders: How a Better Middle East Would Look," *Armed Forces Journal*, November 2, 2007; Mordechai Nisan, "The Minority Plight," *Middle East Quarterly*, September 1996; and Editorial, "Al Aqalliyat al Mashrequiyya Wal Naft" [The Middle Eastern Minorities and Oil], *Sawt al Mashreq*, Beirut, September 1982.
2. See Matthew Sousa and James J. F. Forest, *Oil and Terrorism in the New Gulf: Framing U.S. Energy and Security Policies* (Lanham, MD: Lexington Books, 2006).
3. See National Commission on Terrorist Attacks, *The 9/11 Commission Report: Final Report of the National Commission on Terrorist Attacks Upon the United States*, (New York: W. W. Norton & Company, 2004).
4. See Matt Pyeatt, "Clinton Paid 'Lip Service' to Terror Attacks, Expert Charges," CNSNews.com and NewsMax, December 6, 2001; also see Eleanor Hill, "Hearing on the Intelligence Community's Response to Past Terrorist Attacks against the United States from February 1993 to September 2001," Joint Inquiry Staff, Federation of American Scientists, Intelligence Resource Program, October 8, 2002.
5. See Alec Magnet, "Columbia Dean Admits Taking Saudi Junket," *The Sun*, January 11, 2006; also "His New Book Explores the Rise of the Academic Jihad," *History News Network* and *Front Page Magazine*, September 4, 2007.
6. On Saudi protection of the Taliban before 9/11, see James Risen, "CIA Director Prefers Saudi Plan to Bribe Taliban over Direct Action against Bin Laden," in *State of War: The Secret History of the CIA and the Bush Administration* (New York: Free Press, 2006); as reported in the *Sunday Times* (London), July 25, 2002: "Saudi Arabia had previously given money to the Taliban and bribe money to bin Laden, but this ups the ante. A few weeks after the meeting, Prince Turki sends 400 new pickup trucks to the Taliban. At least $200 million follow." See also Gerald L. Posner, *Why America Slept: The Failure to Prevent 9/11* (New York: Random House, 2003).

7. See United States District Court, Eastern District of Virginia, "Prepared Statement of John Walker Lindh to the Court" (Alexandria, VA, October 4, 2002); see also Cal Thomas, "Jury Failed in Terrorism Case," *Lawrence Journal World and News*, October 29, 2007.

8. See Ian Bremmer, "Prices Transform Oil into a Weapon: Petroleum Politics," *International Herald Tribune*, August 27, 2005; Max Singer, "Saudi Arabia's Overrated Oil Weapon," *The Weekly Standard*, August 18, 2003; and Bahman Aghai Diba, "Iran and Oil Weapon," *Persian Journal*, July 11, 2006. On opposing views see Jerry Taylor and Peter VanDoren, "Oil Weapon Myth," *The Cato Institute Paper*, December 6, 2001.

9. See Roy Licklider, "The Power of Oil: The Arab Oil Weapon and the Netherlands, the United Kingdom, Canada, Japan, and the United States," *International Studies Quarterly* 32, no. 2 (June 1988), pp. 205–226; Dr. Joseph S. Szyliowicz and Major Bard E. O'Neill, "The Oil Weapon and American Foreign Policy," *Air University Review*, March–April 1977.

10. The concept of *Silah al Naft* [The Oil Weapon] has been used frequently on al Jazeera's various live forums such as *al Sharia Wal Hayat* [The Sharia Law and Life], *al Ittijah al Muakess* [Opposite Direction], and *Ma Wara' al Khabar* [Behind the News] 2001–2007.

11. See "Iran Tuhadded Mujaddadan Bi Istikhdam Silah al Naft" [Iran Threaten Again of Using the Oil Weapon], *Mufakkirat al Islam* [Islam Memo], September 18, 2006; Brian Michael Jenkins, "The Threat of Oil Jihad," *United Press International*, March 3, 2006.

12. See Shoshana Klebanoff, *Middle East Oil and U.S. Foreign Policy: With Special Reference to the US Emerging Crisis* (Praeger, 1974); also Tom Barry and Martha Honey, "US Oil Policy in the Middle East," *Foreign Policy in Focus* 2, no. 4 (January 1997).

13. After a deal cut in 2005 with the United States and Great Britain, the Qadhafi regime dropped its nuclear ambitions to get off the terror list and begin rehabilitation internationally. See Eben Kaplan, "How Libya Got Off the List," *Backgrounder*, Council on Foreign Affairs, October 16, 2007.

14. Such as the "European-Sudanese Public Affairs Council" directed by David Hoile, which was established, originally, as the British-Sudanese Public Affairs Council in London in 1998.

15. See Walid Phares, "Education vs. Jihad," *Journal of Homeland Security Today*, November 2006.

16. On these challenges see Tom Turnipseed, "Our Declaration of Independence from Domination by Middle Eastern Oil: Developing a Sustainable Energy Policy," *Common Dreams*, June 30, 2005; Josef Braml, "Can the US Shed its Oil Addiction?" *The Washington Quarterly*, Autumn 2007; Jonathan Powell, "Is Oil Independence Attainable and Desirable?" *PolicyWatch #1085*, The Washington Institute for Near East Policy, March 16, 2006.

17. Congressman Howard Berman (D-CA) introduced a bill on November 15, 2007 that would force disclosure on all foreign contributions (including those of the Saudis) to American universities.

18. See Ronald R. Cooke, *Oil, Jihad and Destiny: Will Declining Oil Production Plunge Our Planet into a Depression?* Opportunity Analysis (July 30, 2004); also see David Kaplan, "The Saudi Connection: How Billions in Oil Money Spawned a Global Terror Network," *U.S. News and World Report*, December 7, 2003.

CHAPTER 5

1. See Irfan Hussein, "Blame It on the West," *Khaleej Times*, August 16, 2007; "Muslims in Europe Blame Non-Islamic West for Their Alienation—Map and Statistics," BBC, December 18, 2006; Mordechay Lewy, "The Islamic Blame Game: 'Shame Culture' vs. 'Guilt Culture,'" *Free Republic*, February 14, 2003; and Timothy Furnish, "Blame the West First: How the Media Misconstrue Jihad and the Crusades," *History News Network*, January 13, 2003.

2. "Mr. X" [George F. Kennan], "The Sources of Soviet Conduct," *Foreign Affairs*, July 1947.

3. The two main ethnic groups in Cyprus, a Greek majority and a Turkish minority, have confronted each other since the early 1960s. They were supported respectively by Greece and Turkey, both NATO members. During the Cold War, it was delicate and tough on the United States to handle two allies almost at war with each other.

4. See Robert Kaplan, *The Arabists* (New York: Free Press, 1995).

5. In his first address to the U.S. Congress, President Sarkozy asserted a new French policy of fighting terrorism alongside its allies, including the United States, but the terms used in the speech didn't identify the Jihadi movement. See "Nicolas Sarkozy reçoit une 'standing ovation' au Congrès américain," *Le Monde*, November 7, 2007; also Elaine Sciolino, "Congress Warms to France's New President," *New York Times*, November 8, 2007.

6. See "Terror and Democracy: The Bombers 'Voted,' and Aznar's Party Lost in Spain," *The Wall Street Journal*, March 16, 2004; also see C. de la Hoz, "Aznar firma que si se cede al terror se implantará la ley islámica en parte de Occidente" [Aznar Affirms that If Spain Cede to Terror, Islamic Law Will Be Established in Parts of the West], *ABC* [Spanish newspaper], March 15, 2007.
7. The UNIFIL is a UN peace force deployed on the Lebanese side of the borders with Israel since 1978 under UNSCR 425. In 2007 UNIFIL was strengthened after Hezbollah's war with Israel and deployed throughout south Lebanon. As of 2008, the force hasn't yet confronted the Jihadist forces.
8. See Bat Ye'or, *Eurabia: The Euro-Arab Axis* (Madison, NJ: Fairleigh Dickinson University Press, 2005). See an opposing view: Ralph Peters, "The Eurabia Myth," *The New York Post*, November 26, 2006.
9. James Kurth, "Europe's Identity Problem and the New Islamist War," *Orbis*, Summer 2006; Alexandr Vondra, "Radical Islam Poses a Major Challenge to Europe," *Middle East Quarterly* (Summer 2007).
10. See Lorenzo Vidino and Steven Emerson, *Al Qaeda in Europe: The New Battleground of International Jihad* (Amherst, NY: Prometheus Books, 2005); John Schindler, *Unholy Terror: Bosnia, Al-Qa'ida, and the Rise of Global Jihad* (Osceola, WI: Zenith Press, 2007).
11. See Christopher Deliso, *The Coming Balkan Caliphate: The Threat of Radical Islam to Europe and the West* (Westport, CT: Praeger Security International, 2007); also Shaul Shay, *Islamic Terror and the Balkans* (Piscataway, NJ: Transaction Publishers, 2006).
12. See Robert Bruce Ware, "Why Wahabism Went Wrong in Dagestan," paper presented at the Central Asia Caucuses Institute, September 2000; also Maj. Gen. Afsir Karim (Ret.), "An Indian Perspective On Central Asia," *Executive Intelligence Review*, July 22, 2005.
13. See Donald Jensen, "Islam in the Caucuses: A Look at Chechya," *CSIS*, May 7, 2004. Jensen is director of communications for Radio Free Europe.
14. "Vladimir Putin declared in Brussels that radical Islamic groups are planning to systematically annihilate non-Moslems and to create a worldwide caliphate. He added that western civilization was at risk of being attacked by terrorists, these attacks are a concerted effort and programme by an organisation which has a global structure and which has the intention to commit murderous atrocities in the name of Islam." In Ambrose Evans-Pritchard and Julius Straus, "West in Mortal Danger from Islam, Says Putin," *London Telegraph*, December 11, 2002.
15. See Gordon M. Hahn, *Russia's Islamic Threat* (New Haven: Yale University Press, 2007).
16. See Anne Bayefsky, *The UN and Beyond* (Washington, D.C.: Hudson Institute, 2007).

CHAPTER 6

1. See Ali Salem, "Thaqafat al Maout al Wajh al Muqabil Li Thaqafat al Aalaam" [The Culture of Death, the Other Face of the Culture of Peace], *Al Sharq al Awsat* (Saudi Arabia), July 1, 2007; Saad bin Tufla, "Tajdeed lil Aahd Maa al Amal" [Renewal of Commitment for hope], *Elaph*, September 2007; and Al Sayed Mohammad Ali al Husseini, "Al Maout li A'adaa' Wilayat al Faqeeh" [Death for the Enemy of the Mandate of the Wise], *As Siyassa* (Kuwait), October 12, 2007.
2. *Uruba* translates literally as "Arabity." It means a politically unique Arab nationalism leading ultimately to a vast and integrated Arab nation. In European languages it could translate into "Arabness" or "Arabity." Comparable to "Francite" or "Africanism," but with a radical ideological dimension, closer to national-socialist "Germanism." See Ralph M. Coury, "Who 'Invented' Egyptian Arab Nationalism?" *International Journal of Middle East Studies* 14, no. 4, November 1982, pp. 459–479; Michael C. Dunn, "Why Is Federalism Rare in the Middle East?" *MEI Journal*, August 12, 2005; Hilal Khashan, "Revitalizing Arab Nationalism," *Middle East Quarterly*, March 2000; and Talib Mushtaq, "Al Baath Muqaraba Baina al Uruba Wal Islam" [The Baath: A Comparison between Uruba and Islam], *Shabakat al Bassra* [Basra Network], June 3, 2007.
3. Faysal Jalul, "Al Liberaliya al Arabiya Ghayma la Tumtir" [Arab Liberalism: A Cloud that Never Rains], *al Mu'tamar* (Yemen), September 11, 2007; Abu Yarub al Marzuqi, "Geneologia al liberaliya al Arabia" [Geneology of Arab Liberalism], *Jadal Magazine*, July 7, 2007; Omran Salman, "Kharafat al Liberaliyun al Arab al Judud" [The Myth of New Arab Liberals], *Aafaq Magazine*, November 11, 2007; Barry Rubin, Laith Kubba, and Tamara Cofman Wittes, "Arab Liberalism and Democracy in the Middle East: A Panel Discussion," Brookings Institute, November 9, 2007.

4. For historical background see Albert Habib Hourani, *Minorities in the Arab World* (London: Ams Pr Inc, 1947); on the current state see for example Saad Eddin Ibrahim, "The Uneven Condition of Arab Christians," *The Daily Star* (Lebanon), December 21, 2004; also Sami Fares in his series of editorials in *Sawt al Mashreq* (Beirut), 1982–1983.

5. For background see Nawal El Saadawi, *The Hidden Face of Eve: Women in the Arab World* (London: Zed Books, 1980); Sheikh Yusuf al Qardawi, "Hal al Mar'a Shar la Budda Minhu?" [Is Woman a Needed Evil?], available at www.qaradawi.net, December 26, 2004; Rayyan Al-Shawaf, "Empowering Women and Minorities in the Arab World," *Al Naqed*, Oct 22, 2006; and "Women in the Arab World: Your Views," BBC, October 5, 2005.

6. See Barry Rubin, *The Long War for Freedom: The Arab Struggle for Democracy in the Middle East* (Hoboken: Wiley, 2005).

7. On the treatment of ethnic minorities see Mordechai Nisan, "Minorities in the Middle East: A History of Struggle and Self-Expression," 2nd ed. (Jefferson, NC: McFarland & Company, 2002).

8. See Bat Ye'or, *The Decline of Eastern Christianity Under Islam: From Jihad to Dhimmitude: Seventh–Twentieth Century* (Madison, NJ: Fairleigh Dickinson University Press, 1996); also Bat Ye'or, *The Dhimmi: Jews & Christians Under Islam* (Madison, NJ: Fairleigh Dickinson University Press, 1985).

9. Assyrians and Chaldeans are the original populations of Mesopotamia and, along with other smaller groups, form the Christian minority of today's Iraq. According to various human rights reports, they are persecuted principally by Jihadi groups. See Christopher Allbritton, "Iraq's Persecuted Christians," *Time Magazine*, September 20, 2004; and "Iraq's Christian Leaders Appeal for Protection From Islamists," *Assyrian International News Agency*, May 10, 2007.

10. On the Islamist view on Umma see Yassir Abdallah al Ghamdi, "Umma Wahida, Imanan, Wa Dinan Wa Daawa Wa Jihadan" [One Umma, in Faith, in Religion, in Knowledge, in Proselytizing and in Jihad], available at http://www.omah1.com/ November 12, 2007; also Sheikh Yassir Burhami, "Wa Inna Hazihi Ummatakum, Umma Wahida" [And This Nation Is One Umma], *Sawt al Salaf*, May 3, 2007. The Pan Arabist view on Umma is found in Arab Nationalist literature, for example Michel Aflaq, *al Baath* (Damascus, 1961).

11. Moshe Ma'oz, "Why the UN Partition Plan Wasn't Implemented: An Examination of Whether or Not the Palestinians and Arabs Actually Rejected the Partition Plan," *Palestine Israel Journal* 9, no. 4 (2002).

12. See Christopher Hitchens, "The Arab Street, a Vanquished Cliché," *Slate Magazine*, February 28, 2005; also Wahid Abdel-Meguid, "The Abused Arab Street," *Al-Hayat* (London), November 6, 2002.

13. From a campaign launched by the Cedars Revolution *Ahubbu al hayat* ("I love life") in 2006.

14. *Vilayet e faqih* is the theological name of the radical religious institution that controls the regime in Iran.

15. www.Elaph.com; CLIME available at http://www.mideastliberty.org/; www.Aafaq.org.

16. See Walid Phares, "An Idealistic Alternative to the Saudi Arms Deal," *New Media Journal*, August 10, 2007.

CHAPTER 7

1. *Les Lendemains qui chantent*, "The Tomorrows That Sing," is a narrative found in the autobiography of Communist essayist and leader Gabriel Péri, who praised the promised achievements of Communism.

2. A more expanded analysis is found in my article "Denying the West Understanding Jihad," *American Thinker*, July 17, 2007.

3. *Taqiya*, or "simulation," an old deception technique used in the historical Jihads. It allows operatives to lie in the objective of winning against the enemy. See Anwar Yassine, "Epitre Druze adressée Aux Noseiris" (Druze Chapter Addressed to the Nossairis), *Esoterikos* (Beirut, 1985), p. 21; also Kamel Mustafa al Shebi, *Al Sila Bayn al Tasauf Wal Tashayuh* [The Link between Sufism and Shiism], (Beirut, 1985), p. 414.

4. Robert Spencer, "Why We Must Label Al-Qaeda Terrorism 'Jihad Martyrdom,'" *Front Page Magazine*, August 10, 2007.

5. See Patrick Poole, "What's in a Name?: 'Jihad' vs. 'Hiraba,'" *The American Thinker*, September 18, 2007; LTC Joseph C. Myers, "The Muslim Brotherhood in America Defined as 'Threat Organization' in DOD Memo," in Doug Farah, *Counterterrorism Blog*, September 10, 2007.

6. See the works of Hassan Banna, Sayyid Qutb, Ayatollah Khumeini, and al Jazeera mentor Sheikh Yussuf al Qaradawi.
7. The Muaatazila is a theological school of thought within Islam that sought to explain Islamic faith in reason. It is also spelled Mu'tazilite. It began in circa 748 A.D/C.E. One of its major writers is al-Qadhi Abduljabbar al-Mu'tazili and his two main works were *al-Mughni fi al-Tawhid wa al-A'dl* and *Sharh Al-Usul Al-Khamsah.*
8. See Omran Salman, "Arab Governments Win the Battle for the 'Hearts and Minds' in America," *Aafaq* [Arab Reformers magazine], November 15, 2007.

CHAPTER 8

1. See Ron Cooke, *Oil, Jihad and Destiny* (Opportunity Analysis, 2004), p. 67.
2. See Stephen Schwartz, "Butchers Enablers," *National Review,* March 10, 2003; also Asaf Romirowsky, "New Book Explores the Rise of the Academic Jihad," *History News Network,* September 4, 2007.

CHAPTER 9

1. From Osama bin Laden speeches. See Raymond Ibrahim, *The Al Qaeda Reader* (New York: Broadway Books, 2007).
2. See James Gordon Meek, "Busted Illegal Alien Was Great Spy, Say Sources," *New York Daily News,* November 16, 2007; Josh Lefkowitz "The 1993 Philadelphia Meeting: Roadmap for Future Muslim Brotherhood Actions in the U.S.," *NEFA Foundation,* November 15, 2007; and Steven Emerson, "Hezbollah's Penetration of the FBI, CIA," *Counterterrorism Blog,* November 14, 2007.
3. "Incidents Involving Jihadist Infiltration into U.S. Government Institutions—Military Infiltration," *Global Strategic Analysis Center,* Report 2004; Jon Dougherty, "Are 'Jihadists' Infiltrating U.S. Military?" *World Net Daily News,* November 18, 2002.
4. See Dave Eberhart, "Muslim Moderate Kabbani Firm on Terrorist Nuclear Threat," NewsMax.com, November 19, 2001; also see Gerald E. Marsh and George S. Stanford, "Terrorism and Nuclear Power: What Are the Risks?" *National Policy Analysis,* National Center for Public Policy Research, November 2001.
5. See, for example, Danny Hakim, "Detroit: 4 Are Charged with Belonging to a Terror Cell," *New York Times,* August 29, 2002; Curt Anderson, "Miami: Defendant Denies Sears Tower Bomb Plot," Associated Press, November 8, 2007; Ben Dobbin, "New York: U.S. Knew of Terror Cell Before 9/11," *Washington Post,* September 16, 2002; Josh Meyer and Jason Chow, "Alleged Canadian Terror Cell May Have Worldwide Links," *Los Angeles Times,* June 5, 2006.
6. See Rod Dreher, "What the Muslim Brotherhood Means for the U.S.: Memo Lays bare Group's Plans to Destroy U.S. from Within," *The Dallas Morning News,* September 9, 2007; Joseph Myers, "Homeland Security Implications of the Holy Land Foundation Trial," *The American Thinker,* September 18, 2007.

CHAPTER 10

1. See "Muhammad Cartoon Row Intensifies," BBC, February 1, 2006; Hjörtur Gudmundsson, "Danish Imams Propose to End Cartoon Dispute," *Brussels Journal,* January 22, 2006; Arthur Bright, "Firestorm over Danish Muhammad Cartoons Continues: Newspaper That Published Cartoons Received Bomb Threat a Day after Issuing Apology," *Christian Science Monitor,* February 1, 2007; "U.K. Terror Suspects Include 2 Doctors," MSNBC, July 1, 2007; "'Terror Ringleader' Is Brilliant NHS Doctor," *Daily Mail,* August 27, 2007.
2. Acknowledging, though, that the continent faces ethnic, Marxist, and neo-Nazi violence as well. Examples of main ethnic terrorism in Western Europe are found in the Basque areas, Northern Ireland, and Corsica. Ethnic conflicts in the Balkans are a separate category. On Marxist and non-Islamist terrorism in Europe see Michael Radu, "The Futile Search for Root Causes of Terrorism," *American Diplomacy,* August 16, 2002; Samuel T. Francis, "The Terrorist International and Western Europe," *The Heritage Foundation Backgrounder* 47 (December 21, 1977); "State Department Terrorism Report: Europe, Eurasia," overview, *Country Reports on Terrorism 2004,* April 27, 2005.

3. Note also that the first historical clash between the United States and Islamic powers took place in the Mediterranean as well as on the Barbary Coast. See Thomas Jewett, "Terrorism In Early America: The U.S. Wages War against the Barbary States to End International Blackmail and Terrorism," *Early America Review*, Winter/Spring 2002; Rand H. Fishbein, "Echoes from the Barbary Coast—History of U.S. Military Actions against Pirates," *The National Interest*, Winter 2001.

4. Bat Ye'or, *Eurabia: The Euro-Arab Axis*, (Madison, NJ: Fairleigh Dickinson University Press, 2005).

5. See Bruce Bawer, *While Europe Slept: How Radical Islam Is Destroying the West from Within* (New York: Doubleday, 2006).

6. In 2002–2003 the first terrorism trial was held in Rotterdam. See Lorenzo Vidino and Erick Stakelbeck, "Dutch Lessons," *Wall Street Journal Europe*, August 7, 2003. A second Rotterdam trial was held in 2004–2005. See Emerson Vermaat, *Nederlandse Jihad* [Jihad in the Netherlands: The Hofstad Trial], *Aspekt*, September 2006.

7. See David Ashenfelter, "Defense Disputes Meaning of Tapes," *Detroit Free Press*, May 10, 2003.

8. See Michael Ledeen, "The Killers: The Dutch Hit Crisis Point," *National Review*, November 10, 2004; "Dutch Filmmaker Critical of Islam Killed," Associated Press, November 2, 2004.

9. See "Teaching Islam in Italy Calls for Reciprocity, Says Martino, Clarifies Previous Press Statements," *Zenith*, March 10, 2006; John Allen, "A Challenge, Not a Crusade," *New York Times*, September 19, 2006; "Pope Urges 'Reciprocity' of Respect in Visit to Turkey," Associated Press, November 30, 2006.

10. "Muslim Cleric Says Attack on London 'Inevitable,'" Reuters, April 18, 2004; Steve Harrigan, "Muslim Extremists Preach Violence in Europe," *Fox News*, November 29, 2004; "Abu Hamza: Controversial Muslim Figure," CNN, May 27, 2004. On Zawahiri threats to Europe see "Al-Qaeda 'issues France threat" BBC, September 14, 2006; Craig Whitlock, "Risk of Attack Rising, Officials In Europe Say New Threats by Al-Qaeda No. 2 Single Out Britain and France," *Washington Post*, December 21, 2006.

11. See B. Raman, "Home Grown Jihadis (Jundallah) in UK and US," *UK and US International Terrorism Monitor*, paper no. 231, South Asian Analysis Group, June 11, 2007; also Owen Bowcott, "Woman in UK 'Groomed' as Bomber," BBC, June 11, 2007; "Jihad Camps Were Preparation for Murder, Court Told," *The Guardian*, October 11, 2007; Vikram Dodd, "Al-Qaida Plotting Nuclear Attack on UK, Officials Warn," *The Guardian*, November 14, 2006.

12. Ayaan Hirsi Ali, *Infidel* (New York: Free Press, 2007).

13. Classical tensions related to social integration in Europe meant that workers decided or were led to stay but not integrate, culturally or sociologically. And because of that they isolated themselves in society.

14. See Alexander Ritzmann, "The Fairytale of the Poor and Angry Terrorists," *American Institute for Contemporary German Studies Advisor*, May 25, 2007.

15. On al Qaeda in Germany, see "Al Qaeda in Germany," on *News Hour* (PBS), October 25, 2002; on Hezbollah, see Mark Dubowitz and Alexander Ritzmann, "Hezbollah's German Helpers," *Wall Street Journal*, April 17, 2007.

16. Matthias Gebauer, "Three Islamist Terror Suspects Arrested in Germany;" *Der Spiegel*, September 5, 2007; Annie Jacobsen, "German Jihadists Targeted Airports and More," *Aviation Nation*, September 5, 2007. On arrest, see Craig Whitlock, "Germany Says It Foiled Bomb Plot: 3 Suspects Allegedly Trained in Pakistan, Planned to Hit Sites Frequented by Americans," *Washington Post*, Thursday, September 6, 2007, A01.

17. Alexander Schwabe, "Germany's Student Train Bomber: Friendly, Unremarkable, and Pious," *Der Spiegel*, August 21, 2007.

18. See Ivonne Marschall, "Homegrown Austrian Terrorism—The End of a Safe Era?" *EUX TV*, September 13, 2007.

19. See Olivier Guitta, "Cuckoo Clocks and Jihadists: What Switzerland Is Now Producing," *Weekly Standard*, July 16, 2007.

20. See Craig Whitlock, "Neutral Switzerland, a Rising Radicalism: Islamic Extremists Newly Seen as Threat," *Washington Post*, July 20, 2006; Olivier Guitta, "Cuckoo Clocks and Jihadists," Swiss Domestic Security Report, Press Release, Federal Office of Police, May 31, 2007.

21. "Norway Jihad: Mullah Krekar: Islam Will Win," *Aftenposten*, March 13, 2006; D. Fjord-man, "Norway: The Country of Peace Meets the Religion of Peace," *The Brussels Journal*, September 18, 2007; "Where Boys Grow Up to Be Jihadis," *Ein News*, November 24, 2007.

22. On Jihadi threats to Denmark see "Denmark Targeted by Jihadists," *Site Institute*, October 2006; Jan M. Olsen, "Danish Police Arrest 9 Terror Suspects," Associated Press, September 5, 2006; Flemming Rose, "Denmark Convict Three Jihadists," *Northern Light*, November 24, 2007. On European liberal resistance to Jihadism see Flemming Rose, "Europe's Politics of Victimology: The Danish Cartoon Editor Argues That Failed Multiculturalism is Killing Europe's Liberal Values," *Blueprint Magazine*, May 17, 2006.

23. I expanded on this crisis in an article titled "Al Qaeda in Iraq Threatens Sweden," *American Thinker*, September 22, 2007.

24. On Islamic rule of Sicily: *Jazeerat Siqliya* [The Island of Sicily] Islamnet.com, May 2006; "Rahla Maa al Lissan al Arabi Wal Wujud al Islami Fi Siqliya" [Journey with Arabic Language and Islamic Presence in Sicily], *al Majalla*, [international Arab magazine], November 11, 2006. On historic background see Paul Fregosi, *Jihad in the West, Muslim Conquests from the 7th to the 21st Centuries* (New York: Prometheus Books, 1998).

25. *Hizb al Tahrir* (Party of Liberation) is an Islamist and Jihadist political movement, founded in 1953 in the Levant, that believes in resurrecting the Caliphate. For more information, please see http://www.hizb-ut-tahrir.org/EN/.

26. My interviews occurred in Madrid at the FAES summer school in July 2006 and in July 2007. *Fundación para el Análisis y los Estudios Sociales* [The Foundation for analysis and social studies], Madrid.

27. The concept of the return to Andalusia (Spain) or *al Awda ila al andalus* was published in "Al Itizar Mina al Muslimeen Litarduhum Mina al Andalus" [Apologizing from Muslims for Removing Them from Spain] in a report on historians' conference on Andalusia in *Shabakat Annaba al Maalumatiya*, November 2007, available atwww.annabaa.org; also see Fakhri al Waseef, "al Awda Ilal Andalus," *Muntadayaat al Tareekh*, May 2002, see www.altareekh.com; Jonathan Dahoah-Halevi, "Al Qaeda: The Next Goal Is to Liberate Spain from Infidels," Research Institute for European and American Studies, May 2007; "Saudi Daily: Andalusian Muslims Recall Mass Exodus," *MEMRI Special Dispatch Series*, no. 873, March 4, 2005, available at http://memri.org/bin/opener.cgi?Page=archives&ID=SP87305.

28. The author participated in the Prague Conference on Security and Democracy. See Kathleen Moore, "World: Democracy and Security Conference Opens In Prague," *Radio Free Europe*, June 5, 2007.

29. On Koso and Jihadism see Khaled Yussef, "*Kosova Jirhul Muslmeen al Nazif: Dalil Unsuriyat Wa Wahshiyat al Masihiya al Gharbiya Wal Ilmaneya*" [Kosovo: the Wound of Muslims and the Evidence of the Racism and Savagery of Western Christianity and Secularism], *Jaridat al Shaab*, August 26, 2007; on opposite view see Ray Robinson, "Kosovo, Albania and Jihad," *The American Thinker*, May 13, 2007; Nathan Burchfiel, "U.S. Accused of Siding with 'Criminals and Jihadists' in Kosovo," *CNS News*, July 21, 2006; "Haradinaj and Thaci met with Osama bin Laden in Tirana in 1995 to Plan al-Qaeda Jihad in Kosovo," *American Council for Kosovo*, May 2, 2006.

30. See "Experts Reassess Changing Face of Europe's Terror Threat," *DW-World*, April 7, 2007; "Bulgarian Police Official Warns Of Jihadist Threat," Associated Press, April 15, 2005; Kathryn Haahr, "Catalonia: Europe's New Center of Global Jihad," *Global Terrorism Alert 5*, no. 11, June 7, 2007; *Violent Jihad in the Netherlands: Current Trends in the Islamist Terrorist Threat*, Ministry of Interior: The Netherlands, General Intelligence and Security Service, 2006.

31. Tariq Ramadan, who has supporters among the apologists toward Islamism as well as their opponents, rejects the concept of a War on Terror and a conflict with Jihadism; he promotes Euro Islamism. See Gideon Lichfield, "Explaining the Terrorists," *The Economist*, September 6, 2007.

32. See "European Union Battle Groups to Sudan?" *Global Power Europe*, July 13, 2007, http://www.globalpowereurope.eu; "U.S. Policy on Sudan Outlined for Lawmakers," The United States Mission to the European Union, September 25, 2005; Soeren Kern, "European Foreign Policy in Lebanon: Is This for Real?" *Strategic Studies Group Briefs*, no. 36, November 21, 2006; Stephanie Levy, "Analysis: Preparing for a French Revolution in Mideast Policy," *Jerusalem Post*, April 22, 2007; P. Parameswaran, "France, U.S. Lead Drive to Force Out Syrian Troops from Lebanon," *AFP*, March 1, 2005.

CHAPTER 11

1. Jihadi doctrinaires have endorsed the concept of Jihad against Russia. See Yusuf al Qardawi, *"al Muslimun wal Unf al siyassi, Nazarat Ta'silya"* [The Muslims and Political Violence: Fundamentalist Views], Islamonline.net, June 6, 2004, http://www.islamonline.net /Arabic/contemporary/2004/06/article01c.shtml. On the background see Paul Murphy, *The Wolves of Islam: Russia and the Faces of Chechen Terror* (Dulles, VA: Potomac Books Inc., 2006).

2. See statement by Duku Amrov, *"Qaid al Muqawama al Chechenya Yadu Li Jihad Dud America, Britania wa Israeel"* [The Commander of the Chechen Resistance Calls for Jihad against America, Britain and Israel], Islamonline.com, November 1, 2007, http://www .islamonline.net/Arabic/contemporary/2004/06/article01c.shtml.

3. A *khanat* was a Turkic or a Mongol principality between central Asia and Mongolia. The major initial *khanats* were Mongolia, Djaghatai in Central Asia, the Ilkhanat of the Hougalites in Persia, and the Khanat of Kiptchak in Russia and Kazakhstan.

4. See Robert D. Crews, *For Prophet and Tsar: Islam and Empire in Russia and Central Asia* (Cambridge, MA: Harvard University Press, 2006).

5. From bin Laden speech in November 2001 on al Jazeera, October 7, 2001.

6. Grand Mufti of Jerusalem Hajj al Amin Husseini joined Adolf Hitler in Berlin in 1941 against the Allies. See the "Record of the Conversation Between the Fuhrer and the Grand Mufti of Jerusalem, November 28, 1941," in *The Presence of Reich Foreign Minister and Minister Grobba in Berlin: Documents on German Foreign Policy, 1918–1945*, series D, vol. XIII, London, 1964, p. 881, available in Walter Lacquer and Barry Rubin, *The Israel-Arab Reader* (New York: Facts on File, 1984), pp. 79–84; also in Ronald J. Rychlak "Hitler's Mufti: The Dark Legacy of Haj Amin al-Husseini," in *Crisis Magazine*, December 5, 2005. On Rashid Ali al-Kilani of Iraq alliance with the Nazis see Chuck Morse, "The Arab–Nazi Connection," *Free Republic*, April 28, 2002. See also Mark Erikson, "Islamism, Fascism and Terrorism," *Asia Times*, November 5, 2002.

7. Followers of the Islamist school of Deband-dar al Ulum in India, founded in 1857. See "Deobandi Islam," *Global Security*, November 2007; "The Flowering of the Deobandi Movement," *Pakistan Link*, April 20, 2001.

8. On post-Soviet Jihad, see for background Hilary Pilkington, ed., *Islam in Post-Soviet Russia* (London: Routledge Curzon, 2002).

9. See John Giduck, *Terror at Beslan: A Russian Tragedy with Lessons for America's Schools* (Golden, CO: Archangel Group, 2005).

10. Basayev was a Jihadist terrorist leader in Chechnya. He was responsible for the Moscow theater siege and the Beslan school massacre. He was killed on July 10, 2006, by the Russian forces. See Jonathan Steele, "Shamil Basayev: Chechen Politician Seeking Independence through Terrorism," *The Guardian*, July 11, 2006; "Basayev: 'We Strike across the Central Russia,'" *Kafkaz Center*, May 27, 2007; Bill Roggio, "Chechen al Qaeda Emir Abu Hafs Killed," *The Long War Journal*, November 26, 2006.

11. On al Qaeda Chechen connection see Scott Peterson, "Al Qaeda among the Chechens: As Russians Bury Their Dead, Officials Look at Terrorist Links to Chechen Rebels," *Christian Science Monitor*, September 7, 2004.

12. See "Russian Missiles to Syria, Venezuela and Iran? Why?" geostrategymap.com, January 21, 2005; also Paul Gigot, "Syria, Iran and Russia Stir up Trouble," *The Wall Street Journal*, December 2, 2006.

13. See Richard Lugar, "The US Russian Front against Terrorism and Weapons Proliferation," *US Foreign Policy Agenda*, July 2002.

14. *Mahakem Islamiya* or Islamic Courts are the Jihadist forces in Somalia, much like the Taliban of Afghanistan.

15. On Russian realignment see Michael Wines, "After the Attacks: In Moscow, Russia Takes Stand against Terrorism, but the Stance Wavers Quickly," *The New York Times*, September 16, 2001; also Graham Allison and Andrei Kokoshin, "A US–Russian Alliance against Megaterrorism," *The Boston Globe*, November 21, 2001.

16. "Four Jihadi militants have been killed during a special operation in the village of Gelinbatan (Novo-Fite) in the Tabasaran district of Dagestan and another two were killed on January 8 and 9, 2008." Al Qaeda-like Wahabis are spreading outside Chechnya. *Interfax*, "6 militants killed in special operation in Dagestan" January 10, 2008.

CHAPTER 12

1. See Amil Imani, Iranian dissident, "Why Confront Islamism?" *The American Thinker,* February 28, 2007; Roger Scruton, "The West and the Rest, On terrorism and globalization," *National Review,* September 23, 2002; also Fiona Symon, "Analysis: The roots of jihad," BBC special, October 16, 2001; for opposite view see Ahmad Ali Ahmad, "Aafaq al siraa fil mintaqa: hassem askari aw silmi" (The struggle in the region and the upcoming ending: military or peaceful?), *al Thawra,* Syria, November 19, 2007.

2. See Jeffrey Imm, "Jihad, Islamism, and the Challenge of Anti-Freedom Ideologies," *Counterterrorism Blog,* September 26, 2007; James J. F. Forest "Countering the Threat of Islamic Militant Terrorism: A New Look," *Family Security Matters,* November 27, 2006; Maria Alvanou, "Symbolisms of basic Islamic imagery in Jihadi propaganda," *ITSTIME* (Rome), January 2003.

3. Lydia Khalil, "Al-Qaeda & the Muslim Brotherhood: United by Strategy, Divided by Tactics," *Terrorism Monitor* 4, no. 6 (March 23, 2006); Joseph Myers, "Homeland Security Implications of the Holy Land Foundation Trial," *The American Thinker,* September 18, 2007; Douglas Farah, "The Little Explored Offshore Empire of the International Muslim Brotherhood," *International Assessment and Strategy Center,* April 18, 2006; on Arabic sources see Yusuf al Qardawi, "Kitaab al Ikhwan al muslimeen, sabun aaman min al dawa wal tarbiya, wal jihad" [The Book of the Muslim Brotherhood: 70 Years of Call, Education and Jihad], available at http://www.khayma.com/; Sylvain Besson, *La conquete de l'Occident: Le projet secret des Islamistes* [The Conquest of the West: The Islamists' Secret Project] (Paris: Seuil, 2005).

4. Often on al Qaeda websites and in al Ansar chat rooms including on paltalk.com. The concept of love of Jihad is found on the web site of the leading Wahabi thinker of Saudi Arabic, Mohammed Salah Alothaimeen, http://www.binothaimeen.com; also on Jihadi media websites such as Islamway.com at http://www.islamway.com/?iw_s=Lesson&iw_a=view&lesson_id=28439; or on Jihadi females at http://www.mojahdat.jeeran.com/.

5. The UN sponsored World Conference against Racism, Racial Discrimination, Xenophobia and Related Intolerance was held in Durban, South Africa, from August 31 to September 7, 2001, http://www.un.org/WCAR. It was criticized for being hijacked by the radicals and used by Jihadists. See Anne Bayefsky, "Terrorism and Racism: The Aftermath of the Durban Conference," *Jerusalem Letter—Viewpoints* 468, December 16, 2001; also Tom Lantos, "The Durban Debacle: An Insider's View of the World Racism Conference at Durban," *The Fletcher School of Law and Diplomacy* 26, no. 1 (Winter/Spring 2002).

6. The author expanded on this analysis in a presentation to the U.S. House of Representatives Caucus on Terrorism on July 5, 2007. It was published in August in the *World Defense Review* under the title "The Iran Plan in Iraq."

7. See Jamie Glazov, "Symposium: Lebanon: The Spark of Liberty in the Middle East," with Joe Baini, Charbel Barakat, Brigitte Gabriel, Joseph Farah, *FrontPage Magazine,* November 3, 2005.

8. Alawites are a Muslim religious sect located in today's northern Syria and in Turkey. They are considered as schismatic by both Sunnis and Shia, and they form 9 percent of Syria's population.

9. See Peter Ackerman and Ramin Ahmadi, "Iran's Future? Watch the Streets: People Power," *International Herald Tribune,* January 5, 2006; Reza Pahlavi, "Iran, Regime Change or Behavior Change," *Hudson Institute Briefing Series,* April 3, 2007.

10. See Sabri Sayari, "Turkey's Islamist Challenge," *Middle East Quarterly,* September 1996; also ten years later see M. K. Bhadrakumar, "Turkey: Islamists Pay a Price for Victory," *Asia Times,* July 28, 2007; Steven A. Cook, "Cheering an Islamist Victory," *Boston Globe,* July 26, 2007; Amir Taheri, "Turkey's Islamist Crossroad," *The New York Post,* November 20, 2007.

CHAPTER 13

1. The triborder area is located between Brazil, Argentina, and Paraguay. Multiple intelligence services have identified a presence of Hezbollah and al Qaeda in that area. See Mike Boettcher, "South America's 'Tri-Border' Back on Terrorism Radar," CNN, November 8, 2002; also "Tri-Border Transfers 'Funding Terror,'" BBC, December 14, 2006; also Joe Pappalardo, "South America Hotspot Garners U.S. Attention," *National Defense Magazine,* June 2005.

2. On this group background see Sayed Askar Mousavi, *The Hazaras of Afghanistan: An Historical, Cultural, Economic and Political Study* (New York: Palgrave Macmillan, 1997).

3. See Zachary Abuza, *Militant Islam in Southeast Asia: Crucible of Terror* (Boulder, CO: Lynne Rienner, 2003); also see Ken Conboy, *The Second Front: Inside Asia's Most Dangerous Terrorist Network* (London: Equinox Publishing, 2006).

4. See Hugh Fitzgerald "Indian Dhimmitude—Remedies and Responses," *Jihad Watch*, March 20, 2006. On background see Sita Ram Goel, *Heroic Hindu Resistance to Muslim Invaders, 636 A.D. to 1206 A.D.* (New Delhi: Voice of India, 1990); Sita Ram Goel, *The Story of Islamic Imperialism in India* (New Delhi: Voice of India, 1996); see for an Islamic perspective Sharif Abdel Aziz, "Maarakat Sumnat: Fath al Hind al Aazam" [The Battle of Sumat: The Great Conquest of India], in *Majallat Aqlaam al Thaqafiya* [Magazine of Cultural Pens], May 18, 2006, http://www.aklaam.net.

5. On Pakistan see Mark Mazzetti and David Rohde, "Terror Officials See Al Qaeda Chiefs Regaining Power," *The New York Times*, February 19, 2007; "Al-Qaeda Gaining Strength in Pakistan, Waziristan Accord Has Failed," *The New York Times*, February 19, 2007; and comments by Daveed Gartenstein-Ross on *The Counterterrorism Blog*, February 19, 2007.

6. *Lebensraum*, literally " living space" in German. Concept used by Adolf Hitler to conquer lands needed for the Reich to expand.

7. Zachary Abuza, "Wake Up Call: 6 Months After the Thai Coup, Islamist Insurgency is Raging," *The Counterterrorism Blog*, March 20, 2007.

8. On Malaysia Islamism see Farish A. Noor, "Islam Embedded: The Historical Development of the Pan-Malaysian Islamic Party (PAS) 1951–2003," *Malaysian Sociological Research Institute (MSRI)*, Kuala Lumpur, 2004, vol. 2, part 2, pp. 730–737. On Thailand see B. Raman, "Raging Jihad in Southern Thailand: An Intriguiung Aspect," *International Terrorism Monitor* 239 (February 6, 2007); also Isaac Kfir, "Southern Thailand and Islamic Terrorism," International Institute for Counter-Terrorism (ICT), February 23, 2007.

9. The Non-Aligned Movement (NAM) is an international organization of states considering themselves not formally aligned with or against any major power bloc. It was founded in 1950s; as of 2007, it has 118 members.

10. Since the 1940s Darul Islam has been an active militant organization dedicated to the foundation of an Islamic state in Indonesia. In the last two decades other Islamist parties emerged, such as the United Development Party (PPP) Prosperous Justice Party (PKS), and the Crescent Star Party (PBB). Other Islamist movements include, for example, the Indonesian Muslim Intellectuals Association (ICMI). A main Jihadist militia is the Laskar Jihad, present on many islands. The principal Jihadist organization identified as terrorist and linked to al Qaeda is Jemaa Islamiya, also present in Malaysia and other countries. Smaller groups exist such as "Kommando Jihad" (Holy War Command). See for example Douglas E. Ramage, "Islam in Asia," Capitol Hill Hearing Testimony, Federal Document Clearing House, July 14, 2004; also see "Indonesia: Islam," U.S. Library of Congress: Country Studies.

11. The main Jihadi force in Indonesia. See "In the Spot Light: Laskar Jihad," Center for Defense Information (CDI), March 8, 2002.

12. For background see Zachary Abuza, *Political Islam and Violence in Indonesia* (London: Routledge, 2007); Simon Elegant Poso, "Indonesia's Dirty Little Holy War," *Time Magazine*, December 10, 2001; also "Asia Letter: Indonesian Islamist Party Is Quietly Gaining Ground," *International Herald Tribune*, April 8, 2004; "Battle for Indonesia's Islamic Vote," BBC, June 4, 1999; "Laskar Jihad," Global Security.org, 2007.

13. John T. Sidel, *Riots, Pogroms, Jihad: Religious Violence in Indonesia* (Ithaca, NY: Cornell University Press, 2006). On background see Muhammad Khalid Masud, "Defining Democracy in Islamic Polity," paper for the conference "The Future of Islam, Democracy and Authoritarianism in the Age of Globalisation," organized by the International Centre for Islam and Pluralism (ICIP), Jakarta, December 5–6, 2004.

14. See Patung, "Southern Philippines Jihad," *Indonesia Matters*, November 6, 2006; also Robert Spencer, "Philippines Capitulates to Global Jihad," *Human Events*, July 19, 2004.

15. See Abu Khalid al Sayyaf, "Al Maghreb al Islami wa Dawrahu fi Fath Ifriqiya wal Andalus" [The Islamic Maghreb and Its Important Role in Conquering Africa and Andalusia], *al Lukah*, http://www.alukah.net/, July 9, 2007; also see *Fath Afreeqiya* [The Conquest of Africa], Arabia.net, http://encyclopedia.aarabiah.net/Africa-history, September 2007; "The Conquest and settlement of Africa," *Journal of Islamic Studies* 1 (1990): 164-167; Abdulwahid Dhanun Taha,

"The Muslim Conquest and Settlement of North Africa and Spain," review by M. Donner, *International Journal of Middle East Studies* 23, no. 2 (May 1991): 274–275; see also Greg Richard, "Primer on Islamic Imperialism," *The American Thinker*, November 19, 2006.

16. See *The Road to Sudan and Darfur, and Brief History of Jihad in Africa*, SITE Institute, May 15, 2006; James Phillips, *To Stop Sudan's Brutal Jihad, Support Sudan's Opposition*, The Heritage Foundation, Backgrounder no. 1449, June 13, 2001; also John Eibner, "Another Front: Genocidal Jihad in the Sudan" *The National Review*, March 25, 2003; "Bin Laden Calls for Jihad in Arabia and Sudan-Web," Reuters, October 23, 2007.

17. Scott Baldauf, "As Islamists Take Over Somalia, Its Western-Backed Neighbor Ethiopia Prepares for War," *The Christian Science Monitor*; Ali Hilnim *"Awdat al Mahakem al Islamiya fil Somaal"* [The Return of the Islamic Courts in Somalia], *al Sharq al Awsat*, March 7, 2004; Christopher Griffin and Oriana Scherr, "Terrorist Threats in the Horn of Africa," AEI.org, July 31, 2007; Gregory Alonso Pirio, *The African Jihad: Bin Laden's Quest for the Horn of Africa* (Trenton, NJ: Red Sea Press, 2007); Douglas Farah, "The Horn of Africa in Decline," *The Counterterrorism Blog*, November 1, 2007.

18. Muammar Al Qadhafi, *The Green Book* (Berkshire, England: Garnet Publishing, 2005); Ahmad al Mujabbiri, *Al Dawa al Islamiya wa Tahaddiyat al Muassira* [The Islamic Dawa and the Contemporary Challenges], *Al Markaz al Aalami Li Dirasat wa Abhass al Kitaaab al Akhdar* [The International Research Center for the Green Book], http://www.greenbook-research.com, September 2007.

19. See Andrew Black, "Recasting Jihad in the Maghreb," *Terrorism Monitor* 5, no. 20 (October 25, 2007); also Olivier Guitta "New Worrying Signs of Activity in the Maghreb," *Le Croissant*, November 5, 2007; Carlos Echeverría Jesús, "Al-Qaida's Obsessive Fixation on the Maghreb," *Strategic Studies Group*, Intellibriefs, November 12, 2007; Andrew Hansen, "Al-Qaeda in the Islamic Maghreb (aka Salafist Group for Preaching and Combat)," Council on Foreign Relations, April 11, 2007; "Al Jamaa al Salfiya Tughayir il Qaeda al Jihad Bi Bilad al Maghreb al Islami" [The Salafist Jamaa Transforms into al Qaeda's Jihad in the Islamic Maghreb], in al shuruq, http://www.echoroukonline.com, January 26, 2007; also "Al Bu'ss wal Jihad fil Maghreb" [Misery and Jihad in the Maghreb], *Le Monde Diplomatique Arabe*, November 2004.

20. Afwaj al Muqawama al Lubnaniyaa, also known as Amal, is a Lebanese Shia movement preceding Hezbollah.

21. Ralph Peters, "The Other Jihad," *USA Today*, August 23, 2005; Moshe Terdman and Reuven Paz, "Islamization and Da'wah in Contemporary Sub-Saharan Africa: The Case of the African Muslim Agency (AMA)," *African Occasional Papers* 1, no. 2 (July 2007); Abdelkérim Ousman, "The Potential of Islamist Terrorism in Sub-Saharan Africa," *International Journal of Politics, Culture, and Society* 18, nos. 1–2 (December 2004).

22. See Gemma Meyer, "Warning from South Africa," *Town Hall*, January 23, 2007; "Terrorists Warn South Africa on Somalia Troops," *Afrol News*, January 11, 2007; Michael Clough and Loubna Freih, "Will South Africa Speak out on Darfur Today?" *Business Day*, April 19, 2005.

23. Douglas Farah, *The Growing Terrorism Challenges from Latin America*, International Assessment and Strategy Center, February 2007; Mark Steyn, "And Now the Latino Jihad," *The Jerusalem Post*, May 28, 2006.

24. Ayman El-Amir, "From Bolivia to Baquba," *al Ahram*, June 15, 2006.

25. Douglas Farah, "Ahmadinejad's Excellent Latin American Adventure," *The Counterterrorism Blog*, January 15, 2007; Pablo Brum y Mariana Dambolena, "Las alianzas estratégicas iraníes en América Latina" [The Iranian Strategic Alliances in Latin America], *El Diario Exterior*, October 3, 2007.

26. "Fundamentalismo islámico en América Latina. Anexo. Texto del llamamiento a la Yihad en Latinoamérica" [Islamic Fundamentalism in Latin America: Annex: Text of the Declaration of Jihad in Latin America], *Paz Digital*, November 4, 2007.

CHAPTER 14

1. Example for strategic direction of the Jihadists versus international law, see "Democracy Runs Counter to Islam, Because it Emphasizes the Sovereignty of the People, Whereas Islam Emphasizes the Sovereignty of Allah," interview with Abu Bakr Bashir, spiritual leader of Al-Gama'a Al-Islamiya in Indonesia, which aired on *Al-Arabiya TV*, October 26,

2007; also see Samir Khalil, "Salafist Islam Spawns Islamic Terrorism," *Asia News*, April 12, 2007.

2. Michael Jacobson, *The West at War: U.S. and European Counterterrorism Efforts, Post-September 11* (Washington, D.C.: The Washington Institute for Near East Policy, 2006); Babu Suseelan, "Close the Door on Jihadi Terrorism: Lessons from the Mumbai Blasts," *India Forum*, July 16, 2006; Charles Feldman and Stan Wilson, "Ex-CIA Director: U.S. Faces 'World War IV'" CNN, April 3, 2003; On background see Norman Podhoretz, *World War IV, The Long Struggle Against Islamofascism* (New York: Doubleday, 2006).

3. Peter Brookes, "The Iran–al Qaeda Axis," *Real Clear Politics*, November 1, 2005; "9/11 Panel Links Al Qaeda, Iran: Bin Laden May Have Part in Khobar Towers, Report Says," *Washington Post*, June 26, 2004; on defining the enemy as Islamist see Daniel Pipes, "The Islamic Enemy Within," *New York Post*, January 24, 2003, and same author, "Vanquishing the Islamist Enemy," lecture at Tufts University, October 24, 2007. On the Jihadi perception of infidel enemy see Abdel Muhsin al Wkaiban, "Li'ay Shai' *al Jihad?*" [Why Jihad?], *al Sharq al Awsat*, October 31, 2004; also "Hikm al Safar Lil Jihad Dud al Kufar al Muhtalleen li Bilaad al Muslimeen" [Edict on Moving for Jihad against the Infidels Occupying the Countries of Muslims], http://www.islammemo.cc/, November 15, 2005.

4. See Osama Bin Laden, "Declaration of War against the Americans Occupying the Land of the Two Holy Places," *al Quds al Arabi*, August 23, 1996; "Declaration of War by Osama bin Laden," al Jazeera, February 23, 1998.

5. See "New Strategies keep Terrorists Ahead," Reuters, March 5, 2007; Phyllis Chesler, "The Legal Jihad Is Already Underway," *Front Page Magazine*, August 14, 2007; Tony Blankley, *The West Last Chance: Winning the Clash of Civilizations* (Washington, D.C.: Regnery Publishing, 2005).

6. Ann Scott Tyson, "Ability to Wage 'Long War' Is Key To Pentagon Plan," *Washington Post*, February 4, 2006; James Jay Carafano and Paul Rosenzweig, *Winning the Long War: Lessons from the Cold War for Defeating Terrorism and Preserving Freedom* (Westminster, MD: Heritage Books, 2005); William Kristol, "The Long War: The Radical Islamists Are on the Offensive. Will We Defeat Them?" *Weekly Standard* 11, no. 24 (March 6, 2006).

7. Yossi Verter, "Netanyahu: Barak Is Responsible for Hezbollah on Our Border," *Haaretz*, July 11, 2007; Michael Rubin, "The Lessons of Lebanon: Iran and Syria Sponsor an Ominous Arms Build-up on Israel's Northern border," *The Weekly Standard* 007, no. 41 (July 1, 2002).

8. See Hamid Bin Abdallah al Ali, "Hal Darb al Kafir ala Arduhu Dakhilan Dumna al Jihad?" [Is Striking the Infidel Inside His Land Part of Jihad?], *Fatawa al Jihad* [Fatwas on Jihad], http://www.h-alali.net, December 13, 2006; Jonathan Feiser, "Bin Laden Lacks a Political Solution," *PINR*, October 9, 2003; Joseph Loconte, "Peace Now: Christian Pacifists Ignore the True Ambitions of Terrorists," *The Wall Street Journal*, November 4, 2005; "L'Ideologie Islamiste contemporaine autorise le genocide" [The Contemporary Islamist Ideology Authorizes Genocide], *MEMRI*, March 24, 2004.

CONCLUSION

1. See *Fact Sheet: National Strategy for Homeland Security: A Comprehensive Guide for Securing the Homeland*, White House press release, October 9, 2007, available at http://www.whitehouse.gov/news/releases/2007/10/20071009–1.html.

2. For a precise identification of the threat see Jeffrey Imm, "Jihad, Islamism, and the Challenge of Anti-Freedom Ideologies," *The Counterterrorism Blog*, October 2, 2007; also by the same author "The Dangerous Denial of Jihad's Threat," *The Counterterrorism Blog*, October 15, 2007.

3. See *Islam Versus Islamism: Voices from the Muslim Center* and *Muslims against Jihad*, two documentaries produced in 2007 by Martyn Burke, Franck Gaffney, and Alex Alexiev. Slated initially to appear on PBS, they were banned from being aired on public television, http://www.islamdocumentary.com.

4. See the author's article "The Strategic Waves of Iraq's Liberation," *World Defense Review*, May 1, 2006.

INDEX